LAND OF
PROMISE

LAND OF
PROMISE

*A history of European Australia
through the lives of seven generations of my family*

RICHARD WATERHOUSE

K
KERR
Melbourne, Victoria

First published 2025
Kerr Publishing Pty Ltd
Melbourne, Victoria

ISBN 978-1-875703-65-4
ISBN 978-1-875703-66-1 (eBook)

Cover design: Paul Taylder
Book design: Paul Taylder of Xigrafix Media & Design
Genealogical charts by Luke Howlin

Typeset in Adobe Caslon Pro 11/15pt

Print of Demand services: Lightning Source

National Library of Australia PrePublication Data Service:

A catalogue record for this
book is available from the
National Library of Australia

NATIONAL
LIBRARY
OF AUSTRALIA

To the memory of my father and to Grace Karskens—the book explains why.

LAND OF PROMISE
A history of European Australia through the lives of seven generations of my family

Contents

LAND OF PROMISE
A history of European Australia through the lives of seven generations of my family

Acknowledgments

I OWE A GREAT DEBT OF GRATITUDE TO JENNY Salter whose brilliant detective work first revealed that Josiah Branchflower, not our shared, ostensible great, great grandfather, William Henry Waterhouse, was the father of my great grandfather, Henry Benjamin Waterhouse, and her great grandmother, Frances Alice Waterhouse. My curiosity to discover the context of this exchange of children was an important factor in my decision to write this book. Jenny and her daughter, Cassie Nancarrow, were also extremely helpful in providing me with material relating to the Branchflower, Waterhouse/Graham family history, and with photographs of her family, photographs which appear in Part 2 of this book.

My thanks to Kath Hayhurst, the historian of Burton in Kendal who provided me with the names of the children of Ann and John Waterhouse and a photograph of the Royal Oak Hotel of which they were proprietors. I am lucky to enjoy Tuesday morning fishing excursions with Kath's son, Jeff, who has shared his knowledge of Burton and photographs of the recently renovated Royal Oak.

I could not have written the section that deals with the Entwistle family of forgers, four of whom were convicted and transported to the Australian colonies as convicts, without the help of Associate Professor Carol Liston who provided me with copies of the Bank of England's Greenfield Papers containing transcripts of materials relating to the trials of Martha and Ann Entwistle.

Jenny and Roger Gifkins now live in the schoolmaster's residence at Belmore River in the Macleay Valley where my grandparents lived from 1912 to 1930 and in which my father Earle Waterhouse and his siblings grew to adulthood. They showed enormous generosity to Earle when he visited their house in 1980 and have looked after both the residence and schoolhouse with loving care. I am deeply grateful to them not only for this reason but also because of their friendship over more than 40 years.

Brad Manera, the Senior Historian Curator at the Anzac Memorial in Hyde Park, Sydney, never met my father, Earle, but his respect for my father's World War 2 achievements ensured that Earle featured in an exhibition in the Gallery to mark 100 years of the RAAF. Because of Brad, Earle Waterhouse finally achieved some of the recognition he deserves.

Thanks to Stephen Garton who encouraged me to persist with this project and read drafts of the entire manuscript. His support was important because I sometimes felt overwhelmed by a project which had seemed modest in the beginning but became increasingly complex and ambitious as it progressed. Stephen also successfully encouraged me not to be equivocal in telling my own story in Part 5

Robert C (Bobby) Allen and I have enjoyed a professional relationship and a personal friendship that extends over more then 25 years. A long time ago he taught me the value and importance of analysing texts in their contexts. More recently, we have spent many hours discussing approaches to and the values of family history, discussions based in part on the insights he has gleaned from teaching a course in family history at the University of

North Carolina at Chapel Hill. His influence is evident in nearly every page of this book.

During the years it took to research and write this book I experienced a number of illnesses that required surgery, hospitalisation and recovery periods at home, and as a result there were times when I was unable to travel to libraries and archives. I am very grateful to Dr Rosemary Kerr who located and copied the teaching records for David Drake and Percival Waterhouse, as well as the bankruptcy papers relating to David Drake (the elder) in the NSW Archives, and more bankruptcy papers dealing with David Thomas Drake in the Sydney branch of the National Archives.

My sister, Annabel Agafonoff, shared her memories of both the Waterhouse and Agafonoff families. My nephew, Dr Stephen Oakley not only recalled my sister Susan Oakley's life but also offered valuable insights into the causes of the post-traumatic stress disorder experienced by his grandfather, Earle Waterhouse. My cousins, Janet Magnin and Bill Waterhouse, shared their memories of their parents, Alan and Doris Waterhouse, as well as their own life stories. They also supplied some fascinating family photos. Linda Fienberg, my cousin once removed, made available an evocative memoir written by her mother Barbara (Hall) as well as childhood letters written by her mother which throw light both on the lives of Barbara's grandparents, Percy and Fanny Maude Waterhouse, and her parents, Rod and Ella Hall.

Our children Margot, Eliza, Isabel and Leo all read sections of the manuscript and offered encouraging and morale boosting comments. I'm grateful that they understood that it was more than just a dad retirement project.

When there were problems in reproducing the illustrations I had chosen for this book, Katherine Martin at the Camera Shop at Erina came to the rescue. I am deeply indebted to her for the capable manner in which she resolved all the issues in a minimum of time.

My deepest thanks to Luke Howlin for drawing the genealogical charts.

I am extremely grateful to my editor, John Kerr, for his encouragement and wise advice, and for his suggestions for changes to the text which have added clarity to my arguments and saved me from some serious and embarrassing errors. I also owe a huge debt of thanks to Paul Taylder for his imaginative designs of the book cover and contents, not to mention his miraculous improvement of the illustrations. I am so lucky to have worked with two such creative and professional people.

But, as always, my greatest debt is to Grace Karskens. When I began this project in 2019, I envisioned it as involving brief explorations of my Branchflower ancestors, my (possible) convict ancestry, and my father's World War 2 experiences. My aim was simply to satisfy my somewhat idle curiosity about these subjects, I had no ambitions to produce a book covering so many generations or to join them to a broader history. But it was Grace who encouraged me to extend this into a major research project through exploring the lives of successive generations of my extended family in evolving European and Australian contexts, in the process connecting the stories of my family to Australia's history. It was only because of her emotional and intellectual support that this book became a reality.

Introduction

URING THE TIME I WAS A GRADU-
ate student in the United States in
the late 1960s and early 1970s I
encountered two rather different versions of family
history. Academic historians began to research
and write family history largely as a result of the
inspiration provided by the Cambridge Group for
the History of Population and Social Structure
which was formed in 1964 by Peter Laslett and
Tony Wrigley. The historians associated with this
group developed a set of techniques that allowed
the systematic, statistical pursuit of demographic
data. Specifically, their main concern was with
family reconstitution, that is, determining when
the traditional 'extended family', which involved
three or more generations living under the same
roof, was replaced by the modern 'nuclear family',
comprising only parents and their children. This
research involved collecting demographic data
on mostly pre-industrial families over several
generations, data which allowed historians to
conclude that, rather than emerging as a product
of the Industrial Revolution, the nuclear family
predated it.[1] This form of social history crossed
the Atlantic to exert a strong influence on the
writing of colonial American history. Histories of
the New England towns of Plymouth, Dedham
and Andover by John Demos, Philip Greven, and
Kenneth Lockridge were highly influential in
shaping historians' understandings of the nature
and roles of families in pre-Revolutionary North
America. In accord with the arguments proposed
by the Cambridge Group they argued that the
English nuclear family was reproduced in the New

World, although with modifications. In focussing
on families of modest social and economic standing they also demonstrated that it was possible for
historians to recover the past stories of 'ordinary'
families, not just those who belonged to the elite
classes.[2]

I spent most of the 1971–72 academic year in
Columbia, South Carolina, carrying out research
in the State Archives, and the Caroliniana Library
for my PhD dissertation relating to the emergence
of plantation slavery in Carolina. This Library,
which holds large manuscript and book collections, was founded both to preserve and promote
the state's heritage, culture and history. At the
foot of the stairs leading to the upper floor reading room there is a large marble tablet, on which
are written the words:

A Tribute of tender love to the Memory of PRESTON S BROOKS

Brooks, a fanatical supporter of slavery and
a member of the House of Representatives,
on May 22 1856 attacked William Charles
Sumner, an abolitionist supporting Senator
from Massachusetts, with a walking cane, which
resulted in the victim suffering near fatal injuries. The fact that this plaque was erected in this
location reflects that, at least until recently, the
Library's administrators viewed the role of the
institution to uncritically promote South Carolina,
as a colony and then as a state which was a bastion
of white southern civilisation. The library contains
a huge collection of genealogical histories focussing on the slave owning merchants, planters

A history of European Australia through the lives of seven generations of my family

and lawyers who constituted the master class which dominated and controlled South Carolina for much of its history. When the older studies refer to slaves they are usually simply counted as numbers, indications of the wealth of their owners. These tomes also contain valorising narratives and bear execrable titles, my favourite being *Little Acorns from the Mighty Oak.* I spent many hours in this library reading the genealogical histories that related specifically to families that lived in South Carolina in the colonial period. They proved to be a valuable resource, allowing me to construct a profile of at least five generations of the colony's colonial elite, through an assessment of the extent to which wealth was passed on from one generation of wealthy colonial families to the next, and to determine how often newcomers emerged from humble economic origins, to become members of the master class.

However, this preoccupation of Carolinians, and indeed of Americans more generally, with family history was a puzzle to me because although the writing of local history had a long tradition in Australia, one stretching back well into the nineteenth century, there was no similar preoccupation with family/genealogical history. I suppose it is commonplace for people who live in settler societies to want to trace their own histories back to the countries from which their families originated some generations in the past. It is a means of establishing a sense of identification and belonging. But during the colonial as well as in the first 70 years or so of nationhood, the stigma of convict ancestry contributed to a widespread Australian preoccupation with creating a selective interpretation of the nation's past which focussed on the claimed achievements of the 'pioneers', free settlers and their descendants, whose 'conquest' of the 'wilderness' brought national prosperity. On the other, the widespread fear of 'the hated stain' of convict ancestry led to an accepted understanding of the Australian past in which the contributions and roles of convicts were minimised and sometimes even written out of the narrative altogether. Because of the limits placed on access to convict records by state governments it was difficult for people to research their family histories but, in

any case, there was a widespread reluctance to do so because in a society in which there was a great emphasis on 'respectability' many Australians feared what they might find. My family placed emphasis on the fact their ancestors had arrived in the post-convict era of the 1860s, which as this book demonstrates, was true of some but certainly not all past family members. I suspect many other Australian families adopted the same convenient understanding.

Although there were a few genealogical and local history societies formed in Australia, beginning in the 1930s, the greatest growth period, both in terms of the number of organisations and members, dates from the 1970s. This coincided with and was directly connected to the Australian middle-class abandonment of its previous long-held obsession with a culture of respectability. In this context it was now possible for Australians of all classes to embrace Australia's convict heritage, an embrace made easier with the emergence of a narrative that claimed that most convicts were victims, men and women who stole to feed their families, and most of whom were transported for trivial offences. Once reviled as the scum of the earth, they were now valorised, in Jack Thompson's words, as 'convict royalty'. I suppose that nowhere is the current willingness of Australians to accept and acknowledge their convict ancestry more evident than in the television series *Who Do You Think You Are?* [3]

The 1980s also marked a much greater emphasis on family history by Australian academic historians. Of particular importance was the publication in 1985 of a ground breaking collection of regional studies demonstrating that the nuclear family was the Australian norm, although age of marriage and family size varied by region, class and ethnicity.[4] Amongst an impressive number of local family history studies that appeared in subsequent years two stand out for their quality and influence. Drawing on Tony Wrigley's family reconstitution techniques, Alan Atkinson's history of family life in Camden in the early colonial era, integrated this subject into the wider context of NSW provincial society. Similarly, relying partly on census data related to the early European inhabitants of The

Rocks, Grace Karskens constructed a complex narrative of the nature of family and community life in this pre-industrial society.[5]

As I indicated above, the period since the 1970s has witnessed the formation of large numbers of family history societies and the publication of an astonishing number of family histories, some of them written by professional historians carrying out commissions, many others by descendants of convict or free settler immigrants. For the most part these focus on constructing family genealogies utilising traditional written sources to provide modestly descriptive and usually uncritical contexts. Individually, these genealogies don't contribute to broader understandings about the Australian past, although collectively they have become valuable resources for historians researching the changing roles of the family in Australian history, allowing them to focus on such issues as family size as well as the extent of social and geographical mobility.[6]

In writing this book my first aim was to construct a genealogy. The genealogical chart I constructed, relied in part on research already carried out by other family members, most notably, Jenny Salter. But it is also based on my own findings, which mostly, but not exclusively, drew on the sources available through Ancestry. Second, I constructed biographies of family members as a means to understand their characters and values as well as the roles they played both in their families and local communities. Third, I connected these family narratives to wider social, cultural, religious, political and economic contexts to understand more fully the factors that shaped the lives of my relatives and how their life experiences related to broader trends in Australian society.

In the first part I have located my Branchflower (Blanchfleur) ancestors within the contexts of the Huguenot exodus from France in the sixteenth and seventeenth centuries, and the silk weaving culture to which they belonged both in the English provinces and London. In this part I also explain the decision of Josiah Branchflower and his wife Mary Susannah to emigrate to Australia, and their negotiation of new lives, in partnership with their four children and Mary Susannah's parents, in the

gold rush society of Marvellous Melbourne.

In the second part the story of three generations of the Waterhouse family is told, first, against the background of northern England Lakes District rural and small-town society and second, within the setting of the late nineteenth and early twentieth century boom and bust economy of Grafton and the Clarence Valley in northern NSW. More specifically, it also relates how in 1867 Mary Susannah Branchflower and William Henry Waterhouse ran away together from Melbourne to northern NSW where they claimed to be a married couple and that Mary Susannah's two youngest children, Henry Benjamin and Frances Alice, who came with them, were the products of their union. They were so successful in constructing and maintaining this narrative that it was accepted not only by their colonial contemporaries but also by their descendants, and remained hidden until Jenny Nancarrow/Salter revealed it as a falsehood in 1999.

Part 3 narrates the stories of my grandfather Percy, the oldest son of Henry Benjamin, and his wife Ellen (Spring) and of my grandmother Maude (Paine) Waterhouse, and their lives in the Lower Macleay Valley where Percy worked as a school teacher. He later served in three subsequent rural schools elsewhere in NSW. Here the focus is on the family's interaction both with the local community and the wetlands environment of Kinchela and Belmore River. This story also follows four of the five Waterhouse children on journeys that took them to England, Sydney, rural New South Wales and the battlefields of World War 2.

The fourth part relates the story of my other great, great grandfather David Drake and the story of the wooden ship building dock he founded at Bald Rock, Balmain, its success and its failure. It also narrates the life of my grandfather, also named David Drake, and his rather different career, as an educator. The Drake narrative is succeeded by the story of my father's career as a teacher, education administrator and RAAF wartime navigator and Squadron Leader. This section also narrates the relationship of my parents, Nancy Drake and Earle Waterhouse, across the period from the 1930s to the 1980s, against a background of changing attitudes towards family values and the roles of women in the family and society more generally.

The final part is a highly personal narrative of my life as a student, teacher, researcher, academic administrator and most importantly as a husband and father. It tells how I became an academic historian and of my evolution from a social to a cultural historian. In this story my personal and professional lives are told as intertwined narratives because each one impacted heavily on the other.

Overall, my purpose in writing this book was not only to recover the lives of my ancestors, stretching as far back as seven generations but also to determine how both international as well as local events impacted and shaped the lives of my extended family over this more than 200-year period. The history of my family is complex and diverse, one marked by tragedy and sorrow as well as triumph and success. In the end, of course, it is not simply a family narrative, it is also an Australian story.

Endnotes

1   E. A. Wrigley, ed., *An Introduction to English Historical Demography*, London: Weidenfield and Nicolson, 1966. The mathematical models listed in the appendices indicate the high level of statistical sophistication employed by the Cambridge Group historians. For a more popular account of the findings of the Group see Peter Laslett, *The World We Have Lost*, London: Methuen, 1965. The Cambridge Group drew much of its inspiration from the French Annales School

2   John Demos, *A Little Commonwealth: Family Life in Plymouth Colony*, New York: Oxford University Press, 1970; Philip Greven, *Four Generations: Population, Land, and family in Colonial Andover, Massachusetts*, Ithaca: Ornell University Press, 1970; Kenneth A. Lockridge, *A New England Town*

the First Hundred Years Dedham, Massachusetts, 1636–1736*, New York; W. W. Norton, 1970.

3   For an assessment of the impact of this series in shaping its viewers' understanding of Australian history see Tanya Evans, *Fractured Families Life on the Margins in Colonial New South Wales*, Sydney: UNSW Press, 2015, pp. 246–52

4   Patricia Grimshaw, Chris McConville and Ellen McEwen eds., *Families in Colonial Australia*, Sydney: Allen and Unwin, 1985

5   Alan Atkinson, *Camden Farm and Village Life in Early New South Wales*, Melbourne: Oxford University Press,1988; Grace Karskens, *The Rocks Life in Early Sydney*, Melbourne: Melbourne University Press, 1997

6   Tanya Evans, *Fractured Families, passim*.

A Note on Method and Sources

IN CONSTRUCTING THE FAMILY GENEALO-gies that form the skeletons of this book I relied heavily on the material in Ancestry. Mostly, I constructed my family genealogies from the rich family materials available from this source. I only relied on the family trees constructed by other Ancestry subscribers when they provided documentation to support the names on their trees. I also relied on other material to construct my own trees, including on-line church registers of births, baptisms, marriages and deaths. In a few cases I depended on material from the Waterhouse family collection, including the Paine family Bible containing the names of the children of Richard Paine, and a letter from an unknown relative to my mother listing the children of David Drake the elder. Kath Hayhurst provided me with a full list of the children of John and Ann Waterhouse.

I was able to more fully trace the lives of my nineteenth and twentieth century ancestors because most of them lived in rural environments both in England and Australia. The rural press concentrated on the lives of local people, while metropolitan newspapers focussed on colonial, state, national and international news. As a result, I found a very large amount of relevant material through both the British Newspaper Archive and the Australian National Library's Trove on-line newspaper collection. The Waterhouse Family Collection in my possession holds a modest collection of letters and postcards relating to Henry Benjamin, Percival, Earle and Richard Waterhouse and David and Nancy Drake. I also depended on a series of written memoirs and oral recollections from Earle Waterhouse, Annabel Waterhouse, Barbara Hall, Judy Thompson, Janet Magnin, Bill Waterhouse and Linda Fienberg. These sources allowed me to recover, at least in part, the lives of those members of my family contained on the genealogical lists that I had first created. It was a metaphorical case, of putting flesh on skeletons, and then locating the characters I had recreated within the wider contexts of changing cultures and societies, first in Europe and subsequently in Australia.

LAND OF PROMISE
A history of European Australia through the lives of seven generations of my family

PART 1

Branchflower Family Tree

John Branchflower — **Grace Branchflower**

- **Mary Brake** — **William Branchflower**
  - **James Branchflower**
  - **Thomas Branchflower**
  - **Sarah Branchflower**

Benjamin Littlejohn — **Elizabeth Paul**

James Armstrong (d. 1869) — **Susannah Cornwell** (d. 1882)

Josiah Branchflower (1801–1870) — **Elizabeth Littlejohn** (1797–1875)

Children:
- **Mary Ann Branchflower** (1824–1829)
- **William J Branchflower** (1825–1844)
- **Josiah Branchflower** (1826–1909)
- **Charles J. Branchflower** (1829–1907)
- **James Branchflower** (1833–1833)
- **John James Branchflower** (1834–1889)
- **Henry Benjamin Branchflower** (1836–1916)
- **Mary Ann Branchflower** (1838–1910)
- **Samuel Branchflower** (1859–1935)

James Thomas Armstrong (b. ca 1833) — **Lydia Parsons**
Mary Susannah Armstrong (1869)

Children:
- **Josiah Branchflower** (1855–1942)
- **James T. Branchflower** (1857–1882)
- **Henry Benjamin Branchflower** (1860–1945)
- **Frances Alice Branchflower** (1865–1947)

Chapter 1

Generations of Huguenot Silk Weavers

Prelude: James and Thomas (Robert) Branchflower

Until 1999, when I was contacted by a distant relative, Jenny Nancarrow (now Salter), a family historian who had researched the Branchflower/Waterhouse connection, I had no idea that I was descended not from the Cumberland-located Waterhouse but instead from the Somerset/Bethnal Green based Blanchflower/Branchflower family. Jenny, also a Branchflower descendant, explained how this was also related to a long-buried family secret, which I will explore in succeeding pages. But the story of the first member of the extended Somerset Branchflower family to voyage to Australia, James Branchflower, is a story of tragedy.

The name Branchflower was originally the French surname Blanchefleur, which was first anglicised to Blanchflower and subsequently to Branchflower, and means, of course, white or pale flower. In some Somerset parishes the name Blanchflower can be found from the 1560s onwards. In the eighteenth century it was sometimes spelled Branchflower either as a mistake or perhaps because some members of the extended family decided to Anglicise their surname even further in the face of anti-Catholic and anti-French sentiments, which they experienced despite the fact that they were Protestants. One example of error can be found in the Somerset Staplegrove parish records. The clerk recording the simultaneous baptisms on November 8 1771 of Thomas and Sarah, two children of John and Grace Blanchflower, first listed them both as 'Branchflower', but then wrote an l over the r.

Another child of John and Grace was baptised as William Blanchflower in 1768. But when William married Mary Brake on June 7 1789, he was listed as William Branchflower. Perhaps he further Anglicised the name in response to the rising Francophobia in England even before the outbreak of Revolution across the Channel.[1]

Altogether John and Grace, who married in 1765, had four children, including William (1768), James (1770), Thomas and Sarah (1771).[2] Their son James was perhaps the James Branchflower, a convict, who was transported to NSW. James was baptised in Staplegrove parish on November 28 1770 while the James Branchflower, tried and convicted in Taunton on March 27 1788, was seventeen years old. So, their ages match.[3] But there is a spanner in the works. A James Blanchflower, the son of Sarah (born Sarah Winter in 1739) and William Blanchflower (born 1724) was baptised in Brompton Ralph Parish, Somerset, on September 23, 1770. He also fits the age profile for James Branchflower the convict. So, there are two candidates for our convict and on the evidence available I find it difficult to separate them.[4]

James was tried at the Taunton Assizes in 1788, convicted of assault and robbery and sentenced to death. He was subsequently reprieved and ordered instead to serve seven year's transportation. Held on the Dunkirk hulk at Plymouth between May 1788 and November 1789, he left England in January 1790 on board the *Neptune,* one of the vessels that made up the Second Fleet, bound for the infant convict colony of New South Wales.[5]

As it turned out James' transportation was a death sentence. The conditions for convicts on

The *Neptune, State Library of Victoria*

the Second Fleet were appalling and those on the *Neptune* were the worst of all. When it set sail there were 421 male and 78 female convicts on board, along with six free wives of convicts and their five children. Before the ship reached Cape Town 46 convicts were already dead and by the time the ship arrived in Sydney only forty-two of the convicts were strong enough to make their own way off the ship. In addition to the many who died between the Cape and Sydney many others died in the hospital to which they were taken on arrival. Indeed, forty percent of those who arrived in Sydney died within a few months of arrival. Altogether, 158 convict men and women on the *Neptune* passed away from dysentery, typhoid, typhus, and scurvy including James who was one of the convicts who died and was buried at sea.

The contractors who organised the voyage and carried the convicts to Australia were the slave traders, Camden, Calvert and King, and the fact that the male convicts were kept in irons and close confinement below deck for the whole voyage—in keeping with the practice on slave ships—ensured the spread of disease, for their bodies were weakened by the lack of exercise and they were perpetually in close proximity to each other.[6]

But there is another puzzling twist to this tale. On March 8 1793 a Thomas Branchflower

was buried in an unmarked grave at St John's Cemetery in Parramatta.[7] In fact, the convict buried at Parramatta was almost certainly Robert Blanchflower, who was tried and convicted at the Norfolk Assizes for stealing a horse. Originally sentenced to hang, his punishment was subsequently reduced to seven year's transportation. Blanchflower came to Australia on an East India ship, the *Royal Admiral*, captained by Essex Henry Bond. A ship's captain, also seeking to become a colonial entrepreneur, Bond was given the Governor's permission to take some of the prisoners directly to Parramatta to work as assigned convicts at his newly opened store, which explains how the 33 year old Robert (Thomas) Blanchflower came to be there. Blanchflower lived in Parramatta for about five months before his death and was buried in an unmarked grave on March 8 1793.[8] Why did he live as Robert Blanchflower and yet was buried as Thomas Branchflower? The sad but likely explanation is that the convicts' gaolers and supervisors quite commonly confused and misunderstood their names.

There were pockets of Blanchflowers not only in Somerset and Norfolk but in other rural counties as well as in East London, which is encompassed by county Middlesex. It is highly likely that Blanchflowers came to England sometime in a period stretching from the mid sixteenth through to the end of the seventeenth century as part of what historians now regard as the first modern refugee movement. During these years probably more than 100,000 French Protestants, or Huguenots, took refuge in England from the persecution of the French monarchy and Catholic Church, almost certainly including the ancestors of James, Robert (Thomas) and Josiah, a man who made his way to Australia more than fifty years later and under somewhat different circumstances from the two convicts.

Josiah Branchflower the Elder

My great, great grandfather, Josiah Branchflower, in company with his wife, Mary Susannah and her parents, James and Susan Armstrong, immigrated to Australia in 1855, leaving Southampton on the ship *Calliance* on October 6 and arriving in the Port of Melbourne on December 31. On the passenger list both Armstrong and Branchflower described themselves as 'agricultural labourers", although that belied the trades and crafts they had previously followed. Almost certainly they described themselves as rural workers, knowing that men with experience of farm work were in demand in the Australian colonies and were therefore more likely to receive assisted passages.

I have not succeeded in tracing Josiah's family origins further back than his father on the Branchflower side and his grandparents on his mother's side. Also called Josiah, his father worked primarily as a silk weaver, first in Taunton, and subsequently in Battersea and Bethnal Green in London. In 1829 the elder Josiah stated that he was born in Staplegrove parish in Somerset but I can't find any record of his birth or baptism either in the Staplegrove or other Somerset parish registers. The 1841 Bethnal Green census listed his age at 35, while the census for 1861 recorded it as 56.[9] Extrapolating back from these two records, we can conclude that he was born in 1805 or 1806. However, given that he married Elizabeth Littlejohn in the parish church of Taunton St Mary on December 2 1821, neither of these dates seem likely, because it means that he was only 15 or 16 when he wed. Contrary to popular understandings people did not usually marry early in pre-industrial England, waiting until they were financially secure, which often didn't happen until they were in their late twenties. When the elder Josiah died in 1870 his age was listed as 69, which means he was born in 1801. It also means that he was 20 when he was married, still a young age to be wed in that era, and four years younger than his wife, Elizabeth.

The Littlejohns had lived in Taunton St Mary's parish and were connected to the weaving industry for at least a century before Elizabeth married Josiah in 1821. The St Mary Magdalene Church parish register reveals that a William Littlejohn, weaver, married Elizabeth Stacy in 1724. Elizabeth, the sixth child of Benjamin and Betty Littlejohn, was born in Taunton on March 25 1797. When she married Josiah Branchflower in 1821 they both signed the register with their

marks, indicating that they were probably illiterate. As a silk weaver Josiah was a skilled craftsman, although the subsequent mechanisation of the industry meant most silk workers, unless they were weaving complex garments or decorative works, now only required basic expertise, but literacy was never a prerequisite for his trade.

As I indicated above, I can't find a record of the elder Josiah's birth in the Staplegrove or for that matter any of the other available Somerset parish registers. In the context of a plausible time frame the most likely parents for Josiah are William (born Blanchflower but when he married listed as Branchflower) and Mary (born Mary Brake). William was baptised in 1768, the eldest son of John and Grace Blanchflower. His siblings included James (the possible convict, baptised 1770), Thomas and Sarah (both baptised 1771). William fits the time frame to be Josiah's father. Moreover, he lived in Staplegrove and when he married Mary Brake on June 7 1789 was listed as William Branchflower. On the other hand, I can only find a record for one child born to William and Mary, Sarah, who was baptised at Staplegrove in 1794. In this era parents were sometimes neglectful in recording the births of children and in having them baptised, so it is conceivable that William and Mary failed to record Josiah's birth or have him baptised. Josiah also probably had a brother, William, who like him moved from Taunton to Bethnal Green, although there is no direct evidence that he was William and Mary's child either. So, I have laid out a speculative suggestion with a modest conviction that it is correct.

Earlier I suggested that the first Blanchflowers/ Branchflower to move from France to England were probably Huguenot refugees. I don't have any direct proof that this was the case but the circumstantial evidence is reasonably persuasive. Stirrings against the teachings and practices of the Catholic Church had grown strong in Europe in the late fifteenth and early sixteenth centuries but Martin Luther's 95 theses, which he nailed to a church door in Wittenberg on October 31 1517, crystallised an inchoate set of protests that had existed sporadically, into a coherent movement to reform the Church. In France, the Crown and Catholic hierarchy responded to the nascent Protestant movement with an Edict, issued in 1535, which called for the extermination of Protestantism. This led to a small wave of migration of Protestants, or Huguenots, from France into countries where Protestantism had replaced Catholicism as the established religion. A larger wave of outward Huguenot movement took place after the State organised massacre of Protestants in Paris and rural areas, beginning on St Bartholomew's Day 1572. Many Protestant exiles from Brittany, Normandy and Picardy joined Walloon refugees, fleeing persecution from the Duke of Alva in the Spanish Netherlands, to settle in London as well as southwest and southeast England. In later years as they came of age the majority of the second generation of these first refugees deserted their Huguenot communities and merged into the surrounding populations.[10]

The Treaty of Nantes in 1598, which gave Protestants a measure of religious toleration, brought a temporary end to the French religious wars but the exodus began again in 1661 when Louis XIV assumed the throne. He lived up to his reputation for anti-Protestant beliefs when in 1681 he introduced the dragonnais, a policy that allowed the billeting of soldiers in Protestant households, followed by his decision in 1685 to revoke the Treaty of Nantes. Now Protestants were excluded from public life, their ministers were exiled, and their children were baptised and brought up as Catholics. Although lay Protestants were refused the right to leave France in the period between 1660 and 1700, tens of thousands did so anyway, with some 40,000 to 60,000 crossing the Channel to settle in England.

In France, the majority of Huguenots had lived in a crescent, which stretched south from La Rochelle to the Mediterranean and then east and finally north from the southern coast to Lyon, a river city in eastern France. In England they tended to join existing French Huguenot communities in London as well as in other cities and towns that were either on the coast or not too far from it, towns that included Norwich, Southampton and Canterbury. Sometimes they moved to cities that had long standing ties to the places they came from. Bristol, which became a Huguenot destination had close fishing and more general trade links to La Rochelle.[11]

Not all of the refugees came from cities and towns located on the French coast. Although, as was the case in the sixteenth century, some of the emigrant Huguenots came from Normandy, others, most of whom were silk weavers, came from the Loire Valley town of Tours and the eastern river city of Lyon. In the 1560s Tours had the reputation for producing the best woven silk in France. Its Huguenot workforce was particularly skilled in lustering, a process that enhanced the appearance of the silk. In the late sixteenth century Lyon supplanted Tours as the capital of the European silk trade and its Huguenot weavers developed their own decorative style, abandoning oriental designs in favour of European landscapes. However, in the aftermath of the Revocation of the Treaty of Nantes, many Calvinist weavers fled Tours and Lyon for England. Those who moved to London mainly settled in Spitalfields, although they also spilled over into the neighbouring community of Bethnal Green. Here the refugees made clothing and household items from pure silk, velvet and mixed wool and silk materials. While most of the Huguenot silk weavers settled in London they also established workshops in Canterbury, Manchester, Norwich and Taunton.[12] In any case, by the late seventeenth century London had usurped Lyon as the centre of the European silk trade.

Silk weaving began in Somerset in the 1670s in the south-eastern town of Wincanton and in the 1750s the industry spread to the nearby town of Bruton. Silk manufacture was given an unintended boost in Somerset with the passage of the Spitalfields Acts of 1773, 1774, 1792 and 1811. These acts allowed London and Middlesex local government officials to set minimum wages and prices in the Spitalfields and Bethnal Green silk factories and workshops, making it the only regulated industry in the country. Fearing these regulations would lead to lower profits some silk manufacturers moved their operations outside London-including to Somerset. Workshops and factories in Taunton, Dulverton, Ichester and Pitcombe parish (Gant's Mill) were established, the locations chosen because they provided both water to power the looms and cheap labour. Here the silk was thrown, a process that involved the conversion of imported single filament into a multiple filament silk thread. The yarn was then sent to London for dyeing and finally returned to the Somerset mills for weaving. The unskilled section of the workforce mostly consisted of young girls, although it also was reliant on small numbers of skilled male workers.

The precise role of Huguenots in the Somerset silk industry is not clear, but given that their role as founders of the London silk workshops, they were almost certainly also the organisers of the Somerset silk trade. We know that there was a Huguenot Dissenting Church in Somerset as early as the 1680s, although it was gone within a decade, suggesting that at this stage the Huguenot presence was not extensive. We also know there were a number of Huguenot descendants living in the Somerset village of Chewmendip in the eighteenth century. And more direct evidence of Huguenot descendant involvement in Somerset silk weaving can be found in Ichester near Yeovil, where in the 1790s William Sevoir was the co—founder of a silk mill.[13]

More specifically, there were Blanchflowers in Somerset from at least the mid-sixteenth century. They were part of the first wave of Huguenot refugees, although I suspect that the Blanchflowers I am concerned with were most likely immigrants from Tours or Lyon, weavers who came in the second, post 1685 migration. An early Huguenot resident was Thomas Blanchflower, a farmer, who lived at Kingston near Bristol in the 1550s. Two Blanchflowers, Thomas and George, became Church of England ministers in the seventeenth century. The Huguenots were the only non-Church of England Protestant religious group that had legal permission to establish their own Dissenting congregations but the fact that George and Thomas chose to become ministers of the Established Church, suggests they were not radical, dogmatic Calvinists. This argument is reinforced by the fact that in 1643, during the

Civil War, George, who was curate of Stoke St Mary, refused to adhere to the Calvinist requirements now required of clergy by the Puritan dominated parliament, and in consequence was deprived of his church living. The seventeenth and eighteenth century parish records reveal the existence of Blanchflowers not only in Devon, Oxford, Sussex, London (Hackney) and Norfolk but also in a number of Somerset parishes. These include Lydeard St Lawrence, Staplegrove, Bridgewater St Mary, Ash Priors, Brompton Ralph, Wiveliscombe, Thurloxton, Milverton, Wellington and Taunton St Mary.[14]

In any case, it is likely that Josiah Branchflower the elder was descended from Huguenot refugees because of his French surname, because he was a silk weaver, and because although he was born, married and for some time worked in Somerset, in 1832 he moved with his family to London, settling first in Battersea but then moving to the long-established Huguenot silk weaving enclave of Bethnal Green. In other words, it seems he was drawn into a community consisting of people with similar working, cultural and religious backgrounds to his own.

St Mary Magdalene Church, Taunton

Elizabeth Littlejohn was baptised in the Taunton Independent Church, which was a Congregational denomination place of worship, although she and Josiah married in one of the local Church of England churches, St Mary Magdalene, and their numerous children were all baptised in Anglican churches. In other words, Elizabeth joined Josiah in maintaining a Blanchflower/Branchflower tradition of conservative Protestantism. Five children were born in Taunton and baptised in St Mary Magdalene.[15] Subsequently, two were born in Battersea and three in Bethnal Green.[16]

Josiah Branchflower the elder. *Photo courtesy of Dave Branchflower via Jenny Salter*

There are indications that life was difficult for Josiah and Elizabeth in Taunton in the 1820s. In essence this was because their family was growing while at the same time the silk industry was facing a set of challenges and changes, which were detrimental to the wages and living standards of the silk workers. An 1824 Act of Parliament lowered the import duty on raw silk, which provided a boon to the throwing industry, but which was also accompanied by the introduction of large–scale sweated outwork. This was usually carried out by unskilled female labour. This same act also lowered the duty on imported cloth, which Josiah Branchflower claimed at a public meeting of silk weavers in Taunton in 1828 had led to an influx of wrought silk from France into England. He also argued that the over supply of silk products like muslin, crapes and sarsnets was further increased because the new power looms manufactured them at a faster rate than the old hand looms. The overall result of this oversupply was to reduce both the prices of silk products and the wages of the weavers.[17]

Josiah's speech at this public meeting suggests he held a certain status amongst his co-workers and was recognised as an important advocate of the silk craft. There are also indications that he was a determined man. In 1826 he took out a lease on a house and garden in Taunton. Two years later his landlord sought to evict him without giving him the half-year's notice specified by the lease agreement. Josiah asserted his legal rights and refused to leave the house until legally required.[18]

It was probably the continued decline of the Somerset silk industry that led Josiah and his family to leave Taunton in 1832 and make their way to London, no doubt in expectation of a more prosperous future. Taunton is 216 kilometres (134.5 miles) from London, which in early nineteenth century terms was a considerable distance. However, the Turnpike acts had led to the development of a relatively extensive road network in the course of the eighteenth and nineteenth centuries. Engineers had also developed smoother and more enduring road surfaces, while travelling was also made more comfortable with the construction of stagecoaches complete with suspension systems. Given their likely modest economic circumstances the Branchflower family probably braved the weather in the two-penny outside rather than enjoying the five-penny inside seats. Either they endured a nineteen-hour or so unbroken trip, or perhaps they broke their journey and took two days to reach London,

The family was first lured to Battersea probably because it had an established Huguenot population and also because it possessed a newly established

Silk Factory Battersea

J.R. Inglis and Jill Sanders, Panorama of the Thames: a riverside view of Georgian London, London: Thames and Hudson, 2015 (a reproduction of Samuel Leigh's 1829 panorama)

silk factory, together with adjacent cottages built specifically to accommodate the workforce. In the eighteenth-century Battersea was known for its market gardens, which were probably established by the Huguenots who had settled not only here but also in neighbouring Wandsworth. These gardens were particularly well known for the quality of the asparagus they produced, a touching co-incidence because subsequent generations of the Waterhouse family regarded both white and green asparagus as amongst their favourite vegetables. Perhaps this rural environment was healthier than the urban milieu closer to the centre of London, although an open sewer ran through the swamp land adjacent to the market farms. In the early nineteenth century factories began to appear along the Battersea riverfront, including a shot foundry, a whitewash works, an enamel factory, breweries, flour mills and a woollen mill which soon became a silk factory. John Ford erected the woollen mill in about 1820, a large 24 bay building built in the same architectural style that marked the cotton and woollen mills that had sprung up in the industrial midlands. In 1824 Ford erected a terrace of 39 workers' houses on York Road, a thoroughfare that was subsequently called 'Silk Lane'. When this wool manufacturing venture failed, three merchants, the Brunskill brothers,

who were City silk traders, took over the operation of the factory and converted it to silk production. Recruiting labour from the Huguenot dominated silk manufacturing workshops in Spitalfields they also appointed another Huguenot descendant, Edward Delaforce, as the works foreman. Perhaps Josiah was also recruited or perhaps he simply saw the new Battersea factory as an opportunity to escape from a declining silk economy in Somerset. In any case the Branchflower family settled into one of the terraces in the 'Ford Building' and Josiah went to work as a weaver. But he and his family found, and they would later find again in Bethnal Green, that the London silk industry was no more certain or reliable than its Somerset counterpart and although the looms were still in situ in 1840 silk production at the Battersea factory had ceased sometime in the late 1830s. It subsequently became a glove factory operated by Fownes but by then the Branchflower family had moved to Bethnal Green in search of further employment in the silk trade.

In fact they were already settled in Bethnal Green by 1836 because another child Henry Benjamin was born there in that year and a daughter, a second Mary Ann, arrived in the following year. Their last child, Samuel was born in Bethnal Green in 1839 but died within the year.[19]

The 1841 census reveals the family living at 84 Seabright Street, where they stayed for more than twenty years. The address is now incorporated into a park named in memory of the weavers who once inhabited the neighbourhood. The same census also revealed that five family members, Josiah (35), Betsy (40), Elizabeth (19), William Alfred (16) and Josiah (14) were working as silk weavers.

Josiah and Elizabeth were joined in Bethnal Green by William and Sarah Branchflower. William, who was almost certainly Josiah's elder brother, also listed his birthplace as Staplegrove Parish, Somerset. Born in 1799 he married Sarah Taylor in Taunton St Mary on December 20 1819, the same church where Josiah and Elizabeth subsequently married, in 1821. By 1841 William and Sarah and their children, Eliza (15), Elizabeth (12) and Sarah (6) were living in North Conduit Street. William and Sarah were both weavers and by 1851 so was Elizabeth. William probably remained in the industry throughout his working life, listed as a silk weaver in the 1851 and as a silk manufacturer in the 1861 census.[20]

What were the prospects for silk weavers in Spitalfelds and Bethnal Green in the 1840s? In fact, the Branchflowers had arrived at the very moment when the silk manufacturing was at the beginning of a steep decline, one that culminated sixty years later with its almost complete extinction.

Since Medieval times this area was connected to a range of trades, including the cloth and brewery industries. It also provided a pool of labour for industries in the City and East End. This was also an area characterised by immigrants, most notably Jews fleeing persecution in Eastern Europe, Irish families escaping extreme poverty in their homeland, and Huguenots seeking refuge from Catholic suppression of their churches. Forbidden as outsiders from settling in the City they were forced to make lives for their families in communities they created outside the City boundaries, which included Spitalfields and Bethnal Green. Walloon refugees from the Low Countries introduced weaving here in the sixteenth century, although by the mid-seventeenth century, throwing rather than weaving was the main silk industry. But the silk trade here was transformed by the arrival of Huguenots from Lyon who brought with them not only silk weaving skills but also new techniques, designs, and

materials. In the eighteenth century a system of production emerged that was based on outwork. The weavers collected silk from the manufacturers or master weavers and then wove it on looms in their own houses, which were characterised by upper stories with large windows to provide light for the workers so that they could labour for long hours weaving the silk. This system of manufacture brought prosperity to the master weavers but those who actually wove the cloth earned little more than subsistence wages and lived in appalling conditions.[21]

Crime and disorder were also endemic to this area. The inhabitants were given to riot when they considered prices too high or wages too low. Moreover, the old pre-industrial custom of St Monday, which involved workers taking the first day of the working week as an extra holiday in order to sharpen their tools and recover from excessive weekend drinking, was widely practised. The governing authorities were sufficiently concerned and alarmed by the power of the Spitalfields 'mob' that it passed the series of acts, to which I have already referred, beginning in the early 1770s, which set wages in the silk weaving industry in Spitalfields and were designed to reduce worker unrest. These acts ensured both a level of worker prosperity and political and social stability. It was the only industry and place in England where wages were regulated.

However, this situation was not to last because from the 1820s the Whig Party became increasingly wedded to the principles of free trade and this had huge implications for the silk industry. In 1824 the Government lowered the duty on raw silk and imported cloth and in 1860 concluded a free trade treaty with France that abolished all tariffs on imported silk products. The impact of the first tariff changes was drastic and immediate. In Spitalfields in the 1830s many families lacked sufficient food, owned only the clothes they wore and were forced to sell their household belongings. The workhouse was full.[22]

What also impacted on silk workers' wages, in particular, was the increasing use of steam-powered looms in silk manufacture. The resulting efficiencies in production led to a 30% decline in wages. Sometimes, in particularly prosperous times, there were increases in the production of silk goods and in wages but the overall trend was one of decline. In 1831 there were 80,000 silk workers and 17,000 looms in Bethnal Green and Spitalfields but by 1901 there were less than 550 workers engaged in silk production in these two areas combined.[23]

Nevertheless, in Bethnal Green Josiah came to be acknowledged as a highly skilled weaver who took pride in his craft and as a spokesman for the silk industry. Faced with 'grievous distress' caused by the Government's free trade policies a meeting of weavers in Bethnal Green in 1837 discussed appealing for public support to ameliorate their poverty. But Josiah expressed reservations about such an appeal, believing it might lead to a wider community perception of weavers, not as skilled craft workers, but as beggars.[24] In 1841 the silk workers of Spitalfields proposed, with Government help, to establish a school of design in the neighbourhood and sought to attract royal support for the project by presenting a silk portrait or landscape to the Queen. The promoters of this scheme included three silk manufacturers and three weavers — one of whom was Josiah Branchflower.[25] But his craft skills received their greatest recognition in 1842. To provide encouragement and employment for the weavers, Queen Victoria and her Consort Prince Albert staged the Plantagenet Ball at Buckingham Palace on April 5 of that year. Victoria was dressed as Queen Phillippa of Hainault and Albert was attired as her husband, Edward 111. The costumes were based on Edward and Phillippa's tomb effigies in Westminster Abbey, and designed by James Robinson Planche. Victoria's gown consisted of gold woven into some 30 yards of silk by Spitalfields and Bethnal Green weavers, including one craftsman who was described as '…one of the best workmen', namely Josiah Branchflower.[26] A painting by Sir Edwin Landseer, of Victoria and Albert dressed in costume for the Plantagenet Ball is held by the Royal Collection Trust.[27]

Despite Branchflower's skills and reputation his extended family faced a constant battle for economic survival and an always present threat of a descent into poverty with all the workhouse consequences which this entailed. For the most part Josiah worked as a silk weaver in Taunton, Battersea and then in London. But on occasions he seems to have ventured briefly into more entrepreneurial activities as a 'silk manufacturer' or 'a commission agent', which suggests that he was ordering and buying finished silk products from the weavers and selling them on to retailers and perhaps even exporters. Oddly, when his daughter Mary Ann married in 1858 her father was listed as a 'woodcarver', which I take to mean either that the clerk or clergyman misheard what Josiah told him or hard times in the silk industry temporarily forced him to apply his undoubted craft skills to another trade.[28] In any case, it seems that difficult times in a declining industry forced him to adapt.

His extended family also faced trying circumstances. In 1847 Josiah appeared before the poor law authorities seeking relief on behalf of the four children of Benjamin Littlejohn, Betsy's brother. Benjamin had abandoned the children leaving them without support, for his wife, the children's mother, had died four years ago.[29] Josiah's own children lived modestly, most of them forced to abandon the silk weaving craft. The eldest daughter, Elizabeth, described as a silk weaver, married the upholster George Staines in 1843. Eldest son William married Rosina Ison, the daughter of a gardener, James Ison, and moved back and forth between the trades of gardening and silk weaving as economic circumstance required. Charles John remained a silk weaver for his whole life. John James also worked predominantly as a weaver, although he also spent some time as a dock worker. In 1854 at the age of 20 or 21 he married Anne Taylor with whom he had nine children. Anne, who worked as a silk winder died in 1885 and John James passed away from bronchitis in Bethnal Green Workhouse in 1889, which suggests the industry did not bring him prosperity.[30] Mary Ann married the silk weaver Thomas Leach and they continued to live with his parents, even as they raised a family of six children. While Mary Ann's husband had followed his father into the weaving industry their sons became printers and compositors, a rising industry, paying higher wages and with a far more certain future than the silk trade.[31]

For Josiah and his family the future was always uncertain, even modest prosperity was not guaranteed. And sometimes the good and bad times must have seemed to him to exist almost simultaneously. I suggested previously that the culture of Bethnal Green was rough and ready, with lingering pre-industrial values, centring on drinking, gambling, illicit sex and violence. The Branchflowers had probably long-ago abandoned Calvinist puritanism and one night in November 1850, Josiah provided a demonstration of the family's relinquishment of this strict Protestantism. At this time, he was enjoying a (probably brief) period of relative prosperity as a silk manufacturer and was carrying a bag of money, totalling £32 in gold and silver coins. Perhaps he was in a mood to celebrate and so he took the bait when a young prostitute, Johanne Driscoll, asked him to walk her home, first stopping at a public house to buy a quart of gin. In the process Driscoll slipped chloroform into his drink. He awoke in a house in Thrawl Street to see Driscoll and a companion removing both his trousers and the money which he had stashed in his pants' pocket. Driscoll was sentenced to six months' hard labour and Josiah kept his cash. His explanation of what happened in his exchanges with Johanna Driscoll was quite disingenuous and obviously designed to whitewash his own actions. He claimed that when Driscoll first approached him he had told her to go away and only agreed to buy her a drink because of her appeal to his sympathies. His intention, he argued before the court, was simply purchase her drink, pay for it and then leave the hotel on his own. Perhaps this moment is indicative of the world in which he lived, a world in which men and women committed illegal and desperate acts alien to the norms of prescribed Victorian morality in order to survive, a plebeian society in which the niceties of Victorian middle-class etiquette had little relevance.[32]

Josiah and his probable brother William were in lockstep throughout their lives. Both were born in Staplegrove and married at Taunton St Mary Church. Both became silk weavers and eventually moved from Somerset to Bethnal Green no doubt in search of more secure and profitable employment in the industry. At different times both were weavers and manufacturers. And they found symmetry in death too, William died of pneumonia aged 71 in early 1870 and Josiah died later in the same year at the age of 69 from peritonitis. They had lived long enough to witness the industry in which they were raised and which had blessed them with fleeting prosperity and more frequently had cursed them with economic hardship reach a stage of accelerating and terminal decline.

Endnotes

1   *A Memoir of Jacques De La Fontaine*, New York: John S. Taylor, 1838. Although a Huguenot, Jacques was often accused by his Somerset neighbours of being a 'Papist'.

2   These are the years in which the children were baptised. Sometimes children were not baptised until some years after birth.

3   This means that if I have the right James he was seventeen years and three months old when his trial ended. It should also be noted that there is no further evidence of James—marriage, birth of children, death—in the Staplegrove parish records

4   Like the other James I can't find further evidence of this James in the Brompton Ralph parish records.

5   *The Times*, April 11 1788; Ancestry, NSW Archives, New South Wales *Convict Indents, 1788–1842*; Ancestry, NSW Archives, *Australian Transportation Registers, Second Fleet 1788–90*

6   David Collins, *An Account of the Colony in New South Wales*, two vols, London: 1798, vol.1, pp. 99–100; 'Sir C Bunbury's Resolutions Respecting Convicts for Transportation', in William Cobbett, *The Parliamentary History of England from the Earliest Period to the Year 1803*, London, 1817, p. 959; Governor Phillip to WW Grenville, 13 July 1790, *Historical Records of Australia*, vol. 1 Sydney, 1914, pp. 188–9; George Mackaness, 'Affair of the Hell-Ship Neptune', *Sydney Morning Herald*, 10 February 1945; Narissa Phelps, ' Convict to Settler: an analysis of the female convicts of the second fleet vessel Neptune from the status of convict to settler and the role they played in the early colonization of Australia during the period 1790–1792, Southern Cross University Thesis, nd, https://research portal.scu.edu.au/discovery/fulldisplay/alma9910112821593802368/61SCU-INST.ResearchRepository

7   Judith Dunn, *The Parramatta Cemeteries: St John's Parramatta, 1991*

8   https:/convictrecords.com.au/convicts/blanchflower/robert123639: *Cumberland Argus*, October 25, 1899

9   Josiah's age listed in the 1851 census located on Ancestry

was crossed out by the census taker and is indecipherable. In this census he is listed as Js Branchflower. Some genealogists have misread the Js as the initial H and then imaginatively turned him into Henry Bowchflores, the father of the elder Josiah. His wife Elizabeth (or Betsy) was also mistakenly listed by the census taker as Emma, which has prompted some family historians to claim her as the elder Josiah's mother. The names of the children listed on this same census as the offspring of Josiah/'Henry' and Elizabeth/'Emma' bear the exact names of the children of Josiah and Elizabeth.

10 B. Cottret, *The Huguenots in England: Immigration and Settlement, 1550–1700*, Cambridge: Cambridge University Press, 1991, pp. 11–18

11 Sir Frank Warner, The Silk Industry in the United Kingdom https://archive.org/details/silkindustryofun00warnuoft pp. 36–43; Robin Gwynn, 'Huguenots in English Port Towns in the Late seventeenth Century' www.lib.kobe-u.ac.jp/repository/81000029.pdf; 'Walloons and Huguenots',www.family/search.org/wiki/en/England_History_Walloons_Flemish_Religions_National_Institute); Gerald B. Hertz, The English Silk Industry in the Eighteenth Century', *English Historical Review*, Vol. 24, October, 1909, 710–27

12 Sir Samuel Smiles, pp. 55–59; https://Jimmcneill.worldpress.com2011/05/21history-of the-silk-industryin-the-Touraine-region-france; Robin Gwynn 'Conformity, Non-conformity and Huguenot Settlement in England in the Later seventeenth Century' in Anne Duncan-Page ed., The Religious Culture of the Huguenots, 1660–1750, London: Ashgate, 2001, p. 28; www.bbccc.uk/legacies/immig_emig/england'; Brookes Gallagher Reusch, 'Huguenot Silversmiths in London, 1685–1715', MA Thesis William and Mary College, pp. 1–28

13 *Victoria County History: Wiltshire*, vol. 3 London: 1974, pp.179–203; *Victoria County History, Somerset*, vol. 7, www.British-history.ac.uk/vch/som/vol 7/, pp. 1–2, 56–9 165–68; www.victoriacountyyhistory.ac.uk/explore/themes/industry/textile-industry www.englandsimmigrants.com

14 The information in this paragraph is gleaned from the various Somerset parish records. These can easily be found on-line.

15 Elizabeth (born ca. 1822), Mary Anne (baptised 14/10/1824), William Alfred (baptised 10/9/1825), Josiah (baptised 15/7/1827) and Charles John (born 1829)

16 James (baptised 19/04/1833) and John James (born 24/3/1833) were baptised in Saint Mary Battersea. Henry Benjamin (baptised 23/03/1836), Mary Anne (born 1837) and Samuel (born 1839) were all born in Bethnal Green. The first Mary Anne had died by 1826, while James and Samuel died in 1833 and 1839 respectively.

17 *Cornwall Gazette*, 28 June 1828. This reference was located by Dave Branchflower

18 Examination of Josiah Branchflower before Two Justices of the Peace for Somerset, 20 May 1829. Copy of original provided by Dave Branchflower

19 Ancestry, London Church of England Births and Baptisms 1813–1917, Wandsworth St Mary, Battersea for the births and baptisms of James and John James. These records also list the trade and address of Josiah. For James' death see London, Church of England Deaths and Burials, 1813–2007, Wandsworth St Mary Battersea, 1813–1876. For Battersea history see 'The Battersea Society' www.batterseasociety.org.uk/history.php; www.panorama thames.com/1829/guide/silk-factory:https:hidden-london.com/gazetteer/battersea/

20 Ancestry, Somerset England Marriage Registers, Bonds and Allegations, 1754–1914 (Branchflower/Taylor); Ancestry, 1841, 1851 and 1861 Censuses, Middlesex, Bethnal Green

21 Peter Linebaugh, *The London Hanged: Crime and Civil Society in the Eighteenth Century* , London: Penguin, 1991, pp. 258–79, 408

22 *The (London) Standard*, 5 April 1837

23 W. H. Court, *A Concise Economic History of Britain from 1750 to Recent Times*, Cambridge: Cambridge University Press, 1954, pp. 48, 58, 152; E. P. Thompson, *The Making of the English Working Class,* New York, Vintage,1966, pp. 147, 157, 261–2;www.spitalfields.co.uk/spitalfields-history; 'The Spitalfields Silk Weavers; London's Luddites', at www.brh.org.uk/site/wp-content/uploads/2012/11/THE-SPITALFIELDS-SILK-WEAVERS

24 *The Examiner*, 5 April 1837

25 *Evening Mail,* 25April 1841;Morning Post, 25 January, 1841

26 *The Examiner*, 25 April 1841

27 https://www.rct.uk/.../queen-victoria-and-prince-albert...

28 Ancestry, Church of England Marriage Banns, 1754–1932, Hackney, St John of Jerusalem, South Hackney, 18/3/1858, marriage of Mary Ann to Thomas Leech (Leach)

29 Ancestry, London Selected Poor Law Removal and Settlement Records, 1847, Testimony of Josiah Branchflower

30 Ancestry, Church of England, Marriage Banns, St Thomas, Bethnal Green, 1851–1886; Ancestry, 1861 Census John and Ann Branchflower.

31 Ancestry, London Church of England Marriages and Banns 1754–1832, St James the Less, Bethnal Green, 13/8/1855, marriage of William Alfred Branchflower to Rosina Ison; St George in the East, Tower Hamlets,26/3/43, marriage of Elizabeth Branchflower to George Staines; Ancestry, 1881 Census, 85 Cyprus Street, Bethnal Green, James Leach, wife Elizabeth, son Thomas, wife Mary Ann and their children

32 John Bennett, *Mob Town: A History of Crime and Disorder in the East End*. New Haven: Yale University Press, 2017, p. 84; *Bell's Weekly Messenger*, 7 December 1850

Chapter 2

Adapting to a New World: Melbourne

Josiah the Younger

Some of Josiah's and William's children, but to my knowledge, none of their grandchildren, followed them into the silk industry, but two members of Josiah's family, Josiah and eventually Henry Benjamin, decided to take more drastic action to escape the diminishing economic opportunities which the silk industry and Bethnal Green now offered. On October 6 1855, in the company of his wife, Josiah sailed from Southampton on the ship *Calliance* in search of a new life in Australia. Fourteen years later Henry Benjamin left England on the *Gresham* to join his brother in Melbourne.

What motivated Josiah to take such a momentous decision to leave England? At the time the 1851 census was taken Both Josiah and Henry Benjamin were still living at home with their parents, with Josiah working as a weaver and Henry not listed as employed. Henry was now fifteen so it is surprising that he wasn't earning a wage, although perhaps in an era of steep decline in the weaving industry there were no openings for new employees.

The Armstrongs

On June 15 1854 Josiah married Mary Susannah Armstrong at St John Hackney. Josiah listed his trade as that of gardener while his father Josiah listed his own profession as commission agent. The witnesses included Josiah's sister Mary Ann and Mary Susannah's father, James Armstrong.[1] Like the Branchflowers, the Armstrongs were East London people, constantly changing their employment to meet evolving economic circumstances. At different times James Armstrong, the

son of John and Mary Armstrong (Ball) was a shoemaker, porter, greengrocer and carman.[2] In 1832 he had married Susannah Cornwell at St Mary Stratford Bow, Tower Hamlets. Susannah's father, George Cornwell was born in Hampshire but subsequently moved to London and when he died in 1846 was buried at St Pancras, Middlesex. James and Susannah had two children, Mary Susannah (b. 1834) and a son James Thomas Armstrong who was baptised in 1833 at St John of Jerusalem in South Hackney. In 1853, when he was just 20, he married Lydia Parsons at St Anne's Westminster. His father was a witness. James Thomas and his new wife, Lydia, remained in London. At the time of his marriage, he was a glass painter but he subsequently moved to Golden Square, Westminster, where he became a 'journeyman tailor', while his wife earned extra family income as a glove maker. By 1871 they had four children Elizabeth (19), James (17), Richard (7) and Ellen (2). Richard was working as a labourer, which suggest that the family was not on an upward economic and social trajectory. Ten years later John Thomas, his wife Lydia and their daughter Ellen were living in Lambeth where he worked as a 'military tailor' and Lydia as a 'tailoress'. Only twelve, Ellen was still at school.[3] As we shall see James Thomas lost contact with his sister Mary Susannah when she moved to Australia but eventually made strenuous, determined and almost certainly fruitless attempts to locate her antipodean whereabouts.

Josiah and Mary Susannah

In 1853 Josiah was still living with his parents but

when he and Mary Susannah married they were both living in Jerusalem Square. By 1855 they had moved to Camden Street in company with Josiah's younger brother, Henry Benjamin. It is clear that they were enduring hard times because William West, a broker, held a warrant to make a levy on their goods. When he tried to enforce it Josiah and Henry not only challenged the legality of his actions but took matters into their own hands, manhandling him out of the house, throwing him to the ground and kicking him in the stomach. A jury found they had a right to resist the levy but that the degree of force they used in doing so was unjustifiable. They were each sentenced to two months imprisonment.[4]

For Josiah perhaps this was the straw that broke the camel's back. Faced with difficult economic circumstances, which were only likely to worsen, and sentenced to gaol for defending his property against an illegal attempt to deprive him of it, gold rush Melbourne, with all the exaggerated stories of the prosperity it promised, may have seemed to offer a more certain and promising future. His father-in-law James Armstrong was experiencing even harder times, turned out of the depot (workhouse) for refusing to work. When the immigrant ship *Calliance* left Southampton on October 6 1855 its passengers included Josiah, his wife Mary Susannah, their infant son Josiah, James Armstrong and his wife Susannah.[5] Henry Benjamin didn't join his brother in Australia until 1869, his decision to emigrate probably at least partly shaped by the family crisis that encircled Josiah in Collingwood sometime around 1867.

As I indicated above both Josiah and James described themselves on the passage lists as agricultural labourers. In the immediate years before he left London Josiah had worked as a gardener and so perhaps his job description was not too inaccurate. But the urban raised James had never worked in agriculture or in gardens and when he reached Melbourne he retained his preference for city life by once again taking up the trade of shoemaker.

Fortunately for the Branchflowers and Armstrongs the conditions on ships travelling between the UK and Australia had improved greatly since the early days of convict

transportation. Leaving Southampton on October 10 1855 and carrying 314 passengers, including 42 married couples, 155 single men, 20 single women and 20 children, the *Calliance* arrived in Melbourne on December 31 of the same year.

The Melbourne Rate Books indicate that by the early 1860s both families were living in Collingwood, and perhaps they had moved there immediately after disembarkation. As a place to live Collingwood had serious disadvantages. In the first place, it possessed the highest mortality rate in the city, the marshes along the Yarra restricting drainage runoff from the streets and houses that extended back from the River and creating a breeding ground for enteric disease. This disease environment was reinforced by a sewerage system that flowed directly into the Yarra. What further exacerbated this situation was the practice of employees of the local tanning and wool washing workshops of disposing of the entrails of slaughtered stock by throwing them into the river. Finally, pollutant gases from the smokestacks of the numerous breweries, flour mills and other factories located in Collingwood also contributed to what constituted an extremely unhealthy inner-city environment.

But for artisans and unskilled labourers alike the suburb also had its attractions. In the first place, there was a range of employment in its factories, especially in the boot and shoe workshops, which by 1890 were more common in Fitzroy and Collingwood than elsewhere in the City. At the same time, because of its proximity to the city centre, many unskilled Collingwood workers found employment in downtown Melbourne as cleaners, storemen and draymen. In this context it is not surprising that most of Collingwood's population was made up of either tradesmen or unskilled workers. Second, until the 1880s, when Collingwood real estate became expensive, it was a suburb in which workingmen could afford the cheap rents and even purchase the small wooden detached dwellings that characterised the suburb. They valued these more highly than the noisier and less private terrace houses that were typical in other inner suburbs.[6]

James Armstrong quickly adopted to the new

economic environment and his income as a shoe-maker allowed him to save enough so that by 1867 he owned two houses on Yarra Street, one of which he rented out. Josiah was a trained silk worker but there were no opportunities to continue this trade in Melbourne. Instead, he resumed work as a gardener, a trade he had followed in his last years in London. In the early 1860s he rented houses on Vere Street but by 1866 he too had achieved enough prosperity to become a house owner. Josiah remained a resident of Vere Street until he moved to Launceston sometime around 1890.[7]

The Branchflowers arrived in Melbourne with their infant son Josiah. In the following years three more children were born to them, James Thomas in March 1857, Henry Benjamin on December 28 1860, and Frances Alice on November 24 1865.[8]

The skimpy available evidence suggests that Josiah was neither an ambitious nor a particularly savvy person where entrepreneurship was involved. In Melbourne and its surrounding gold rush towns and villages there was money to be made by those who engaged in the commercial and industrial operations that supported mining activities. But Josiah's one recorded attempt at profiting directly from mining was a failure. In 1863 in partnership with three miners he entered an agreement worth £525 with the Collingwood Mining Company to sink a shaft measuring 133 feet deep. The operation came to a complete halt at a depth of only 43 feet because water flooded the mine. When the mining company refused to pay the sum speci-fied in the contract, Josiah and his partners took it to court, claiming damages of £500 for wrongful discharge of the agreement. But the jury awarded them only £11, which almost certainly meant that for Joseph and his fellow contractors the whole exercise was a costly failure.[9] After this disaster Josiah returned to his trade as a gardener, although whether he worked for homeowners, local coun-cils or the colonial government is not clear.

But he was also a loyal, kind, generous and even brave man. In 1879, together with a policeman, the fifty-two year old Josiah went to the assistance of a man who was being viciously attacked by two assailants. Josiah, it seems had the characteristics of a good Samaritan.[10]

He was also a good son-in law. His father-in-law, James Armstrong, died on July 28 1869, and sometime after his death, his wife Susannah moved in with Josiah. Perhaps initially she contributed to the household, cooking and cleaning like so many other working class Victorian wives and moth-ers. But towards the end of her life, at least, Josiah found it necessary to hire a person described vari-ously as 'a girl' or 'woman' to look after her during his absences for work and leisure. The fact that he judged that Susannah needed constant supervi-sion may indicate that she suffered from an illness, most likely dementia. But in the end Josiah's precautions were in vain, for on one night in early July 1882 when Josiah was at work, Susannah's carer 'stepped out', leaving the seventy four year old on her own. Somehow, perhaps because she had a fit and fell into the fire, her clothes caught alight, and although the flames were extinguished by a neighbour, it was too late. Admitted to hospi-tal with burns to her legs, thighs, abdomen and right hand, she died some hours later.[11]

Josiah's second son James Thomas, an unmar-ried labourer, died in August of the same year. Before these two tragedies unfolded, Josiah's oldest son, also named Josiah, had moved to Tasmania where on December 28, 1881 he married Annie Preece.[12] During his Tasmanian years the youngest Josiah, his wife and children, lived in Launceston, where he earned his living as a grocer. By 1892 his father, the sixty-five-year old Josiah, had also moved to Launceston, perhaps driven out of Collingwood by the really hard economic times that hit Melbourne in the 1890s, and lured to Launceston by the prospect of living near his oldest son. But Tasmania also experienced a severe depression in the 1890s and the fact that by 1896 Josiah and his son and family were now sharing the same house, combined with the evidence that the younger Josiah had difficulty meeting rent payments, indicated that the Branchflowers were facing serious financial problems.[13]

By 1903 the extended Branchflower family had moved back to Melbourne, taking up resi-dence first on King Street and then at Punt Road in Richmond. The younger Josiah became a tinsmith and sheet metal worker, while his sons Adye Hinton and George John took up the trades of rubber worker and trimmer, respectively.[14] The retired Josiah, silk worker, gardener and failed mine shaft digger, now described himself as 'gentleman', perhaps less a sign of his own real social status than a genuflection in the direction of his father's ranking as a highly skilled silk weaver, a leader of the artisan 'aristocracy'.[15]

Mary Susannah's Vanishing Act

The story I have related about the Branchflower's Melbourne history has focussed very much on Josiah, and his relations with his in-laws and his son Josiah. But what about Mary Susannah and her connection to Branchflower family life? On December 28 1865 she signed the registration form recording her daughter Frances Alice's birth on November 24, listing her address as Gillingham Cottage, Vere Street, Collingwood.[16] But that is the last record we have of her as a member of the Branchflower family. Sometime in the late 1860s, probably in 1867, she left her family, taking her two youngest children, seven-year-old Henry Benjamin and two-year-old Frances Alice with her. In company with William Henry Waterhouse she travelled on the ship *Alpha* to the North Coast of New South Wales, where they first settled at Wardell before subsequently relocating to Grafton.[17] Throughout the rest of his life William Henry maintained that he and Mary Susannah were married and he raised Henry Benjamin and Frances Alice as his natural children. How the thirty-three-year old Mary Susannah met the twenty-six-year old William Henry and why she abandoned her husband and two eldest children and fled to the NSW North Coast is a complex mystery, a story which I will explore in the following chapter.

Her flight must have caused distress and consternation in the family. Perhaps it partly or even wholly explains the arrival of Josiah's brother, Henry Benjamin Branchflower, on the *Gresham* in 1869. It is possible that his mission was both to console and assist his brother, with whom he had a close relationship when they both lived in London, as well as to escape the grinding poverty and limited economic opportunities that marked

the Bethnal Green and Spitalfields economies. Almost certainly these difficult circumstances had also limited his marriage prospects for he arrived in Australia as a thirty-three year old bachelor. But if Henry Benjamin had undertaken the voyage as a mission to provide family support, he also found Melbourne to be a place of opportunity. On June 22 1870 he married Emma Elizabeth Thompson, a domestic servant, and also an immigrant from London, who was the daughter of a police officer.[18] He was also far more successful as a tradesman and entrepreneur than his brother Josiah. Describing himself as a chairmaker when he married, in the 1880s he established a furniture making company on Elizabeth Street in the City, specialising in reproducing fashionable traditional and contemporary items. The factory subsequently moved to Guildford Lane off Latrobe Street. After Henry Benjamin died in 1916 the business was carried on by his son Herbert Arthur, and Herbert's son, Eric Arthur Branchflower. By the late 1930s it was regarded as one of Melbourne's premier furniture companies.[19]

Henry Benjamin Branchflower, and son Herbert Arthur and grandson Eric Arthur

Josiah died on October 4 1909 aged 82 (although the death certificate listed his age as 85) only three years before his son Josiah also passed away at the age of 57.[20] In his co-authored book on post World War 2 immigration to Australia my former academic colleague, Richard Bosworth argued that immigration is always a tragedy for the first generation. Josiah's story in Melbourne is not one of rags to riches but apart from what I suspect were difficult economic circumstances in the 1890s he managed to make a living, become a homeowner and ensure that his son Josiah achieved a modest level of economic security as a semi-skilled and skilled worker. Unskilled workers lived in poor conditions and faced the prospect of uncertain employment and poor wages. But semi-skilled and skilled workers made up a larger portion of the workforce, earned far higher wages and often owned their own houses. Unlike their English counterparts they did not live constantly on an economic precipice.[21] Certainly, Josiah faced some terrible personal tragedies, including the loss of his son John Thomas at the age of 25, his wife's abandonment of him, his mother-in-law's tragic death, and the disappearance of his two youngest children, Henry Benjamin and Frances Alice, children that he never saw again. Perhaps he took consolation in the company of the family of his son Josiah and in the knowledge that life in Melbourne provided more security and certainty than Bethnal Green and Spitalfields.

Epilogue: the Branchflowers in Family Memory

In late 1999 I received an unexpected telephone call from Jenny Nancarrow (now Salter) who was then completely unknown to me. She asked me if I was the son of Earle Waterhouse, and when I indicated that I was, she told me that she and I were distantly related and that she had a family story involving a long-buried secret to tell me. Her family history research, she told me, had revealed strong evidence to suggest that Henry Benjamin and Frances Alice Waterhouse were in fact the children not of my ostensible great, great grandfather William Henry Waterhouse but of Josiah Branchflower.[22]

This was certainly a different narrative from the one my father told me. On the rare occasions on which my he showed me the photo albums which he had inherited from his parents, my father always pointed to the photos of William Henry and Mary Susannah, identifying them as my great, great grandparents. That is the story which his parents had passed on to him and he had no reason to disbelieve it. In the years before his death my father took great care to label those photos in the collection that he regarded as the most important, and these included portraits of William Henry and Mary Susannah. When he talked about the Grafton family he always emphasised the respectability of William Henry and his son Henry Benjamin as solid North Coast citizens. He also said that because William Henry arrived in the 1860s the family was free of 'the convict stain'. At this time, Australians regarded such ancestry as reflecting poorly on a family's social status. But my father's suggestion was, of course, rather naïve because as I discovered when years later I began to explore the family genealogy more closely, there were other paths to a family convict inheritance, paths to which I will also refer in the next chapter.

In any case when I related Jenny's research findings to other Waterhouse family members some were indifferent, a few thought it was interesting and exotic, and one distant relative, who already possessed a sense of grievance toward Percy Waterhouse (Henry Benjamin's son and my grandfather), claimed that it proved the hypocrisy of the whole Waterhouse clan. My sister Susan was quite strongly affected when I told her this story of deception and perhaps betrayal. She told me that her identity was closely tied to her understanding that respectability, decency and community service were family hallmarks and that the Mary Susannah and William Henry saga cast a shadow over that legacy.

I am fascinated by the unanswerable question relating to how long the knowledge that Henry Benjamin and Frances Alice were Josiah Branchflower's children remained in family memory. Mary Susannah's parents, James and Susannah Armstrong must have remembered her but they didn't acknowledge her in their wills. Their loyalty was with their son-in-law Josiah and his extended family. When Josiah's brother, Henry Benjamin married soon after his arrival Susannah was a witness. At the inquest after Susannah's death in 1882 Josiah testified that she was a widow with no family, which was untrue because she left a son in England and a daughter in Grafton. Perhaps Josiah wanted no difficulties with the execution of her will. Yet when Josiah died in 1909 his daughter-in-law, who was the informant for his death certificate, provided the names of all four of his children, including Henry Benjamin and Frances Alice. So, amongst the Melbourne Branchflowers, the memory of the two youngest of Josiah's children lasted, at least for one more generation. Many years later, in NSW, Frances Alice and Henry Benjamin left their children with what were probably more deliberately fragmented memories. In his last years Henry Benjamin lived at Yamba with his daughter Beatrice (Farlow) and her family. Beatrice was the informant for his death certificate, and named his place of birth as Melbourne, his father as William Henry and his mother as 'unknown'. Given that Beatrice was born in 1887, grew up in Grafton, and was seventeen when her grandmother died it is quite remarkable that she couldn't remember Mary Susannah's name. When Frances Alice died in 1947 the informant for the death certificate was one of her two sons, probably Clarence, who listed her father as William Henry, her mother as Mary Susannah and her birthplace as Collingwood. The fact that Henry Benjamin and Frances Alice's children recorded their births as taking place in Melbourne were the only fragments now remembered by the Waterhouse family of this truly remarkable Branchflower saga.

One other family member from her own generation remembered Mary Susannah and made a brief but determined effort to locate her. In 1892, her London based fifty-nine-year old brother, James Thomas Armstrong, placed advertisements in *The Queenslander* and the *Brisbane Courier* inquiring about her whereabouts.[23] Perhaps he chose to seek information about her location exclusively in the Brisbane press because the Branchflowers had some information, which they passed on to James Thomas, that when she left Melbourne, she had travelled north. There is no evidence that the fifty-five-year old Mary

Susannah, now a long-term resident of Grafton, either read or responded to her brother's message.

The family story recounted to me by Jenny Salter also as it turned out contained a remarkable coincidence. At that time, I was Head of the School of Philosophical and Historical Inquiry (SOPHI) at the University of Sydney. My supervisor was the Dean of the Faculty of Arts, Stephen Garton, who later became the University's Vice-Chancellor. I am the great grandson of Henry Benjamin Waterhouse (Branchflower). Jenny's researches revealed that Frances Alice, Henry Benjamin's sister, married William John Graham in 1884. One of their daughters, Ruby Violet Graham, married Leslie Garton. Their son Robert married Mary McBride, whose eldest son is Stephen Garton.[24] Jenny revealed that my boss was also my cousin several times removed.

There is also a tragic story attached to this speculative narrative of memories. For more than 15 years dementia gradually destroyed the mind and body of my beloved sister Susan. For the last few years before her death in 2021, she couldn't see, speak, or walk. Effectively, she lost the capacity to understand what was happening in the world around her. Only recordings of hymns and readings from the Bible brought her any solace. But the last time I saw her, which was at least a year before she died, because Covid and my lack of courage, combined to prevent any visits in the last year or so of her life, I was struck by the uncanny resemblance she bore to the member of the Waterhouse family she always admired most—our father Earle. Perhaps the values that he embodied and she admired—bravery, a commitment to education, an appreciation of English literature, a deep love of family, and an adherence to a simply defined and non-institutional form of Christianity—constituted a set of 'Waterhouse values.' However, rather than comprising principles passed down over many generations, as some family members have always insisted, this Waterhouse family cultural inheritance, as succeeding chapters indicate, extended no further back than Earle's parents, Percy and Maude.

Endnotes

1 Ancestry, London, Church of England, Register of Marriages and Banns 1754–1832, St John, Hackney

2 Ancestry, St John of Jerusalem, South Hackney, Baptisms, January 16 1833 (James Thomas Armstrong), February 19, 1837 (Mary Susannah Piggott Armstrong); Ancestry, 1851 Census, Bethnal Green; Ancestry, London, Church of England Marriage Banns ,1754–1832, St John, Hackney, Josiah Branchflower, Mary Susannah Armstrong)

3 Ancestry, London, Church of England Births and Baptisms, 1813–1911, St John Jerusalem, South Hackney; Ancestry, London, Church of England Marriages and Banns, 1754–1953, St Anne Soho; Ancestry, 1871 Census, St James Westminster, Golden Square; Ancestry, 1881 Census, Lambeth, Kennington First, District 35

4 Ancestry, 1853 England Election Rolls, Tower Hamlets; *The Standard*, 16 August 1855; Ancestry, England and Wales Criminal Registers,1791–1892, Middlesex, 13 August 1855

5 Josiah was baptised in St Simon Zelotes, Bethnal Green on March 17, 1855. The baptismal register for the church can be located at Ancestry

6 Graeme Davison, *The Rise and Fall of Marvellous Melbourne*, Melbourne University Press, Carlton, Vic., 1978, pp. 14, 44, 150–151; Seamus O'Hanlon, *Together Apart: Boarding House, Hostel and Flat Life in Pre-War Melbourne*, Australian Scholarly Publishing, Melbourne, 2002

7 The rental and home ownership careers of James and Josiah can be traced through the Ancestry collection of Collingwood Rate Book Records from 1864 to 1888.

8 Ancestry, Victorian Birth Register (birth records for James Thomas, Henry Benjamin and Frances Alice); Ancestry, St Peter's Eastern Hill Baptisms, 1845–1915 (Henry Benjamin's baptism)

9 *Argus,* 19 November, 1863

10 *ibid.*, 31 May 1879; *Mercury and Weekly Courier,* 31 May, 1879. From the newspaper accounts it seems Josiah acted dispassionately for there is no evidence that he knew either of the men involved in the attack.

11 *Argus,* 6 July 1882; *Weekly Times,* 6, 8 July 1882; *Age,* 7 July 1882; Victoria Archives, Series V, PRS 24, Consignment No., P000, Unit No., 440

12 Ancestry, Australian Marriage Index, 1788–1950, Marriage of Josiah Branchflower to Annie Preece, Launceston, 28 December 1881

13 Ancestry, City Directory, Launceston; *Launceston Examiner,* 3 September 1896

14 Ancestry, The Victorian Death Register, records Josiah's death on 17 September 1912. He was survived by his widow Annie and his children George John (27), Adye Hinton (25), Margaret Elizabeth (20), and Frederick Josiah (13). Two children, William James Arch and Percy Henry had predeceased him.

15 Ancestry, Australian Electoral Rolls, Yarra, Richmond West, 1903, 1905, 1906, 1909, 1912

16 Ancestry, Victorian Register of Births, Frances Alice Branchflower 24 November, 1865

17 *Clarence and Richmond Examiner,* 23 March 1897

18 Ancestry, Victorian Marriages, District of Bourke, 1870 Henry Benjamin Branchflower, Emma Eliza Thompson

19 Ancestry, Victoria Wills and Probate, 1841–2009, records his death on 12 May 1916. He and Emma had five children Florence Emily (1873–1951; Henry George (1875–1898), Herbert Arthur (1877–1940), Ernest William 1878–1880), Emma Elizabeth (1883–1883) For this information see Jenny Salter (Nancarrow) *The Branchflower Family*, typescript in possession of the author; *The Argus*, 22 September 1937; *The Age*, 30 November 1895-marriage of Florence to John Cuthbert; *The Age*, 29 September 1896, recording the death of Henry after a short illness; *The Australian Home Beautiful*, 1 May 1930; *The Age*, 6 February 1937

20 Ancestry, Victoria, Register of Deaths, Josiah Branchflower, 4 October 1909, 2

21 Shirley Fitzgerald, *Rising Damp: Sydney 1870–1890* , Sydney: Oxford University Press, p 115; Graeme Davison, *The Rise and Fall of Marvellous Melbourne*, pp. 41–71, 175–89

22 Jenny confirmed the details of this conversation in a letter to me dated 4 February 2000. Waterhouse Family Collection

23 *The Brisbane Courier*, 4 March 1892; *The Queenslander*, 5 March 1892

24 Jenny Nancarrow (Salter), *Descendants of Josiah Branchflower*, copy in possession of the author

PART 2

*River Valley People:
the Waterhouse Family in England
and the Clarence Valley*

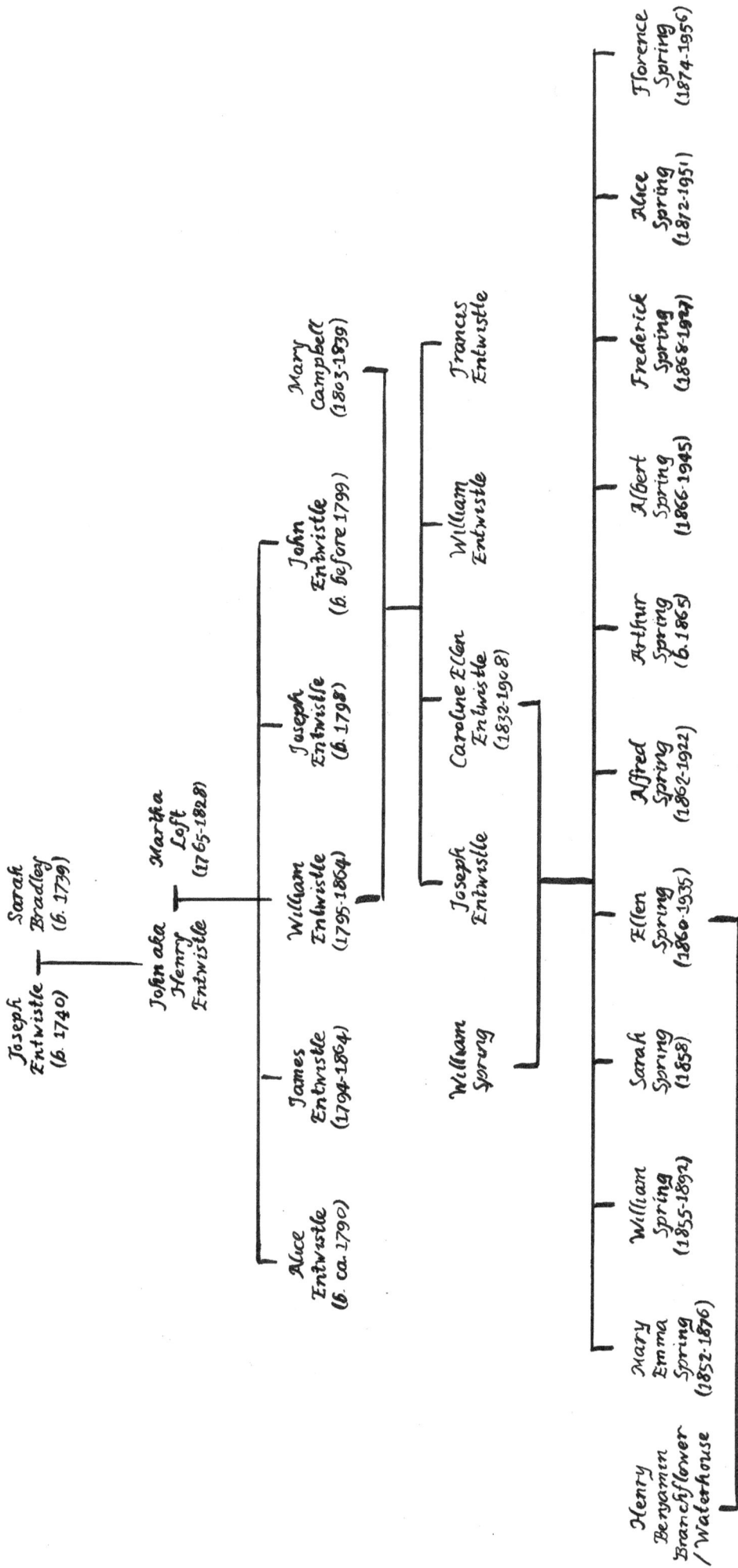

Joseph
Entwistle
(b. 1740)
—
Sarah
Bradley
(b. 1799)

John aka
Henry
Entwistle
—
Martha
Loft
(1765-1828)

Alice
Entwistle
(b. ca. 1790)

James
Entwistle
(1794-1864)

William
Entwistle
(1795-1864)
—
Mary
Campbell
(1803-1839)

Joseph
Entwistle
(b. 1798)

John
Entwistle
(b. before 1799)

William Spring
—
Caroline Ellen
Entwistle
(1832-1908)

Joseph
Entwistle

William
Entwistle

Frances
Entwistle

Henry
Benjamin
Branchflower
/ Waterhouse
—
Mary
Emma
Spring
(1852-1876)

William
Spring
(1855-1892)

Sarah
Spring
(1858)

Ellen
Spring
(1860-1935)

Alfred
Spring
(1862-1922)

Arthur
Spring
(b. 1865)

Albert
Spring
(1866-1945)

Frederick
Spring
(1868-1927)

Alice
Spring
(1872-1951)

Florence
Spring
(1874-1956)

Chapter 3

A Northern English Family of Publicans: Ann Harrison and John Waterhouse

THE CIVIL WAR ERA IN ENGLAND LASTing from 1642 to 1660 witnessed a proliferation of Protestant religious sects, including the Quaker movement, founded by George Fox in 1653. Eschewing clergy, church organisation and religious ceremony, the Quakers preached a Christianity of religious equality, insisting that the presence of God existed in every woman and man. The area encompassed by what is now Cumbria was the centre of Quakerism, reflected in the large size of Quaker congregations in places like Padshaw, Kirkby Kendal, Kentmere and Keswick. Swarthmore Hall, a house to which Fox moved when he married its owner, Margaret Fell in 1669, became the sect's organising centre.

In the eighteenth and nineteenth centuries the name Waterhouse was particularly common in the northern counties. Amongst their number were Richard Waterhouse and his wife Esther who were both Quakers and belonged to the Quarterly Meeting of Westmorland. Richard was born in about 1736 and Esther in about 1740. They were both later buried in the Kendal Quaker Burial Ground. However, Richard outlived his wife by 39 years. She died in 1788, but Richard survived to be 91, passing away in 1827. Their son, John Waterhouse, who was born in Greyrigg, Westmorland in about 1767 and his wife, Hannah Scott, born in Caldbeck, Cumberland in 1769, were also Quakers.[1]

Like his father John was a husbandman, which meant he was a small tenant farmer or landholder. His social and economic status was higher than

that of an agricultural labourer but lower than that of a yeoman farmer. To qualify as a yeoman a landholder needed to possess freehold property worth an annual rent of at least 40 shillings.

Because their income was at the mercy of regular slumps in the agricultural economy the status of nineteenth century husbandmen tended to be precarious. However, it seems that John managed to retain his status. At the time of his death in 1837 he was listed as a farmer, a term that was now commonly used in place of husbandman or yeoman.[2] Perhaps he was the owner of 70 acres of land in Beetham, near Burton-in-Kendal, land which was listed for sale in 1828.[3]

John and Hannah had a total of six children born between 1790 and 1803. But it is John junior, born in 1802, and the father of my ostensible great, great grandfather, William Henry Waterhouse, who is the focus of the narrative that follows.[4]

Burton-in-Kendal

The elder John, who died in Kirkby Kendal in 1837 remained a Quaker for his whole life, eventually belonging to the local monthly meeting.[5] But his namesake son apparently abandoned the sect in favour of the Church of England. The 1753 Marriage Act recognised marriages conducted by the Society of Friends, while the ethos of the Quaker movement stressed the necessity for Quakers to be married in the Quaker fashion. Nevertheless, in 1828 John, now aged 26, applied to the Consistory Court of Lancaster, in the Diocese of Chester, for a licence to marry Ann Harrison of

Arnside, in the parish church at Beetham.[6] And it seems that John Waterhouse senior approved of the match because his consent was sworn to before the court.[7] John and Ann married on July 21 1828 and their first child Ann (listed as Anne in the church register) was baptised on 31 January the following year. That means, of course, that she was born some time before that date. Did John senior give his consent to the marriage because Ann was certainly already pregnant? Would a Quaker congregation have approved John's marriage in a Quaker 'ceremony' to a woman who was both pregnant and almost certainly a non-Quaker? Sect members did not forbid the drinking of alcohol although they opposed drinking to excess. The fact that both John and Ann became publicans also indicates at the very least an absence of a strong Quaker commitment given that it is hard to imagine a desire of hotel owners to insist on moderate drinking habits in their public houses.

Altogether, between 1829 and 1844 John and Ann had ten children, including Ann, Mary, Jane, John Harrison, Hannah, Robert Scot, Jane, Margaret, William Henry, and Sarah. Two children were called Jane because the first Jane died young.[8] The children were baptised in the Church of England which is further and conclusive evidence that John had abandoned the faith of his parents and grandparents

At the time of their marriage John was farming in the vicinity of the village of Warton, Lancashire. Their first child, Ann, was born here, although by 1830 they had moved about one and a half miles to Yealand (Conyers) where John became a merchant and their second child, Mary, arrived.[9] Not too long afterwards, in 1832, they moved again, this time to Burton-in-Kendal, where John became proprietor of the Cross Keys Inn. If he rather than his father was the owner of the land put up for sale in Beetham, it's conceivable that he bought the hotel with the profits from that transaction. A year later he became owner

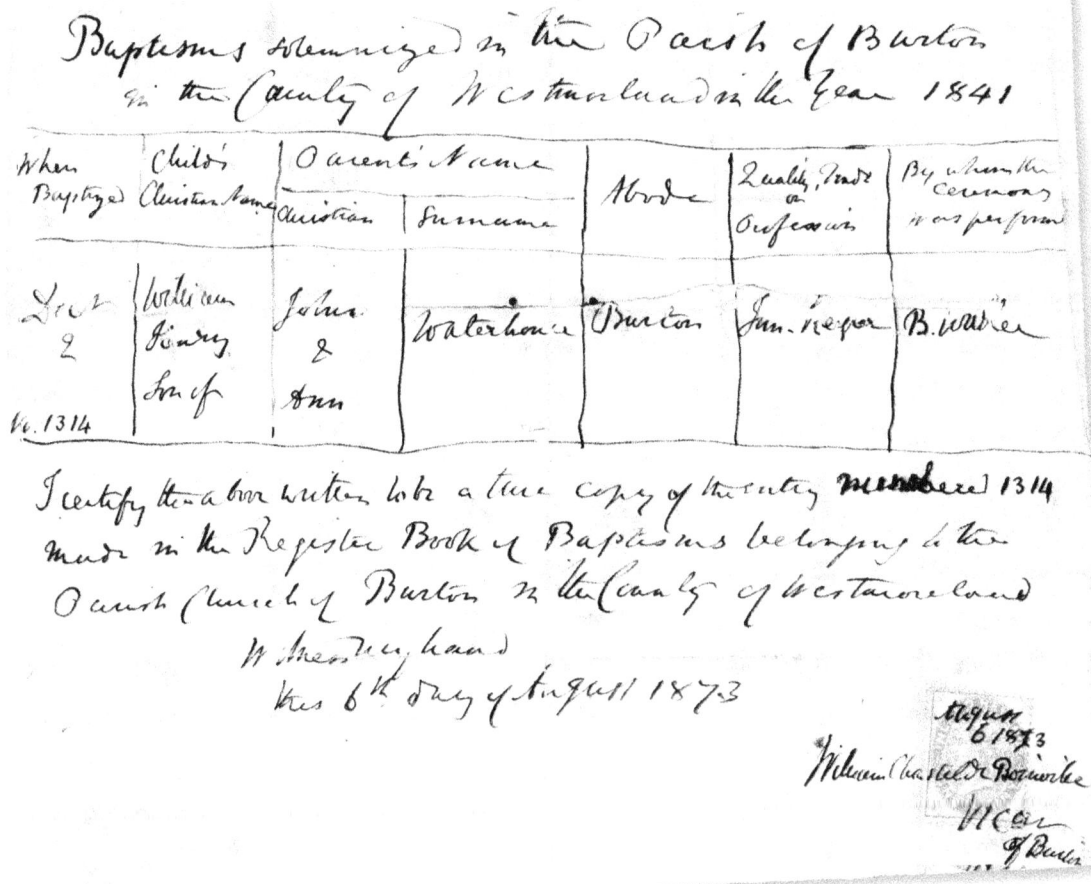

Baptismal Certificate for William Henry Waterhouse. *Copy obtained by Bob Garton*

of the more substantial Royal Oak Hotel, later known simply as the Royal Hotel. Choosing an establishment in Burton-in-Kendal was probably a modestly shrewd business decision. Located midway between Lancaster and (Kirkby) Kendal it was a regular stopping and horse changeover place for commercial and privately owned coaches. It is an indication of John's financial shrewdness in farming and trade that a comparatively young man, from a modest social background, was able to purchase such a substantial business.

In an earlier chapter I referred to how research into the Branchflower and Waterhouse families had revealed the coincidence that Stephen Garton, my former Sydney University 'boss', is also my distant relative. In researching this chapter, I found another coincidence. Jeff Hayhurst and I became friends during the years we both commuted by train from Tascott to the City. We also became and remain fishing companions who spend a couple of hours or more together on the water on a weekly basis. On one of our expeditions, I referred to the fact that I had discovered that my ostensible great, great, great grandfather was the publican of the Royal Oak in Burton-in-Kendal.

To my surprise Jeff informed me that his family had lived and farmed in the neighbourhood of Burton for several generations and that as a young man he was a regular at the Royal Oak. The hotel closed some years ago although at the time of writing renovations of the building are taking place. In the future it will consist of apartments and a bar.

During his tenure as innkeeper of the Royal Oak John demonstrated a keen and continuing interest in agriculture, which no doubt reflected his upbringing as a farmer's son and his own former career as a husbandman. The local agricultural society dinners were held at the Royal Oak and John acted as the society's treasurer. He also seems to have engaged in small scale farming on the side, perhaps utilising the land he owned adjacent to his hotel, for one of his pigs won the society's best sow award in 1833.[10]

At a time when schooling was not compulsory John and Ann were concerned nevertheless to ensure that their children, including their daughters, received an education, and so they were sent to the local Commercial and Mathematical or Grammar School. Ann was awarded prizes in 1837 and 1839 for Reading, Geography and the

The Royal Oak Hotel, Burton-in-Kenda. *Source: Kath Hayhurst Collection*

English Classics while Mary earned awards in 1838 and 1839 for proficiency in reading the Old Testament, Letter Writing, and the mysteriously named, 'the like of Scotland'.[11]

John put the hotel and the adjacent land up for sale in 1836, but neither found buyers. The 1841 census revealed that the family was still occupying the hotel and they remained there for most of the ensuing decade.[12]

Southport

In 1849 the Waterhouse family moved to the much larger seaside resort town of Southport in North Meols Parish in Lancashire. Perhaps John had tried to sell the Royal Oak earlier because Burton was a small town, providing certain but limited economic opportunities, mostly through the travelling trade. In any case, he took over the licence of the eleven-year-old Hoghton Arms Hotel in the coastal holiday resort town of Southport near Liverpool, one of many newly established hotels catering to the fast-growing tourist trade.

This hotel was particularly popular with visitors from nearby Wigan, a rapidly growing mill and coal mining town. Located just north of Liverpool, Southport was regarded as more upmarket than Blackpool, and boasted baths, promenades, a large number of hotels and a pier that stretched more than 4,000 feet (1219 metres) into the ocean. It was also a town with promising future growth prospects, for the Industrial Revolution had fuelled a new era of commercial tourism catering to emergent middle-class and skilled working-class families.[13]

But the Southport move was quickly followed by tragedy. On November 14 1850 John Waterhouse, aged 48, died leaving his wife Ann with two major responsibilities.[14] First, she took over the management of the hotel and was listed in the 1851 census not as a widow but as an innkeeper. Second, she had to care for the large number of children still living at home, including Mary (20), Hannah (16), Jane (13), Margaret (11), William Henry (9) and Sarah (7). She also had to pay the boarding fees for Robert Scot (14) who was now at school in nearby Churchtown. Her sister Elizabeth, who had lived with the family when they occupied the Royal Oak was also still present. Finally, Ann and Elizabeth's widowed mother, also named Ann, had now joined what

Still Open for Business: The Hoghton Arms Hotel

was very much an extended family. The older children together with Elizabeth almost certainly worked in the hotel. But in an era in which people aged more quickly than in contemporary society, it is unlikely that Ann's 67-year-old mother was a major contributor to the work of the inn.

The 1861 census revealed that Ann was still managing the hotel and that her sister Elizabeth and a number of her children were still living with her. Elizabeth was listed as an 'assistant maid', and Margaret (21), Hannah (26) and Sarah (17) no doubt also contributed to the running of the hotel. Two sons were also living at home. John Harrison, now a widower had returned to live under his mother's roof along with his son, three-year-old, John Alexander Waterhouse. William Henry, now nineteen, had chosen not to go into the family business, but was working in 'building sales.' This census represents the last contemporary historical record on which he can be certainly identified until 1874 when he placed an advertisement in a Grafton newspaper offering a reward for the return of horses that had strayed from his property.[15]

In 1871 Ann was still running the hotel with the assistance of Elizabeth, Hannah and Sarah. By 1881, however she had retired, although she was still living in company with Hannah, Sarah, and another daughter, Margaret Shenton, who had returned to the family when she became a widow. The three daughters were all described as 'property owners', which suggests that they now lived from their earnings as landlords rather than from wages as pub workers. The family was now well off and when Ann died on June 21, 1881, she left an estate of £23,442/5/6, evidence that she was not just a determined and strong woman, the matriarch of a (mostly)close knit family, but she was also a very successful hotel keeper. [16]

Ann was buried in the churchyard of Christ Church, Southport. When she married John in a Church of England ceremony, she effectively indicated that she preferred the safety of the established church to the quirkiness of the Quaker faith to which her husband's family had adhered for generations. It seems sadly ironic that while the Hoghton Arms still stands, the site of her retirement home at 54 Duke Street is now occupied by a Jehovah's Witnesses Hall of worship. I suspect that given a choice between the gentle eccentricity of Quakerism and the harshly asserted certainties of the Jehovah's Witnesses sect Ann would certainly have opted for the former.

Endnotes

1   Ancestry, *England and Wales Quaker Births, Marriages and Deaths Registers, 1578–1837*

2   *ibid.*

3   *Lancaster Gazette*, 16 August 1828. Jenny Salter (Nancarrow), *The Waterhouse Family Story*, typescript. I am grateful to Jenny for providing me with a copy of this history.

4   William (1790–1857), Mary (1794-), Hannah (1798-), Richard (1800–1847), John (1802–1850) and Isabella (1803–1832).

5   Kirkby Kendal is a market town, which in previous centuries was also home to cloth, tobacco and snuff manufactories. It is located 31 kilometres north of Lancaster. It is not to be confused with Burton-in-Kendal, a much smaller town located in the extreme south of Cumbria, half way between Lancaster and (Kirkby) Kendal.

6   Beetham is just north of Burton-in-Kendal and Arnside is a coastal settlement just west of Beetham

7   Ancestry, *Archdeaconry of Richmond, Church of England Marriage Bonds, 1611–1861*

8   Ann (baptised 31/1/1829), Mary (b. 24/8/1830), Jane (baptised 26/1/1832, buried 24/2/1832), John Harrison (1/8/1833 – 11/12/1902), Hannah (baptised 10/2/1835), Robert Scot (baptised 5/8/1836 – 14/2/1878)), Jane (baptised 14/1/1838), Margaret (baptised 12/2 1840) William Henry (b. 1/10/1841), and Sarah (baptised 5/10/1844 – April 1926). Ann's baptism and Mary's birth and baptism are recorded in Ancestry, *Warton St Oswald, Births and Baptisms, 1813–1911.* The baptisms of Jane, John Harrison, Hannah, Robert Scott and Sarah are recorded in the *Burton Parish Register 1653–1837.* The 1841 census lists Ann aged 12 as the daughter of John and Ann. The 1851 census lists Mary aged 20 as the daughter of John and Ann. William Henry's birth certificate is held by the General Register Office. Jenny Salter obtained a copy on 17/1/2000. A copy of William Henry's baptism certificate was obtained by Bob Garton. For Sarah see Ancestry, *Civil Registration Death Index 1916–2000.* My thanks to Kath Hayhurst, who has an expert knowledge of Burton-in-Kendal's history and historical records, for providing me with the names of the Waterhouse children listed in the Burton church records and to Jenny Salter for sending me a copy of her carefully documented Waterhouse family genealogy.

9   The registers recording the births of Ann and Mary indicate Ann and John's places of residence and John's professions.

10   *Lancashire Gazette*, 19 November 1833, 24 October 1935, 1 September 1838

11   *ibid.*, 1 July 1837, 1 September, 13 October 1838, 6 July 1839

12   Mary and Margaret, are missing from the 1841 census but are listed in the 1851 census, which means either that they were away from home when it was taken or the census collector made an error.

13   James Walvin, *Beside the Seaside: A Social History of the Popular Seaside Holiday*, Allen Lane, London, 1978; Frank Robinson, *A Descriptive History of the Popular Watering-Place of Southport in the Parish of North Meols, on the Western Coast of Lancashire,* http://southportworld.co.uk/history/southport-in-1848.php

14   *Westmorland Gazette,* 16 November 1850 I am grateful to Cassy Nancarrow for this reference

15   *Clarence Richmond Examiner and New England Advertiser*, 4 August 1874 (Hereafter *Clarence Examiner*)

16   *Cheshire Observer,* 2 July 1881; Ancestry, *National Probate Calendar Index of Wills and Administration, 1858–1895*

Chapter 4

Mary Susannah and William Henry's Excellent Adventure: from Collingwood to Grafton

Escape From the City

In the north of England in the 1860s there were men named William Waterhouse who married and had children.[1] But it is extremely unlikely that any of them were William Henry Waterhouse the future immigrant. In 1897 William claimed that he had arrived in the 'northern districts' of NSW 30 years ago, that is in 1867, although that should be treated as an approximate date given that he was remembering back over many years. [2]

When Mary Susannah died in 1904 her death notice in the local press indicated that she had arrived in Grafton in 1872 after a residence 'of some years' at Wardell.[3] So, we know William left England for Melbourne sometime after 1861 and that he and Susannah travelled from Melbourne to Wardell either in 1867 or slightly later, Perhaps, it is our William who was acting for a Manchester auctioneer who advertised for sale four lots of growing oak trees in Cheshire in April 1867. Cheshire is adjacent to Lancashire, so if he was working there it is not inconceivable that he had left his home in Southport and moved to the adjacent county in search of employment. Moreover, the trees were probably destined for use in building construction, which means as a building materials salesman, William was qualified to promote their value.[4] However, that means that he must have left England very soon after, met Mary Susannah in Melbourne, eloped with her and her two youngest children and arrived in Wardell, perhaps in late

1867 or more plausibly sometime in the succeeding one or two years. This is a possible but highly unlikely time frame scenario.

For reasons relating to the need for colonial governments to demonstrate fiscal accountability, assisted passengers were often more carefully recorded than those making their own way, and given there is no record of William's passage it is likely that he was a full fare paying immigrant. He probably travelled directly to Melbourne, choosing a city and a colony where the continuing gold rush was sustaining a long building boom and economic opportunities for men of his trade were greater than elsewhere in Australia. It is likely that he specifically based himself in Collingwood because the opportunities in timber sales here were excellent. Houses under construction in Collingwood were mostly free-standing wooden structures, whereas in other suburbs they were more likely to be terraces built of brick.

The most frequently referenced William Waterhouse in the Victorian press at this time was a wonderfully colourful and tragic character who combined the trades of auctioneer and slaughterman in Ararat, Ballarat and Melbourne in the late 1850s and through the 1860s. He was continually facing court charged with drunkenness, disorderly conduct in company with 'disreputable women', 'furious riding' and insolvency. He is probably the William Waterhouse committed to the Yarra Bend Asylum in 1873, as 'a miserable imbecile old man…' Given that our William didn't arrive until sometime after 1861 and moved north in the late 1860s this is clearly not him.[5]

I failed to find any written record of his stay in Melbourne and so we don't know how he met Mary Susannah Branchflower. In later life, to conceal the facts that he was not legally married to her and that Henry Benjamin and Frances Alice were not his children, William Henry sometimes falsified legal documents. For example, as informant on Mary Susannah's death certificate he indicated that they were married in Hackney Wick in 1854, when Mary Susannah was twenty years old.[6] In fact, this information is partly true because, as already noted, Mary Susannah did marry in Hackney in 1854 at the age of 20, but it was to Josiah Branchflower, not William Henry Waterhouse. Moreover, in 1854 William was only thirteen years old, too young to be marrying.

He provided a different account of his 'marriage' to members of his own family because his death certificate, based on information provided by his children, indicated that he and Mary Susannah had married in Melbourne on a date 'not known'. His family surely knew his approximate if not his specific age and so a claim that he had married in London in 1854 at the approximate age of thirteen was unlikely to have seemed credible to his children and their family members.[7] However, when he reminisced about when he and Mary Susannah arrived in the northern rivers area he had no reason to tell untruths so credence can be given to his version of how and when he and his family arrived in Wardell and then Grafton.

In his 1897 recorded reminiscence, he noted that he had settled in Wardell on the Richmond under contract to the sawmill owned by the partnership of Ingpen and Carter, a business that also operated a mill in Grafton. At that time most of the timber harvested in the Richmond Valley was transported to market in sailing vessels. Waterhouse and his new family arrived on the north coast on board one of these small timber carrying ships, the schooner *Alpha*.[8] We know that when William Henry arrived in Melbourne he resumed his career in 'timber pursuits', and that, no doubt, is how he came in contact with the northern

rivers firm of Ingpen and Carter, a company that relied on the *Alpha* to ship cedar, pine and beech to the fast-growing city of Melbourne.[9] One of the partners in Ingpen and Carter was Thomas Carter who arrived in Melbourne as an immigrant from England in 1855. Noting the high prices that builders were paying for softwoods from Tasmania and New Zealand and learning of the high quality of the small shipments of pine from the Clarence and Richmond, he bought William Kirchner's mill on the Clarence and then, in addition, built a mill for his son Ernest on the Richmond at Wardell. However, he maintained a connection to the Wardell operation, serving as its agent. It is probable that Carter met William Henry in Melbourne because they were both associated with the timber and construction industries, and that Carter then hired Waterhouse to manage his newly established sawmill at Wardell.[10]

In this era, it was common for working class families to earn extra income by taking in boarders, especially young working men and women who were living away from their families.[11] Perhaps William met Mary Susannah when he boarded with her family or more likely in the home of one of the Branchflower's Collingwood neighbours. As will become clear he was a flamboyant and forceful personality and perhaps he convinced Mary Susannah that he could offer her and her youngest children a bright and prosperous future. Josiah was almost certainly a decent and well-meaning man, but his modest record as family provider suggests he lacked effectiveness and ambition.

In any case it seems likely that the escape was carefully planned, involving Waterhouse securing employment in Wardell and then organising the voyage on the *Alpha* for himself and his newly acquired family. In his own much later written words, the Wardell district in the Richmond Valley was in 'wild condition', by which description he was probably referring to the crude nature of the local housing and working facilities, and the typical unruliness of the timber workforce.[12] It was an isolated and (in European terms) 'undeveloped' settlement. Located approximately 1500 hundred kilometres from Melbourne it was also a place where the secret of William Henry's real

Mary Susanna Armstrong/Branchflower/Waterhouse portrayed as a respectable Grafton wife and mother.
Waterhouse Family Collection

relationship with Mary Susannah and her children could be well hidden. Between 1964 and 2014 the village of Wardell was most noted for its lift span bridge carrying Pacific Highway traffic across the Richmond River, while also still allowing sugar cane carrying vessels to make their way up and down river. When Waterhouse lived there the sawmill was the town's most vital institution, providing employment for the locals who processed the timber, which was then carried by sailing vessels to the ports of Sydney, Melbourne and beyond.

By 1873 William and his family had moved from Wardell to Grafton. In that year both Frances Alice (kindergarten) and Henry Benjamin (third class) were enrolled in the town's public school and both received proficiency prizes at the annual awards ceremony.[13] In 1874, when William Henry placed an advertisement in the Grafton Press offering a reward for the four horses that had strayed from his Mary Street home, he was probably in his third year of residence in this fast-growing Northern Rivers town.[14] He was now manager of Ingpen and Carter's Grafton sawmill, which

was equipped with up-to-date saws and planing equipment. Originally owned by Patrick Fraser by 1875 it had passed via Ingpen and Carter into the hands of William Kinnear, one of the earliest selectors on the Clarence who abandoned farming in favour of operating a sawmill, a sugar mill and a boat building yard. By the early 1880s the mill had once again passed into Fraser's ownership and when he died in 1891 it was purchased by his brother William in partnership with William Norrie. Sometimes identified by the name of whichever individual owned it at that particular time, the business was also frequently referred to simply as Grafton Sawmills. Moreover, throughout these changes of ownership William remained manager of this mill, only relinquishing the position when he and Mary Susannah travelled to England for a three year stay in 1897. Under his direction it eventually emerged as the largest sawmill in Grafton.[15]

A Growing and Prosperous City: Grafton 1830-1914

The Selection Acts which were passed by colonial

legislatures in the 1860s and 1870s briefly created hundreds of thousands of small farms in colonies across Australia. Combined with the boom in wool and wheat production and export that extended from the 1850s to the 1890s, this provided a stimulus to the growth of the Australian rural population including both town and country. Not only did many existing towns expand in size but new ones were founded and prospered. Grafton was settled on both sides of the still interchangeably named Big or Clarence River around 1840 as a port as well as a site of stores, workshops and a hotel. In fact, for the rest of the nineteenth and into the early twentieth century Grafton grew faster than most NSW towns, its population more than doubling in the 1860s and rising by more than 70% in the succeeding decade. The prosperity that accompanied the town's growth in this era was reflected in the building of a new courthouse, gaol, customs house and hospital and the extraordinary increase in the number of banks, hotels, schools and churches.

where food remained relatively abundant, especially in and near the river, there was less conflict between the invaders and the Indigenous occupants. However, in the upper Clarence where sheep and cattle replaced kangaroos, Aborigines inevitably turned to killing and eating the introduced species with the result that conflict and the murder of Aboriginal peoples was more common. In the end there was an unequal accommodation, with Aborigines often working for European farmers, cutting scrub and husking maize on the land that was stolen from them. They were also shifted to reserves where in the absence of native tucker and provided with meagre rations they also became maize farmers. For Indigenous inhabitants of the Big River, a partial adoption of European ways became a necessary means of survival.

In the Clarence as in the other north coast river valleys the cedar cutters were the first European arrivals and it took only a few years for them to clear the river banks of cedar in the lower sections of the Valley. Many of the timber getters in the

Grafton from Water Tank.

Postcard of nineteenth century Grafton. *Waterhouse Family Collection*

Of course, this process involved the displacement of the original owners and occupiers of the Clarence, the Bandjalong, Jigara, Kumbainggiri and Jakambal peoples, who had lived in the area for at least 5,000 years. In the lower Clarence

Clarence were men who had earlier cut cedar on the Macleay River.

However, the economy and European population of the Clarence Valley in general and of Grafton in particular grew faster than in the towns of the other northern river valleys because the Clarence was uniquely situated both in terms of its location and its climate. In the first place, Grafton became a port not only for produce grown in the Clarence but also for wool and wheat from the northern tablelands. This produce was brought down on hastily and crudely built roads from Armidale, Glen Innes and Tenterfield. Even when the rail line from Newcastle reached Armidale in 1876 the tableland farmers and graziers still found it cheaper to send their produce destined for Sydney and elsewhere via Grafton.

Second, whereas in river valleys located further south, timber getting was succeeded first by maize growing, and then dairying, with cattle raising mostly confined to the upper, inland areas, the Clarence developed a more complex rural economy. Timber, including both softwood and hardwood remained important to the economy, and was processed in Grafton mills and shipped to Sydney, Melbourne, New Zealand and even Germany. The discovery of gold in the Upper Clarence in 1853 also contributed a modest boost to the local economy because the metal was first transported to Grafton before it was shipped to Sydney. Grafton was also a stopover for miners on their way to and from the goldfields, although I suspect it was the Grafton publicans who were the chief beneficiaries of their patronage. Agricultural goods shipped to larger metropolitan markets included not only maize but potatoes, onions and eggs. Dairying remained a modest industry catering to local consumption until the 1880s when new technology, especially refrigeration, allowed the shipping of butter to Sydney and beyond. This led to an expansion of the industry everywhere on the north coast, although in the Clarence it tended to be concentrated in the Lower Valley, especially around Southgate. Most importantly, sugar growing, which had failed in valleys further south, where the climate was too cool, became a major source of income for Clarence Valley farmers, beginning in the 1860s. Traditionally grown on large plantations in the West Indies, using slave or bonded labour, what emerged in the Clarence was a unique system of small-scale production. For many farmers it provided a far more prosperous source of income than maize.

Sugar must be processed within a day or so of being cut and so a whole series of mills sprang up in the Clarence, including not only those built by CSR but others established by local entrepreneurs as well as by farmer co-operatives. Nor were sugar mills the only manufacturing plants in the Valley. By the 1880s, Grafton and surrounds also boasted a meatworks, a soap and tannery factory and a brewery. In addition, by the 1890s there was a network of creameries in the Clarence serving butter factories at Grafton and Ulmurra.[16]

To sum up, in the second half of the nineteenth century the Clarence Valley hosted a complex and prosperous economy, providing opportunities in farming, mineral resources, industry, public service and commerce. Members of the Waterhouse and other families with which it intermarried, engaged with this prosperous rural and large town economy, some with more success than others. The Waterhouse family called Grafton home for two generations, and here, far from Melbourne, William Henry's secret remained safe. And if his family didn't reach the level of wealth achieved by some Grafton entrepreneurs it maintained, with occasional lapses, a measure of modest economic security and prosperity.

A Contradictory Life: How William Henry Re-invented Himself (Twice) in Grafton

William Henry's life in Grafton can be divided into two distinct periods. In the first, he became obsessed with acting as a guardian of Victorian respectability and morality to the point of caricature. In particular he engaged in crusades which favoured temperance and vilified Catholicism. In the second, adopting a more measured personae, he assumed the role of a senior Grafton citizen, serving on the City Council and as a magistrate, and abandoning membership of organisations dedicated to bigotry in favour of supporting more moderate institutions.

In the twentieth century masonic lodges became essentially male social organisations but in the nineteenth century many of them were founded and operated as vehicles to espouse certain ideologies and social reform agendas. At various times William Henry belonged to a total of four Grafton lodges including the Graftonia No. 79 Lodge (1878), the Loyal Orange Lodge (ca.1880), The Good Templars Lodge (1881), and sometime later the Royal Leopold Lodge. He also held the highest office, as 'Worshipful Master', in the Loyal Orange and Good Templars Lodges. Moreover, both of these Lodges had social, political and religious agendas. In the case of the Loyal Orange Lodge movement, Sabbatarianism, opposition to gambling, and temperance were all part of the reform agenda. As a member of the Royal Orange Lodge Waterhouse often organised the annual July 12 Battle of the Boyne celebrations, which involved picnics and public meetings addressed by evangelical clergy. Usually these were Methodist or Baptist ministers, men who delivered zealous speeches promoting the broad ideals of Protestant belief and culture, and denouncing Catholicism as a totalitarian faith opposed to personal liberty. These events also included band music and programs of competitive sports.[17] Apart from a term as leader of the Loyal Orange Lodge Waterhouse at other times served as Lodge Librarian and Secretary of a committee that raised funds for the purchase of monuments to erect over the graves of Protestant clergy. He was also a driving force in a Loyal Lodge aligned movement to erect a Protestant Hall in Grafton, the foundation stone of which was laid in 1880.[18] The speeches given by evangelical clergy at the meetings held to raise funds for this Hall, as well as those subsequently delivered in the new building, apart from their obligatory denunciations of Catholicism, were filled with praise of past and present military and religious Protestant leaders, including Gustavus Adolphus.[19]

The Order of Good Templars was a lodge that emerged out of the reform movement that swept the United States in the first half of the nineteenth century. It was a movement that witnessed the emergence of new religious sects, including the Mormons, and of reform organisations that embraced the abolition of slavery, women's political and legal rights and temperance. Branches of the Lodge were established in Australia, probably

in the 1870s, including one that was operating in Grafton by 1880, with William as one of its officials.[20] It's not clear how the child of publicans in Burton-in-Kendal and Southport became an anti-alcohol advocate but he made his position very clear when at a temperance meeting in 1881 he spoke of alcohol as Satan's 'right hand destroyer'.[21] He became very active in this Lodge and the temperance movement more generally, organising steamer excursions offering 'temperance refreshments' and joining a deputation of Good Templars who lobbied a group of visiting cabinet ministers from Sydney on the virtues of local option polls as a means of 'restricting the traffic in strong drinks'.[22] Local option polls, which allowed each electorate to decide whether to reduce or eliminate the hotels within its boundaries, were in fact introduced in NSW in 1882. However, the Good Templars were committed to total prohibition, and William's public comments suggest he was too.

William Henry Waterhouse in his lodge regalia.
Waterhouse Family Collection

Local Option Polls didn't guarantee that, because they gave electors the choice of voting to eliminate, reduce or maintain the number of hotels in their electorate, but perhaps the Templars saw them as a necessary compromise.[23]

If I didn't know that William Henry was the son of Westmorland and Lancashire publicans John and Ann, who had married in the Church of England, baptised their children in the same Church and had never exhibited signs of religious zeal or bigotry, I might have concluded that he was an immigrant from Ulster, who was born and raised in an atmosphere of Protestant extremism and anti-(Irish) Catholic fervour and fanaticism. How then do we explain William's actions and attitudes? One possibility is that there was alcoholism in his family, which might explain the relatively early deaths of his father John at the age of 48, and his brother Robert Scot aged 42. Conceivably, William's advocacy of temperance resulted from his observations of the damage alcohol may have caused in to people he loved and knew. Of course, this doesn't explain his support for organisations that were also virulently anti-Catholic. Another possibility is that the surprising cultural diversity of Grafton population aroused William's insecurities. By the 1870s Catholics made up almost 25% of the city's population and they were served by two churches, a school and a convent. Another 10% of the town's population was made up of German Lutherans, who laboured on the local stations and farms and worked in Grafton's soap and candle factory. By 1876 they also had their own church. On the one hand, as members of the foundation Protestant Reformation Church, Lutherans posed no threat to William's religious understandings. On the other, Lutherans didn't see alcohol as a moral evil, but rather enjoyed beer and wine in abundance. Together, Grafton's Lutherans and Catholics may have challenged William's moral and religious understandings.[24]

But I suspect that it is most likely that William adopted a personae of religious and moral righteousness because he was determined to present himself as a person of honour and good morals, a man committed to serve his adopted community tirelessly and selflessly. And that determination was driven by his secret knowledge that in fact he was an imposter, who was pretending to be Mary Susannah's legal husband and Henry Benjamin and Frances Alice's legal father. Instead, he was an adulterer and a liar, an exemplar of what a respectable middle-class Victorian husband and father should not be.

In the late nineteenth and through the twentieth century the Bush was promoted, mostly by radical writers and journalists, as both the birthplace and permanent site of the typical Australian (male) character, one based on mateship, egalitarianism and an inherent distrust of authority. However, despite this characterisation of the 'typical' Australian by late nineteenth century *Bulletin* journalists, and subsequently by nationalist school historians, the Bush was marked by a rigid social hierarchy that in turn engendered endemic conflict, especially between selectors, itinerant workers, including shearers, rouseabouts and boundary riders on one side, and pastoralists on the other.

Rural towns too, were marked by social and economic hierarchy. At the top were the local pastoralists who usually had little to do with local town society because their focus was on the social life of the capitals. Next came the professionals-doctors, business owners, lawyers, clergy, bank managers and school headmasters, A third level consisted of clerks, teachers, small business owners, police and stock agents. At the bottom were waged blue collar workers. The social differences were rigidly maintained, with the wealthier citizens dismissing those at the base of the social pyramid as 'rabble', while those at the bottom resentfully labelled the elite as 'the umbrella mob'.[25]

So, this was the social milieu, which William Henry, carrying the heavy cultural baggage of deceit and adultery, was required to negotiate. In an era in which the temperance movement had developed strong support amongst middle class and religiously minded rural town dwelling Australians, the fact that both his parents were publicans, may have deepened his sense of insecurity and his need to hide his past, as well as sharpening his zeal for temperance.

However, beginning in the late 1880s, William

Henry began to pursue a different path to ensure and maintain his status as an entitled member of Grafton's respectable middle-class community. He was no longer an advocate of the causes championed by zealous, evangelical, anti-Catholic Protestants. Although William was still organising 'Battle of the Boyne' commemorations on behalf of the Loyal Orange Lodge in 1885 he subsequently abandoned this Lodge in favour of the Emulation Lodge whose purpose was purely to teach the formal rituals of the lodge movement to members of regular lodges. In 1877 The Royal Leopold Lodge, named in honour of Prince Leopold, Queen Victoria's youngest son, was founded in the Surrey Masonic Hall. A branch of this Lodge, which was dedicated to male fellowship, opened in Grafton in 1880. William became a member, a sign both of his loyalty to the crown and of his social status in the Grafton community.[26] Moreover, he was now so well-known and accepted that he was appointed and elected to a number of important local offices. He became Auditor for the City Council and Member of the Council of the Clarence Pastoral and Agricultural Society (CP and A), Treasurer of the Grafton School of Arts, Alderman of the Borough, a Justice of the Peace who jointly presided over the Grafton Police Court, and a member of the Grafton Chamber of Commerce. He was still engaged in fundraising but for secular not religious or moral causes, for he was Collector both for the Grafton Hospital and the CP and A Society. Although he still organised fund raising picnics and river excursions, now it was to raise funds for the Grafton School of Arts. The narrow-minded zealot had transformed into the generous and benevolent citizen.[27]

There were also changes in his professional career. In August 1887 he established an electric baths therapy business, which involved exposing customers sitting in a hot bath to low voltage electricity. Waterhouse promoted the treatment as a cure for neuralgia, liver problems, muscular tremors, muscular and joint soreness, gout, sterility, uterine disorders, irritable bladders, constipation and asthma. Decorum was maintained by offering women a separate apartment in which to change and bathe, and clients were encouraged to sign

up for multiple visits, given that the electrical currents passed through rather than remaining in their bodies. He charged £3/5/ – for a course of seven baths. Nor did he just confine his promotion of the baths to local citizens, for he also targeted visitors to Grafton, especially travellers attending major race meetings.[28]

William operated this business while also continuing to manage Grafton Sawmills. When he returned from England in 1900, he re-opened the baths after installing new equipment in the form of a thermal bath cabinet.[29] This form of medical treatment was developed in the late eighteenth and early nineteenth centuries and a few highly qualified physicians treated patients using this method. At Guys Hospital in London an electrifying room was set up and integrated into the treatment of patients with 'nervous disorders'. Physicians only promoted its value in treating psychiatric disorders, although unqualified charlatan promoters of 'electric baths' claimed them as a cure-all for most diseases. Although still popular in the United States, electrotherapeutic treatment fell out of favour in England in the late nineteenth century, which suggests that William's timing in promoting its curative properties was a little late. He advocated for his 'electric baths' treatment as a cure-all which suggests he too was more interested in quick profit than in providing genuine curative treatment.[30]

In April 1896 Waterhouse advertised to purchase samples of native Tulipwood, (Black) Bean Tree and Rosewood.[31] These proposed acquisitions were in preparation for a planned business trip to England. Although he claimed to have acquired farms to sell to prospective immigrants, more central to his purpose was a plan to persuade prospective English buyers, who presently considered Australian hardwoods too difficult to cut and shape, of their virtues and usefulness. Overall, his hopes were to develop a direct timber trade linking the Clarence and English ports.[32]

William left for England on the *Orizaba*, a comfortable Royal Mail Ship on April 18, and returned, brimming with optimism, in January of the following year. He claimed he had succeeded in persuading English engineers of the usefulness of Australian hardwoods for railway sleepers and street wood paving. He also insisted that the potential English demand for Clarence timber was so great as to require the services not only of Fraser and Company but of other Clarence River mills. He indicated that there was '…an increased activity in the timber business in the Clarence', prompting the need to engage a ship to carry timber directly from Grafton to England. This ship, he suggested, would be the first of many.[33]

An academic historian, trained to be sceptical, might come to the conclusion that William was at least partly engaging in exaggerated self-promotion. The subsequent history of his involvement with this project provides strong evidence to support this judgement. Almost immediately upon his return he announced that he was making a second journey to London, this time accompanied by Mary Susannah. Clearly intended as involving a longer stay than his first trip William announced that now that he had established a trade in timber with the 'old country', he would act as Fraser's agent in London, although also undertaking other commissions.[34]

By this stage of his life William was modestly prosperous. He and Mary Susannah sailed for England aboard the twin screw mail ship, the *Ophir*, a ship noted for its elaborate and expensive interiors. But the venture was not a financial success and his claims that he had previously developed valuable connections with English engineers and timber merchants turned out either to indicate a misjudgement or were deliberately untrue. The couple returned to Grafton in 1900 with William blaming English middlemen for extracting huge profits from Australian exports at the expense both of Australian exporters like himself and English consumers. Unsuccessful as a timber exporter he had turned to selling Australian honey direct to English customers and bypassing the brokers. But he had no more success either with this product or this strategy.[35] His three-year experience as a timber exporter in London had failed to produce the results that his previous visit had led him to expect because he had misjudged the English timber market. There was nothing left to do but rationalise the experience as he did in later years by

suggesting that he and Mary Susannah returned to Grafton because the English climate did not agree with her.[36] And yet there are fragments of evidence to suggest the voyage to England and their London experiences were remembered perhaps as (another) great adventure. Frances Alice's granddaughter, Edna Winter, recalled hearing stories when she was a child about her great grandparents visit, and related that Frances Alice owned a set of teaspoons inherited from her mother, which bore the *Ophir* insignia.[37]

Family Matters: Siblings

Altogether, as I noted earlier, William Henry had seven sisters and two brothers. The first Jane died only five weeks after she was born but the others lived to adulthood.[38] The eldest child, Ann, was listed with the family in the 1841 census when she was 12, but had left, probably to get married by 1851. Her husband was a Londoner, Daniel Thomas Marshall. At some stage Ann moved to Southport where she died in 1857.[39]

I have only managed to find a scant amount of material relating to the lives led by Mary and the second Jane. The prize-winning school scholar Mary was not living with her parents in 1841, when she was ten but had returned to her mother's home when the 1851 census was held. Then she vanished from the record, which was probably because she married, although there is a possibility that she became a domestic servant.[40] All we know about Jane is that like Mary, she was not listed with the Waterhouse family in the 1841 census but was recorded as living with them in 1851. She was probably the (unmarried) Jane Waterhouse who died in Preston, Lancashire, in 1919 aged 81.[41]

Two daughters, Hannah and Sarah, never left their mother's side, staying with her in the Hoghton Arms to work as 'hotelkeepers assistants'. They even joined Ann in retirement at 54 Duke Street. After Ann's death in 1881 Hannah became the head of the household and the women lived comfortably on their inheritances from their mother. They were joined by another sister, Margaret, who sometime before 1871 had married a glass manufacturer, Thomas Shenton. When he died, she joined Hannah and Sarah at

Duke Street as a property owner of independent means. Sarah died in 1895 leaving her estate of £1568/19/ – to Hannah. By 1911 Hannah was in ill health because she was employing a nurse companion. She died the same year, leaving an estate of £11,690.[42] In the meantime, Margaret had moved to a house on Leyland Street. She died in Christchurch, Hampshire, in 1914.[43]

In 1851 John Harrison Waterhouse was boarding in Shoreditch, London, and working as a draper's assistant. By 1861 he was a widower and had returned to live with his mother and sisters in Southport, along with his three-year old son, John Alexander Waterhouse. Eventually he both remarried and returned to London, where he established a prosperous millinery business. Given the fact that men did not usually train as milliners it is likely that his wife, Sarah Ann, was the expert milliner, while John Harrison managed the business. He does not seem to have had children by his second marriage. His son from his first marriage, John Alexander Waterhouse, married Emily Hamlen at Walcot St Andrew, Somerset, on June 15 1885.[44] Altogether John Alexander and Emily had five children, Florence Emily, John Alexander Stalman, John Herbert, Beatrice Margaret, and William. The two eldest children both died very young. By the time Beatrice Margaret was born in 1896 John Alexander was an accountant living in Hackney.

At some stage, probably after he retired, John Harrison and his wife Sarah moved back north where John died in Liverpool in 1902. He left an estate of more than £5300 to be divided amongst his wife, son and a William Ross, tutor. He and his wife, who died in 1907, were buried in the Duke Street cemetery, Southport, close to where his mother and sisters had lived. Their large and solid gravestone makes no reference to his son or three surviving grandchildren.[45] In fact, John Alexander died at Stoke Newington in 1903, not long after his father. He left an estate of just over £2300 to his widow, Emily. Intriguingly, his daughter, Beatrice Margaret, although none of his other surviving children, would be remembered and care taken to ensure that she had at least a measure of financial security by a distant relative in a distant land, for

she was the only one of William Henry's English relatives to be named in his will.

Robert Scot, followed a different career path from those of his two brothers. He joined a cavalry regiment, the 6th Dragoon Guards (Carabiniers), a regiment that served in England and Ireland (before 1855), in Crimea (1854–6), India during the Mutiny (1857–59), and which returned to the UK in 1870. It's not clear when Robert Scot joined this regiment so we don't know whether he served in Crimea or India. However, he was already a soldier when he married Fanny Colborne in the Islington Parish Church in 1870. Two years later, probably suffering from injuries or illnesses relating to his army experiences, Private Waterhouse was admitted to the Royal Chelsea Pensioner Hospital. By 1872 he had moved to Preston, Lancashire, where he worked as the night watchman in the local prison.[46] He died at a property in Christian Road, Preston, Lancashire, in February 1878.[47] William Henry and Beatrice Margaret, both had a probable, and also improbable, connection to this property.

Mary Susannah, William Henry and Family Life

In Victorian England and in the Australian colonies middle class women were expected to be guardians of the home and creators and maintainers of domestic, family values. Many working-class women worked, as did their children, but that was because the wages of unskilled and semi-skilled male workers were insufficient to maintain a family. But in families that had pretensions to middle class status, wives and mothers were confined to domestic roles as True Women, whose duties were to promote private family enjoyments marked by religiosity and restraint. And because women's roles were confined, their lives received little public attention.[48] This dichotomy between the public lives of men and the private lives of women was reflected at a specifically local level in the story of Mary Susannah and William Henry. As an outspoken community activist William Henry left a public record of his public life. As a mid and late Victorian wife and mother, Mary Susannah left virtually no record of her exclusively private

FITZROY STREET, GRAFTON.

FITZROY STREET, GRAFTON.

William Henry and Mary Susannah in middle-age. *Waterhouse Family Collection*

life, nor evidence that she engaged in community events and causes. She died of an 'internal growth', which was probably cancer, on December 20 1904, after a painful three-month illness. One obituary listed her as 'a very old and respected citizen'.

I suppose that in 1904 the age of seventy was considered very old. I suspect she would have been pleased to find herself described as 'highly respected' because that was confirmation that the secret of the nature of her relationship with William had survived for the 30 odd years she had lived on the Clarence. She was buried in the Anglican section of Grafton cemetery and her epitaph described her as the 'beloved wife' of William Henry. It also featured the following aphorism:

When the toil is over comes rest and peace

Grace Karskens and I visited her grave a few years ago and in a wonderfully thoughtful act Grace cleaned the headstone and weeded and planted flowers on the grave itself. When I reflect on the words carved into the headstone, I find myself hoping that her life was not just one of work and hardship but that she also found happiness in herself and her family. Perhaps she sometimes missed her two oldest children and that led to regrets about the consequences of her momentous decision to abandon Josiah for William Henry.[49]

William Henry was almost 60 when he and Mary Susannah returned from England. It is not entirely clear how he earned his living in the years before Mary Susannah died, although, as I have already indicated, he revived and refitted his electric baths business. He also resumed a role of service to the community, becoming a collector for the local hospital and chairing the City's band committee.[50] William had served on the Grafton Council before his trips to England and in 1904 he ran again for Council, although this time he was unsuccessful.[51] After Mary Susanna's death he qualified as an auctioneer and moved to Coffs Harbour where he sold goods, land and buildings. Perhaps he also wanted to be close to Frances (Fanny) who was now living at Coffs Harbour with her husband, William John Graham, the town's lighthouse keeper.[52] He seems to have also retained ecumenical if not evangelical leanings because in early 1907 he attended the laying of the foundation stone of the Coffs Harbour Presbyterian Church.[53] But in early 1907 his health began to fail and he returned to Grafton, perhaps relying on the modest rental income from his properties for financial support. The same year he fell while attending the hospital ball and after that his health decline accelerated. Admitted to hospital in 1910 he lingered for a few weeks before dying on May 29. The causes of death were listed as 'Uraemia' (kidney failure) and 'Coma', the latter no doubt resulting from the former.[54] It is an

indication of his closeness to his two children that Fanny travelled from Coffs Harbour and Henry from Kempsey to visit him in hospital before his death.

There is no evidence that Mary Susannah kept in touch with her family, including her husband, children and parents in Melbourne and her brother in London. As I indicated in the previous chapter, her brother made at least one attempt to contact her, although the fact that he placed notices seeking her whereabouts in the Brisbane press suggests he only had vague information about where she was living. But William Henry kept in close contact with his English family. In 1878 he placed a notice in the local press to commemorate the death of his brother, Robert Scot (Scott) Waterhouse on February 17 of that year.[55] Moreover, Robert Scot was on such terms with William that he almost certainly left his house in Christian Road, Preston to him.[56] Again, when his mother passed away in 1881 William Henry recorded it with a notice in the Grafton press which referred to her as the 'beloved mother of Mr W. H. Waterhouse…'[57] And when John Harrison

Photograph taken in London during William Henry and Mary Susannah's visit: William Henry is in the centre. The man on his right may be his nephew, John Alexander Waterhouse. The young man on his left may be one of John Alexander's two surviving sons, most likely John Herbert who was born ca. 1885. *Waterhouse Family Collection*

Waterhouse died in late 1902 William ensured it was recorded in the *Clarence and Richmond Examiner*.[58] I also think it's likely that in the period between 1897 and 1900 when he and Mary Susannah lived in London he connected with members of the family who lived there. This may have included John Harrison, although perhaps by then he and his wife had already returned to Liverpool/Southport. However, given that in his will William left a house in Preston to one of John Alexander's children, Beatrice Margaret, it is fair to assume that he was familiar with that particular branch of the family as the above photograph suggests. Moreover, he must have kept in touch when he returned to Australia, because apart from his knowledge of the death of John Harrison, his will, which he made in 1908, referred also to the passing of John Harrison's son, John Alexander in 1903, and to his widow Emily's remarriage.

In his will, William Henry left his estate, in Australia, valued at £899/13/ – to his daughter Frances Alice Graham and his daughter-in-law, Ellen Waterhouse (Spring). He chose to leave half of his local inheritance to Ellen rather than her husband, almost certainly because Henry Benjamin had debt and bankruptcy problems. It was a strategy designed to avoid the claims of creditors. The modest house in Preston, valued at £292 sterling, which had passed from Robert Scot to William Henry, was now bequeathed to his nephew John Alexander's daughter, Beatrice Margaret Waterhouse.[59] Fifteen years later, in 1925, Beatrice wed Wilfred Carruthers Bell, who became the proprietor of the Southcliffe Hotel in the parish of Morte-Hoe in Devon.[60] In short, she had married a publican and the wheel had turned full circle. I suspect that this is not what William Henry, the zealous temperance campaigner, had in mind. Nevertheless, he had worked to earn a reputation as a hard-working, respectable and committed member of the Grafton community, and in death he was acknowledged as 'one of Grafton's formerly prominent men.'[61] But his time, as this obituary rather tactlessly noted, had passed. In the meantime, his children were already making their own marks.

Endnotes

1 *Leeds Mercury*, 22 August 1864; *Liverpool Mercury*, 25 October 1865, 24 February 1868; *Preston Herald*, 24 February 1866

2 *Clarence and Richmond Examiner*, 23 March 1897

3 *ibid.*, 24 December 1904

4 *Manchester Courier and Lancashire General Advertiser*, 20 April 1867

5 *Age* 26 February 1858; *Argus*, 12 April 1858 14 November 1861, 14 July 1862; *Ballarat Star*, 13 September 1859; *Ovens and Murray Advertiser*, 9 January 1873

6 Jenny Salter (Nancarrow), *The Waterhouse Family Story*,

7 NSW Registry of Births, Deaths and Marriages, *death certificate of William Henry Waterhouse*, 29 May 1910

8 *Clarence and Richmond Examiner*, 23 March, 1897

9 *Macleay Chronicle* 19 June 1910. The obituary for W.H. Waterhouse which appeared in this newspaper was surely written by his stepson, H.B. Waterhouse, who was its owner and editor. It refers to William Henry working in the timber industry in Melbourne when he first arrived in Australia.

10 Louise Tiffany Daley, *Men and a* River: *Richmond River District 1828–1895*, Melbourne: Melbourne University Press, 1966; reprint edition Lismore: Richmond River Historical Society, 2011, pp. 130–31. My thanks to Robyn Brathwaite from the Society for providing me with a copy of this valuable work

11 I am grateful to Grace Karskens for the plausible suggestion of how Mary Susannah and William Henry met.

12 *Clarence and Richmond Examiner*, 23 March 1897

13 *ibid.*, 23 December 1873

14 ibid., 4 August, 1874

15 *ibid.*, 27 May 1873; Terry Kass, *Grafton Jacaranda City on the Clarence*, Grafton: Clarence Valley Council, 2009, pp. 71–4, 175; Brett J. Stubbs, *A Thematic History of the City of Grafton, vol. 2*, Grafton: Clarence Valley Council, 2007, p. 91

16 In compiling this summary I have relied on Kass, *op. cit.*; Stubbs, vol. 2; B. W. Higman, 'Sugar Plantations and Yeoman Farmers in NSW', *Annals of the Association of American Geographers*, vol. 58, December 1968, pp. 692–719

17 For but one example see *Clarence and Richmond Examiner*, 4 July 1885

18 *ibid.*, 20 November 1880

19 *ibid.*, 13 January 1880, 28 May 1881

20 *ibid.*, 28 September 1880

21 *ibid.*, 19 February 1881

22 *ibid.*, 18 June 1861

23 Richard Waterhouse, *Private Pleasures, Public Leisure: a History of Australian Popular Culture Since 1788*, Melbourne: Longman, 1995, pp. 108–9

24 Terry Kass, *Grafton*, pp. 48, 54, 101

25   Richard Waterhouse, *The Vision Splendid; a Social and Cultural History of Rural Australia*, Fremantle: Fremantle Arts Centre Press/ Curtin Books, 2005, p. 33

26   *Clarence and Richmond Examiner*, 31 December 1887; *Grafton Daily Examiner, 31 May 1910,* 8 July 2016.

27   *Clarence and Richmond Examiner*, 24 January, 19 December 1991, 23 March 1997; *Grafton Daily Examiner*, 31 May 1910

28   *Clarence and Richmond Examiner*, 9 August 1887, 6 July 1889

29   *ibid.,* 6 October, 1900

30   Iwan Rhys Marus, *Frankenstein's Children: Electricity, Exhibition and Experiment in Early Nineteenth Century* London, Princeton: Princeton University Press, 1998, pp. 231–36

31   *Clarence and Richmond Examiner,* 14 March 1896

32   *ibid.*, 4 April 1896

33   *Sydney Mail*, 23 January 1897

34   *Clarence and Richmond Examiner*, 23 March 1897

35   *ibid.*, 29 September 1900

36   *The Grafton Examiner,* 31 May 1910

37   I am grateful to Cassy Nancarrow for providing me with this information.

38   Ancestry, *Lancashire Church of England Deaths and Burials 1813–1980, Bolton-le-Sands 1830–1839*

39   Ancestry, Church of England, *Births and Baptisms, 1813–1911,* Warton St Oswald (1829)

40   Ancestry, *Census of 1901*, School Street, Walton-le-Dale Lancashire lists a Mary Waterhouse, aged 69 and born in the village of Hoghton, Lancashire, working as a servant for the family of James and Mary Burton. Her age fits with the (approximately) known birth year of our Mary. Intriguingly, John and Ann lived in Hoghton Street Southport and owned the Hoghton Arms Hotel. Mary was actually born in Yealand, but perhaps either she or the census taker became confused in naming her place of birth. At one time she had lived at the Hoghton Arms.

41   Ancestry, *Civil Registration Death Index, 1916–2007.* We know John and Ann's daughter Jane was born in 1838 and the Jane who died in Preston was listed as 81, so she was also born in 1838. We also know that at least one of Jane's siblings lived in Preston which is what may have attracted her to the town.

42   *Yorkshire Post and Leeds Intelligencer,* 4 August 1911; *Southport Visitor*, 10 June. 1911

43   Hannah can be traced through the censuses of 1881, 1891, 1901 and 1911 all of which are available on Ancestry. For Sarah see the censuses of 1881 and 1891 and Ancestry, *England and Wales National Probate Calendar*. For Margaret see the censuses for 1861, 1871, 1881, and Ancestry, *Civil Registration Death Index, 1837–1915*

44   Ancestry, *1851 Census* Shoreditch, Family of Henry Pocock. John Harrison boarded with this family; Ancestry, *1861 Census*, Ann Waterhouse family, Southport. He was a witness at his son's wedding and listed himself as a milliner. Ancestry, *Somerset Marriage Register, Bonds and Allegations, 1754–1914*, Walcot Parish, 15 June 1885, marriage of John Alexander Waterhouse to Emily Hamlen

45   Ancestry, *England and Wales, National Probate Calendar, 1858–1995*

46   *Preston Herald*, 6 July 1872

47   Ancestry, *Church of England, London Marriages and Banns, 1754–1963* (Parish Church Islington); Ancestry, *Royal Hospital Chelsea, Pensioner Admissions and Discharges 1715–1921*

48   William E. Houghton, *The Victorian Frame of Mind, 1830–1870,* New Haven: Yale University Press, 2013 (reprint edition), pp. 342–3

49   *Grafton Argus and Clarence General Examiner,* 22 December 1904; *Clarence and Richmond Examiner* 24 December 1904

50   *Clarence and Richmond Examiner, 15 March, 9* November 1901

51   *Richmond River Herald,* 8 July 1904

52   *Clarence and Richmond Examiner,* 8 December 1906; *Raleigh Sun,* 25 January 1907; *Grafton Examiner*, 31 May 1910; Ancestry, *NSW Public Service Lists, 1868–1960, 1910,* William John Graham

53   *Coffs Harbour Advocate,* 5 March 1907

54   *Death Certificate for William Henry Waterhouse*, Registered at Grafton, 25 June 1910, Waterhouse Family Collection; *The Macleay Chronicle,* 19 June 1910; *The Clarence and Richmond River Examiner*, 31 May 1910; *Grafton Argus,* 30 May 1910

55   *The Clarence and Richmond Examiner,* 18 May 1878

56   Robert Scot died at his home in Christian Road, Preston. In William Henry's will he named a house in 'Cushan' Road, Preston, which he left to Beatrice Margaret. There is no 'Cushan' Road in Preston but there is a Christian Road. It is a fair assumption that the house which William Henry bequeathed to Beatrice was the same house that belonged to Robert Scot and that W.H .Waterhouse acquired it by bequest

57   *ibid.*, 3 September 1881

58   17 January 1903

59   Probate on the will was granted on September 7 1910. I am grateful to Jenny Salter, Cassy Nancarrow and Judy Fuller for providing me with copies of the will, which is held in the NSW Archives, *Deceased Estate Index 1880–1939 INX-15–170956* ; Ancestry, England and Wales *National Probate Calendar* (Index of Wills and Administration 1858–1995), Will of WH Waterhouse of Grafton

60   *North Devon Journal*, 25 January 1934; *Western Morning News*, 15 February 1934; Ancestry, *Halley-Frame Family Tree*

61   *Grafton Argus,* 30 May 1910

Chapter 5

The Journalist and the Descendant of Convict Royalty: Henry Benjamin Waterhouse and Ellen Spring

Apprenticeship and Marriage

As I noted in the previous chapter, Henry Benjamin Branchflower was born in East Collingwood on December 28 1860. He was seven years old when he travelled from Melbourne to Wardell aboard the *Alpha* along with his mother, his two old sister, Frances Alice, and the man who became known as his father, William Henry Waterhouse. He left Melbourne a Branchflower and arrived in Wardell as a Waterhouse. How much he remembered of his Melbourne family and how he dealt with those memories is a mystery because he took them with him to his grave. There is no surviving evidence relating to the family's brief stay in Wardell, although the material relating to his subsequent life and career is more extensive. When his family moved to Grafton Henry first attended Miss Wagner's private school and subsequently enrolled in the newly built public school. Ellen Spring, who subsequently became his wife, also attended these two schools.[1] After primary school Ellen went on to further education at Mrs Currey's Ladies Seminary but rather than continue his school education in 1874 Henry was apprenticed as a printer to the office of the *Clarence and Richmond Examiner*.[2]

Under the terms of his apprenticeship William was at first entitled to board, lodging, clothing and washing and a salary of 1/ – a week. His pay was increased to 2/6 in his second, 7/6 in his third, 10/ – in his fourth and 15/ – in his fifth year. During his apprenticeship he worked 6 am until 6pm six days a week and was required to live on the premises and be home every evening by 9 pm. Although the printing press at the *Examiner* was updated from a hand to machine press during Henry's apprenticeship the available resources for reporting events outside the Clarence remained very limited. Because there was as yet no telegraph line from Sydney to Grafton the *Examiner* staff copied stories relating to international and colonial matters from the Armidale press.[3]

Either there were no printing jobs available for Henry in Grafton when he finished his apprenticeship or he decided that having experienced the Bush he now wanted to try Sydney. In any case, for the next few years he worked in Sydney and surrounds, first at the printing works of S. E. Lees, then at the Government Printing Office and finally and briefly with the *Cumberland Mercury*. Henry then spent a year as foreman at the *Forbes and Parkes Gazette*, no doubt lured there by the offer of more senior and better paying employment. However, not yet twenty-one he returned to Grafton when a position at the *Examiner* became available. Formerly, Henry was employed exclusively as a printer but now he also worked as a journalist. As an accomplished and enthusiastic cricketer, who was a founder of the Grafton Cricket Association, he was certainly qualified to write articles on local cricket matches for the *Examiner* under the name 'Bails'. In his time as an apprentice printer his favourite pastimes included attending performances by visiting circuses and

Albert Cricket Club, 1899 – 1900 : Back Row: J Waterhouse (Scorer), F I Shafer (V/Pres), C Everingham (Patron), W Ford Snr (Pres), R Barnier (V/Pres), H B Waterhouse (V/Pres). Middle Row: L Klaus, Albert Ford, L Everingham, T Ford (Capt), A Clarke, W Crispin, A Starr. Front Row: Child, W Ford Jnr, G Brindle, T Michael, W Hall. – Photo published in The Sydney Mail, July 21 1900.

HB as cricket enthusiast: In this group portrait of the Albert Club, Vice-President H.B. is standing at the far right in the last row. His son John (Jack), the club scorer, is standing at the far left in the same row.
Judy Fuller Collection

the annual (July) Grafton horse race meetings. He now utilised his impressive knowledge of horse racing to become a successful newspaper racing tipster. Later in life he became handicapper for the Nambucca races at Bowraville and a steward for the Grafton race club. In any case, by 1880 the tradesman printer had also become a sports journalist.[4]

However, a job with his old newspaper was not the only benefit of Henry's return home. On November 15 1882, about two years after his return to Grafton he married his former school-mate, Ellen Spring, in a Baptist ceremony at her parents' home.[5] I suspect the marriage took place at the bride's parents' house because her family were Baptists, while Henry Benjamin and his parents were Anglican. Perhaps the two families could not agree in which church the ceremony should take place and so it became a home wedding. In the end however, it was Ellen who 'converted' for both she and Henry became dedicated members of the Church of England. Yet while Ellen's parents belonged to a church which placed a

strong emphasis on what it interpreted as a strict and upright code of Christian moral conduct, her ancestors had behaved in ways that were neither moral nor upright, which is in fact how they and she came to be in Australia.

Ellen Spring's Convict Ancestry

In the early eighteenth century the British Parliament considerably increased the number of crimes that were punishable by death. This was reflected in the 1723 Black Act, which created more than 200 capital offences.[6] One of Ellen's ancestors, John Henry Entwistle, was executed for one of these crimes. Although he was baptised as John Entwistle into the Church of England faith in St Mary, Manchester on August 29 1763, he was more commonly known as Henry. His parents, Joseph Entwistle (b.1740) and Sarah Bradley (b. 1739) were married in St Mary on the following day.[7] Henry married Martha Loft (b. ca., 1765) from Manchester in 1792.[8] They had six children that I can identify, and probably more.[9]

The Entwistle family were well and truly

entrenched in the plebeian class, for Henry and his sons were agricultural labourers in the Lancashire village of Edgworth. Their economic circumstances were probably made more difficult by the fact that large scale enclosure was taking place in the area around the village, enclosure that as a result of an act of Parliament in 1795, also included the local common. This meant not only that the family's opportunities to own and farm land in the area were greatly diminished but it was also denied access to once shared common's land on which the inhabitants had collected firewood, grazed stock, grown crops and hunted game.[10] In any case, the family turned to crime in the form of larceny and forgery as a means of improving their collective economic circumstance or perhaps even to avoid the workhouse and starvation.

In 1809 the 46-year-old Henry and his son John were brought before the Lancashire Assizes charged with forgery. Although a John Entwistle, the son of Martha and Henry, was baptised in 1799, John was certainly born many years earlier, because at the time of his trial he was married to the 22-year-old Ann (Nuttall) and the couple had two young children.[11] Henry, who probably instigated the crime, was indicted on one count of uttering a forged note but was freed when the court found there was insufficient evidence to convict him. Originally charged with the capital crime of uttering forged notes on three occasions John was instead found guilty of the lesser charge of having forged notes in his possession and sentenced to fourteen years transportation.[12] He left for Sydney on the *Indian* in July 1810 and upon arrival was send to Hobart, presumably on one of the small intercolonial vessels. In Van Diemen's Land John was a model prisoner, 'universally known', and held in 'respect and esteem'. By early 1817 he was living in the remote north coast settlement of Port Dalrymple. On January 24 he left the settlement in company with the Government Messenger to ride to Hobart. However, when he attempted to cross the New River, which was swollen and fast running because of recent rain, his horse bucked and John was thrown into the water. Presumably he drowned for his body was never found. Convict life was held cheaply in Van Diemen's Land but

his death was genuinely mourned.[13]

John was the first but not the last of his family to be transported. Fortunately, those who followed managed to lead longer and more modestly prosperous lives, despite the initial hardships of transportation and colonial convict life. In 1812 Henry's wife Martha and her daughter-in-law and John's wife, Ann Entwistle (born Nuttall), entered a tailor's shop in Bolton and sought to buy some dress cloth with a forged £5 note. Although Martha left the shop before the forgery was discovered she was soon apprehended. Two days later constables visited the family home at Edgworth and arrested Ann and her sister-in-law Alice. Left handcuffed in a lock-up room for five days Ann nevertheless escaped by jumping from a window eighteen or twenty feet above the ground. Injured, and leaving a pool of blood where she had landed, she managed to disappear and remained at liberty for some time.

In the meantime, Martha was tried, convicted and sentenced to death, although the judge subsequently commuted this to transportation for life.[14] But Marsha's harsh odyssey was far from over, for in 1812 England and the United States were at war and travelling the seas was a risky business for English ships. Martha was on board the relatively small vessel *Emu* which left England in October 1812, carrying just 49 female convicts. The transport was intercepted in the Atlantic by an American privateer and its captain dumped the crew and convicts of the *Emu* at Porto Grande in the Cape Verde Islands, while claiming the ship as a prize of war. The crew and convicts waited there for twelve months before they were picked up by the *Isabella* and returned to England. Martha then spent some time on a hulk in Portsmouth before boarding the *Broxbornebury* in January 1814 along with 122 other convicts and travelling uneventfully to Sydney, where the ship arrived in July of the same year. She was joined on the voyage by Ann, who was eventually caught, pleaded guilty and sentenced to fourteen years transportation. Martha had pleaded not guilty, claiming she had received the forged £5 as change in another shop. But Ann told the deputy constable when he arrested her that Martha had given her the note she passed in the tailor's shop.[15] In any case, both paid a heavy price for their involvement in the attempted forgery. The two voyages took a particularly heavy toll on Martha's physical and mental well-being, while Ann lamented leaving two destitute children behind and pleaded with the Governors and Directors of the Bank of England to provide her with relief, for she lacked any means of securing 'the smallest necissary (sic.) for the voyage'.[16]

Upon arrival Martha and Ann were both initially assigned to the newly established Lunatic Asylum at Castle Hill, where Martha, despite having no training in the profession, became the nurse. George Suttor was appointed the first superintendent and Ann was probably given the role as his servant. In reality, Martha's role was probably a combination of servant and medical assistant. On the one hand she probably assisted in bloodletting and administering castor oil. On the other, she may have maintained the garden as well as sewing and mending clothes.[17] A recent scholarly study, which is cited below, acknowledged Martha as Australia's first mental health nurse. Seven generations later her direct descendant, Leo Waterhouse, and his wife, Mai Nguyen, are mental health nurses at Cumberland Hospital in Westmead, not that far from Castle Hill. History can be so wonderfully and accidentally symmetrical

The eighteen months at sea left Martha with long term trauma. She had lost all her clothes on the *Emu* and Suttor petitioned Governor Macquarie on her behalf to belatedly replace them. Moreover, when Ann was given permission to travel to Van Diemen's Land to be with her husband, John, Suttor wrote to Macquarie to indicate that after spending several days considering the matter Martha had decided she didn't want to accompany Ann because her previous long voyages had caused her considerable suffering.[18] This was surely a painful decision for Martha to make, and one that Suttor indicated that she thought about for some time, presumably because not only did it mean that she was losing Ann's company, but also forgoing the opportunity to reunite with her son. As it turned out, because of

his subsequent tragic death in 1817, she missed her last opportunity to see him.

Suttor was constantly in conflict with the hospital's surgeon, Thomas Parmeter, and the situation became so dysfunctional that in February 1819 Macquarie dismissed them both.[19] Martha left the hospital too, and was moved to Port Macquarie, a settlement established as a place of secondary punishment for recidivist convicts. Because she wasn't in the repeat offender category, she probably went there in the more privileged position of an assigned servant to a government official.

At Port Macquarie Martha met and married another convict, Thomas Carpenter. Born in about 1775 Carpenter was tried, convicted and sentenced to fourteen years transportation by a Coventry court. With 199 other convicts he left England on the *Fortune* in November 1812 and arrived in Sydney in June 1813. Although he received a conditional pardon in 1818, two years later he was again in legal trouble when he was convicted of receiving stolen goods, sentenced to a further fourteen years, and despatched to Newcastle, then a place of secondary punishment.[20] In September 1823 he was moved to Port Macquarie, where he met and married the approximately 57-year-old Martha, who was about nine years his senior. His record didn't suggest that he was likely to prove the most reliable husband, but in the closely supervised penal settlement in which they lived his prospects for committing further crimes were limited. Martha seems to have had more privileges than most of the other prisoners and in 1826 was even given permission to visit Sydney. Perhaps this trip was for the purpose of re-uniting with her son William, who had arrived as a convict in 1819, and her daughter-in-law Ann, now remarried and living in Parramatta. Martha died in 1828 and was buried in the churchyard of St Thomas in Port Macquarie. Her husband Thomas survived her until 1837.

In February 1815 Suttor reported to Macquarie that Ann Entwistle was 'desirous' of joining her husband in Van Diemen's Land and was grateful to the Governor for giving her permission to travel to the settlement there. In fact, there is no evidence that Ann went to Van Diemen's Land, despite her expressed desire to do so. Instead, it seems that soon after her request was granted she met William Rafter, a 22 year old Irish convict who had arrived on the *Archduke Charles* in 1813 to serve a seven year sentence. Their first child, William, was born on November 16 1815 and baptised in St John's Church of England on December 24 of the same year. Two more children followed, Maria in 1817 and Mary Ann in 1821. On February 14 1821 William Rafter and Ann Entwistle applied as persons professing the Roman Catholic faith to marry in the Roman Catholic Church. Ann, it seems, had decided to leave the Anglican in favour of the Roman Catholic Church. Why did they wait until at least two of their children were born before marrying? Convict women who had left husbands behind in the United Kingdom when they were transported often didn't hesitate to remarry in Australia even though that meant they were technically guilty of bigamy. But it was known to the authorities in NSW that Ann had a husband in Van Diemen's Land. Perhaps she only learnt of his death some years after it took place and that cleared the way for her re-marriage. Another possibility is that initially Ann was reluctant to convert to Catholicism, which may be reflected in the fact that her first child with William Rafter was baptised in the Church of England. When they finally married William was free by servitude while Ann was still a convict.

The Census of 1828 revealed that they now had four children including William, Maria, Mary Ann, and Richard (b. ca 1824). Another child, John, was born after the census was taken but in the same year. The couple lived out their lives in Parramatta, where William practised as a barber. He died in 1853 at the age of 52 and Ann died in 1871 aged about 84, although the inscription on her tombstone specified her age as 96.[21]

The transportation of John, Martha and Ann failed to prevent those members of the family who remained in England from engaging in further criminal activity. In 1810, in partnership with John Nuttall, who was probably either Ann's father or brother, Henry was charged with stealing, a prosecution that in the end did not proceed. However,

in 1813 Henry and three of his sons William (aged 19), James (aged 18) and Joseph (aged 15), were charged, convicted and each sentenced to seven year's transportation on charges of larceny. In the case of William and James the theft had involved stealing items from a shoe shop They were all sent to the hulks but for reasons that are not clear were not transported but instead released after five years' incarceration.[22]

Immediately, Henry and William returned to committing what was the Entwistle trademark offence, that is, forgery. On 17 October 1818 they were arraigned for uttering forged Bank of England notes. At Henry's subsequent trial, witnesses testified that he was one of a gang of five utterers in Bolton and had sold £1 notes on numerous occasions, including to a man who was an informer to the chief constable. Without needing to retire the jury convicted him and he was sentenced to death. Many of the prisoners sentenced to hang at the Lancaster Spring Assizes were subsequently reprieved but not Henry. Not long after his trial my great grandfather four times removed was hanged in Manchester Castle on April 17 1819.[23] Since discovering this unwelcome episode in my family history I find myself angry with him for acting so recklessly in endangering not only his own life but that of his son, William. But I also find myself shaking my head about a law which made a crime that didn't involve death or physical injury to others subject to capital punishment. This was a legal system that placed a premium on the defence of property, not on compassion and the humane treatment of those who lived under its governance.

William was also originally charged with uttering Bank of England notes but in the end was allowed to plead guilty to the lesser charge of being in possession of such notes. He was sentenced to fourteen years transportation.[24] Perhaps here we can find at least a dash of humane treatment, because as this case illustrates, judges were reluctant to sentence two members of a family to death, at least at the same time.

In 1819 William came to Sydney on the *Malabar*, one of 117 convicts carried by the ship on what turned out to be an uneventful voyage.

On arrival in Sydney he was assigned to Gregory Blaxland to work on his Field of Mars property. A free immigrant from a wealthy Kent family, Blaxland accumulated thousands of acres of land by grant and purchase both around Eastwood to the northwest of Sydney and also on the Emu Plains to the west. On these properties, and relying on the labour of 40 assigned convicts, he raised and grazed cattle. He also engaged in speculation in commercial goods. Along with William Charles Wentworth and William Lawson he was a member of an expedition that crossed the Blue Mountains in 1813 in search of more and even better grazing country. Later mythologised as a pioneer, who contributed to the emergence of Australia as a great pastoral nation, in fact he was simply a colonist on the make, more interested in his own than in future national prosperity.[25]

By 1828 William, who now had a ticket of leave, had moved to Sydney and was working as a servant for Gregory's son John at his residence in George Street. He was now a paid employee, but the fact that he had remained with the same family suggests trust on one side and loyalty on the other.[26]

Twenty-seven-year-old, Mary Campbell, was a Protestant Irish convict who came to Sydney on the *Asia* in 1830. Originally from Londonderry she worked as a straw bonnet maker as well as doing 'all work' before she was convicted for stealing flannel and sentenced to seven years' transportation in Tyrone in 1829. She was assigned to the Wilshire family who also lived on George Street and who owned a number of business enterprises, including a slaughterhouse and the largest tannery in the colony.[27] Presumably, Mary and William met because they were close neighbours. They needed permission to marry because William only held a ticket of leave and Mary was still a convict, permission which was granted in September 1831. Their first child, Joseph, was born in Parramatta a few weeks later, followed in subsequent years by William, Francis, Caroline Ellen (b.23/12/1832) and Nancy. Mary died in 1839 and was buried in St John's Anglican cemetery in Parramatta. William subsequently married Francis Day, an eighteen-year-old free immigrant seamstress from Sussex.

From convict to respectable citizen: the grave of William Entwistle

They had a further five children, including Alfred, Ann, Mary Jane, Sarah and James. Francis died in 1851 and was also buried in St Johns cemetery.[28]

Moving to Parramatta with Mary soon after his first marriage, William remained there for the remainder of his life. There is no evidence that he committed any crimes after his arrival in Australia in 1819. For his exemplary behaviour he received his certificate of freedom in 1833.[29] He became a shopkeeper and dealer, in the process accumulating two brick cottages and a respectable collection of goods. He achieved sufficient status to have his name included on a list of eligible jurors, and I cannot help but think he was particularly qualified to assess charges of forgery. Although there is no evidence that he served as a juror in a forgery trial he was a member of a Supreme Court Jury in a case of conspiracy to defraud creditors. The jury found the two defendants not guilty and the judge indicated that he agreed with the verdict. When he died on July 29 1864, William was referred to as 'an old and respected colonist'. In his youth he was misled into reckless criminal activity by an irresponsible father but by the time of his death he had become a thoughtful and considerate colonist. In his will he provided that his property should not be sold until his youngest child turned 21 and then the proceeds were to be divided equally amongst all his children. Clearly, he cared equally for them all, whether they were men or women, whether they were the children of Mary or Francis. He had become a far better man than Henry. Despite all the tragedies that had befallen the Entwistles, William's life, like those of Martha, John and Ann, was a true redemption story.[30]

William Spring: Not Quite a Yeoman or a Farmer

In his will William Entwistle named two of his children and his son-in law, William Spring as his executors. William Spring was born in 1828 in the village of Pidley in Cambridgeshire, the son of William (b. 1796) and his wife Sarah Ann (Shanks). His father was a farm labourer, a low paid trade that was also followed by son William and his brothers John (b. 1819) Phillip (b.1832) and Thomas (b. 1837). In the area encompassed by the East Anglia fens life was made even more difficult by the draining of the land, a process that had begun in the mid seventeenth century but was given final impetus after 1840 with the introduction of highly efficient coal fired pumps. The wetlands of the fens were commons on which the local population had the right to gather reeds, shoot wild fowls and catch fish and eels, but as the land was drained it was divided into privately owned farms, which produced crops for the exclusive benefit of their owners.[31]

In 1849 at the age of 21 William emigrated as an assisted passenger to NSW on board the *James Gibb*, in company with his 30 year-old brother John, the latter's wife Sarah (Fulstone) and their small child Barron. William reported that he was a Baptist and that he could read and write.[32] Two years later, despite his proclaimed affiliation with the Baptist Church, William married William Entwistle's daughter, Caroline Ellen Entwistle, in St John Church of England in Parramatta. In marrying Ellen (as she was generally known) in an Anglican Church, Spring was clearly deferring to his new father-in-law's wishes. Their first two children, were also baptised in St John.[33]

For some years William worked as a labourer in Parramatta but by 1858 the family had moved to Grafton where eight more children were born, including Henry Benjamin's future wife Ellen.[34] Like her, some of the children remained in Grafton and married locals. These included Mary, Alfred and Albert. Mary, who married George Shore, died suddenly at the age of 23 after a short illness. Some of the others drifted away, especially in the direction of Sydney. Arthur worked on the tramways and lived in Leichhardt, Alice married James Short and eventually moved to Hornsby, while Florence married William Crowcroft and lived first in Tempe and later in Sutherland.

William Spring had grown up in rural England and worked as an agricultural labourer. The chances of someone of his status acquiring and working his own land in England were very remote, but what I suspect drew him to Grafton in the late 1850s was the approaching passage of the Selection Acts and the prospect of farming lots becoming available in the Clarence Valley. The time payment system, which was an integral part of the proposed acts, allowed many families with limited capital to acquire land for farming.

However, William failed to become a selector, probably because he never earned sufficient income as a labourer to afford a first payment on a selection. Under two land acts passed in NSW in 1861 any person could select a block of Crown land between 40 and 320 acres at a fixed price of £1 per acre. One quarter of the amount was to be paid immediately. At one stage Spring operated a small business as a sawyer but it didn't prosper and he found himself in the Insolvency Court with debts of almost £98, while his total assets only amounted to £12.[35] He was a brave and strong man who once caught an intruder who broke into his house with the intent of theft or perhaps even the sexual molestation of his daughter Sarah Ann.[36] But he never escaped from his humble status as an uneducated and unskilled labourer, which meant his income remained quite low. When he immigrated, he attested that he could read and write but he signed both his marriage certificate and his will not with his signature but with his mark.

Yet although he and Henry's father belonged to different levels of Grafton society a religious bond held them together. William Waterhouse

A moving photo of Ellen and H.B. with their surviving children and Percy's new family. In the front row from the left are Beatrice, H.B., Ellen, baby Dorothy and her mother (Fanny) Maude (Paine). In the back row Percy is on the right behind his wife and daughter. His two brothers John and Reginald stand beside him. John (Jack) is probably the one on the far left. *Nancarrow/Salter family Collection*

was formally an Anglican, but more importantly he was an evangelical Protestant. In 1880 he joined William Spring and six other Grafton men in appealing for funds to build an interdenominational Protestant Hall. Four years later both men served on the building committee supervising the construction of a new Grafton Baptist Church. When William Spring died in 1898 he was acknowledged as a pioneer of the district, although that was more a reflection of the fact that he had, by the standards of that time, lived to a comparatively old age, than an acknowledgement of a great contribution to the Clarence community.[37]

Ellen and Henry Benjamin's Family Life

Ellen and Henry Benjamin had eight children born between 1884 and 1899, including Percival Ernest (1884–1974), John Harrison (1885–1975), Beatrice Mary (1887–1959) Harold Arthur

(1888), Reginald Abner (1890–1950), Mabel Irene (1892–1902), Leslie Clarence (1894 – 1897) and Redvers Clarence (1899). Two of them, Harold and Redvers died in infancy and two more, Mabel and Leslie, did not survive beyond childhood. On a family visit to Woolgoolga in 1897, Leslie was feeding a horse when it knocked him down and kicked him in the head, fracturing his skull. A doctor at Grafton Hospital decided to operate on Leslie but the procedure was abandoned when it was discovered that skull pieces had penetrated and damaged his brain. He died a few hours after admission.[38] Mabel died in 1902 at the age of ten of what at the time was incomprehensively described as a 'complicated attack', but which 30 years later was recalled as 'sunstroke'.[39]

Percy's story will be narrated in the following chapter but John Harrison, surely named after William Henry's brother, moved to Woolgoolga, a small coastal town 25 kilometres north of Coffs Harbour, where he became a newsagent and

Ellen Spring/Waterhouse. *Waterhouse Family Collection*

married Alice Leeding, the daughter of an English immigrant farmer.[40] They had two children, Douglas and Joyce. Beatrice married Peter Farlow from Richmond and moved to Yamba at the mouth of the Clarence. Reginald Abner ('Abbie') married Emma Louise Hacking (1893-) in 1911. He worked for the railways, tried his hand at farming on the Nambucca and then finally joined John as a storekeeper in Woolgoolga. In keeping with family tradition, he also served as the local correspondent for the (Grafton) *Daily Examiner*.[41] He and Emma had five children, including John Ross (1919–1991), Ellen 'Nell' Louise (1912-), Henry Leonard (1914-), Allan Arthur, and Nita.

When Ellen died in 1935, she was described in an obituary as possessing a 'retiring disposition' and 'gentle kindly nature'.[42] I suspect this was generally true, although she also had a temper and a sense of social superiority towards those of lower status. In 1910, when she and Henry were living in Kempsey, suspecting that the children who lived next door were stealing her fowls, she took to them with a whip. Because of a complaint laid by Henry and herself the children's mother was also charged

and convicted of stealing the Waterhouse fowls, despite the defence lawyer suggesting with some justification that the evidence was thin and the magistrate biased. [43]

Still, she was a caring mother who for the rest of her life mourned the children who died before her, which is reflected in her wish to be buried in the Anglican Section of Grafton cemetery, alongside Mabel, who predeceased her by 33 years. As Barbara Welter has argued, the Victorian Cult of True Womanhood emphasised the pivotal role of women as guardians of the home. However, she also noted that this ideology carried within it a fundamental contradiction. For if it was true that women were morally superior to men didn't it logically follow that they should assume the role of the moral guardians of society more generally? And, indeed that is exactly what late Victorian and Edwardian women did, not only in Australia, but also in Great Britain and the United States. In particular women's organisations became powerful advocates for temperance and the rights of women to vote and hold political office.[44] In a modest way Ellen was part of this movement, especially from the time when her children had grown old enough to look after themselves, and when World War 1 stirred her compassion and patriotism. Always a staunch member of the Church of England she now became active in the Red Cross and War Chest, knitting hundreds of pairs of socks for soldiers in the trenches. After the War she continued her life of service as a volunteer at Casino Hospital during the Spanish Flu epidemic. Henry was a long-term member of the Manchester Order of Oddfellows, a lodge formed in Manchester in 1810 and which was established in the Australian colonies in 1840. Its primary purpose was not to encourage fellowship or promote moral or religious causes but to raise funds to support the poorer members of the community, especially through the provision of affordable health insurance policies. Ellen too, became a member of this Lodge during the time the couple lived in Casino.

We don't know how much Ellen knew of her Entwistle family background. In an era when possession of convict ancestry was regarded as a major social disadvantage the Spring and

Entwistle families probably did their best to ignore or disguise it. This task was made easier by the fact that William Entwistle lived a long, respectable life, including many years as a free man, which allowed his criminal past to be obscured and forgotten. When she died Ellen was mourned as a beloved wife and mother who endeared herself to everyone who came in contact with her. The restlessness and loneliness that Henry exhibited after her death suggests how much he valued her and how these cliché sounding phrases also contained real truths.[45]

Henry's career as a newspaper manager, entrepreneur and journalist involved success and failure. After many years at the *Examiner* he left the paper in 1893 to start up his own newspaper *The South Grafton Mercury*. But these were hard times in the Australian colonies and the Clarence economy was not immune from the deep Depression that gripped the continent. Moreover, a series of floods that inundated Grafton in the nineties had the effect of severely depressing property prices. Henry found himself in a difficult position when many of his debtors were unable to pay, while at the same time the two properties he had used as securities against his own bank borrowings, declined steeply in value. Henry had also accumulated a modest set of debts with Sydney and local providers, including solicitors, printers, advertising agents, storekeepers, tailors and bootmakers. To extricate himself from his financial difficulties Henry decided to sell the newspaper but he was tipped into bankruptcy when he was unable to pay the commission on the sale of the *Mercury*. Perhaps what was worst of all about this situation was that it unfolded at a time of great family tragedy, for it was in October 1897, when the bankruptcy proceedings were in full swing, that Henry's son Leslie was killed when kicked by a horse. Apart from the emotional trauma that this caused the family, the medical and funeral expenses were an additional burden on a man who had few remaining financial resources.[46]

In August 1899 the Supreme Court of NSW ruled that there was no misdemeanour or misconduct involved in Henry's bankruptcy and he was issued a certificate of discharge. But his financial

H B Waterhouse the respectable newspaper editor and defender of Grafton middle-class values and virtues. *Waterhouse Family Collection*

troubles lingered for more than a decade. When he was first bankrupted in 1896 he was unable to find employment and although he later worked as a compositor in Grafton, his earnings only totalled between 30/ – and 35/ – shillings a week, a low wage on which to support a wife and six children. Ten years later, in 1908, he was still desperate enough to sell his household furniture, furnishings, crockery and kitchenware at auction. As I previously indicated, when William drew up his will two years later, he left Henry's inheritance to Ellen, a tactic designed to circumvent outstanding claims by Henry's creditors.[47]

By late 1896 then, Henry had returned to work at the *Examiner*, first in the printing department and later as a journalist. In 1907 he became editor and manager of the *Raleigh Sun* and *Coffs Harbour Advocate*. This was followed by a brief stint as editor of the *Nambucca News* and then a two-year period owning and editing the *Macleay Chronicle*, beginning in 1910. Then, probably because of the intense competition that this paper faced from the well-entrenched *Macleay Argus*, Henry sold the *Chronicle* and returned to Grafton. Here he combined managing the printing press with serving as sporting editor at the *Examiner*. In 1915 he moved to Casino as literary editor of the *Casino Express* and in 1916 he became the paper's editor, a position he held until 1924. After his resignation from that post, he held relieving positions on various papers, including the *Casino Express*, the *Daily Examiner* and the *Lower Clarence Advocate*. He had experienced periodic ill-health since about 1910 but by 1937 his medical symptoms had worsened to the extent that he was forced to retire from the newspaper business and forsake his community commitments.[48]

William and his son both engaged in the Grafton community through their support of political and religious institutions. Like his father Henry became a member of the local Council to which he was elected an alderman in 1932. He also became a Justice of the Peace, although unlike William he didn't serve on the bench of the Police Court. Although both father and son were active in religious institutions, Henry never displayed evangelical inclinations, confining his commitments to serving as a churchwarden and member of the Diocesan Synod. It is an indication of their different values, that in the first decade or so that he lived in Grafton, William joined lodges that embraced evangelical and moral causes. In contrast, Henry became a member of the Manchester Unity Order of Oddfellows in 1880 and remained a member and officeholder until ill-health forced his resignation in 1936. His membership gave him the opportunity to support fundraising for the purpose of caring for lodge members as well as those who lived in the wider community. The Grafton Manchester Unity Lodge, in keeping with the traditions of the organisation more generally, focussed on raising funds to provide health insurance for those who could not afford it. Finally, while there is no evidence that William took any interest in sport, Henry belonged to the local racing, cricket, shooting, rowing and bowling clubs, acting both as an administrator and participant. In the late nineteenth and early twentieth centuries the cult of 'muscular Christianity' emphasised that participating in amateur team sports encouraged manliness while also inculcating Christian morals. Like other men of his generation Henry probably believed that physical activity on the sports field was more likely to influence male moral behaviour than the self-righteous and highly prejudiced lectures of evangelical clergy.[49]

Henry Benjamin and Ellen's Place in Grafton Society

In 1924 Henry was described as probably one of the best-known journalists on the North Coast.[50] This suggests that he and his family belonged to the respectable middle class and that his professional abilities had earned him a reputation that extended beyond the Clarence. But status was not simply dependent upon profession and proficiency, it also required wealth, and that meant that he sometimes found himself in a precarious social position. His forced sale of the *South Grafton Mercury* in 1896 to another proprietor, who changed its name to *The Clarion*, marked the beginning of many years of financial difficulty for Henry.[51] Until 1915 he drifted from Raleigh to Coffs Harbour, from Bowraville to Kempsey, editing marginal newspapers that probably failed to yield the highly profitable returns he was seeking. Long term financial security finally came when he took up a position with the *Richmond River Express* in 1915, a position which lasted until 1924.

But despite these financial setbacks Henry seems always to have thought of himself as a member and defender of respectable middle-class society on the North Coast, and there is one ethnographic moment in Grafton's history that demonstrates this point. When Henry established the *South Grafton Mercury* in 1893, his newspaper quickly became engaged in a battle of words with another local newspaper, *The Grip*, edited by Tom Penrose, and dedicated to promoting union and working-class causes. Penrose not only possessed an argumentative and divisive personality but he also enjoyed a reputation as a heavy drinker, womaniser and as affiliating with people with criminal records and reputations. Penrose was not a member of the Grafton establishment, but one of its sternest critics. For several years he constantly engaged in vitriolic and sometimes libellous exchanges with other newspaper editors as well as impugning the reputation of one of Grafton's most respected and loved citizens.

The exchanges between Penrose and Waterhouse culminated in 1895 when, probably threatened with legal action, Penrose was forced to withdraw some negative comments which *The Grip* had published about Henry and his paper. In an article on November 29 1895 the *Mercury* triumphantly referred to this retraction as constituting an 'abject and grovelling' apology. Further, it described Penrose as a 'whipped cur' and derided his qualities as a journalist:

> …we do not want to be interrupted by men who would be better employed in disseminating the theory of how to suck eggs than in attempting to edit a newspaper.[52]

These words outraged Penrose. The next day when Waterhouse, having left his South Grafton workplace, arrived by ferry at the foot of Prince Street near his home in Grafton, Penrose was waiting with whip in hand. He managed to get in at least two cuts across Henry's face, before Waterhouse, an amateur athlete as well as a journalist, wrested the whip away from him and Penrose fled in a cab. Just over a week later Penrose pleaded guilty in the Police Court to the charge of assaulting Henry and was fined £4 plus costs.[53]

However, this was not the end of Penrose's assaults on the local establishment. In 1896, without specifically naming him, *The Grip* apparently questioned the medical proficiency of the most highly qualified and respected doctor in the Clarence, Dr Charles Hedley. A graduate of the University of Melbourne, Hedley had practiced in Hamilton, a suburb of Newcastle, working tirelessly to improve the health of working men and women. In 1889 he moved to his wife's home town of Grafton and soon accumulated a large number of patients. He became the Government Medical Officer, Senior Medical Officer of the Hospital and Visiting Surgeon to the Gaol and Aborigine's Home. He also served the local community more generally, for he was appointed to a number of service committees, including one to organise a vice-regal visit to Grafton. A fellow member of several of these committees was W. H. Waterhouse, another stalwart of the Grafton establishment.

Because he had not specifically named Hedley in the derogatory article Penrose was able to argue it didn't actually refer to him. In response Hedley withdrew the complaint. But resentment towards Penrose lingered in the Clarence, in large part because of his unwarranted claims against Hedley, although perhaps also because his attack on Henry involved a cowardly retreat once Waterhouse wrested the whip from him.[54]

In 1899 Penrose sued both Margaret Burt of the *Clarence Advocate* and T. J. Houghton for libel, and in Houghton's case, slander as well. In Burt's case the jury dismissed the claim, although the judge subsequently ruled that defamation had occurred according to law. However, although the defendant in the end agreed to a settlement in which she paid costs Penrose didn't get the £200 he had claimed in damages. In the Penrose vs Houghton trial, a constable who attended the meeting at Ulmurra where Houghton had allegedly slandered the plaintiff, claimed that the defendant referred to Penrose as a 'dirty wretch' and 'drunken brute' as well as 'the most immoral man in the Clarence'. In his testimony Penrose admitted to past court appearances for affiliation, a conviction for whipping H.B. Waterhouse, and being under the influence of alcohol in public. He had sought £1000 but the jury awarded one farthing in damages.[55] This was probably the last straw for Penrose because he left *The Grip* in the same year and it was taken over by his sister Susan, one of the first women to edit a newspaper in the colonies. She was joined as co-editor by the well-known *Bulletin* journalist, E.J Brady.[56] In any case, this story of the bohemian labourite Tom Penrose, and his skirmishes with the Grafton establishment, demonstrate both the power of that establishment and that the extended Waterhouse family was one of its staunchest defenders.

Henry Benjamin, Frances Alice and the End of Their Stories

After he retired from the editorship of the *Richmond River Express and Casino Kyogle*

Advertiser in 1924 Henry and Ellen returned to Grafton where they took up residence in Oliver Street. But he remained active both in the community and at work. In 1932 he was elected to Grafton Council, and for a decade he continued to take on occasional relieving work for newspapers in Grafton, the Lower Clarence and Casino. But after Ellen's death in 1935 his health deteriorated. In 1936 he resigned from the lodge in which he had held membership and office for 57 years, and two years later he quit the newspaper profession permanently. Appropriately, the last position he held was at the Grafton *Daily Examiner*, the very same newspaper which had hired him as an apprentice 65 years earlier. Soon after Ellen died Henry moved to Victoria Street but sometime later, as his health worsened, he travelled to Yamba to live with his daughter Beatrice and her family.[57] Indeed, from the time his children left home to pursue their own lives Henry ensured that he remained in touch, with postcards serving as the main means for organising family get togethers. In my collection of family memorabilia are a small number of postcards written by Henry in the early years of the twentieth century to his

son Percy who was then teaching at Kinchela in the Macleay Valley. Written in small, sometimes indecipherable handwriting, and signed 'HB' the postcards relate Henry's travels across the North Coast to meet and stay with his sons at Woolgoolga, and his plans to visit Percy and his family in the Macleay Valley.

Henry lived almost until the end of World War 2, dying on May 4 1945. The conflict must have caused him some anxiety since nine of his grandsons served in the forces, including all three of Percy's sons. Fittingly, members of the Manchester Order of Oddfellows acted as pallbearers at his funeral, which was held in Grafton Cathedral and attended by 'a large and respectable gathering'.[58] He was buried in the Church of England section of Grafton Cemetery, but not next to Ellen and Mabel, probably because of a lack of space. My grandfather Percy and my father Earle only mentioned him occasionally and briefly to me when I was a child, although I grew up knowing that the Waterhouse family had originally lived in Grafton. My sister Annabel recalls Percy speaking with some pride of Henry's role as a pioneer journalist and newspaper editor on the North Coast.

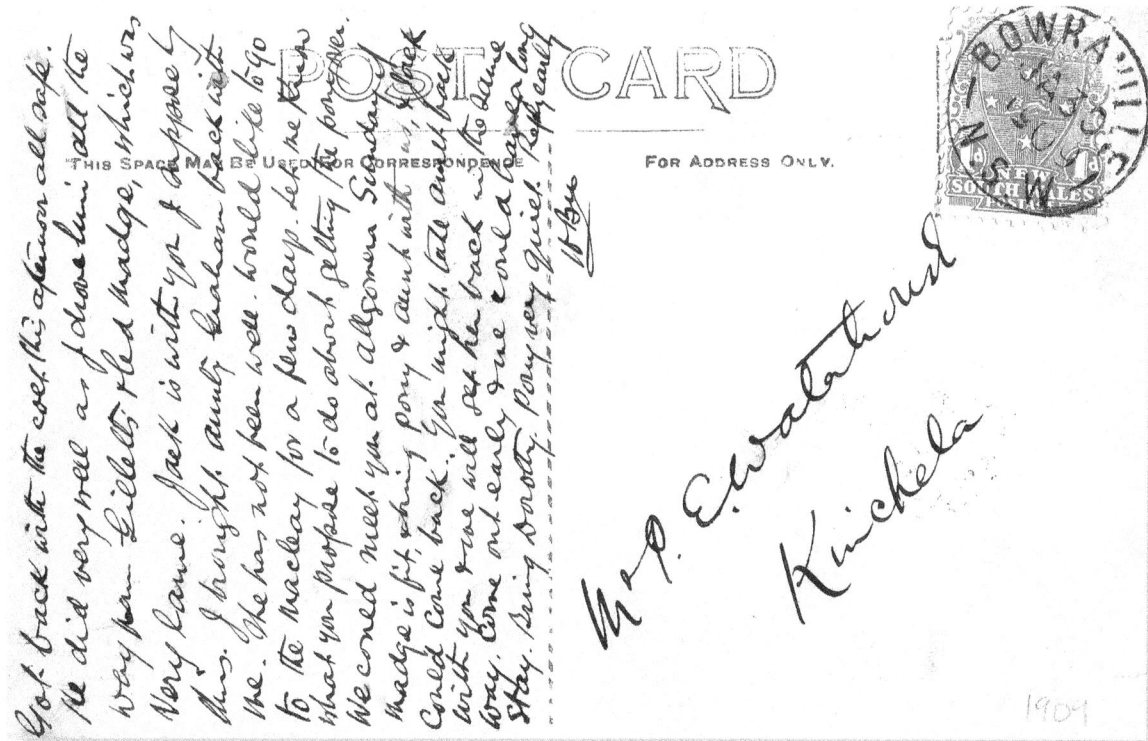

Postcard written by Henry to his son Percy in 1909: Henry was then living at Bowraville where he edited The Nambucca News. Concerned with Frances Alice's health Henry was arranging for her to stay with Percy and Maude at Kinchela. *Waterhouse Family Collection*

In Henry I can see traits that I also recognise in Percy and Earle, that is a commitment to serving the community and a love of sport. However, I can't find any evidence that Henry loved English literature, although his son and grandson were both passionate about it. When I read over what I have written about him he seems far more familiar than William, but I suppose that understanding is coloured by my conviction that W. H. was always role playing and that from the time he left Melbourne he was obsessed with concealing his real self.

Frances Alice's identity was also transformed by the move north. Born Frances Alice Branchflower in Collingwood in 1865, in Wardell and subsequently Grafton she became Fanny Waterhouse. She was educated at Grafton Public School, winning a proficiency award in 1873 when she was still an infants' student.[59] I can't locate any evidence about when she left school and how she spent her post-school years, although at that time it was common for middle class girls to finish their education at the age of 14 or 15 and then live and help at home until they married.

Fanny married the Irish born Presbyterian, William John Graham, in Grafton on December 20, 1884. She was nineteen and he was 29. In 1892 he joined the NSW Public Service and subsequently became the lighthouse caretaker at Coffs Harbour. Later, he was promoted to Harbour Master (Wharfinger), first at Woolgoolga and then at Coffs Harbour. Because he held positions of authority he was known as 'The Boss'.[60]

Fanny and William had five children.[61] Their oldest son Con also became a Harbour Master first at Woolgoolga and subsequently at Byron Bay.[62]

When William retired, he and Fanny moved from their government owned cottage near the Coffs Harbour jetty to a house up on the hill. Later, the couple moved to Sydney, living in a flat in Clovelly on the proceeds of his state government pension. Here he busied himself with membership of a masonic lodge and as verger of the Randwick Presbyterian Church. Apart from Con, their other children also eventually moved to Sydney. Clarence, known as 'Little Boss', ventured even further afield, enlisting in the First AIF in October 1916.

William died in 1933 and was buried in the Presbyterian section of Randwick General Cemetery. Fanny lived for another fourteen years. But one day in late 1947 she had difficulty getting off a tram and was admitted first to a private hospital near Moore Park and subsequently to the orthopaedic ward of St Vincent Hospital, where she died. A subsequent examination revealed she had suffered both from bone and breast cancer. Her family remembered and remembers her as a gregarious, talkative and much-loved matriarch. She lived on in the memory of the Graham family far more strongly than Henry was remembered by the Waterhouse descendants.

Although I think it is likely that Fanny and Henry only had intermittent contact once she moved to Sydney, while she remained on the North Coast the Graham and Waterhouse families continued to socialise, evidence perhaps of continuing affection and companionship between Fanny and Henry.[63]

Finally, I am intrigued by a photo from the Nancarrow/Salter family collection, taken in the vicinity of Coffs Harbour, and which shows Henry and Frances Alice posing next to a car

Frances Alice Branchflower/Waterhouse/ Graham.
Nancarrow/Salter Collection

From the Left: Henry Benjamin, Frances Alice, Mildred Walsh, Cecil Walsh, Patricia Walsh. *Nancarrow/Salter Family Collection*

along with Frances Alice's daughter Mildred, her husband Cecil Walsh and their daughter Patricia. Both William and Ellen are missing from the photo, which suggests it post-dates their deaths in 1933 and 1935 respectively. Moreover, Patricia, who was born in 1922, looks to be in her late teens, so I suspect the photo was taken at Coffs Harbour in the mid to late 1930s and recorded a visit by Frances to the North Coast to meet both those of her children and grandchildren who still lived there, and Henry who by now was living in semi-retirement in Grafton. It may well record one of the last meetings of the Branchflower/Waterhouse siblings and reflects a determination to maintain their connection even after 75 years.

Endnotes

1   *Grafton Daily Examiner*, 15 November 1932

2   *Richmond River Express and Casino Kyogle Advertiser*, 28
     March 1924

3   ibid.

4   *ibid.*; *Grafton Daily Examiner*, 7 May 1945

5   NSW Registry of Births, Marriages and Deaths, *Marriage
     Certificate of Henry Benjamin Waterhouse and Ellen Spring, 15
     November 1882; Examiner*, 21 November 1882

6   Peter Linebaugh, *The London Hanged*, p. 18

7   Ancestry, Lancashire, *Church of England Baptisms, Marriage
     and Burials, 1538–1567–1936*

8   Ancestry, *Manchester Marriages and Banns, 1754–1930*
     (Cathedral)

9   These included Alice (ca. 1790), James (1794–1864),
     William (1795–1864), Joseph (1798-) and John (baptised
     1799, but born many years earlier). Alice was named as
     Martha Entwistle's daughter at her mother's trial in 1812.
     A witness estimated her age at 22 or 23. The ages of Henry,
     James and Joseph were named at their trial in 1813. https:/
     www.ourfamilypast.com/node/10972/tree, Vicky Parslow
     Stafford, *HAA007 Court Case Study: William Entwistle*. I
     have extrapolated their approximate birth years from these
     figures. Stafford's account names John instead of Joseph as
     one of the defendants but John was not on trial in 1813 with
     his father and two brothers because he was already a convict
     in Van Diemen's Land. For John's baptism see Ancestry,
     *Lancashire Bishop's Transcripts, Church of England Baptisms,
     Marriages and Deaths, Bolton-le—Moors Parish, 1790–99;* A
     Solomon Entwistle was baptised in a Manchester Baptist
     Church on 23/5/1793 and his parents were listed as John
     and Ann. This indicates that he was another child but the
     fact that he was baptised in a Baptist Church is surprising,
     given the strong connection between St Mary, Manchester
     and Henry and Martha Entwistle. There is enough doubt to
     exclude him as a certain child of our John/Henry and Ann

10   Grace Karskens, *People of the River: Lost Worlds of Early
     Australia*, Sydney: Allen and Unwin, 2020, p.76

11   Bank of England, Greenfields Papers, *Petition of Ann
     Entwistle to the Governors and Directors of the Bank of
     England* 11 January 1814 M5/314: 15 September 1813–11
     January 1814.

12   *Lancaster Gazette* 12 August, 28 August 1809; *Manchester
     Mercury* 29 August 1809

13   *Hobart Town Gazette and Southern Reporter*, 1 February 1817

14   *Lancaster Gazette*, 21 March, April 18 1812

15   http://convictrecords.au/ships/emu; Toby Reeborn, Carol
     Liston, Jarrad Hickmott, Michelle Cleary, 'Life of Martha
     Entwistle: Australia's First Convict Mental Health Nurse',
     International Journal of Mental Health Nursing (298), 27, pp.
     455–63; Bank of England, Greenfields Records, *Deposition of
     Thomas Barrett*

16   Bank of England, Greenfields Records, *Petition of Ann
     Entwistle*, 9 February 1814. I am grateful to Associate
     Professor Carol Liston for providing me with copies of all
     the Greenfields Records I have cited in this and previous
     footnotes

17   *ibid.*

18   *ibid.*, pp.458–9; Ancestry, *Colonial Secretary Main Series
     of Letters Received*, George Suttor to Governor Lachlan
     Macquarie, 12 February 1815; Suttor to Macquarie 1 April
     1815

19   James Dunk, *Bedlam at Botany Bay*, Sydney: NewSouth
     Publishing, Sydney, 2019, pp. 101–24

20   *Sydney Gazette*, 5 August 1820; Ancestry, *Colonial Secretary*,
     Convicts Index, 4/4430 reel 74, p. 105; Ancestry, *Colonial
     Secretary, Copies of Letters Sent*, J.T Campbell to Major
     Morisset, 22 September 1820; Ancestry, *Colonial Secretary*,
     Special Bundles, 1794–1823 15–5 June-August 1820;
     Reeborn et al., 460

21   https://Australianroyalty.net.au/purnellmccord.ged/
     individual/124786/William-Rafter: Ancestry, *St John's
     Church Parramatta, Baptisms, Marriages and Burials
     1790–1918* (William); Ancestry, *Colonial Secretary, Requested
     permission of a person professing the Roman Catholic Religion
     to marry in a Roman Catholic Church*, 14 February, 1821.
     Ancestry, *Australian Birth Index, 1788–1922* (John). The
     family can also be traced through the 1823, 1824, 1825
     General Muster and the 1828 Census.

22   *Manchester Mercury*, 11 September 1810, 2 February 1813;
     Liverpool Mercury, 23 April 1813; Ancestry, *Lancashire
     Quarter Sessions, Records and Petitions, 1648–1908; Vicki
     Parslow Stafford, 'Our Family Past: Convict Case Study'
     https:www.ourfamilypast.com/node/10972/tree*

23   (London) *Statesman*, 30 March 1819; *Lancaster Gazette*, 27
     March 1819; *Lancaster Gazette*, 10 April 1819

24   *Lancaster Gazette*, 20 March 1819; *Liverpool Mercury, 2 April
     1819*

25   Jill Conway, 'Gregory and John Blaxland', *Australian
     Dictionary of Biography*, vol. 1, Melbourne, Melbourne
     University Press, 1966

26   Census of 1828

27   D. R. Hainsworth, *The Sydney Traders: Simeon Lord and
     His Contemporaries*, 1788–1821 Melbourne: Melbourne
     University Press, 1981, p.191

28   Ancestry, *NSW Register of Convicts' Applications to Marry
     1826–1853*, William Entwistle and Mary Campbell, 20
     September 1831; Ancestry, *NSW Convict Indents, 1788–1842,
     Asia 1830* (Mary Campbell)

29   *NSW Government Gazette*, 13 November 1833

30   Vicki Parslow Stafford, *Our Family Past; New South Wales
     Government Gazette*, 11 July 1832, 13 November 1833;
     Sydney Morning Herald, 21 April 1843, 1 August 1864

31   James Boyce, *Imperial Mud The Fight for the Fens*, London:
     Icon Books, 2020, pp. 127–45, 157–62

32   Ancestry, NSW Assisted Passengers Lists, 1828–1896, *Lists
     of Passengers per Ship James Gibb*

33   Mary Emma (1852–1876), William James (1855–1892)

34   Sarah Ann (1858), Ellen (1860), Alfred Henry (1862–1922),
     Arthur Ernest (1865–1903), Albert Thomas (1866–1945),
     Frederick Phillip Entwistle (1868–1927), Alice Martha
     (1872–1951), and Florence Emily (1874–1956).

35   *Sydney Morning Herald*, 9 April 1873

36   *Grafton Argus and Clarence River General Advertiser*, 21 July,
     27 September 1875

37   *Clarence and Richmond Examiner*, 13 January, 1880, 27
     September 1884; Ancestry, *William Spring, Will, 21 May
     1898*, NSW Wills, 15923; *Sydney Morning Herald*, 21 May
     1935

38   *Clarence and Richmond Examiner*, 2 October 1897

39   *Ibid.*, 5 April 1902. The *Daily Examiner* 15 November
     1932 published a story commemorating Ellen and Henry's
     Golden Wedding anniversary. The family history recounted
     here was probably provided by Henry.

40   Ancestry, Australian *Marriage Index, 1788–1950:* Ancestry, *Unassisted Passenger Lists, Zealandia, 1912*

41   *Daily Examiner,* 24 November 1950

42   *Daily Examiner,* 21 May 1935

43   *The Macleay Argus,* 25 November 1910

44   Barbara Welter, 'The Cult of True Womanhood', *American Quarterly,* vol. 29, Summer, 1966, pp. 151–74; Marilyn Lake, *Progressive New World How Settler Colonialism and Transpacific Exchange Shaped American Reform* Cambridge, Massachusetts: Harvard University Press, 2019, passim.

45   *Daily Examiner,* 21 May, 6 June 1935; *Sydney Morning Herald,* 21 May 1935

46   Archives of NSW, Bankruptcy Files, NRS 13655-1-[10/23129]-File1141. See especially 2 December 1896, H.B. Waterhouse Evidence Before District Registrar in Bankruptcy; 9 May 1899, Affidavit in Support of Application for Leave to Apply for Certificate of Discharge;7 August 1899, Testimony of H. B. Waterhouse in Supreme Court of NSW; 17 August 1899, Certificate of Discharge

47   *NSW Government Gazette,* 6 November 1896, 4 July, 20 December 1899; *Clarence and Richmond Examiner,* 13 June 1908

48   *Grafton Argus and Clarence River General Advertiser,* 10 April1916; *Richmond River Express and Casino Kyogle Advertiser,* 28 March 1924; *Daily Examiner* 7 May 1945

49   *Casino and Kyogle Courier and North Coast Advertiser,* 24 September 1924; *Daily Examiner,* 23 January 1930, 7 May 1945; *Northern Star,* 23 November 1931

50   *Casino and Kyogle Courier,* 28 March 1924

51   *NSW Government Gazette* 6 November 1896, 4, 26 November 1899; *Evening News* (Sydney), 18 August 1899; Kass, p. 160

52   *Albury Wodonga Express,* 20 December 1895, repeated the *Mercury* article in full. *The Mercury* is not included in the Trove digital collection and it is not held by the State Library

53   *Northern Star,* 30 November 1895; *Dungog Chronicle,* 13 December, 1895; *Evening News* (Sydney), 7 December 1895

54   *Clarence and Richmond Examiner,* 11, 18 July 1896, 24 January 1899; *Grafton Argus and Clarence River General Advertiser,* 23 January 1899

55   *Grafton Argus,* 23 October 1899; *Clarence and Richmond Examiner,* 14 November 1899

56   *Northern Star,* 1 December 1916

57   Grafton Daily Examiner, 15 November 1932, 7 May 1945; Ancestry, *Commonwealth Electoral Roll,* Cowper, 1930 and 1936

58   *Grafton Daily Examiner,* 5, 7 May 1945

59   *Clarence and Richmond Examiner,* 23 December 1873

60   Ancestry, *New South Wales Public Service Lists,1858–1960,* 1910; Jenny Nancarrow/Salter, Descendants of Josiah Branchflower, (2000), typescript; Ancestry, *Australian Marriage Records, 1787–1950* (Frances Waterhouse/William Graham); Ancestry, *Australian Electoral Rolls, 1903–1980,* 1913 ,NSW, Raleigh, Coffs Harbour Jetty

61   William Henry Conly (Con) (1886-), Mildred May (1888–1951), Ruby Violet (1890–1966), Clarence John (1893-) and Mary (1905–1905).

62   Nancarrow/Salter

63   *ibid.;* Ancestry, *Australian Death Index 1787–1885* (William John Graham); Ancestry, *Australian World War 1 Service Records,* 1914–1920 (Clarence John Graham)

PART 3

Pastoral Pleasures, the Perils of War and the Challenges of Peace: Two Generations of Waterhouse Family Life in the Macleay Valley and Beyond

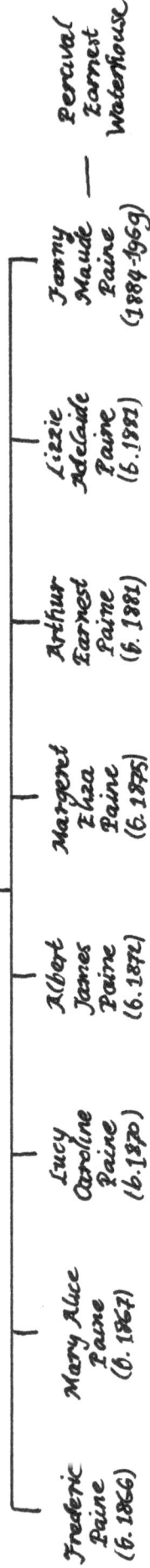

Thomas
Paine
(1738-1826)

Mary
Stevens
(1755-1826)

William
Paine
(1787-1876)

Philadelphia
Watson
(1786-1859)

Richard
Paine
(1842-1933)

Caroline
Thomson
(1844-1902)

Frederic
Paine
(b.1866)

Mary Alice
Paine
(b.1867)

Lucy
Caroline
Paine
(b.1870)

Albert
James
Paine
(b.1872)

Margaret
Eliza
Paine
(b.1875)

Arthur
Earnest
Paine
(b.1881)

Lizzie
Adelaide
Paine
(b.1883)

Fanny
Maude
Paine
(1884-1969)

Percival
Earnest
Waterhouse

Chapter 6

When Percy met Maude

A Close Encounter of the Love at First Sight Kind

While two of Henry Benjamin and Ellen's sons sooner or later followed their father's example by becoming small businessmen, their oldest child, Percival Ernest Waterhouse, chose the teaching profession. Perhaps his father's business experiences made Percy wary of entering the world of private enterprise while, on the other hand, in an age still scarred by the depression of the 1890s, the public education sector offered security of employment and a guaranteed income. However, while there is no evidence that his parents loved reading and learning, Percy's career as a teacher revealed that he was passionate about both, which suggests that his choice of a profession was not simply motivated by economic concerns.

Sydney Teachers' College was not established until 1906 so Percy was trained through the 'pupil teacher' system.[1] Sometime around 1900 he was assigned to two crudely built half-time schools in the Bellinger River district, one of which was built with cedar offcuts. It is also likely that both schools lacked windows and floors.[2]

During school holidays Percy returned to live with his family in Grafton, taking advantage of the recreational facilities available on the Clarence, facilities not available in the scrublands of the

This photo of the Bellingen school named either 'Best' or 'Dingle' was taken after Percy had left for Kinchela. It was forwarded by his replacement, Stan Moody, as a Christmas card to Percy and Maude. It contains an identification notation written by Earle Waterhouse on the back. *Waterhouse family collection*

Bellinger. It was common for charitable, church and commercial bodies to organise passenger steamer excursions that plied between Grafton, Harwood Island and Maclean. On one of these trips, probably in 1905, Percy met Fanny Maude, the youngest child of a Southgate farmer, Richard Paine. Because she had three older brothers and five older sisters, she had more leisure hours than most farm girls, hours for reading, fancy work, drawing, dressmaking, church activities and, of course, trips on passenger steamers. According to my father's account, which was probably based on what his parents told him, the attraction and commitment between Percy and Maude were immediate and determined. They were married on April 21 1906 by a Methodist minister, Robert Mowbray, at Richard Paine's Southgate farm, Lyndon.[3] William Henry Waterhouse gave them an expensive tea and coffee set. In his account of how Percy and Maude met and married, their son Earle noted that the path was not 'smooth' and that there were 'obstacles' to their union. He was probably referring to the fact that Henry Benjamin and Ellen were dedicated members of the Church of England and that Percy's confirmation in Grafton's Christ Church Cathedral in 1902 suggested that at this stage of his life he too was a committed Anglican.[4] In contrast Maude's father Richard, like his father James before him, was a devoted Methodist. The fact that they were married by a Methodist minister indicates a concession from the Waterhouse family. However, Maude was pregnant when she married Percy, which was undoubtedly a major factor in securing her family's permission to marry. Their first child, Dorothy was born in Grafton on October 6 of the same year.[5]

The Paine Family: Sussex, The Hunter and the Clarence

At least from the eighteenth century onwards, the Paine (also sometimes spelled Payne) family from which Maude was descended lived in the eastern part of Sussex, more specifically in the town of Rye and the nearby villages of Beckley and Peasmarsh. William Paine and Elizabeth Mitten were both born about 1710 and married on June 1, 1732 in Elizabeth's home town of Warbleton in east

Sussex.[6] Their son, Thomas (1738–1826), married Mary Stevens in Beckley on May 11, 1784. He was 46 and she was 29. Perhaps this was a case of a second marriage for Thomas and even for Mary although I can't find evidence of first marriages for either. Their son William (1787–1876) was born in Peasmarsh and married Philadelphia Watson (1786–1859) on May 18 1812. William and Philadelphia's children included James (1814–1895), who was born in Beckley, Harriet (1821–), and probably other unidentified children as well.[7] The Paines were members of the Church of England, baptised, married and buried according to its rites. But their socio-economic status was low. The second William was an agricultural labourer, who together with his new wife signed his marriage certificate with his mark. I suspect his father and grandfather were also unskilled rural workers.

Through the eighteenth and into the early nineteenth century rural Sussex enjoyed a period of sustained prosperity. It produced a variety of primary products, including corn, lamb and fruit for the nearby London markets. But the end of the Napoleonic Wars was followed by Depression in Surrey, Kent and Sussex, which produced particular hardship for agricultural labourers. The result was that a significant number of families from Peasmarsh, Beckley and surrounding villages took advantage of the assisted passages offered to agricultural workers and emigrated to New South Wales. They included Maria Ann Smith and her husband John and Henry and Ann Packham. Maria was later to cultivate the 'Granny Smith' apple in the settlement of Eastwood, now a Sydney suburb, while Henry and Ann's son, Charles Henry, created the Packham pear at Molong.[8]

Another emigrant from the same area was James Paine, the son of William and Philadelphia, and, like his father, an agricultural labourer, who left for Australia as an assisted emigrant with his wife, the Beckley born Sarah Ann Larkins (1816–1891), in 1839.[9] Bringing with them two small children born in Beckley, they settled at Bolwarra in the Hunter Valley where they became parents of a further twelve children.[10] Tragically, the last five children died either at birth or soon after.

Apart from the fact that he was an emigrant, what distinguished James from previous generations of his family was that as a young man he became a devoted and demonstrative Methodist. Later in life he lamented the loss of evangelical fervour in contemporary Australian Christianity and spoke longingly of 'the good old days of revival and blessing'. His conversion almost certainly occurred after he arrived in Australia, where he was subject to the strong Methodist revival movement that swept both the Hawkesbury and Hunter Valleys. In contrast to the formality of Church of England services the itinerant Methodist ministers spoke passionately and compellingly in the same informal language as their listeners. James was demonstratively eccentric in the expression of his religious beliefs but no-one doubted the sincerity of his faith.[11] His Methodist legacy was to remain in his family for at least one more generation.

The Paine family remained in the Hunter for about twenty years. When Richard Paine was christened in 1842 his father was described as a labourer. In fact, it was difficult for families like the Paines to acquire large amounts of the land in the Hunter Valley because from the beginning land was allocated and sold by the Governor on the basis of the wealth of the applicants. Moreover, those who obtained land were given a convict worker for every 100 acres of land they 'improved'. Most of the small farms in the Hunter were leased from large land owners who depended more on rents than pastoral or agricultural production for their income.[12] Given the high cost of land in the Hunter it was hardly surprising that when the Selection Acts of 1861 and beyond allowed the sale at reasonable prices of land in the areas previously designated as beyond the limits of location (legal settlement) that families like the Paines decided to take advantage of the opportunity. James Paine's decision to move his family to the Clarence was well informed because there the soil was rich, the rainfall was reliable and the markets for rural produce were easily accessible. However, like other farmers on the Clarence the family did face one major difficulty in the form of the regular floods which damaged their lands, crops, stock and houses.[13]

When she was a child Percy told my sister Annabel that when the Paine family left the Hunter they drove a herd of cattle to the Clarence. Probably this involved a long trip via the road from the Hunter Valley up to the Tablelands and then another route from Glen Innes down into the Clarence Valley. Earle told a different story, one which he probably learnt from his grandfather Richard Paine, who in later life lived with Percy's family at Belmore River. He recounted that James Paine and his family arrived in the Clarence in a small wooden sailing ship, as part of the first group of farmers to usurp land from the local Indigenous people under the Selection Acts.[14] Perhaps they did both, with the women and children arriving by ship and the men driving cattle up from the Hunter to the Tablelands and then down into the Clarence. James acquired land in the Great Marlow District on the north west side of the River. His sons also purchased land for farms, Richard and William on adjoining land at Southgate, and Benjamin at Carr's Creek and subsequently at Great Marlow. Although Richard's obituary praised the family for doing 'their share of the pioneering work of the Clarence', the fact is that the Selection Acts involved large scale appropriation of the country of the Indigenous Peoples.[15] It was not land that the Europeans 'settled', it was occupied land that they confiscated, although no acknowledgement of that reality was made when it was sold to European farmers like the Paines.

Richard made a trip back to the Hunter in 1864 where he married Caroline Shaw Thomson, from Dunmore near Maitland, in the Wesleyan Chapel at East Maitland. To mark the occasion Caroline was given a King James Bible in which either she or Richard subsequently noted the names and years of birth of their nine children. When Earle acquired the Bible after Percy's death, he and his wife, Nancy, added details concerning the subsequent births and deaths of close and extended Waterhouse family members. Richard Paine took the Bible wherever he went and Earle remembers a passage that his grandfather often quoted to him, a passage that impressed him so much that he never forgot it:

Honour your father and Mother so that your

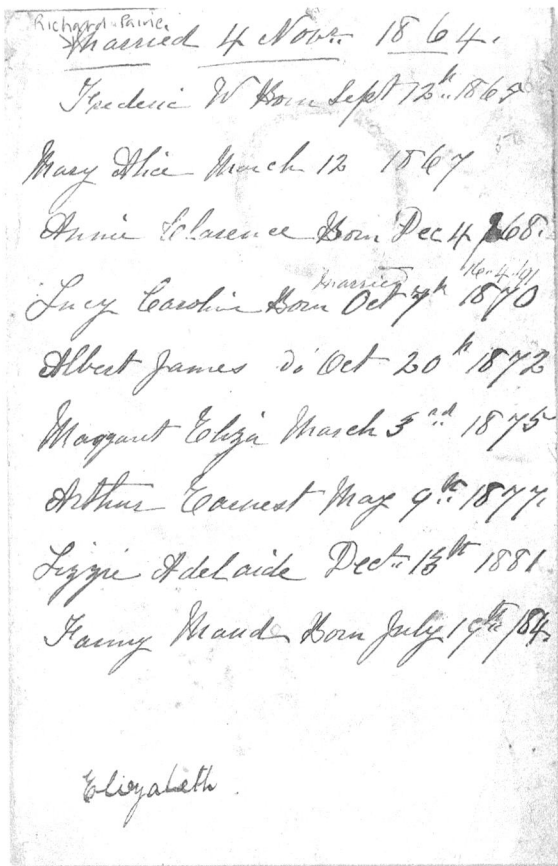

The inside cover of the Bible given to Caroline Shaw Thompson on her marriage to Richard Paine. Either Caroline or Richard inscribed the names of their children in this space. *Waterhouse Family Collection*

days may be long and all may be well with you in the land the Lord has given you[16]

This Bible is the oldest piece (excluding photographs) in the Waterhouse family collection.

Caroline died on October 10 1908 at the age of 58, but Richard lived to be 92, passing away on July 7 1933. Accepting the statement in Psalm 90, verse 10, 'The days of our years are three score and ten', he handed over his farm to his sons when he reached 70, no doubt in the expectation that he now had little time to live. Instead, he survived another 22 years, spending the rest of his life visiting and staying with his children. For a number of those years, he lived with Percy and Maude and their family in the schoolmaster's residence at Belmore River on the Lower Macleay. In 1980 when my father and I visited this house where Earle had grown up, he pointed out the bedroom to the right of the entrance hall as the room which Richard had occupied for many years. Richard also joined the Waterhouse family on their Christmas

camping holidays at Maguire's Crossing and fished off the beach with Earle.[17]

Like his father Richard was a committed, although less strident Methodist. He was the Superintendent of the Southgate Methodist Sunday School and was also a lay preacher. Perhaps the fact that he was a teetotaller contributed to his longevity. Nor was he the only member of his generation of Paines to be an involved Methodist, for his brother Benjamin was also an active member of the same denomination.

Unfortunately, Caroline left nothing in the written record that allows us to measure and understand her character and values. We can be certain that she contributed to the work on the family's Southgate dairy farm in addition to raising nine children. Still, the words on her tombstone are parsimonious, including just basic family details and the short phrase 'Asleep in Jesus'. Their children included, Frederick (b. 1866), Mary Alice (b. 1867), Annie Clarence (b. 1868), Lucy Caroline (1870), Albert James (b. 1872), Margaret Eliza (b. 1875), Arthur Earnest (b.1877), Lizzie Adelaide (b. 1881), and Fanny Maude (b. 1884).[18] My grandmother, Maude, grew to be a woman of slight build and only 150 centimetres in height. She was called Maude by the Paine family and her husband. Her sons, who revered her, always addressed her as 'Mater'.

While some of Richard's children stayed in the Clarence to farm or, as in the case of Annie, to marry a farmer, one of them chose life in the city. When her first husband, died leaving her with an inheritance of £300, Mary Alice moved to Sydney to set up a dressmaking business and remarry, this time to William Ronneberg.[19] Another sister, Lucy Caroline married William Leeson and moved to the Darling Downs. She occasionally sent Maude photos and postcards of Toowoomba and surrounds.[20]

The Lower Macleay Valley

The Djangadi people had inhabited the Macleay Valley for at least 10,000 years before the invasion of their lands by Europeans, who first arrived in the 1820s but whose numbers accelerated in the subsequent decade. In the Lower Valley, where the

Indigenous people mostly relied on the river and the ocean for their food, the arrival of Europeans may not, at first, have resulted in widespread disruption to their supply of tucker. There were cases of conflict and white reprisal massacres, for example at Yarrahapinni, but not on the scale that occurred in the Upper Valley. Here the Europeans created a grazing economy with disastrous consequences for the Indigenous people and their way of life. The introduced stock monopolised water supplies, competed with native animals for fodder and ate the roots that Aborigines collected as food. Wallabies and kangaroos were driven from the area leaving the Indigenous hunters little choice but to spear cattle and sheep, although they probably also killed the stock as a guerrilla war tactic. The European response was to conduct a series of reprisal massacres. Not until the arrival of a contingent of Native Police from Queensland in 1856 was large scale frontier conflict in the Upper Macleay brought brutally to an end. Yet in both the Upper and Lower Macleay, including areas where there was continuing conflict, and in those in which it was more sporadic, the number of Indigenous inhabitants declined sharply from the early 1840s. Disease was the main contributor to this rising Aborigine death rate.[21]

In the late nineteenth century Macleay Valley Indigenous people became determined to acquire secure land tenure at a time when white appropriation of their lands was increasing. The response of the white authorities was not to listen sympathetically to Indigenous voices but rather to gather First Nations people into reserves. In effect what was established was a form of apartheid. However, what happened at Kinchela was somewhat more complicated. In 1880 an Indigenous man, William Drew, took up 26 acres near the village with the intention of farming the land. He applied to the NSW Government for secure tenure but instead was granted 'permissive occupation', which meant he held it temporarily at the government's pleasure. Nineteen years later, in response to a white farmer's claim on the land the Protection Board defended Drew's residency but only by transferring the title to an Aboriginal Reserve. Subsequently, the size of the Reserve was shrunk while the number of

Indigenous people in residence was increased as they were moved from other long inhabited homelands. In 1918 some of the land was leased to a white farmer, while in 1924 more of the land was appropriated for the Kinchela Boys Home. In the same year the Indigenous residents of three islands in the Macleay were moved to the Kinchela Reserve. Throughout all these changes the Indigenous farmers cultivated the land with great success, even as the number of people to be supported increased and the land available for cultivation continued to shrink.[22] In the years the Waterhouse family lived in Kinchela they were within walking distance of the Reserve, including the site of what later became the Boys' Home. In later life, as reflected in his memoir letters, Earle was deeply troubled by the injustices perpetrated at the Boys' Home.

In some ways the European occupation of the Macleay mirrored what also happened in the Clarence. The first Europeans to move into the Macleay were also mostly ex-convict cedar cutters who arrived in the late 1830s and quickly cleared the river and creek banks of the cedar trees. By 1842 most of the easily accessible timber was gone.

Just like the Clarence too, the cedar workers were succeeded by small farmers who focussed on growing maize both for the local and Sydney market. Many of these farmers also raised pigs, cattle and sometimes a small number of sheep. The Selection Acts of 1861 and after gave a stimulus to small scale farming, allowing modest agricultural holdings to replace the large pastoral leases on the northern side of the river. However, maize production suffered in the aftermath of a major flood in 1864 while a depression in the Sydney maize market in 1867 led to lower prices. In response farmers and capitalists turned to sugar growing, which was seen as a more profitable crop than maize. Small mills were built at Kempsey, Frederickton, Kinchela and Summer Island and a major one, owned and operated by CSR, at the junction of the Belmore and Macleay Rivers at Gladstone. But sugar failed to become a major crop in the Macleay, in part because the growers were ignorant of how to produce high quality cane. More importantly, the climate was too cool for growing a high standard product, with regular winter frosts causing particular damage. The CSR mill ran at a loss for three seasons and in response the company moved it to the Clarence. Within a decade, most of the smaller mills had also shut.[23]

In the late nineteenth century dairying became a major rural industry in the Macleay. The rapid multiplication of small-scale dairy farms was stimulated by technological innovation for the creation of the centrifugal cream separator allowed butter making to become a more profitable commercial industry. At first the process took place in small factories spread throughout the Lower Macleay, although in the late 1890s household separators came into more common use. Now farmers did their own processing and then organised transport of the processed product to the cheese and butter factories at Smithtown, Kempsey and Frederickton. However, the farmers around Kinchela, probably lacking the funds needed to purchase separators, still had their unprocessed milk collected twice a day and transported by boat to the Bacchus Marsh factory at Smithtown. Two other factors gave stimulus to dairying in the Macleay. First, a fall in the prices of maize and beef in the 1890s persuaded more farmers to turn to dairying. Second, the passing of the Closer Settlement Act of 1901 by the NSW Parliament, an act which provided for the purchase of large properties by the Government, which were then divided into small lots and sold at auction, led to an increase in small dairy holdings in the Macleay. In 1900 there were 66 dairy farms carrying 2428 head of cattle in the region but by 1906 that had increased to 759 farms and 43,000 head of cattle. An improved milking machine came onto the market in 1904 but again many Lower Macleay farmers lacked the capital to purchase and maintain milking equipment and they continued to use family labour, including children. For most dairy farmers, I suspect, the labour was hard, and the rewards were modest.[24]

Idyllic Childhoods: Family Life in Kinchela and Belmore River

Kinchela

Kempsey and the Macleay were not a complete mirror of Grafton and the Clarence. The failure of sugar in the Macleay meant the opportunities for rural prosperity were more limited. Moreover, Grafton became a port for the export not only of local but also produce brought down from the New England Tablelands. But Kempsey never became a conduit for inland produce because the route from the Tablelands was steep and arduous, causing a long delay in constructing the road to Armidale, which was not completed until the early twentieth century. Grafton became a prosperous trade centre and a provincial capital. Kempsey remained a relatively small river town.

Percy's Department of Education salary was not large but the family was to some extent self-sufficient, especially at Belmore River. Later in life Percy and Maude spoke affectionately of the years they spent in the Macleay and I can't remember them ever referring to hard times. For Earle, memories of his childhood were a consolation in the most difficult period of his life — the War years. Navigating a Beaufort Bomber at 10,000 feet en route from Richmond to Horn Island in Torres Strait in 1942, he set a course that took the plane over the Belmore River School and residence. 'As I looked down,' he later wrote, 'I thought I was near one of earth's fair places'.[25] I doubt even despite his later travels to other parts of Australia as well as to Europe, Japan and North America, that he ever changed that view. Like most people in the Valley, farmers and townspeople alike, the family lived frugally but they were also resourceful and independent. Earle's memoir describes a happy and united family. But Maude and Percy had ambitions for their children that extended beyond the Macleay and believed the path forward was through education. In the Macleay years they devoted themselves to providing the means for their children to take advantage of the opportunities that formal learning provided.

In 1906, Maude and Percy moved to the small town of Kinchela, located at the junction of

Kinchela. *Waterhouse Family Collection (photo by Percy Waterhouse)*

Kinchela Creek and the Macleay River. Although Dorothy was born in Grafton their succeeding four children, Earle, Ella, Alan and Barry all arrived during the family's residence in Kinchela.[26] Now bypassed by the road running from Kempsey to South West Rocks, the village consists only of a small set of houses. But in 1906 the road ran through Kinchela and along the riverbank and, apart from the houses, a blacksmith's workshop, a cattle dealership, two stores, a butcher shop, and three cheese works were located within its precincts. The township also boasted a wharf at which steamers called regularly to convey passengers, deliver goods and to pick up maize, meat, milk and cream.[27] What Kinchela did not possess was a school, although there were three in the vicinity. The school at Summer Island (opened 1881), originally called Tacking Point, was built on the site of the Kinchela village reserve, which was several hundred metres down the road towards South West Rocks. A little further down the same road was Kinchela Aboriginal School which opened in 1892 and was eventually attached to

Waterhouse family home, Kinchela (photo by Percy)

Waterhouse Family Collection

the Kinchela Aboriginal Boys' Home. But the oldest school of the three (opened 1874), and the one to which Percy was appointed, was Kinchela Creek Public School, located on the right bank of Kinchela Creek three and a half miles (5.6 kilometres) from the village.[28]

Although the Summer Island school possessed a schoolmaster's residence, the school at Kinchela Creek did not and so the family lived successively in two small rented wooden houses. The first was close to the Summer Island school and residence while the second was located behind the main wharf near the junction of the Macleay River and Kinchela Creek . Although in dilapidated condition it was still standing in 1980 when Earle pointed it out to me. A year or so later, when it became available for sale, at what now seems an absurdly cheap price, I considered purchasing it as a family holiday home. However, daunted both by the size of the mortgage Grace and I held on our house in Annandale in Sydney and by the number of repairs required to make the Kinchela structure properly inhabitable, I baulked. It was perhaps for the best but I still possess some feelings of regret about my decision, especially since the ultimate purchaser, rather than renovate the house, demolished it and replaced it with a more modern dwelling.

Dorothy undertook her primary education at Summer Island School, passing her High School qualifying certificate in 1918, but Earle, was taught by his father at Kinchela Creek School.[29] On school days Percy and his son, travelled to and from Kinchela Creek School by horse and either sulky or buggy. In subsequent years, Ella, Alan and Barry also enrolled at Kinchela Creek School. The other students were from dairy farms and those over six years old helped with the milking before coming to school. As a result, sometime around mid-morning, many of them fell asleep at their desks. Given this cohort Percy sought to implement a curriculum that balanced teaching the children practical farming skills while they also learned the prescribed subjects. So, they were taught to test milk for quality and keep records of rainfall and temperature as well as writing, spelling, grammar, arithmetic, geography, history,

music (with a focus on English songs) and art.[30] Each Thursday Percy read stories about ancient Greek, Roman and Norse heroes, relying especially on Charles Kingsley's *Heroes* to tell the stories of Theseus, Perseus and the Argonauts. I don't know about the impact of 'Thursday Stories' on the other children that Percy taught but it left an indelible impression on Earle, inculcating in him a life-long love of English literature. Later in life he could still quote from Shakespeare's tragedies and history plays, Gray's *Elegy Written in a Country Churchyard* and the King James Version of the Bible, especially the Old Testament, with great ease. His literary education was continued at home where the children were encouraged to read Dickens, Kingsley (*Westward Ho!*), Thomas Hughes (*Tom Brown's Schooldays*) as well as Australian poetry and short stories, which were Maude favourites. Teaching English literature was probably what Percy liked most. Judy Thompson, Percy's granddaughter, recalls staying with Percy and Maude at Glenbrook shortly after World War 2 had ended while Ella, her mother, was hospitalised. Every night, at bedtime, Percy read her stories from Kipling's *The Jungle Book*. Percy, certainly, was a natural communicator and teacher.[31]

Indigenous Encounters

Apart from those who lived on what became the site of the Kinchela Boys' Home there were a number of other Indigenous families who lived in other areas in the vicinity. One family lived in an abandoned house in the village until they were evicted when the house was demolished to make way for the construction of Ball's store and residence. A few more families lived in three or four huts made of timber, bark and corrugated iron about a kilometre from Kinchela alongside the Hat Head Road where the rich alluvial farmland is replaced by forest heath. The residents lived on rations distributed from the nearest police station and money earned working for local Europeans. Maude employed three women from the camp to do the family's washing every Monday, for which they were paid 2/-.

Fishing became a life-long passion for Earle and he first learnt to cast a line when he was occasionally allowed to hold his father's handline when Percy fished from the Kinchela wharf. Then Earle took the initiative of raiding his mother's sewing box for a reel of cotton, which he used as a line, and a purposefully bent pin which became the hook. For bait he found some dead house flies. By some miracle he actually caught some small tailor and saltwater herring. But while he was facing the water fishing, his catch was picked up from the wharf by two emaciated Indigenous children from the family living in the abandoned house and taken home to feed an impoverished family. Many years later Earle recalled the guilt he felt, even though a small boy, because it was clear that these boys were very hungry.

The Kinchela Boys Home, in which between 400 and 600 Indigenous boys and girls were incarcerated between 1924 and 1970, was not opened until six years after the family left the village, but in later life Earle often expressed remorse about the treatment of these children. Although the boys were trained as dairy and agricultural labourers, when Earle wrote his memoir letters in 1987, he couldn't recall ever meeting any farmhands who were trained at the Boys Home during his time in the Macleay Valley. Perhaps many of them eventually returned to their families in the Macleay and beyond. What then did the Boys Home training achieve? When he got homesick while boarding in Kempsey during his high school years, he contemplated how painful it was for eight-year-old Indigenous children to be permanently removed from their families. This sense of injustice remained with him for life, recalled in his memoir and voiced to me over many family Sunday lunches in the last years of his life.[32]

The Europeans on the Lower Macleay kept apart from the Indigenous residents. Even as late as 1947 and again in 1960 the parents of children attending what was now Kinchela Lower School successfully opposed a merger with Kinchela Aboriginal School. Earle noted too that when he attended Belmore River Public School there were no Aboriginal students. He also recalled that not a single Indigenous student attended high school in the Macleay during the five years he was enrolled at West Kempsey High School.

There is no record of Aboriginal parents petitioning to enrol their children at the Belmore River School but that was probably because they knew their enrolment applications would be rejected. In 1928 W.H. Gray appealed the Department of Education's decision to exclude his eleven-year-old daughter from Upper Belmore River Public School. Acknowledging that she was 'probably classed as Aboriginal' he indicated that she was as 'well dressed as any other child'. In rejecting his appeal, the Department's Under Secretary indicated that parents of white children had objected to his daughter's enrolment and that it was the Department's policy to exclude 'colored' children in that case.[33]

The Waterhouse family were perhaps more sympathetic to Indigenous causes than other families both at Kinchela and Belmore River. Earle noted that a Mr Davis was a prominent local First Nations leader, an organiser of concerts with Indigenous performers to raise funds to cover the transport and accommodation costs of deputations to State Parliament. There they demanded the provision of resources and electoral rights for the Indigenous inhabitants of the Macleay. The Waterhouse family attended these concerts.[34]

Belmore River

The impact of World War 1 reached into the Kinchela village community. The attachment of recruitment posters to the front wall of the Post Office was followed by the arrival of recruitment marches. Farmers with German names were harassed and then arrested and confined to Trial Bay Gaol. The growing lists of casualties posted on the Post office noticeboard, inevitably began to contain the names of locals. Families of men who had enlisted presented studio portraits of their sons in uniform to the Waterhouse family. I suspect these were young men whom Percy had taught. Percy or Maude pasted them in the family photograph album, no doubt as a sign of respect, and looking at them now I wonder which of them returned. On the announcement of War Percy, rather than engaging in patriotic rhetoric about King and Country, pronounced with some foresight that it was 'a gravely serious matter'. I suspect

H DUNFORD   1ST AIF

Photo Given to Maude and Percy by an enlisted
former student. There are several more photos of
this kind in the family collection. *Waterhouse Family
Collection*

The Belmore River School Master's Residence now in
the caring hands of Jenny and Roger Gifkins. (Photo
by Richard Waterhouse). *Waterhouse Family Collection*

that he was grateful that his three sons were far too
young to go to War, although during the course of
World War 2 all three of them enlisted.[35]

But another event that was to have a significant impact on the family's lifestyle began to
unfold in early 1918. On January 11, in a letter to
the Department of Education the local District
Inspector proposed that Percy exchange positions
with the teacher at Belmore River. In support of
his plan Inspector Harvey argued that Percy had
never had a school with a residence, and that he
needed and deserved one more than the current
occupant, Mr Turnbull, in part because he had five
children. Harvey also suggested that Percy was
not only a more formally qualified teacher than
Turnbull, but a very capable educator, which was
particularly relevant because Belmore River was a
bigger school than Kinchela Creek. It seems that
Harvey was also anxious that the curriculum in
schools in his inspectorate include material relating to Macleay Valley agriculture. Noting that

there was a piece of land attached to the Belmore
River that was suitable for agricultural experi-
ments, Harvey concluded that the Waterhouse
family were capable of carrying out those experi-
ments, but Mr Turnbull was not. The Department
accepted Harvey's recommendation and although
Turnbull attempted to delay the exchange, falsely
arguing his ill wife was 'unable to be moved', the
swap of schools took place in May. The children
and the family's belongings were transported
up the Macleay and then the Belmore by a flat
wheeled paddle steamer, or drogher, while the two
parents drove in horse drawn vehicles along the
tracks that passed as roads that ran beside the two
rivers. So began a period in the family's history
that Earle and his parents were to remember as
amongst the happiest in their lives.[36]

To meet both the Inspector's and their own
needs, one of the first acts of the family when they
arrived at Belmore River was to lay out an intricate
garden in the school grounds and to clear the residence area in preparation for a fruit tree orchard
and flower and vegetable gardens. Within a year
or so the Waterhouse gardens were so well known
that people came from as far away as Kempsey
to view the flowers and share the vegetables. At
first, the family bought milk from neighbours,
with Earle walking across the fields each morning to collect a supply from a nearby dairy farm.

Eventually the family produced its own dairy products, acquiring three cows, a separator and a butter churn, which was also used to make soap. They also kept honey producing beehives. The boys hauled the Belmore for prawns with a chaff bag serving as a net, and trolled for perch ('Australian bass') in the family rowing boat, using a spoon-bait lure.

My father later taught me to troll for tailor on Brisbane Water using the same carefully preserved and now vintage lure. Because both hands were needed to row the boat his practice was to tie the line around a big toe and then grab it with his hands when a fish hit the lure. I found this technique worked well when catching small fish but one day when a large greenback tailor latched onto the lure my toe was lacerated as the line tightened quickly and sharply around it. While the Belmore River was located only about twenty-five metres to the west of the schoolhouse, the Swan Pool was to be found several hundred metres to the east. Here the boys hunted for ducks from the family boat ,which was pointed at both ends. The greatest hazard from this form of hunting was that snakes took refuge in the boat when the boys left it to wade through the swamp to get close to their targets.[37]

Percy earned just under £450 a year at Belmore River, a salary supplemented by a small annual amount paid to Maude for teaching sewing to the girl students. However, there was an annual deduction £42 from Percy's salary for rent on the school residence.[38] In fact the family was able to save a reasonable proportion of the parents' earnings because it was largely self-sufficient, providing its own fruit, vegetables, milk, butter, soap, honey, eggs, poultry and wildfowl. The children contributed to splitting wood, milking, churning cream to butter, washing and drying up, and making jams and preserves. I'm sure that the boys undertook the outdoor jobs while the girls focussed on the indoor tasks. Their mother did both, working in the garden, cooking family meals and making clothes for the family—pyjamas, nighties, bloomers, singlets and even shirts. On week nights she worked until 9 p.m. Because of the sheer volume of work involved in making clothes for seven people

Four of the Waterhouse Children Dorothy, Earle, Ella and Alan The identification labels on these, and other photos in the collection, were written by Earle in the 1980s. *Waterhouse Family Collection*

Barry, the last of the Waterhouse children.
Waterhouse Family Collection

she probably found sewing quite arduous but it was also something she enjoyed. On our annual visits to my grandparents' home in Glenbrook when I was a small child, she always gave me a pair of short pants which she had sewed with a small flap in place of a button or zip fly. I loved the shorts, simply because they were gifts from my Nana, but I was always a bit embarrassed about the flaps because other kids made fun of them.

The indoor recreational activities of the family focussed on reading, writing and visiting. Maude was an avid reader who worked her way through the family and school libraries as well as regularly perusing the *Sydney Morning Herald*. In particular, she loved and never discarded, her copies of Henry Lawson's stories and poems, which I eventually inherited, including *Joe Wilson* and *While the Billy Boils*. When I was a postgraduate student in the United States in the late sixties and early seventies my father regularly sent me letters in the form of aerogrammes but only mailed me a parcel once. It contained a book, *The Poetical Works of Henry Lawson,* and on the title page he inscribed the words, 'You are sure to find a few grains of gold among the doggerel'. I was puzzled by his choice of books, for at this stage of my life I was arrogantly dismissive of Australian literature and indeed of Australian culture more generally. Only

when I read his memoir letters many years later did I realise that this gift was an attempt at perpetuating his mother's literary tastes in the mind of one of her grandsons. Ironically, in the aftermath of my intellectual conversion from researching and teaching American to Australian history in the 1980s, I wrote about the Bush poets and their important contributions to the creation of an influential Australian literary tradition.

Maude was also a prolific letter writer and was constantly in touch with friends, relatives and also children after they left home for study and work. The broader Waterhouse and Paine families also kept in touch and visited at least occasionally. Apart from Richard Paine, Percy's father H.B. Waterhouse, his 'Aunty Graham' (Frances Alice), and his brother Jack were all Kinchela and later probably Belmore River visitors.[39] In 1933, when Percy and Maude were about to leave Lower Portland School on the Hawkesbury for a new posting at Stuart Town on the Central Western Slopes they made the long journey to Grafton, in company with Earle and Barry, for a re-union with H. B. and Ellen. It was probably the last time they saw Ellen, for she died the following year.[40]

Percy and Maude also engaged in community service and activities including Empire Day celebrations and the annual Harvest Festival. In

Belmore River School as restored in 2023, thanks to the work of Jenny and Roger Gifkins. (photo by Richard Waterhouse). *Waterhouse Family Collection*

The Club That Percy Founded. The Maguire's Crossing Surf Life Saving Club. *Waterhouse Family Collection*

keeping with family tradition Percy was a founding member of the local lodge which met at Gladstone. When the family left Belmore River Percy continued to pay his annual fees to this lodge only ceasing in 1973 when he was made an honorary life member. He also established the Maguire's Crossing Surf Club in 1923. Located on the long beach that stretches from Crescent to Hat Head the Crossing features a rough surf and at times a strong rip. It's an isolated location and the Surf Club was probably established to cater to the small groups of families who camped there in the Christmas Holidays. At this time the Macleay community was not beach going and very few men from farming families were strong swimmers. Percy, however, was a very good and confident surfer and on one occasion he saved Alan's life when his son got caught in a rip at Maguire's Crossing. Although, the local farm-based recruits enjoyed and were competent at the land-based drills, most were so intimidated by their experiences in the surf that they quickly abandoned the Club.

The Club was short-lived not only because of a quick decline in membership but also because in 1924 the Club stalwarts, the Waterhouse family, decided to move their summer camping

destination. In that year, in partnership with another family, Percy, Maude and their children, became the first Europeans to camp at Hat Head, a large headland at the southern end of a beautiful beach that stretches almost 20 kilometres to Smoky Cape. In a way this was an odd decision because the camping ground which the family chose was extremely inhospitable. Now Korogoro Creek extends from the Hat Head beach several kilometres inland, almost connecting to the Swan Pool. But in 1924 it only reached two or three hundred metres inland before it expanded into a very large wetland. The only possible camping spot was a high knoll on the northern side of the creek, which like the surrounding water, was infested with sand flies and mosquitos. Indeed, at night the sound of the mosquitos amounted to a continuous dull roar.

As they had done at Maguire's Crossing the family cut tent poles from the local trees and erected four tents, one for the parents, one for the girls, one for the boys and one for dining. They also constructed an additional small tent over a pit that served as the toilet. The daily routine consisted of several swims in the surf and long periods fishing off the beach for whiting, using beach worms and pippies caught at low tide. They

Camping at Maguire's Crossing with family friends. The Waterhouse campsite at Hat Head probably looked similar.

scorned rods, instead casting handlines rigged with multiple hooks. At night they fished from the rocks for bream, although this was less productive than beach fishing. The catch was boiled in a water filled kerosene tin over an open fire and eaten with bread and butter. Whiting is a beautiful sweet fleshed fish to eat, especially when fried in butter and oil and drizzled with lemon juice when served. From the perspective of 21st century Australian culinary tastes the Waterhouse whiting recipe seems pretty crude, but Earle always remembered this method of cooking fish with a sense of nostalgia.

There is an ethnographic moment which Earle and I shared in 1980 which movingly illustrates how much he valued his Belmore River childhood. In what was his first visit to the Macleay since his parents had left the Valley in 1930 Earle spent some of this Hat Head holiday exploring familiar places from his childhood, including Kinchela and Kempsey. At first, he didn't venture up the Belmore River Road in search of the old schoolhouse and residence because his brother Barry had told him that they were both swept away in the floods that devastated the Macleay Valley in the early 1950s. But one afternoon when the tide was out, the wind was blowing, and the fish unlikely to be biting, he asked me to drive him from Hat Head to Gladstone and then follow the road beside the Belmore River so that he could at least revive pleasant childhood memories by visiting the site of his boyhood home. After we had driven some five kilometres, we came around a bend and there in front to us on the riverfront was a giant casuarina tree. Recognising it as growing there when he was a child, he next noticed the familiar and still neatly painted paling fence, a fine garden and behind it the old school residence as well as the schoolhouse. I stopped the car in front of the fence and Earle was out the car door, through the front gate and into the garden before I could suggest that perhaps we shouldn't intrude on the residents. As I later discovered, the school had closed in about 1970 and was subsequently purchased by the family of Jenny and Roger Gifkins, who were now living here. Roger was working in the front garden, surprised to be confronted by a very excited old man, who immediately related his connection to the house and then dragged his son, who was cowering with embarrassment in the car, into the garden to meet the owners. Roger and then Jenny were extremely generous and hospitable, inviting us into the house and asking Earle questions about its original room layout.

It was an extraordinary and emotional experience for Earle, for not only did it revive childhood memories, but provided him with re-assurance not only that the two properties had survived but that they were in good and caring hands. A few days later, when Grace, then my fiancée, arrived from her parents' house in Coonabarabran to join the family holiday group, I took her back to Belmore River to meet Roger and Jenny. At that time, she was working for the National Trust and was so impressed by the residence and schoolhouse that she subsequently organised for them to be listed on the National Trust Heritage Register. Roger later became an internationally recognised wood-worker, and Jenny an internationally recognised quilt maker. Grace and I remain friends with them more than 40 years later. In my heart I remain deeply grateful to them for the generous recep-tion they gave to Earle, a reception that gave him so much joy.

My sister Susan's family first began to visit Hat Head for the Summer holidays in the late 1970s, and from 1980, the extended Waterhouse family, including Nancy and Earle, as well as Annabel and Richard, their partners and children, joined them. I fished from the beach with a rod and reel but Earle maintained his life long tradition of using a line wrapped around a small, round, olive oil bottle. Because he was suffering from advanced emphysema fishing was a struggle for him. He could only throw his line a few metres into the surf, which was advantageous, because whiting feed in close. When he hooked a fish, instead of winding the line back around the bottle, he put it over his shoulder and walked up the beach drag-ging the fish out of the water and onto the sand. At night he walked over to the creek and usually came back with a couple of bream. I realise now that I have read his memoir letters over and over that even though he later lived in rural towns on both sides of the Divide as well as in Sydney, the Macleay remained his country, the place to which he felt most emotionally attached. We moved to Gosford from Orange in 1955, when I was eight, and my parents decided to spend most Sundays in spring, summer and autumn at Avoca Beach. On one of our early visits, I looked from the south-ern headland towards its northern counterpart and said to my father that I thought it was a big

and beautiful beach. I can't remember his exact response but effectively he said 'Wait until you see Hat Head'. Thirty years later when he wrote his memoir letters, he acknowledged a feeling that he must have carried for the whole of his adult life:

Part of me seem(s) chained forever to Hat Head as well as Kinchela and Belmore.

Percy continued to teach the same curriculum at Belmore River as he had previously at Kinchela. Although his reputation as an inspiring educa-tor was passed down through the family and still remembered by his former pupils in the 1980s, it was not without blemish.[41] I remember Percy as an even-tempered man, who never raised his voice in anger on any of our family visits. But in 1906 he was censured for 'unjustifiable corporal punishment' of two children and cautioned not to repeat it. In 1928 a parent accused Percy of hitting her son over the head with three books and then pushing him into a desk, leaving him with a split lip. An inquiry revealed that the boy was engaged in an argument with his sister who pushed other students into him. When Percy caught the boy's arm to make him get up from his desk and come to the front of the class, he tripped over the leg of the desk and hurt his lip. When the true facts were revealed the boy's mother responded with the claim that Percy was 'too gentle' with her chil-dren, too sparing with the cane. Nevertheless, the Department of Education warned Percy of his need to 'strictly adhere' to the prescribed regula-tions in future. In this era physical punishment was the school norm, and remained so into the 1960s, so I suspect that Percy's occasional harsh punishments were not unusual, although some-what excessive. In any case, he was never again accused of exceeding the regulations, although he could sometimes be excessively strict, and on one occasion, as I indicate below, he caned a student, who was also his grand-daughter, because she wrote with her left hand.

Earle experienced some unhappy time in these years. When the children had completed their primary schooling, they enrolled in West Kempsey High School (now simply Kempsey High School), which meant that they needed to

Percy Standing Outside the Children's Toilet Facilities at Belmore River. These were later used as a chook pen. *Waterhouse Family Collection*

board in Kempsey in school terms. Early each Monday their father drove them in a horse and sulky to Gladstone where they transferred to a small bus for the trip to Kempsey. On Fridays they made the reverse journey. In Kempsey they sometimes boarded in private homes but most of the time they lived at St George's Hostel. Located in Angus Avenue this was a large house acquired and converted by the Church of England in 1920 for the specific purpose of accommodating children attending the local high school. At first only boys were admitted but later girls stayed there too. Earle arrived in 1921, in his own words 'a thin, undersized, shy, gullible, good lad from the wetlands'. A culture of bullying was quickly established at the hostel and given his youth, size and naivety Earle became a prime candidate for abuse. This involved young and vulnerable boys forced to run a gauntlet while beaten with knotted towels, having their faces rubbed with (the appropriately named) blady grass, and beaten with brushes while their heads were held between a window and its sill. The warden of the hostel was the Reverend

C. H. Clark, who also served as curate of All Saints Church. Clark's son Manning later wrote that his father's skill at billiards, his talents as a story teller and his relaxed attitude to discipline, qualified him for the position. But for the rest of his life Earle blamed Clark for his indifference to the bullying that was carried out by the older boys under his nose, and his failure to show any interest in the educational progress or social needs of those in his care. Clark rewarded those boys who were diligent in maintaining the grounds and tennis court by playing games of billiards with them, but in retrospect, all this signified to Earle was the warden's indifference to the welfare of the victims of abuse. At the time rumours circulated in the Kempsey community about Clark's allegedly scandalous behaviour and Earle took some vindictive satisfaction in recording in his memoir letters that the curate not only had a reputation as a heavy drinker, but was forced to leave both the hostel and the town when his family's maid became pregnant with his child.

Archdeacon Curtis, who replaced Clark in the middle of 1921, ended the bullying, and introduced a strict and fair schedule of study and contributions to hostel maintenance. However, although Clark was warden for only the first six months of the several years Earle spent at the hostel, his bullying experiences resulting from Clark's negligence, left an indelible imprint on his memory. In 1987, when compiling his memoir letters, he took great care to check out the veracity of the scandalous stories about Charles that had circulated in 1921. He consulted Rex Jeffrey who was a fellow boarder at St George's and also subsequently became an Inspector of Schools, a man whom Earle trusted. Jeffrey's confirmation that such rumours had indeed circulated during Clark's tenure as warden, was enough for Earle to believe they were true, even though, as far as I know, Jeffrey offered no supporting evidence. In fact, Charles Clark did father a child by the family's maid, Marjorie Thompson, during his residence at the hostel, although that was only confirmed some years after Earle's death.

In any case, his dislike and resentment of Charles carried over into his attitude towards his son, Manning. At our weekly Sunday lunches in the 1980s he often asked my opinion of the successive volumes of Manning Clark's *History of Australia*. He indicated approval of my answer that I thought the volumes were in the historiographical tradition of the nineteenth century moralistic, nationalist and progressive narratives of Macaulay (Great Britain), Michelet (France) and Bancroft (the United States of America). However, Clark differed from his European and American counterparts in that he did not embrace their views of inevitable human progress because of his pessimism about human nature. He always nodded in approval when I suggested that Clark's histories were anachronistic, given that most historians now focussed on pluralistic understandings of the Australian past. In 1987 he recalled listening on the radio to a talk given by Manning Clark to the National Press Club. 'Sometimes I think he's more a novelist than a historian,' Earle mused, 'and sometimes the prophecy is more the voice of Manning than a pronouncement of the Oracle'.[42] Earle was biased in his assessments of Manning Clark's judgements, but I suspect he was right to question Clark's qualifications as an oracle.[43]

After they sat for the Leaving Certificate and then left high school three of the children, Dorothy, Earle and Ella, moved to Sydney to study at the University and the Teachers College. Alan and Barry, to their parents' disappointment, at least according to what Earle later told me, only attended high school until they had each completed the Intermediate Certificate and then joined the Bank of NSW (now Westpac) and the Commercial Bank (now NAB) respectively. With the children now supported by teaching scholarships or wages, their parents sold the cows, horses, buggy, sulky, separator, and butter churn, bought themselves a red Rugby touring car and two sets of golf clubs and joined the Kempsey Golf Club. They had obviously decided it was time to live for themselves.[44]

Percy and Maude left Belmore River in 1930 for another one-teacher school, Lower Portland, which is located on the site where the Colo and Hawkesbury Rives join. When they arrived, they found that white ants had eaten the floorboards of the residence to the extent that the ground could be seen beneath the floors and the wooden toilet was so ravaged by this infestation that it leaned dangerously and was unusable. Although the Department was reluctant to spend money on remedial work, a report from the Repairs Staff was so dire that it was forced to act to make the house appropriately habitable.[45] Although the area of Lower Portland on the east side of the Hawkesbury is subject to regular flooding, most recently in 2021 and 2022, the School and its residence are on a ridge located on the west side of the River and the northern side of the Colo, a ridge that overlooks a small floodplain fronting the Colo that was once covered with orchards.

In 1933 they moved to the school at Stuart Town, a small NSW inland town located about 60 kilometres north of Orange. In the nineteenth century it was a booming gold mining town, then

A photo of boarders at St George's Hostel in the post Clark era, with notations on the back by Earle. Taken after he had left It includes his brothers, Alan and Barry. The woman at the front is Belle Smith, who assisted the Archdeacon's wife to manage the boarding house. *Waterhouse Family Collection*

Percy as a guest at the 1961 100th anniversary celebrations of the founding of Lower Portland Public School. *Waterhouse Family Collection*

Percy and Maude on a rare visit to Sydney, perhaps to attend the graduation either of Dorothy or Earle. *Waterhouse Family Collection*

called Ironbark, with a reputation for immoral and lawless behaviour. Well before Percy and Maude arrived it had metamorphosed into a town of only a few hundred people with an economy reliant on sheep, cattle and fruit growing. As she had done at Belmore River Maude taught sewing to the girls at Stuart Town, and did it with such skill that several of her students won prizes in state-wide sewing competitions. As a result, she was remembered longer in the local community than her husband. Percy's final appointment was as headmaster of Glenbrook Primary School in the Lower Blue Mountains, a position he held from 1941 until his retirement in 1948.[46]

The couple had spent almost the first 50 years of their lives in the river valleys of the NSW east coast and so needed to adapt to the different environments and life styles of the Western Slopes and Lower Blue Mountains. But there was also a degree of continuity in their lives for they were committed to engaging with their new communities. The School at Lower Portland was situated above flat riverfront land at the junction of the Hawkesbury and Colo Rivers, land that was used

for large-scale citrus farming. Percy served as chairman and convenor of the Citrus Fruit Growers of the Hawkesbury Area, no doubt putting into practice the lessons he had learned from cultivating his own orchard at Belmore River.[47] At Stuart Town he became President of the Golf Club and in 1939 had the pleasure of handing out the A grade winning trophy to his son Barry and the ladies championship cup to his wife Maude. My father sometimes recalled that his mother didn't hit the ball more than a maximum of about 70 or 80 metres but her accuracy and precision ensured she was a competition level player.[48]

The war years were increasingly stressful for Maude and Percy as Earle, Alan, Barry and sons in law John Lipscomb and Rod Hall joined the armed forces and were sent into combat. Many years after the War Maude told me that they fully expected that at least one of these men was likely to be wounded or even killed and they still felt grateful that they had all returned (more or less) safely.

At Glenbrook the couple lived at first in rented accommodation, although eventually they built a small, modest house on a double block of land on Brook Road. At the back of the block they created a large vegetable garden and fruit orchard. They also constructed a fern house and a crudely built outdoor sewing room made of bark and tree branches, which sheltered Maude's pedal driven sewing machine. Next to it was a toilet, which consisted of a small square structure holding a large 'dunnycan', complete with a wooden lid on top. The full can was collected once a week by the 'night soil' workers and a new can installed. At night visitors to the 'dunny' found their way through the garden with the help of a candle collected from a table at the back door of the house.

Percy's favourite room in the house was a partially enclosed veranda with a cobblestone floor. Here he sat in a comfortable chair while he smoked his pipe, read books and newspapers and drank an occasional whisky, oblivious to the cold that enveloped this half open space for much of the year. He also loved conversation and recounting yarns about his past life and his present neighbours and extended family. I remember that he often referred, in antiquated English, to men he had known or knew as 'rum' or 'queer' 'coves'. One of his favourite stories was about Earle and Nancy's dog Patch, which they gave to Maude and Percy when Earle left Mudgee in 1942 to become an RAAF navigator. Earle had trained the animal never to tread on the vegetable garden in the backyard of their house in Mudgee. One of Percy's Glenbrook neighbours once borrowed the dog with the intent of using him to round up his hens and roosters and drive them into a coop. But the birds soon learnt that the backyard vegetable garden was a dog safe zone because he refused to set foot on it. The animal was returned in disgrace to Percy's care. In summary, my grandfather was an extremely gregarious person who was also fascinated by people (and animals) who were different and who he considered to be intelligent and knowledgeable.

In Maude's combined kitchen dining room there was always the smell of nasturtiums (and sometimes freesias), as well as of stewing fruit and roasting meat. At night my grandparents sometimes moved into the living room to listen to the radio, which was always tuned to the ABC. A few

Not quite a mansion. Percy and Maude's Glenbrook house in the early 1950s. *Waterhouse Family Collection*

years after television was introduced to Australia their daughter Dorothy shipped them a 17inch television from England. It was a generous gesture although it involved some modification to fit Australian frequency and electrical requirements. Like the radio it was immutably tuned to the Australian national broadcaster. Sometime after they moved to Glenbrook Maude gave up golf. So did Percy, who took up bowls instead, making regular trips to Penrith, then no more than a small town on Sydney's outskirts, to play both competitive and social bowls.

My family stayed overnight with them every January on our annual trip from Grenfell and then Orange to holiday at my other grandparents' beachside house at Salamander Bay on Port Stephens. I was always excited and impatient to get to Salamander because I loved the fishing and swimming that were integral to our holidays. But Maude and Percy always disguised whatever hurt my insensitive attitude caused to show me the garden, take me for walks to the local lookout and present me with the clothes my grandmother had sewn for me. My two sisters and I slept on camp stretchers in the kitchen/ dining room and on the veranda. There was always competition for the kitchen because even in summer the veranda was cold. Percy and Maude's great grandson, Stephen Oakley, recalled travelling with his parents from Yass to Glenbrook to stay with Percy in about 1970, a few years after Maude had died. In keeping with family tradition Stephen, aged four, and his brother Pat, aged two, were assigned to sleep on the veranda on the same camp stretchers.[49]

Despite their modest circumstances I am sure they enjoyed their retirement, although I sometimes wonder if they had ever contemplated moving back to the Clarence or Macleay after Percy retired. Maude died of a heart attack preparing to go to bed on December 21 1964. Although she had suffered arthritic pain for some years, her heart attack came as a surprise. For the rest of his life Percy believed she might have lived if the ambulance had arrived earlier. A few days before her funeral I remember my father bringing me an early morning cup of tea in bed. The pain, the sadness and the tiredness that I saw on his face at that moment has lived in the back of my memory ever since. When I reflect on the affection that he demonstrated towards his mother in the memoir letters and the great sense of loss which he obviously felt when she died, I realise the depth of love that some or perhaps many children always hold in their hearts for their parents.

Between 1969 and 1973 I lived in the United States while studying for a postgraduate degree. When I returned, I made no attempt to visit Percy, still living alone at Glenbrook. Early in February of the following year he suffered a stroke and lay on the cobblestones of the veranda for some time before he was found. Earle and Barry arranged for him to be moved to an aged care facility in the Drummoyne/Fivedock region. They had to take what was available, which turned out to be a shared room in a poorly equipped facility. When Earle took me to visit my grandfather he was already in a coma, and once again I watched Earle's extreme distress as he mourned his other much-loved parent. After Percy's death on 12 February 1974, I visited Glenbrook to collect a few items which still remained after other family members had made their choices. A neighbour came over, introduced herself and asked who I was. I told her that I was Percy's grandson and that I hadn't visited him after I returned from the US because I was informed that my grandfather disapproved when he was told by a member of my family that I now had an American accent, an American moustache, a (temporary) American wife and wore American style clothes. The neighbour assured me that this was not at all true and that my grandfather had spoken with great pride about my academic achievements both in America and at home. What a spectacular own goal, my misplaced sensitivities deprived me of the chance to re-connect with an admired grandfather who was both an inspiring teacher and a deeply caring father, and husband, and who embodied so many of the values to which I aspired.

Endnotes

1   Alison Mackinnon and Helen Proctor, 'Education', in Alison Bashford and Stuart Macintyre eds., *The Cambridge History of Australia, vol. 2, The Commonwealth of Australia*, Port Melbourne, Cambridge University Press, 2013, p. 430

2   Earle Waterhouse, *Letters on the Lower Macleay River, NSW 1908–1920*, 1987. This is a collection of letters written in 1987 and addressed to Billie Crawford, a retired ABC journalist. Earle responded in a series of letters to successive requests made by Ms Crawford relating to aspects of his childhood and family life at Kinchela and Belmore River. The letters are written in an evocative and beautifully crafted style. In 1987 Earle was increasingly suffering from the impact of emphysema, which is evident in the fact that the letters written towards the end of the year became more and more brief. He died in July the following year. Copies of these letters are held in the Macleay Valley Historical Society and Waterhouse Family Collection. The original letters are in the Oakley Family Collection

3   Certificate of Marriage, Percival Ernest Waterhouse and Fanny Maude Paine, 21 April 1906, Waterhouse Family Collection

4   Confirmation Certificate, Percival Ernest Waterhouse 7 July 1902, Waterhouse Family Collection

5   Birth Certificate, Dorothy Waterhouse, 6 October 1906, copy in Waterhouse Family Collection

6   Ancestry, *East Sussex, Church of England, Baptisms, Marriages, and Burials*, 1538–1812 (William and Elizabeth)

7   Ancestry, England, Select Deaths and Burials; Ancestry, East Sussex, Church of England, Baptisms, Marriages and Burials 1538–1812 (Thomas and Mary);Ancestry, Census of 1841 and Census of 1851 (William and Philadelphia); Ancestry, England and Wales, Civil Registration Death Index 1837–1915 (William)

8   Megan Martin, *Smith, Maria Ann (1799–1870)* Australian Dictionary of Biography, https://adb.anu.edu.au/biography/smith-maria-ann. Accessed 28/6/2022; Rosslyn Finn, *Packham, Charles Henry (1842–1909)*, *Australian Dictionary of Biography* https://adb.anu.edu.au/biography/Packham-charles-henry. Accessed 28/6/2022

9   Ancestry, NSW Assisted Passenger Lists, 1828–1896 (James Paine)

10   Mary (1836–1879) and James (1838–1917), were born in Beckley. William (1839–1916), Richard (1842–1933), James (1844–1855), Harriet (1840-), Benjamin (1848–1926), Edward (1851–1892), Stephen Charles (1853–1931), Charles (1855–1856), Isaac (1856-), Martha (1858–1858), Sarah (1860–1860), and Olive (1861–1861) were born in the Hunter.

11   *The Methodist*, 5 October 1895; Grace Karskens, *People of the River Lost Worlds of Early Australia*, Sydney, Allen and Unwin, 2020, pp. 458–9. For the information relating to his children, I have I have relied on Ancestry, *Mitchell Family Tree*

12   D. N. Jeans, *An Historical Geography of New South Wales to 1901*, Artarmon: Reed Education, 1972, pp. 124–5; T. M. Perry, *Australia's First Frontier: The Spread of Settlement in New South Wales*. Melbourne: Melbourne University Press, 1963, pp. 52–78

13   *The Methodist*, 5 October 1895; *Grafton Daily Examiner*, 25 June 1926 (Benjamin Paine's obituary)

14   Earle Waterhouse to Roxanne Agafonoff, 17 March, 1975, Annabel Agafonoff Collection.

15   *Glen Innes Examiner* 22 July 1933 (copied from *Grafton Daily Examiner*); *Grafton Daily Examiner* 25 June 1926

16   Earle Waterhouse to Roxanne Agafonoff

17   Personal conversation, Earle Waterhouse with Richard Waterhouse, Belmore River, January 1980

18   Paine Family Bible, Waterhouse Family Collection

19   Ancestry, Marriage Certificate, Mary Alice Blake and William Ronneberg, 1 January 1900; Annie married Edwin Pateman who farmed in the lower Clarence. He died in 1915 and she survived him by 35 years.

20   The photos and postcards are in the Waterhouse Family Collection

21   Geoffrey Bloomfield, *Baal Belbura The End of Dancing The Agony of the British Invasion of the Ancient People of the Three Rivers: the Hastings, the Manning, and the Macleay in New South Wales*, Chippendale: Alternative publishing, 1986, pp. 28, 37, 40–2, 46–52; H. A McNaughton, *Early Settlement of the Upper Macleay*, typescript, Kempsey Heritage Centre Archives pp. 1–14; Marie H. Neil, *Valley of the Macleay: The History of Kempsey and the Macleay River District*, Sydney: Wentworth Books, 1972, pp. 41–2, 88

22   Heather Goodall, *Invasion to Embassy Land in Aboriginal Politics in New South Wales, 1770–1972*, St Leonards: Allen and Unwin/Black Books, 1996, pp. 80–81, 112, 142

23   Marie H. Neil, *Valley of the Macleay*, p.73

24   Neil, 78–9; Richard Waterhouse, *The Vision Splendid, A Social and Cultural History of Rural Australia*, pp. 91–3; Earle Waterhouse, *Letters on the Lower Macleay River*, letter, 3 May 1987

25   Earle Waterhouse, letter, 3 May 1987.

26   Earle (5/9/1908), Ella (7/3/1910), Alan (30/10/1911), Barry (4/7/1913) These birth dates can be found in Ancestry, *Australian Birth Index, 1788–1922*

27   Earle Waterhouse, letter, 21 May 1987

28   Ibid., 3 May 1987; Centenary Committee, *Kinchela Public School Centenary*, n. p. 1981, pp. 10–14

29   *Daily Examiner* (Grafton), 7 February 1918. This news was probably inserted by Dorothy's proud grandfather, Henry Benjamin Waterhouse, who, of course, worked for this paper. Earle indicated that he attended Kinchela Creek School in Earle Waterhouse, letter, 21 May 1987

30   The small collection of Percy's books that are now in my possession include *McDougall's British Songster*, London: McDougall's Educational Company, no date. This book contains songs recommended by the Board of Education for use in English schools.

31   Earle Waterhouse, letter, 3, 21 May 1987; personal communication by Richard Waterhouse with Judy Thompson, 16 June 2022

32   Earle Waterhouse, letter, 21 May 1987

33   State Records of NSW (hereafter SRNSW), Belmore River School Files, NRS 3829 5/14578.1. W.H Gray letter 19 November 1928; S. H. Smith, letter 6 December 1928

34   Earle Waterhouse, letter 21 May 1987

35   ibid.

36   SRNSW, Department of Education Administrative File NRS 3829, 5/14877A, memo from Inspector W G Harvey 11 January 1918; memo from Deputy Chief Inspector, 1 May 1918; Earle Waterhouse, letter, 3 May 1987. The school closed in about 1970 and was bought by the Gifkins family soon after.

37   Earle Waterhouse, letter 3 May 1987. This information is

also based on the stories that Earle told me at bedtime about his boyhood. It was his custom to sit by my bed and read me a chapter from a novel (*Treasure Island* was my favourite), and sometimes he also recounted stories of his early life at Kinchela and Belmore River, stories which I found enchanting

38   Ancestry, *New South Wales Public Service Lists, 1928* (Waterhouse P. E.)

39   Postcard From H. B. Waterhouse to Percy Waterhouse, postmarked 30 January 1909, Waterhouse Family Collection

40   *Grafton Daily Examiner*, 16 January 1934

41   There were still some of Percy's former pupils living in Hat Head and vicinity in the 1980s and when he was on vacation Earle usually visited them to talk about shared childhood experiences. On a few occasions he reported to me that these former students still fondly remembered Percy's classes.

42   Earle Waterhouse, *Memoir letter*, 20 October, 1987

43   *Ibid.*, 10, 20 October, 1987; Manning Clark, *The Puzzles of Childhood*, Melbourne: Viking, 1989, pp. 61–64, which is a nostalgic and romanticised description of his father and his tenure in Kempsey; Mark McKenna, *An Eye for Eternity; The Life of Manning Clark*, Melbourne: Miegunyah Press, 2011, pp. 50, 74–80, reveals the truth of the rumours that Charles Clark fathered a child by Marjorie Thompson.

44   Earle Waterhouse, *Memoir Letters*, 4 June 1987

45   *History of Lower Portland Public School 1867–1967*, no author, no place of publication, no pagination. The copy in the Waterhouse family collection was probably presented to Percy when he attended the school's centenary celebration.

46   Stuart Town Bicentennial Committee, *Whispers From Ironbarks*, Molong: Cabonne Printers, 1988, p. 48; SRNSW, NR 15320 (P.E. Waterhouse) *School Teachers' Rolls and Career Cards*

47   *Windsor and Richmond Gazette*, 24 April 1933

48   *Wellington Times*, 14 December 1939

49   Personal communication with Stephen Oakley, 27 August 2022

Chapter 7

A Siblings Diaspora: Dorothy and John, Ella and Rodney, Alan and Doris, Barry and Lesley

Dorothy and John

As I have indicated above, Dorothy was born in 1906 and attended Summer Island and West Kempsey Schools. When she entered high school she was awarded a bursary, which was no doubt welcomed by her parents, because it helped defray the costs of her education. She passed the Intermediate Certificate in 1921, and although the majority of boys and girls left school after obtaining that qualification, Dorothy stayed two more years to complete the Leaving Certificate and become eligible to enrol at Teachers' College or University. Her matriculation performance was excellent for she obtained second class honours

in English and History, an A in French and Bs in Maths I, Maths II, Latin and Chemistry. These results were sufficient to earn her the West Kempsey High School Leaving Certificate Medal, and the choice of a two-year Teacher's College Scholarship or an Exhibition Scholarship to study Arts at the University of Sydney.

Dorothy chose to earn her teaching qualifications by undertaking a university degree, followed by a Diploma of Education at the Teachers' College. She occasionally struggled with French, which meant that at the end of her first year she was required to take a supplementary exam in the subject (often referred to as a 'post'). But she performed well in History and especially English to the extent that she completed an honours degree in 1926, graduating with Second Class Honours in English. Her parents made the long trip from Belmore River to attend her graduation and were photographed proudly standing on the lawn in front of the Quadrangle. She competed her Diploma in Education at the Teacher's College the following year and began her teaching career in 1928. Her achievements were noted and recorded in the northern rivers press no doubt in part due to the influence of her grandfather. Sometimes referred to as Henry Benjamin Waterhouse's granddaughter, she was also described as 'handsome and clever'.[1]

Dorothy Waterhouse: teacher and socialite.
Waterhouse Family Collection

Dorothy's first appointment was to Cleveland Street Intermediate High School in Sydney's inner city at a salary of just over £224 a year, less than a male teacher with the same qualifications received. However, her brother Earle, who had completed his Teachers College Certificate and was now teaching at Granville Public School, was earning the lesser sum of £171/12/-. He was now also enrolled as a part-time Economics student at the University of Sydney. Her tenure at Cleveland Street was brief because a month later she was transferred to Wollongong High School. In 1929 she returned to the familiar landscape of the northern rivers when she was appointed to Grafton High School, where she spent a year living in close proximity to her grandparents. The following year she was re-assigned to Tamworth and then in 1931 she was moved Sutherland Intermediate High School where she remained until she resigned from the NSW Department of Education on March 7 1937.[2] In that era teachers were required to take positions in rural schools before they were appointed to schools in urban areas. Given the way that Dorothy had developed a taste for Sydney social and cultural life I suspect that she was relieved to complete her country service at the end of 1930 and return to Sydney.

By 1927 Dorothy was involved in social events organised by professional, sporting and cultural societies connected to the University of Sydney. In that year she attended the Law Society Dinner, a Musical Society and Glee Club's dance, and the Dismal Desmond dance held to raise funds for the annual Remembrance (Day) Ball. She was also an active member of the 'Renown Canteen' and her service in this organisation was recognised when she was presented to the Duke and Duchess of York at Government House.[3] The girl of humble social origins from the Macleay wetlands was now mixing with Sydney's wealthy upper class. I suspect her posting to Wollongong and more especially to Grafton must have disappointed her, although perhaps she could appreciate the irony of returning to her family's roots not too long after escaping from them. But in Grafton, at least, she made the best of it, by joining the local amateur opera company. Performing in a musical, *Going*

Up, she was praised for her talent, vivacity and 'delightful personality'.[4]

Soon after Dorothy returned to Sydney to teach at Cronulla Intermediate High School in 1931 she became engaged to Charles Sabine-Pasley a stockman who lived in Darlinghurst, although his widowed mother was a Cronulla resident. While the extended family now lived in Sydney, it held large pastoral interests in Queensland. However, the engagement didn't last and by 1934 Charles had married someone else and was the father of an infant daughter.[5] In retrospect it doesn't surprise that this marriage didn't eventuate because I suspect Dorothy's expectations for her life far exceeded the more limited ambitions likely to be held by a member of a family of pastoralists. In particular, graziers were suspicious of higher education, believing their children needed practical training, not the 'distractions' of cultural education.

While Dorothy taught at Cronulla, she lived in Darlinghurst, which made it a long journey to and from work, but easier to re-connect with upper class Sydney society. Once again, she relied on university affiliated organisations, like the tennis club, to attend prestigious social functions in the houses of wealthy eastern suburbs families.[6] She both directed and performed in plays staged by the Chelsea Book Club and demonstrated that she was an actor of considerable talent by also appearing in at least one major role with Doris Fitton's semi-professional Independent Theatre Company, the most important and influential repertory theatre troupe in Sydney.[7]

It was most likely through the social circles in which she mixed that Dorothy met a young doctor from Darling Point, a man whose family had a tradition of involvement both with the medical profession and the Roman Catholic Church. Dorothy's resignation from the NSW Department of Education in 1937 was directly linked to her romantic entanglement with Dr John Lipscomb.

He was born on July 18, 1908 to Beatrice Mary and Thomas Walter Lipscomb, a surgeon. The Lipscombs were a well-known eastern suburbs Catholic family, resident in Darling Point and later Edgecliff. John and his older brother Griffin were educated at St Ignatius College, Riverview, and then, in keeping with family tradition, studied medicine at the University of Sydney. During his time as a student, he also engaged in sporting and social activities, acting as Secretary of the University Rugby Club and attending fundraising balls organised by the staff of local Sydney hospitals.[8] After graduating with honours in 1933 he took up a series of 'house appointments' in Sydney before departing for the UK, together with Griffin, to study for his FRCS qualifications as an Ear, Nose and Throat specialist. In England his brother practiced in London, while John worked at Guy's Hospital for more than three years before passing his specialist qualifying exams in 1939.[9]

Sometime before he left for England John had met Dorothy Waterhouse, probably at a social function organised by a University of Sydney sporting, social or charity organisation. It is unlikely that it was a match of which his parents approved for Dorothy and John's social and religious backgrounds were in stark contrast. In particular, the divide between Catholicism and Protestantism still ran deep in Australia and interdenominational marriages were uncommon and often fraught with conflict. Perhaps John's parents wanted him to marry a woman of the same faith. On the other side, Percy, whose views and prejudices about Catholicism were probably formed in part by his relations with the Catholic farmers of Irish descent who lived in the Lower Macleay, viewed this form of Christianity as a superstitious and outdated religion.[10] In any case, in 1937 Dorothy resigned from the Department of Education and followed John to England. At that time one of Frances Alice Graham's granddaughters, Doris (Dee) Walsh, was working as a nurse in Surbiton and had a brief social encounter with Dorothy, one that left her with an unfavourable impression of her relative. Reporting that Dorothy was '…chasing some lad who is over here getting his FRCS…' Dee suggested that she had come to England to ensure that '…he didn't get away from her…' Somewhat cruelly Dee contrasted Dorothy's distancing herself from her family in Australia as well as those relations, like Dee herself, now living and working in England, with the fact

that she currently held a modest employment position involving 'something to do with gas stoves'. So, Dee accused Dorothy of behaving pretentiously by assuming a social status to which she was not entitled and disowning her extended family, in short, behaving like a 'mad ass'.[11] This assessment held some truth for it reflected Dorothy's obvious ambitions to leave her modest Macleay Valley social origins behind. But I also suspect that Dorothy and John were simply a couple in love and that they married in England first, because John wished to complete his specialist qualifications at a prestigious London hospital; and second, because they wanted literally to distance themselves from the family criticisms that were likely to come in consequence of their marriage. John's parents left for England to visit John and Griffin in the same month that Dorothy resigned her teaching position. I can't help but wonder whether their trip was designed to attend or prevent the wedding.[12] In any case Dorothy and John were married sometime before the end of September that year and for the next few years lived in Surrey, Dorothy working as a 'cooking adviser' for a gas company, while John studied for his specialist qualifications.[13]

With the outbreak of World War 2 John chose to join the Second AIF rather than the British Army. Enlisting in London he was assigned to an Australian Army Medical Corps unit attached to the Ninth Division. He served at Tobruk where he ran into Bill Paine, from Maclean in the Clarence Valley, a cousin of his wife Dorothy.[14] Her brother, Barry, also fought at Tobruk with the Ninth Division although there is no record of him running across Captain Lipscomb. Dee had claimed Dorothy did not 'recognise the Waterhouses in Grafton', so I wonder if Bill provided John with a lesson in the Waterhouse family's Grafton history.[15] After further service in North Africa and the Middle East, the Ninth Division returned to Australia and then was sent back into combat, this time in New Guinea. In 1943 John was awarded a Mention in Despatches bravery award for 'gallant and distinguished service in the Middle East between May 1 and October 22, 1942', and by War's end he had achieved the rank of Major.[16]

Although it proved a long, difficult and probably dangerous voyage, in 1944 Dorothy followed John to Australia. She was probably concerned that the Pacific War might last for some considerable time, especially given that in allied strategy it had a lower priority and allocation of resources than the European War. At the same time, Dorothy, as she later told me, understood that eventually the AIF Divisions were to be de-mobbed in Australia and it was not clear how long it would take John to get back to England even in peacetime. At first, she lived in a flat in Darling Point, not far from her in-laws in Edgecliff, finding employment with the Sydney County Council and socialising with her sister Ella.[17] Sometime in 1945 she followed John to Brisbane where the couple's first son David was born.[18]

Dorothy and John returned to the UK in 1946, travelling, at least from Mumbai, to Southampton, on the *Stirling Castle*, a troop ship, that was probably headed for England to be converted back to its original purpose as a mail, cargo and passenger vessel. A second son, Anthony, was born late in the succeeding year.[19] John returned to work as an Ear, Nose and Throat specialist, working for Kent County Council, Farnborough Hospital, Queen Mary's Hospital, Sidcup, and the Dartford group of hospitals. At some stage John and Dorothy bought a comfortable two storey house with a beautiful and well-cared for garden in Pett's Wood, Orpington, Kent.[20]

Their two sons were both educated at Tonbridge, an exclusive private school in Kent. Both also went on to study medicine with David becoming a respiratory physician and Anthony a paediatrician. David and Anthony married Isabel Mary and Penelope (Penny) respectively. David's family includes three daughters while Anthony's consists of (at least) one child, Gemma.[21]

I first visited Dorothy and John at their home at Pett's Wood, Orpington, in 1970. At that time, I had just completed the first year of my PhD studies at Johns Hopkins and was spending the summer in the UK, combining tourism and researching a seminar paper for submission in the next academic year. I was chaperoned on the train trip from Charing Cross by my cousin Prue

(Barry's daughter) who was now living in London. Ironically, this was only the second time I had met her, even though we had both lived in Sydney at the same time. I was subsisting on a very modest graduate student stipend from Johns Hopkins and while it was bad enough that I was outfitted in Target and K-Mart clothing, what made it worse was that even my best outfit was worn and shabby. John, Dorothy and their two sons treated me generously and with great hospitality, although they seemed quite bemused by the fact that I was an Australian student, albeit with an already developed American accent, studying American history at a US university. It was still much more common for Australian students to pursue postgraduate studies in the UK. I also guessed that as staunch advocates of British culture and institutions they were not warm admirers either of America or its universities.

Fourteen years later when I travelled to London as part of a research trip, which also included visiting libraries in Boston and Washington, I was picked up from my hotel in South Kensington by Penny and Anthony and driven down to Pett's Wood for lunch. In a heart-warming display of hospitality Penny insisted that I move out of my accommodation and spend the rest of my stay with them in their beautiful terrace house in Islington. This time I was not only better dressed — I was now a Senior Lecturer in History at the University of Sydney — but I also brought with me a photo album featuring Grace, Margot and Eliza (Isabel and Leo as yet unborn) as well as my extended kin, that is, my parents and my siblings, Annabel and Susan, and their families. On this occasion John and Dorothy wanted to engage me more frequently on public affairs both in Australia and the UK. As I might have expected, their views were more conservative than mine. They very politely disapproved of me calling newly elected Australian Prime Minister Bob Hawke 'a great man' and of my expressions of dismay about the hard-line economic policies of Prime Minister Margaret Thatcher. They spoke with pride of what they had attained in England and of the achievements and careers of their sons. I was left in no doubt that they considered that they had made the right choice in making lives for themselves and their children in the UK. There were just a few touches of nostalgia for the land of their birth. They told me that they had very recently attended a rugby test match between England at Australia at Twickenham and had cheered Mark Ella and the Wallabies to victory. Dorothy proudly pointed out a stunted blue gum, which she had planted in her front garden and was struggling to grow in this unfamiliarly cold climate. When I mentioned that the extended Waterhouse family was once again holidaying at Hat Head at Christmas, she immediately recalled waving smelly fish heads in the shallow water behind the retreating tide to lure worms to stick their heads out of the sand so they could be caught between nimble fingers and used for whiting bait. John and Anthony looked so surprised that it occurred to me that Dorothy had rarely talked to her own family about her childhood.

Even before they left Australia to live in the UK, John and Dorothy, like many pre-World War 2 Australians, probably identified themselves as more British than Australian. This strong association with British culture and institutions no doubt strengthened as the years passed. In this context, I suppose it was hardly surprising that when they travelled internationally it was to Europe and not Australia. One of their earliest post-War trips was to Paris in 1952, where John travelled to hospitals to observe cancer surgery, while Dorothy breakfasted in bed before visiting expensive shops to 'try on' expensive jewellery and fur coats. In describing these excursions to her parents, she was adamant, and unconvincing, in insisting that she was looking but not buying. She also took pride in explaining that they were now leading 'a wonderful life'. Later the couple began regular visits to Malta. Dorothy loved the climate, although while she acknowledged the locals as 'delightful' she also, perhaps with a large dash of ethnocentricity, dismissed them as 'incredibly inefficient'. In making this judgement by what I imagine was some kind of ideal standard of Englishness she was acting consistently with a set of values that she had held from the time she arrived in the United Kingdom. Travelling by car through Wales by car in 1939 she

dismissed the Welsh landscape as consisting of 'slate quarries, crags and slag heaps' and the Welsh people as 'a sour faced lot', without pausing to reflect that the poverty and land depredation she saw were the products of the impact of an English driven industrial impact. And finally, there were the skiing holidays at Austrian Alps ski resorts, which Dorothy referred to with enormous enthusiasm. She recorded these excursions in postcards sent to her parents in Glenbrook. What Percy and Maude, living in a humble house on a very modest superannuation pension, made of their daughter's extolling of the good life she and her family were living, is unrecorded. But my judgement of their characters leads me to believe that pride in what their daughter and her family had achieved, took precedence over any resentment that Dorothy's comments may have provoked. [22]

After his retirement John continued his hobbies of squash and golf. He died at Orpington on June 7 1986, aged 78. Dorothy lived to be 88, dying at Basingstoke in Hampshire on January 4 1995. Sadly, David passed away suddenly a few months later from disseminated adenocarcinoma on October 30 1995. He was remembered as a fine physician and sportsman, who was characterised by a direct, energetic and competitive personality. I suspect his character, at least in part, mirrored his parents' personalities. Anthony is now a retired paediatrician, a golfer like his father, a gardener like his mother and a mountain lover in the tradition of both parents.[23]

Ella and Rodney

Ella, the third of Maude and Percy's children was born on March 7 1910. She performed at a high level at primary school with the result that she was awarded a bursary tenable at West Kempsey High School.[24] Like her mother and older sister she was slight of build but she excelled not only in her studies but at sport, theatrical performance, and socialising with her peers. She was the school 50-yard breaststroke champion and also a representative tennis player. She appeared in a number of productions by the West Kempsey School Dramatic Society, and as Secretary of the School's 'Social', played a key role in organising dance concerts and sporting events.[25] She was also a highly competent student, matriculating in 1927 with an A in Maths 1 and Bs in her other subjects, results that qualified her for entry to an Arts degree at the University of Sydney. It is unlikely that the natural environment of the Macleay left the same lasting impact on Ella that it had on Earle, for after all it was only the boys who spent so much time outdoors hunting in the wetlands and fishing in the rivers and ocean. In any case, while Earle engaged in extensive reminiscing about Kinchela and Belmore River in his later life, Judy Thompson recalls that her mother rarely, if ever, talked to her family about her Macleay Valley childhood.[26]

When Ella enrolled at university in 1928 it seemed that she was destined to follow Dorothy and Earle's paths by qualifying as a schoolteacher through securing the requisite qualifications from the University of Sydney and the Teachers College. However, at some stage, either during her first or second year of university study, Ella became more preoccupied with social justice issues than her university studies. This new passion was connected

Ella Waterhouse. *Waterhouse Family Collection*

to the fact that at this time she met and became romantically entangled with a young Teachers College student, Rodney ('Rod') Hall who had come to believe in communism as the means of achieving political and economic reform and equality.

Rod was born on July 10, 1909, in the small South Australian copper mining town of Riverton, the son of Robert ('Bob') Hall (1855–39) and his wife Mary (Vaughan) (1863–1943) who was nearly 50 and already the mother of three daughters when he arrived. Subsequently, the family moved to Broken Hill where Rod completed the Leaving Certificate in 1928 and was awarded a scholarship to study at Sydney Teachers' College. In Broken Hill this was considered a major achievement and when Rod and two other Teachers College Scholarship students caught the rail express to Sydney to commence their studies a large crowd of fellow high school students and teachers farewelled them from the local railway station.[27]

Ella maintained her interest in her university studies through to the end of her first year as an Arts student, for she was listed as passing a deferred, or 'post' examination in Philosophy 1.[28] But by 1929, both Ella and Rod had discontinued their studies, presumably to focus on political and social issues. Ella worked in a range of unskilled and semi-skilled jobs although Rod found it difficult to retain long term employment in any one workplace because employers objected to his zeal in enrolling fellow employees in unions.[29] In late 1929 Ella became pregnant, and on February 2 of the following year the couple married. Both sets of parents disapproved of the marriage. I suspect Percy and Maude were disappointed that their daughter had abandoned the chance to secure a first-class education and permanent white-collar employment, which their own frugality and hard work was designed to make possible. Instead, she had chosen an uncertain future with a man whose political views and affiliations ensured his economic prospects were at best uncertain. Did they also disapprove because Ella became pregnant before she married? Perhaps, but looking back I can't say I ever thought of them as likely hypocrites. The fact that their own eldest child was also conceived out of wedlock, may have tempered any moral disapproval they felt. In Rod's family his mother apparently believed that Ella had seduced her son, in the process destroying his career opportunities in the NSW Department of Education.

Facing increased hardship in a Depression hit Sydney the couple travelled to Broken Hill to brave the censure of Rod's family and await the arrival of their first child, Barbara, who was born on June 26 1930. For the next two years the family lived with a group of other unemployed Australians at Menindee. Their home was a lean-to shelter built of packing cases, sacking and corrugated iron and the floor was simply dirt. In those days the unemployed in NSW did not receive cash payment benefits but instead were given sustenance, known as 'susso', which took the form of food and some other goods to the value of 22/-. To qualify for sustenance applicants needed to be registered as unemployed at a labour exchange or local police station. The campers at Menindee supplemented the handouts they received with fruit and vegetables grown on the land on which they squatted and sheep which they stole from the neighbouring graziers. It was, of course, a difficult and unhealthy environment in which to bring up a small child and it was unsurprising that Barbara contracted dysentery.[30]

The family returned to Sydney in 1932 but economic conditions had only worsened in the years in which they were away. Rod gained employment working for the Communist Party for a mere 5/ – a week, while Ella worked in a cakeshop and as a waiter. However, by about 1936 or 1937 the family was in such difficult financial circumstances that while Rod remained in Sydney, Ella and Barbara moved to Stuart Town to live with Percy and Maude. In her memoir Barbara suggests that Ella's parents, motivated by a concern that Rod was incapable of looking after his wife and child, and their conservative dislike of his political views, unsuccessfully sought to persuade Ella to leave Rod.[31] Instead, after a year in the Bush mother and daughter returned to Sydney, where the family was fortunate enough to be given a lease on a Council flat in McElhone Street Woolloomooloo. It was modest accommodation

which included a combined laundry and bathroom but it provided the family with a secure and reasonably comfortable place to live. For the next few years Rod worked on the construction of roadwork approaches to the Harbour Bridge and as a rigger at Mort's Dock in Balmain, while also attending East Sydney Technical College to complete the qualifications to practice as a health inspector.[32]

Both Ella and Rod also continued to work for the Communist Party, Ella as a bookseller at the Communist owned Anvil Bookshop and Rod as a teacher of classes on the current political situation and the fundamentals of Marxism and Leninism, classes which were held on the bookshop premises.[33] Not only their political but also their social lives, and subsequently those of their daughters, centred on the Party, which seems to me to have operated more like a religious denomination than a modern political party. Instead of a religious icon or a picture of the Virgin Mary or Jesus on the Lounge Room wall theirs featured a portrait of Lenin. The creed of the communist congregation consisted of the pronouncements that came from the Party leadership, both at home and abroad, most particularly the Soviet Union, pronouncements to which members were anxious to adhere. There was also a streak of puritanism in Rod, reflected in his determination to publicly demonstrate the Party's moral superiority. When he took his child Barbara to City picture theatres on Saturday afternoons he refused to stand when 'God Save the King', was played, while cheering when a scene in an American Western showed a Native American shooting a cowboy. He was appalled to learn when he was serving overseas that his young teenage daughter was socialising with a GPS schoolboy. When he returned to his family after the War he tried to impose strict rules on his now teenage oldest daughter, including forbidding her to wear lipstick and insisting she be home from Party organised dances no later than 11pm.[34]

Party loyalty was most clearly demonstrated by his refusal to join the armed forces in the fight against Germany and Japan until the Non-Aggression pact of 1939 was broken by

Germany when it launched an invasion of Russia in 1941. In consequence, in 1942, Rod joined the Royal Australian Electrical and Mechanical Engineers as a gunner and served in New Guinea (1944) and the 'mopping up' campaign in Bougainville launched by the AIF in 1944 when it replaced American troops departing for Philippines battlefields.[35]

Life didn't become any easier for Ella during the War years. For part of this period she worked in the small business of a Hungarian refugee, while Barbara was despatched to Glenbrook once again to live with her grandparents. In this period, Barbara's unfavourable opinion of Percy, first nurtured at Stuart Town, deepened as she decided he was difficult to converse with and not a 'lovable grandfather'. This view probably hardened when as a student in his class at Glenbrook Primary School, Percy caned her for writing with her left hand.[36] Her relationship with her grandmother, however, was much warmer. From her Barbara learnt cooking and sewing skills and the two shared their opinions about other family members. When Earle's wife Nancy visited Glenbrook in 1942, Barbara simply recorded her arrival. However, when the family received a letter from Barry's wife, Lesley, Barbara, no doubt echoing her grandparents' views, noted in her own letter to her father:

We had a letter from Lesley today. She is in Mugee (sic.) and we hope she stays there.[37]

Barbara didn't record what Lesley had written to cause such offence, although I suspect Barry's wife just couldn't help behaving like the wealthy squatter's daughter.

A second daughter, Judith, who was born in 1944, also lived with Percy and Maude for a short time after the War when her mother was hospitalised and Rod was busy with work as he aimed to improve the family's dire financial position and establish a career as a health inspector. Her recollection of her relationship with her grandfather is less negative, for she fondly remembers Percy reading to her at bedtime, especially Kipling's *Jungle Book*.[38]

The end of the war also brought a reconciliation

Four Hall generations. Percy and Maude, Ella, Barbara Fienberg and Judy Hall, Linda and Anna Fienberg feature in this photo. Missing are Ella's husband Rod Hall and Barbara's husband Len Fienberg. Rod was probably the photographer. *Fienberg Family Collection*

between Rod and Ella and her parents. I suspect a critical element in this was the fact that Rod, although he retained his Marxist world view for the rest of his life, became a successful local government official with a secure income. Ironically, with his shock of white hair and his ever-present pipe he resembled a stereotype conservative politician, there was even a dash of Menzies in the way he looked. In any case, the family reconciliation was reflected in the fact that a few years after the War Percy and Maude began a tradition of spending Xmas with the Hall family in their small Rose Bay semi-detached house.[39]

After completing the Leaving Certificate at Sydney Girls High School, Barbara, supported by a Teachers Scholarship, enrolled for a BA at the University of Sydney. However, at the end of her first year of study she was allowed to transfer to the Teachers College, with credit allowed for the university subjects she had already completed. At this time she also met a young medical student, Len Fienberg. They discovered that they had few specific interests in common, but shared the same 'basic attitudes to life', which meant they felt completely at ease with each other. Inevitably, they married in 1953. After spending two years in the UK, where Len completed his qualifications in Obstetrics and Gynaecology, they returned to Sydney where Len served as Superintendent of South Sydney and then Ryde Hospitals

After completing further teaching qualifications, Barbara became a teacher librarian at Chatswood Primary School. Their eldest daughter Linda became a furniture designer and cabinet maker as well as teacher of sustainable design both at the University of Sydney and UTS. Their younger daughter Anna held a number of positions relating to creative writing, including as editor of the NSW Department of Education's *School Magazine*. She also became a well-known children's author, especially through the *Tashi* series which she co-authored with her mother. According to Anna the idea for the plots often came from Barbara while Anna then took on the task of 'firming up' the story.[40]

Although they were attached to their Council flat and especially their friends and neighbours

in the Woolloomooloo community Ella and Rod, together with their younger daughter Judy, moved to a semi-detached house owned by Len's father in Rose Bay in 1953. Some years later, in keeping with what had become a Waterhouse family tradition, Judy enrolled in Arts at the University of Sydney and subsequently completed her Diploma of Education at Sydney Teachers' College. Although most of her cousins, including Earle and Alan's children, became teachers in humanities and social science subjects, Judy became a Maths teacher. Soon after graduating she married Jeff Thompson, an executive with an international chemical company. Their two children, Ben and Emma and their families, both live on the Central Coast. Jeff died in 2024.

When I enrolled at the University of Sydney in 1964, Judy, who was already a third-year student, introduced me to the coffee culture of the Student Union's Manning House and we shared a cup there most week days before attending classes or studying in Fisher Library. Sometimes, I also visited the family on Friday nights to talk politics and history with Rod. I didn't gain the impression that Ella was now much interested in radical politics but Rod remained a dedicated communist. If I made any comments about the fields of study I was then most interested in, that is the histories of the United States and the United Kingdom, which he considered varied from Marxist orthodoxy, he simply shook his head and said 'Can't see it Richard'. These visits also involved Rod reminiscing about his role in the Party in in the thirties and early forties, including stories he related about proposed acts of violence which his Party comrades envisioned taking against the hated fascist leaning New Guard. In this earlier period of his life Rod was subject to surveillance by the Special Branch of the NSW Police, the predecessor of ASIO. On one occasion the family flat in McElhone Street was raided and books as well as the portrait of Lenin were confiscated. At the time this happened Ella's brother Barry and his new wife Lesley were staying with the Hall family, and Lesley, the daughter of a no doubt conservative squatter, was reduced to tears. However, the fact that the books and portrait were returned and

Rod was subsequently allowed to enlist in the AIF suggest that he was not regarded as a violent agitator or as a threat to Australian security.[41]

In the mid 1960s Len's father sold the Rose Bay residence that the Hall family had occupied for more than a decade and Rod and Ella became true Australian suburbanites when they purchased a California Bungalow in the northern Sydney suburb of Willoughby. Ella had not enjoyed good health for many years and the keen gardener didn't live long enough to fully recreate the garden at Willoughby to her own liking because she died of cancer on April 25 1969. Rod continued to work as a health inspector for some further years and also took up lawn bowls as a means of providing both outdoor exercise and companionship. But Rod never lost his Marxist commitment, siding with China in the Sino-Soviet split which occurred in the aftermath of the Russian leadership's denunciation of Stalinism and its embracing of peaceful coexistence with the West. In contrast, China condemned Soviet revisionism and adopted a much more aggressive stance towards the West. I have often since wondered how Rod balanced his fervent adoption of Mao Zedong-style Marxism with what had become his own identifiably middle-class suburban lifestyle. In the end, I suppose, he found comfort and enjoyment in both. Like Ella, he died of cancer on March 27 1987. Apart from relatives and friends his funeral was attended by a significant contingent of men with whom he had served in the AIF in World War 2, men who still remembered him as a mentor and guide. The rebel, it seems, was also a leader, a role that was fittingly acknowledged by the presence of his former mates at his final farewell.[42]

Alan and Doris

Percy and Maude's fourth child, Alan, was born on October 30, 1911. Like his siblings he was educated at Belmore River Primary and West Kempsey High School. However, unlike Dorothy, Earle and Ella, he completed only three rather than five years of high school, leaving after qualifying for the Intermediate Certificate. In 1927 Alan joined the Bank of New South Wales as a clerk and was posted to Gladstone a mere 14

kilometres (9.1 miles) from Belmore River. A year later he was moved to Wingham in the Manning Valley while his subsequent postings in the years leading up to his enlistment in the Second AIF in 1943 included Griffith and Cootamundra. Senior bank officers usually lived in bank-owned accommodation, with managers assigned apartments on the second storey of the bank business premises. However, junior staff usually rented rooms in local hotels or in private residences, where such accommodation was available. Alan may have lived in both kinds of accommodation, although at the time of his enlistment he listed his address as the Hotel Cootamundra. He also participated in the sporting and social life of the towns in which he lived. He was an active member of the Cootamundra swimming club, both as a competitor and official. He also played competitive golf and bowls and in the post War years won a number of bowls club championships. After they married in 1950 his wife Doris also participated in those sports. Like his father, grandfather, great grandfather, and brother Barry, Alan was a member of the masons as well as a justice of the peace, a handy office for a bank official to hold.[43]

Alan in his AIF Uniform. *Waterhouse Family Collection*

Alan enlisted on June 3 1943. During the latter half of that year and in the early months of 1944 he underwent training, including a course in signals. He was subsequently classified as competent in this means of communication and entitled to proficiency pay. He trained and served with a number of Australian military units before departing from Cairns for Lae in New Guinea in late April 1944. Several months later, in October 1944 he arrived in the Treasury Islands located south of Bougainville where he joined the Seventh Australian Infantry Battalion, probably as a signaller. It was a militia battalion and Alan was probably assigned to it because it was an Australian Army practice to bring militia units up to strength by assigning non-militia personnel to them. Originally based in Mildura, the Battalion had served from February 1942 through April, 1943, in Darwin, where along with the 8th and 27th Militia Battalions it became part of the 23rd Brigade. The Battalion then returned to Melbourne before moving to the Atherton Tablelands in November 1944 to undergo intensive training in preparation for combat service in Bougainville.

The Treasury Islands were recaptured by New Zealand troops in 1943. The Australian army subsequently relieved American forces who were guarding a strategically located airfield but were deemed to be more useful in the allied assault on the Philippines. With no land battles to be fought a number of Australian soldiers crewed American PT boats in raids on Japanese controlled islands in New Ireland and New Britain. In April 1945 Alan and other members of the Seventh Battalion moved to the town of Torokina on Bougainville and in June it became engaged in the 'mopping up' of Japanese resistance when it replaced the 27th Battalion at Pearl Ridge. By the end of the War 7th Battalion had captured 25 Japanese positions.

In September with the War over the Battalion moved to Fauro Island to guard the captured Japanese soldiers. When the last of them were repatriated in February, 1946, the remaining members of the Seventh returned to Australia where the Battalion was disbanded in May. However, although most of his comrades were discharged Alan remained in service for several more months once peace was declared. Although he expected to be discharged in late 1945 it seems that the Australian Army took advantage of his finance and accounting skills, for he was employed for some months in the District Accounts Office in Rabaul. During this time he made two trips back to Australia for undefined purposes, but a third was clearly for medical reasons because he was admitted to Concord Repatriation Hospital in Sydney and subsequently discharged both from the hospital and the Army. What roles he played during the major part of his military service, especially the time he served in Bougainville, is not precisely clear, although as I have already suggested, I suspect he was assigned to a militia battalion because it lacked skilled signallers. He had performed well in his training, achieving a 'Distinguished Pass' for one of his signalling courses, and the fact that he was promoted to Lance Corporal in late 1945 suggests he was competent in carrying out his duties in the field as well.[44]

When he returned from the War Alan re-joined the Bank of New South Wales, working in branches in several towns and one city located in southwestern NSW and the Australian Capital Territory, including Junee, Tumut, Canberra and Boorowa.[45] During his tenure at Junee he met Doris Lehmann (b. 1918) who he married in December 1950. Although not the youngest of Percy and Maude's children, he was the last to marry; he was 40 and Doris was 32. They were to have two children, Janet born in 1953 in Tumut and Bill who was born in Boorowa in 1955.

Doris was one of two daughters born to Florence May Dietrich (1888–1962) and Charles Louis Edmund (Ted) Lehmann (1876–1961). Her father was a farmer who owned two modest grazing and wheat properties 'Ingomar' (851 acres) and 'Monte Cristo' (377 acres) located on the outskirts of Junee.[46] Ted was also a keen cart horse breeder and supporter of harness racing, entering his mares in the Junee show, owning and training trotters, and holding office as a committee member and clerk of scales for the Junee Trotting Club.[47] His grandson Bill Waterhouse holds the view that when Ted and his and his wife sold up and retired to Wagga in the early 1950s , they deliberately bought a house that was in walking distance of the local trotting course.[48]

Doris was a multi-talented child who grew up to be a multi-talented young woman. From the age of eleven she entered her embroidery work in local show competitions. At about the same age she began to participate in dancing contests, including those involving the Highland Fling, Sailors' Hornpipe, Irish Jig and Russian Dance, and won or placed on a number of occasions. She was also an able athlete, representing Wagga Wagga High School at hockey in 1933.[49] Unlike most high school students of her era, girls especially, she didn't leave school at the Intermediate Certificate but completed two extra years of study leading up to the Leaving Certificate. Unfortunately, illness prevented her from sitting for the final exams and her father, who didn't believe girls needed any form of advanced education, declined to allow her to repeat the final year. This experience later made her determined to encourage her own children to pursue education to the highest level of which they were capable.[50]

When Doris left school at the end of 1935, Australia was still recovering from the effects of the Great Depression, and there were few employment opportunities available. So, she created her own. First, making use of her sewing skills, she opened a dressmaking business.[51] Second, she became a dance instructor, working first as Director for the Wallace School of Dancing which operated dancing schools in a number of towns in the Wagga Wagga vicinity, including Junee, and subsequently running her own school.[52] However, Doris also had ambitions to become a professional ballet dancer and in 1939 she moved to Sydney with the ambition to pass the Royal Academy of Dance examinations by studying for a year at the Frances Scully Dance Studio, one of the city's well-known classic dance schools. During this year of study, she also continued to perform, travelling as far as Newcastle to appear in a grand concert.[53] However, realising she lacked the physique required of a ballet dancer, she abandoned this quest and returned to Junee, to resume her roles as dance teacher and presumably also as a dressmaker.[54] In any case, the prospects for professional ballet dancers were bleak at this time because there were no Australian based professional ballet companies.

Alan and Doris's Wedding. Earle, the best man, stands on the left. *Bill Waterhouse and Janet Magnin Collection*

The Japanese invasion of Malaya in early December 1941, followed by the fall of Singapore on February 8 1942, stimulated a rush of men and women to enrol in the Australian armed forces. Doris Lehmann joined this movement when she enrolled in the RAAF Women's Auxiliary on March 24 of that year. The number of women seeking to join the RAAF was overwhelming and the majority were rejected but Doris was assessed as a 'good capable type', of 'smart appearance' who was suited to a role as drill instructor, the position to which she had nominated herself. She served in the RAAF in this capacity for the next five years, with time spent in Canberra, Sydney, Melbourne and Brisbane. She was finally discharged on April 3 1947, long after most of those men and women who had volunteered for the three services had returned to civilian life.[55]

After a brief stay in Melbourne, where she discovered she was not suited to waitressing, she returned to Junee where she resumed dance teaching and opened a new dressmaking business Sometime over the next few months she met Alan, who was acting in a relieving role at the Junee branch of the Bank of NSW. They married in December 1950. Earle travelled from Grenfell to serve as Best Man, and Doris's sister acted as Matron of Honour. At about the time of their marriage Alan was transferred briefly to Canberra and then on to Tumut for a two and a half-year period before taking up a promotion to accountant at the Boorowa branch in 1954.[56]

In 1960 Alan was appointed relieving manager of the Bribbaree branch of the bank which is some 100 kilometres west of Boorowa. The family continued to live in Boorowa and he came home on weekends. On the Sunday night of May 1960, he took a break on the long drive to Bribbaree to stop at the Young Bowling Club and drink two five-ounce glasses of beer ('ponies') in company with a fellow bowler and retired police inspector, William Fitzgerald. The latter later testified before a coronial inquiry that Alan was not affected by alcohol when he left the Club to resume his drive. Another witness, Gordon Alan Greensmith, a farm labourer, told the coroner's court that he observed Alan's car travelling at a legal speed down the road just before the accident. Very soon afterwards Alan seems to have fallen asleep at the wheel, the car left the road and collided with a tree. He suffered a fatal injury in the form of a fracture at the base of his skull.[57]

Alan's death caused enormous emotional suffering to Doris and her children, while at the same time placing them in difficult financial circumstances. Because Alan was not yet 50

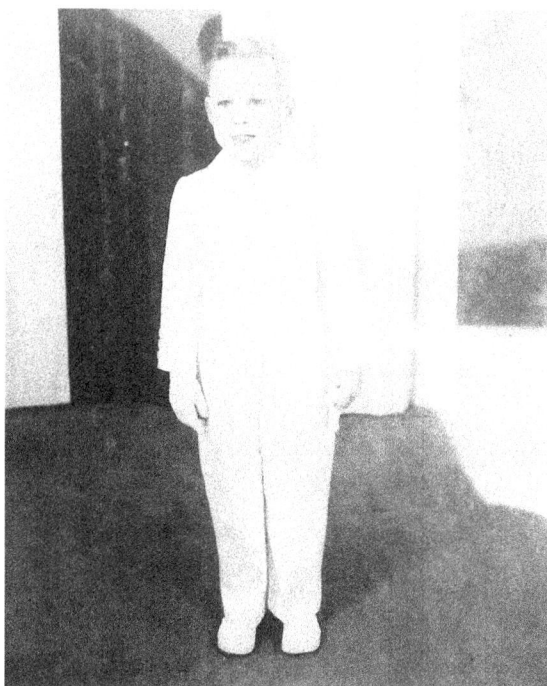

Bill and Janet carrying on their mother's performing tradition. *Bill Waterhouse and Janet Magnin Collections*

when he died, the bank pension Doris received was small. Moreover, its value diminished over the years because at this time neither publicly nor privately funded pensions were cost of living indexed. The family was also required to vacate the bank provided residence in Boorowa and so Doris and her two children moved to Wagga Wagga to live with her parents who had sold the farms in Junee and were now retired. Her father helped Doris buy into a small children's wear shop.

Both Doris's parents died in the next three years and she used her share of the inheritance to buy out her sister's share of the house. After a few years she sold the shop and earned income first from making curtains and later from working in a shop selling sewing machines and dress materials.

While Alan was alive the family maintained occasional contact with his parents and Earle. Janet remembers a trip to Glenbrook to visit Maude and Percy where she was entranced by their huge garden, with all its nooks and crannies, and by Dorothy's television set which took pride of place in the living room. I also remember accompanying my father on a visit to Alan's family when they were holidaying at The Entrance. On another occasion Alan visited us at Gosford on his own and I remember how good natured he was, showing interest in my sporting activities and eagerly demonstrating how to accurately throw a cricket ball and skip stones on the water. He seemed so much more approachable than my own father who was still in his stern Squadron Leader/ Headmaster phase.

But after Alan's death, for reasons that remain incomprehensible to me, the broader Waterhouse family took little interest in the welfare of Doris and her family, and as a result were oblivious to the financial difficulties she faced. Earle sent an annual Christmas card and Barry, perhaps concluding that if he and Lesley liked dachshunds, Doris and her family must too, once travelled to Wagga to present Bill with a puppy of that breed. In fact, the dog proved a hindrance rather than a comfort, developing a taste for the neighbours' chickens. At least, in his will, Percy directed that she receive the equal portion that was originally intended for Alan, and as executor, Earle ensured that these terms were carried out.

Janet performed well at both primary and secondary school and fitted the model, in her own words, of a 'goody two-shoes'. In contrast, as he grew older Bill demonstrated a rebellious nature that resulted in some conflicts with local police officers. In the end, believing that he couldn't break from the friends who were helping to lead him down a path he didn't want to take, Bill persuaded his mother to send him to boarding school in Bathurst. When Janet graduated from high school she took up a Teachers' Scholarship to study for a B.A at the University of Sydney and a Dip.Ed. at Sydney Teachers' College. During these years of study, she lived at the Women's College on the University campus. When Bill completed his Higher School Certificate, he moved to Wollongong to study at Wollongong Teachers College. He subsequently completed a B.A. at the University of Wollongong while teaching at Bulli High School. In the meantime, Doris decided to sell her house in Wagga and move to Wollongong to be near Bill and her widowed sister. She continued to work, finding employment once again in a sewing machine shop.

Bill taught at Bulli High School for 25 years where in 1977 he also met an English, History/ Geography teacher, Lesley Carter. They moved in together in that same year and have been together ever since. They never felt the need to marry although Les changed her name to Waterhouse. Three children were born to them John, (1983), Jo Alexandra (1986), and Jess O'Neil (1989). In 2002 Bill was promoted to Head Teacher at Braidwood Central School, and so the couple purchased a rural property at Majors Creek to which Les travelled from Bulli every weekend. Bill was subsequently promoted to Senior Education Officer and worked for the Department of Education Consultancy until his retirement in 2015. However, he still works part-time as a teacher at Braidwood Central and Captain's Flat Public schools.

When Les retired and moved to live full-time at Majors Creek she and Bill established and still run the Majors Creek Wombat Refuge, rescuing and caring for native animals, and releasing those that recover back into their natural habitats.

During the time he taught at Bulli Bill also played lagerphone and banjo in bush bands in Sydney and surrounds as well as performing as an actor in amateur and semi-professional theatre companies. He still occasionally performs Australian bush ballads at local concerts and conducts a program dealing with local issues on a Braidwood radio station.

Les and Bill's children have had quite remarkable careers. John lives in Canberra with his wife Emma Dixie Waterhouse (Nelson) and their two sons, Django and Tully. He works as a cameraman/grip/editor in the Canberra film industry. Jo Alexandra lives in Millicent, South Australia with her husband Simon Hughes and their two sons, Hunter and Dusty. Simon works as a skilled tradesman in the local paper mill and Jo is employed in HR at the same plant. Jess, is a talented actor and singer in the Canberra theatre scene and also works in HR in the gym and fitness industry.[58]

After graduating from university Janet taught English at St Mary's and Wiley Park High Schools and also completed an MA in English Literature at the University of Sydney. She then took a break to travel in Europe for two years where her experiences working in Bordeaux nurtured a desire to teach French. That is exactly what she did when she returned to Australia to take up a position at Cremorne Girls High School and, when it closed, at Killara High School. However, in 1988 when she was offered the chance to enrol for a year in a Language Centre located in the city of Besançon in eastern France, she saw it as a great opportunity. While she was studying, she met a young Frenchman, Jean-Michel Magnin, who was about to leave for Sydney to take up a position at the French School at Maroubra. Travelling back to Australia together they lived in Janet's small rented apartment in McMahon's Point before marrying in 1990.

After two years living together in Australia, in 1991 they decided to move back to France. Jean-Michel had found it difficult to make friends in Australia and in any case had ambitions to renovate his house which is located in a village outside Besançon. Several hundred years old and

originally used for church purposes it was not yet fully adapted for modern living. The couple also had ambitions to have children.

In France Janet found employment teaching English and after at first focussing on house renovation Jean-Michel also returned to teaching. They also became the parents of two children, Tom born on 10 February 1993 and Zoe born on 3 November 1994. Doris visited them three times, trips which provided her both with re-assurance and happiness. When she first learnt that Janet and her husband were planning to live in a village she became quite concerned, probably because she thought that French villages were dry, dusty and isolated, just like Bribbaree. Instead, she found that they lived in a picturesque rural environment not far from the beautiful city of Besançon. Second, her visits also provided her with the opportunity to spend precious time with her grandchildren. I am sure that she would be very proud of what they have become, too. Tom is now a pharmacist and Zoe a production secretary/director/administrator, in the world of French cinema.

When Doris became more frail she moved into an aged care facility. In 1998 she became extremely ill and despite an operation, died of peritonitis on 27 June. Unfortunately, Janet was unable to return to Australia at this time and so the funeral arrangements were handled by Bill. Doris had a difficult life after Alan's death but I think she approached it stoically and above all appreciated her children and grandchildren as extraordinary gifts. She once told Janet that she had a good life that was marred by one great tragedy, Alan's death.[59]

In 2018 Grace and I travelled to Besançon for a memorable reunion with Janet and equally memorable first meeting with Jean-Michel. We were taken to visit Roman, Medieval, Early Modern and contemporary sites in Besançon, dined at a fine country restaurant, and toured the town of Arbois and its museum celebrating the life of Louis Pasteur. The wider Waterhouse family had shown a high level of indifference to Doris and her children after Alan's death, so I found it both sad and ironic that when I saw Janet on Besançon Railway Station for the first time in so many years, I realised that she looked just like her grandmother Maude.

Four years later in 2022 Grace and I travelled to Majors Creek to meet Bill, Les and two of their children, John and Jess. It was an occasion marked by enjoyable drinking and eating and an enlightening tour of the wombat refuge. The selfless and tireless work which Les and Bill contribute in such a worthy cause earned our admiration and made us think that it deserves much wider acknowledgement. I came away from that experience convinced that it felt more like meeting a lost brother than a lost cousin. In any case when I think of the hardships that Doris, Janet and Bill endured and how, nevertheless, they managed to lead such rich and contributing lives, it re-enforces my faith in what individual and family determination can achieve.

Barry and Lesley

Barry, the last of Percy and Maud's five children, was born in Kempsey on the fourth of July 1913. He was educated at Belmore River Primary and West Kempsey Intermediate High Schools, although there is no extant record of any academic achievement or participation in school cultural or social activities. However, he was apparently a good swimmer, winning the 50 yards Junior Handicap at the West Kempsey School swimming carnival in 1927.[60] Like his brother Alan, Barry left school once he had completed the Intermediate Certificate and joined the Commercial Bank (now absorbed into NAB). He was first posted to Bellingen and was subsequently moved to Molong (1934), Gilgandra (1937) and Wellington (1939).

He was not a sentimental person and tended to admire men who he considered to be physically strong and mentally hard. Nevertheless, he was strongly attached to his extended family. In 1934, he travelled from Bellingen to join Earle and his parents on a trip to Grafton to visit Henry Benjamin and Ellen, and the following year, although now working at Molong, he took the time to visit his recently widowed grandfather in Grafton.[61] When he was stationed at Wellington in the years before he married, he often travelled to Stuart Town on weekends to play golf with his parents.

At Gilgandra he met Lesley Wake, who was born in Dubbo in 1913, and described in the local press as 'a charming Gilgandra lady'. Lesley was the daughter of a grazier, Percival (Percy) H. Wake (1884–1958) and his wife Emily Alice (Skevington, 1887–1939).[62] Percy owned a sheep property, Holmlee, which was located near Gilgandra. He was not a woolgrower but a sheep breeder, who raised and sold Border Leicester stud rams and ewes.[63] It was a profitable business, one that allowed Lesley to live the privileged and leisurely life of a squatter's daughter. From the age of eight she competed in horse riding events at agricultural shows in neighbouring towns and was accomplished enough to win some of these competitions. She also became a talented tennis player, competing not just in country tournaments but also in the annual Country Week competition in Sydney, and earning an acknowledgement that she was one of the most promising players to emerge from the State's west.[64] In keeping with her status as the daughter of a well off grazier Lesley also led a busy social life, attending balls in Sydney and the bush, and was even presented to the Governor of NSW as a debutante at the Narromine Show Ball in 1932.[65] Lesley took holidays in style, enjoying a four month holiday in New Zealand in 1934.[66]

But a shadow was thrown over her family's life in 1936 when an unexplained incident occurred which nearly cost Lesley her life. She had prepared a cake and intended to cover it with icing sugar. But when she tasted the icing sugar its was extremely bitter and its effect on Lesley was to cause her to collapse. However, the subsequence responses of Lesley and her parents was quite astonishing. First, her parents scraped the icing sugar off the cake and ate it without any ill effect. Second, Lesley put the remaining icing sugar into the pig bucket and threw it to the pigs, six of which subsequently died in agony. Dubbo police suspected an attempt was made to poison the family and called in detectives from Sydney.[67] However, no subsequent reports of their findings were ever published, which suggests there was insufficient evidence to draw any concrete conclusions or identify any possible culprits. Strychnine has a bitter taste which suggests it was the poison which Lesley ingested. It was and is used on rural properties for the control of rodents and wild dogs, including dingos. The poison is a strong, white, odorless, bitter crystalline powder, and only a little is needed to produce severe illness. Perhaps, the strychnine used by Lesley, which was intended to be used as a pest poison, was mistaken for icing sugar and put in a kitchen food container rather than in one used to hold poisons. However, if this incident was actually an attempt to murder one or more members of then Wake family it would not be the last, as a tragic and brutal event on April 23 1986 subsequently demonstrated.

In the same year Lesley became engaged to A. R. Mackellar, although I can't determine whether he was related to the famous pastoral family of that name.[68] But the liaison didn't last because just over two and a half years later in April, 1939 she announced her engagement to Barry Waterhouse.[69] This was an unusual step up the social class ladder for Barry because the daughters of prosperous graziers didn't usually marry bank clerks.[70] The couple and her family

Barry Waterhouse Ninth Division Second AIF.
Waterhouse Family Collection

originally planned a wedding in Sydney, perhaps in the fashionable St Stephens, followed by Lesley moving to Wellington where Barry worked in the local branch of the Commercial Bank. However, Barry who had joined the militia in January, was called into camp, and so the marriage was brought forward, and the couple were married in St Ambrose Anglican Church, Gilgandra, on 16 September.[71] Barry was already discharged from the Militia to enable him to join the Second AIF. He was assigned to the 2/17 Infantry Battalion, Ninth Division, which departed for the Middle East on October 19 1940.

When Barry departed Lesley was pregnant with twins who were born on May 12 1941. Tragically, one was stillborn and the other died sixteen days later. With Barry abroad, Lesley was left with the burden of burying and mourning for her lost children without her husband to comfort her.[72] When the Ninth Division returned to Australia in February 1943 Barry took leave to visit Lesley in Gilgandra and at Rose Bay in Sydney in December of the same year, she again gave birth to another set of twins, Terence Edward and Prudence Lyndal.[73]

During the Second World War the Ninth Division was in combat longer than any other Australian Division. The 2/17 Battalion to which Barry belonged first engaged in battle on the Tobruk perimeter in April 1941. The Battalion subsequently engaged in bloody infantry fighting at the First and Second Battles of El Alamein in July and October of the same year. Withdrawn to Australia the Battalion saw its first combat in the Pacific War when it participated in the amphibious landings at Lae and Finschhafen in New Guinea, in September and October 1943. The Division was then returned to Australia for an extended period but returned to combat duty in 1945. The 2/17 Battalion participated in another amphibious landing at Brunei Bay in Borneo in June. Barry and his Battalion returned permanently to Australia in September 1945. When he was discharged on October 30, 1945, he had served in the AIF for a total of 2003 days, 1134 of them outside Australia. During that time, he had fought in several strategically important and long remembered battles, namely, Tobruk, El Alamein and Lae, and risen through the ranks from Private, to Corporal (1940), to Sergeant (1942) and finally to Lieutenant (1943). During the Pacific campaign he was wounded in one of his legs and awarded a Mention in Despatches for bravery.[74]

Lesley and Barry didn't return to rural life after the War. Barry's bank moved him to Sydney and they took up residence in a house in Balgowlah in Sydney's north. Eventually Barry was promoted to manager and he and his wife moved to accommodation above a branch of the Commercial Banking Company of Sydney on the corner of Mowbray and Willoughby Road in Willoughby. Terry and Prue were educated at exclusive private schools, not just because their parents wanted them to receive a first-class education, but because they believed the social contacts they made were likely to benefit them in their future careers.[75]

During the years my family lived in rural towns it had no contact with Barry's family but when we moved to Sydney in 1962 there was more social interaction. I thought that both Prue and Terry were sophisticated and street wise and I was extremely grateful for the clothes that Terry handed down to me, which were so much more stylish than mine. Earle and Barry attended Lodge meetings together on a weekly basis and on occasional weekends Barry took me sailing on his small half cabin yacht. As I indicated earlier, Barry admired men with courage who took risks, and I was put to the test. On one occasion he put me in a flimsy bosun's chair and hauled me up to the top of the yacht's mast to release the sheet (rope) that was used to haul the mainsail to the top of the mast, a sheet that was caught in the pulley at the masthead. For me it was a terrifying experience because of the flimsiness of the bosun's chair, the height to which I was pulled, and the fact that the masthead swung widely from one side to another every time the wake of a passing boat hit the yacht. I suspect that if I had ever told Earle about what Barry had asked me to do he might well have reacted angrily. Unlike his brother he didn't associate risk taking with manliness.

At this time, Barry and Lesley were alienated from Terry because of major disagreements

between them, mainly relating to what they considered to be their son's reckless, irresponsible and hedonistic life style There were also allegations of violence, with parents and son accusing each other. In a sense, I think that Barry hoped that I might prove an occasional weekend substitute for Terry, but in the end I failed the test. I was too bookish and too risk averse to measure up to his standards of manhood.

Neither Terry nor Prue completed the full five years of high school. Terry became a department store window dresser and when he left that job spent the rest of his life engaging in a succession of investment and entrepreneurial activities with the expectation of making quick wealth. In 1972 he was living in Western Australia where he had met and married Jill and had a daughter, Vanessa, by her. Subsequently they moved back to Sydney and not too long afterwards they divorced, with Jill and Vanessa returning to Western Australia. Terry subsequently married Zar with whom he had a son, Zac.

Prue left school to go into show business. She enjoyed some success appearing in modest roles in Sydney theatre productions but then was encouraged to travel to England with the Doyle Carte Gilbert and Sullivan Operetta Company, which had just completed an Australian tour. In the UK she appeared in a cameo role in one movie but subsequently, while still maintaining an interest in opera and ballet, became a financial entrepreneur, describing herself as a company director and business consultant.

In his role as a bank manager Barry experienced unexpected, violent trauma. His bank was robbed several times, and on the last occasion he was bashed and locked in the vault. Unsurprisingly, he decided to take early retirement and move to a house which he and Lesley had built at Lighthouse Beach near Port Macquarie. While he was still working the couple had divided their time between the bank residence during the week and the Lighthouse Beach house on weekends. Unfortunately, Barry's retirement, marked by illness, was short. Probably suffering from post-traumatic stress disorder, which his bank robbery experiences only exacerbated, as well as from emphysema, he became a heavy drinker. Lesley tried to hide the Scotch but he usually found it.[76] Terry once told me that he had provided his father with whiskey, believing it was an act of generosity for a dying man. Barry died on November 11, 1976, only 70 kilometres from his childhood home on the Belmore River.

Lesley continued to live in the Lighthouse Beach house until April 23 1986. On that day she was unexpectedly and brutally murdered, an intruder crushed her head and cut her throat. Her body was not discovered until a fire was started in the back of the house the following day, almost certainly by the murderer returning to the scene of the crime in an attempt to hide evidence. The fire brigade and police officers found blood in the kitchen, bathroom and garage. Although the murder weapon was never discovered, the police believe the murderer used an axe, a knife or a scythe to inflict terrible injuries. The perpetrator of this violent and unexplained crime remains undiscovered, despite a review of the case by the Unsolved Homicide Squad in 2004.[77]

Sometime after Lesley's death, Terry and his wife Zar moved to Port Macquarie but Zar refused to live in the house in which Lesley had died and which Terry and Prue had inherited. Eventually Terry moved into the dwelling by himself, although his tenure was brief, for he died of unexplained causes on July 31, 1993.

Prue became a highly successful manager, serving as a director of Conservation Management Ltd., the British Youth Opera, the English National Ballet School, the English National Ballet, and Errigal Productions. She resigned all these positions between 1994 and 2005. For some time after that, at least, she remained active in supporting the Arts in the UK, attending an after party for the launch of Mikhailovskys *Swan Lake* in London in 2010.[78] But she subsequently vanished from the accessible record. Unless she is deceased, I suspect that she is living a carefully circumscribed life, although given her previous public profile, I doubt she has altogether faded into obscurity. In a way Prue's status as an enigma seems fitting because when I think about her family's history overall it also seems filled with

unresolved questions and quite removed both in terms of its characters and the lives they led, from the histories of the families of Barry's siblings.

Afterword

In one of his memoir letters Earle referred to the joyous Friday night reunions of parents and children when the latter arrived home from boarding in Kempsey:

> On Fridays we made the reverse journey, rejoicing moderately at the sight of Dad waiting patiently at Gladstone and with full hearts as we embraced mother and lifted her off her feet in the Belmore kitchen.[79]

What this and other expressions of devotion to family in this memoir suggest is that the children were strongly attached to their parents, an attachment that continued, although in lessened form, after they left home. From England, Dorothy regularly sent postcards, and on one occasion a television set, while the other children visited Percy and Maude when they could, especially after the couple moved to Glenbrook, which was accessible to most of them. But the siblings drifted apart from each other as their lives took different directions. Because of the educations they received, the professions they adopted, the places they lived, and the partners they chose, they tended to adopt different 'world views', which meant that as time passed they had less and less in common. In one sense, what happened to this generation was not unusual, because families are always in the process of cultural and demographic change. What was unique about Percy and Maude's children, and other families of their era, was not that they grew apart, but that they experienced such a wide range of rewarding, fulfilling, stressful and tragic times, a range wider than you might expect of just one generation, until you realise that they lived through the worst Depression and the most calamitous War that the world had yet seen. Their brother Earle and his wife Nancy also experienced these trying times marked by economic hardship and war and the story of their successes and failures in negotiating through the most eventful years in the nation's history is a major concern of the next section of this book.

Endnotes

1   *Northern Star* (Lismore) 3 March 1919, 30 January 1924;
    Macleay Argus, 16 December 1921, 24 January 1924;
    Richmond River Examiner, 22 February 1924; *Sydney
    Morning Herald*, 27 February 1924, 8 March 1925; *Daily
    Examiner* (Grafton), 31 March 1927; *Macleay Chronicle*, 30
    January 1924, 6, 29 April 1927

2   SRNSW, *Teacher Rolls and Career Cards*, NRS
    15320-1-59-4

3   *Macleay Argus*, 29 April 1927; *Daily Telegraph*, 4 July, 3
    August 1927; *The (Sydney) Sun*, 6 August, 1927

4   (Grafton) *Daily Examiner*, 9 May 1929

5   *Sydney Morning Herald*, 21 February 1931, 1 December
    1934; Ancestry, *Electoral Roll East Sydney, Darlinghurst, 1930*

6   *Sydney Morning Herald*, 10 December 1934

7   *Sydney Mail*, 18 May 1932; *Sydney Morning Herald*, 28
    September 1932, 28 August 1936; *Daily Telegraph*, 9
    September 1936. Dorothy's place of residence was listed
    as Darlinghurst and her profession described as teacher in
    the electoral rolls for 1934 and 1936, which can be located
    on Ancestry, *Electoral Rolls, East Sydney, Darlinghurst, 1934,
    1936*. There were no fully professional repertory companies
    in Sydney at this time. Fitton's company, which included
    both professional and amateur performers, was the only
    Sydney company to consistently stage legitimate theatre in
    the form of stage classics and major contemporary plays.

8   *Catholic Weekly*, 29 December 1932; *Sydney Morning Herald*
    27 May 1930, 27 November 1933; *Daily Telegraph*, 4
    September 1931

9   *The Sun*, 19 March 1937; *Sydney Morning Herald*, 19
    December 1939; Royal College of Surgeons, Plarr's Lives of
    the Fellows, *John Francis Lipscomb*, livesonline.reseng.ac.uk
    (accessed 5 September 2022)

10 When he recounted stories of his Lower Macleay
    upbringing to me at bedtime, my father sometimes told
    me that his father had told him that his task in educating
    and 'enlightening' his students was hindered because they
    belonged to the Catholic faith. My father inherited some of
    Percy's anti-Catholic views.

11 Dee to Gran (Frances Alice Graham), 18 August 1937,
    Nancarrow/Salter Family Collection. I am grateful to Cassie
    Nancarrow for providing me with a copy of this letter

12 *The Sun*, 19 March 1937

13 Ancestry, England and Wales Civil Registration Marriage
    Index, 1916–2007 July/August/September 1937; England
    and Wales Register 1939 (Surrey)

14 *Daily Examiner* (Grafton), 6 September 1941

15 Dee to Gran 18 August 1937

16 Royal College of Surgeons, *Plarr's Lives of the Fellows*, *John
    Francis Lipscomb*, unsourced newspaper clipping reporting
    the award of his Mentioned in Despatches (*probably the
    Sydney Morning Herald*) in Waterhouse Family Collection

17 Ella Hall to Rodney Hall, 28 June 1944, Fienberg Family
    Papers in possession of Linda Fienberg. I am grateful to her
    for providing me with copies of the letters in this collection

18 *Catholic Weekly*, 9 March 1944; *Sydney Morning Herald*, 31
    October 1945; personal conversation, Richard Waterhouse
    and Dorothy Lipscomb, Pett's Wood, Orpington, 1970

19 Ancestry, *England and Wales, Civil Registration Birth Index,
    1916–2007*, October/November/December 1947

20 Ancestry, *Incoming Shipping Lists, 1878–1960* (Dorothy
    Lipscomb)

21 https:history.replondon.ac.uk/inspiring-physicians/

    David-john-lipscomb. (Accessed 6 September 2022); *Essex
    County Standard*, 27 January 2001

22 Dorothy to parents, 18 July 1939, 27 May, 10 September
    1952 (postcards from Paris); Dorothy to parents, two
    undated postcards from Malta; Dorothy to parents, 10
    February 1972, Tirol, Austria (year not listed but the
    reference to the Olympic disqualification of Austrian
    skier Karl Schranz dates it to 1972), Waterhouse Family
    Collection

23 Royal College of Surgeons, *Plarr's Lives of the Fellows*
    (John Francis Lipscomb); Lipscomb, David John, *inspiring
    physicians*; Ancestry, *England and Wales Civil Registration
    Death Index 1916–2007* (Dorothy Lipscomb, John
    Lipscomb)

24 *Grafton Daily Examiner*,14 February 1923

25 *Macleay Chronicle* 22 September 1926; *Macleay Argus*, 17
    December 1926, 24 June, 26 July 1927, 13 March 1928;
    Manning River Times, 27 August 1927;

26   Richard Waterhouse, personal communications with Judy
    Thompson, 16 June, 10 August, 2022

27 *Barrier Miner*, 9, 17 March 1928

28 *Sydney Morning Herald*, 8, March 1929

29 Richard Waterhouse, personal communications with Judy
    Thompson, 16 June, 18 August, 2022

30 Barbara Fienberg, Undated memoir of her family ca. 1930
    – 1969, copy in possession of Richard Waterhouse. I am
    grateful to Linda Fienberg for providing me with a copy of
    this document. Joan Beaumont, *Australia's Great Depression:
    how a nation shattered by the Great War survived the worst
    economic crisis it has ever faced*, Crow' Nest: Allen and Unwin,
    2022, pp. 185–9

31 Barbara Fienberg, *memoir*. In support of her argument that
    Percy and Maude were political conservatives, Barbara notes
    that they listened to 'church music 'and the 'country report"
    by which she is perhaps referring to 'The Country Hour' on
    the ABC. But this evidence may simply indicate that like
    many radio listeners of their generation they listened to all
    ABC programs, in defiance of the offerings of commercial
    stations.

32 NAA, B883 NX200117, War Service Record, Rodney Hall;
    Richard Waterhouse, interviews with Judy Thompson, 16
    June, 10 August 1922

33 NAA, A6126, 750, Security File for Rodney Trevalier Hall

34 Barbara Fienberg, *undated memoir;* Ella Hall to Rodney Hall,
    20 March 1945, Fienberg Family Papers

35 NAA, B883 NX200117, War Service Record, Rodney Hall

36 Personal conversation, Richard Waterhouse with Linda
    Fienberg, 24 May 2024

37 Barbara Hall to Rodney Hall, 2 May 1942, Fienberg Family
    Papers.

38 Richard Waterhouse, personal communication with Judy
    Thompson, 10 June 2022

39 Barbara Fienberg, Memoir

40 Anna Fienberg, *valedictory address at the funeral of Barbara
    Fienberg*, 24 October 2022. Barbara died on 15 October
    2022, Her husband Len had died on 4 December 2020 and
    according to Anna, Barbara was inconsolable without him.

41 NAA, A6126, 750 (security file on Rodney Hall). See
    page 8 for the reference to the confiscation of communist
    literature; Barbara Fienberg, memoir

42 Richard Waterhouse, personal communication with Judy
    Thompson,31 January 2023

43 *Cootamundra Herald*, 12 May 1940, 1 August 1941; Janet Magnin (Waterhouse), *Personal Memoir,* 1 March 2022; Bill Waterhouse, *Personal Memoir*, 10 February 1922. Copies held by Richard Waterhouse

44 Alan Waterhouse to Earle Waterhouse, 16 January 1945, Waterhouse Family Collection; NAA B883 NX201338, Alan Waterhouse, War Record; Australian War Memorial, www.awm.gov.au/collection/U56087 (7th Australian Infantry Battalion); Gavin Long, *The Final Campaign,* The Official History of Australia in World War 2, Series 1, Army, vol. 7, Canberra, Australian War Memorial, 1963), pp. 343–4.

45 *Cootamundra Herald*, 12 May 1950; *Boorowa News*, 24 September 1954

46 *Daily Advertiser* (Wagga Wagga), 4 October 1952

47 *Albury Banner and Wodonga Express*, 10 September 1926; *Daily Advertiser*, 29 March 1929

48 Bill Waterhouse, *Notes for Janet and Richard,* typescript memoir, 2022, copy in possession of Richard Waterhouse

49 *Daily Advertiser*, 15 August 1929; *Wagga Daily Express*, 28 August 1929, 26 September 1931; *The (Sydney) Sun,* 2 January 1930.

50 Janet Magnin (Waterhouse), *typescript memoir,* 2022, copy in possession of Richard Waterhouse

51 Bill Waterhouse, *Notes for Richard and Janet, 2022*

52 *Narrandera Argus and Riverina Advertiser*, 6 March 1936; *Albury Banner and Wodonga Express,* 30 September 1938; NAA, A9301, War Record, Doris Lehmann, p. 25, *Application for Enlistment as an Airwoman*

53 *Newcastle Morning Herald*, 25 February 1939. In this article she was listed as a Sydney resident, which, combined with the newspaper evidence that she was living and working in Junee between 1936 and 1938, suggests that she studied ballet in Sydney in 1939. Family memory is unclear on this date.

54 On her application to join the RAAF Women's Auxiliary she listed her profession as dancing teacher

55 NAA, A0301, 93453, RAAF Women's Auxiliary. Doris Lehmann personnel file

56 *Cootamundra Herald*, 12 May 1950; *Boorowa News*, 24 September 1954

57 SRNSW, *Inquests and Coronial Inquiries, 1851, 1916–1963*, NRS 345 (13/8615), INX-97–42912; Janet Magnin, *Memoir*

58 Bill Waterhouse, Notes

59 Janet Magnin, *Memoir*

60 *Macleay Argus*, 24 June 1927

61 (Grafton) *Daily Examiner*,16 January 1934, 11 July 1935

62 Ancestry, *Waterhouse/Wake Family Tree*

63 *The Farmer and Settler,* 24 September 1948. The article noted that Percy had operated this enterprise since the 1920s

64 *Dubbo Dispatch*, 29 April 1921; *Dubbo Liberal*, 16 September 1924, 9 June, 1934; *Sydney Morning Herald*, 9 May 1924; *Daily Telegraph*, 24 January 1935

65 *Narromine News and Trangie Advocate*, 6 May 1932 *Sydney Morning Herald*, 2 April 1937

66 *Daily Telegraph*, 27 March 1934

67 *Truth* 12 January 1936

68 *Daily Telegraph*, 1 August 1936

69 *Gilgandra Weekly and Castlereagh,* 6 April 1939

70 Barry was described as a bank clerk on his enlistment papers

71 *Daily Telegraph*, 28 September 1939; NAA, B883, NX14133, *War Record, Barry Waterhouse*

72 *Sydney Morning Herald*, 15 May 1941; *Gilgandra Weekly,* 29 May 1941. The twins were born eight months after Lesley and Barry married, which perhaps indicates that they were premature and may explain why they died. However, perhaps Lesley was already pregnant when they married, and this fact may explain the real reason why the wedding was brought forward.

73 Gilgandra Weekly, 24 December 1943

74 NAA, War Record, Barry Waterhouse; Mark Johnston, *An Australian Band of Brothers, Don Company, Second 43rd Battalion, 9th Division*, Sydney, New South Publishing, 2018, pp. 44,52, 205, 295–6302, 346–7; the extended history of the Ninth Division can be found in the *Official History of Australia in World War 2*, Series 1, vol. 3 (Barton Maughan), Canberra, Australian War Memorial !966, and vol. 7 (Gavin Long), Canberra, Australian War Memorial, 1961); *Gilgandra Weekly*, 16 December 1943, 27 March 1947

75 I remember overhearing Barry making this comment to Earle, who later told me he strongly disapproved of Barry's reasons. This was not surprising given Earle valued education for its own sake.

76 Jill Waterhouse to Richard Waterhouse (Messenger), 5 February 2020

77 *Port Macquarie Gazette*, 15 June 2004

78 www.gettyimages.co.uk/detail/newd-photo/lady-alexander-and-prue-waterhouse-attend-the-yota-news-photo/102871913

79 Earle waterhouse, memoir letter, 7 May 1987

PART 4

An Unlikely Connection: the Drake and Waterhouse families

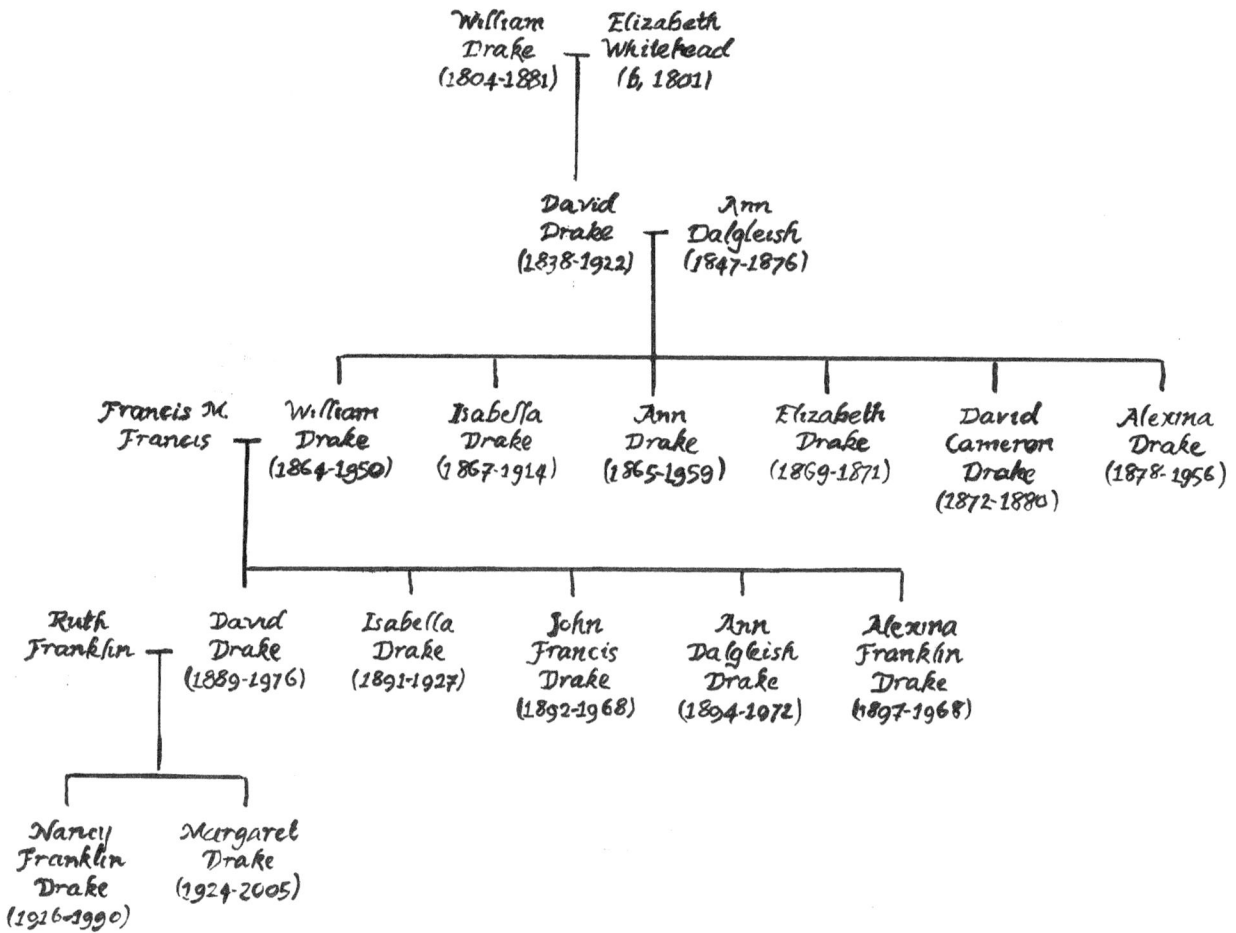

Chapter 8

David Drake and his Docks

My grandfather, David Drake, standing beside a statue of Sir Francis Drake, in Plymouth. The belief in a family connection was embedded in Australian Drake family folklore. *Waterhouse Family Collection*

A Scottish Immigrant

David Drake, my great, great grandfather was born in Limekilns, Dunfermline, Scotland, in 1838, one of at least five children born to his parents, William and Elizabeth Drake. William may have subsequently operated a shipbuilding business in the town of Beauly, Inverness.[1] David Drake's grandson, also named David Drake, once told my sister Annabel that although the first David had emigrated to Australia from Scotland, the family did not originally come from there. Indeed, it seems that it was widely believed in the family that it was at some stage connected to Devon and Cornwall and included as its most famous member,

none other than Sir Francis Drake. This was a belief that extended beyond the Australian branch of the family. In 1922, Francis Drake, an officer aboard the Royal Navy vessel *Meteur*, which was visiting Sydney, and who claimed to be a descendant of Sir Francis, also identified himself as the grand-nephew of David Drake, then a retired shipbuilder living in Balmain.[2] However, although Sir Francis Drake married twice, he had no children. His estate, including his title as baronet, passed to his brother Thomas and through him the male line lasted through generations of Drakes until 1794 when the last Drake baronet, Sir Francis Henry Drake, died without leaving a male heir. There were still descendants of Thomas Drake but they came through the female line and did not carry the surname of Drake. Contemporary male descendants of sixteenth century Tavistock Drakes are not directly connected to Sir Francis or any other male members of his immediate family. In this context, the relationship claims of the Scottish and Australian Drakes were rooted in family lore but not family reality.

After serving an apprenticeship with his father and then working in the Glasgow shipbuilding industry, my great, great grandfather came to Sydney as a ship's carpenter in 1861. Initially, he worked on the first Glebe Island Bridge, which was completed in 1862, and then became a foreman at Chowne's shipbuilding yard in Pyrmont.[3] However, an indication that he already had plans to establish his own shipbuilding business is reflected in his decision in 1863 to pay a deposit to assist the immigration into Australia of his brother Alexander McKay Drake with whom he then worked closely until Alexander's untimely death in 1873.[4]

In 1864 Drake was living in Bowman Street Pyrmont, where he operated a small boat building business. However, the first ship he built, with the assistance of Alexander and 'two boys', was a schooner named the *Annie Dean,* a contract he completed at a shipyard on the Manning River for a distant relative, Daniel Cameron Dalgleish. In fact, this project might have ended Drake's career as a shipbuilder before it had properly begun. He received only part payment for the vessel during the period in which it was under construction and completing its final seaworthy trials in 1868. When he presented his final bill to Dalgleish the owner procrastinated. Unfortunately, in the same year the ship was lost at sea, although Dalgleish then promised to pay his debt when the insurance came through. But when these funds arrived, he still delayed payment. Further delay in Drake receiving his owed moneys occurred when Dalgleish lost his life in a fall from a horse. In the end Drake took Dalgleish's widow, Emma, to court seeking £400 in owed money. The jury awarded him £254/5/11, which no doubt was an important contribution in keeping his business afloat. While building the *Annie Dean* Drake had also completed a six-ton

ketch, *Evelyn,* in a Balmain shipyard.[5]

Although possessing access to only limited finance Drake's business ambitions grew. In 1872 with shared capital totalling £60 he and James Bower opened a large shipyard at the foot of Murray Street Pyrmont. Within four years they were in financial difficulty and declared insolvency when a creditor, John Carr, filed a bill to claim a mortgage over the *Maris,* a schooner nearing completion. The vessel was mortgaged to the Commercial Bank of Sydney for £1000, although it was valued at £2000. Drake and Bower indicated that they planned to sell the vessel to pay the mortgage and the suppliers to whom they were also indebted. What also exacerbated the firm's financial difficulties was the fact that it secured fewer commissions to build other vessels than expected. However, later in the decade business opportunities for building steam-tugboats and ferries improved and in 1880 the firm was discharged from bankruptcy.[6]

Apart from the stress of bankruptcy, the 1870s marked a difficult and tragic chapter in Drake's life. In this period three close family members passed away, including his daughter, Elizabeth (1872), his brother, Alexander (1873), and his first wife Ann (1876)

Ann Dalgleish

Ann was the daughter of William Dalgleish, a Scotsman who was born in Liberton, Midlothian, in 1807. He married Isabella Short (1806–1881) at St Cuthbert's (Presbyterian) Church in Edinburgh and the couple emigrated to Van Diemen's Land in 1833, arriving on the *Edward Coulston,* a ship probably named after a Bristol slave trader, Edward Colston. This was a time when free immigrants were arriving in the colony in unprecedented numbers. William and Isabella had eleven children, the first four born in the United Kingdom, the following seven in Hobart. Ann, who arrived in 1847, was their tenth child. William and Isabella were Scottish Presbyterians but he had no connection to the shipping industry for he worked as a stonemason in Hobart. When David Drake sued the widow of Daniel Cameron Dalgleish in 1870 he indicated that Dalgleish was a 'distant relative'. If Daniel was related to William Dalgleish then so was David Drake. Perhaps David and Ann met because they were part of the same extended family circle. In any case David and Ann were married in Sydney in 1863.

During the period of their marriage David and Ann lived in modest circumstances indicated by the fact that in 1876 the total value of their furniture and clothing was estimated at £20.[7] They became the parents of six children, William, Isabella, Ann, Elizabeth, Daniel and Alexina .[8]

Mary Florence Taylor

Three years after the death of Ann, in 1879 David Drake married Mary Florence Taylor (1856–1898) the daughter of Surry Hills residents Augustus Banks Taylor (– 1878) a broker who later became a customs officer, and his wife Rebecca/Newnham (1821–1873). Her parents were immigrants who came from Kent in England and were members of the Anglican Church.[9] When they married Mary was 23 and David was 41. David Drake mixed largely in Sydney's Scottish community, a mixing made easier when he moved his business and residence to Balmain in 1889, a suburb which contained a large Scottish Presbyterian population. At the centre of this social and cultural life was the Campbell Street Presbyterian Church for which the foundation stone was laid in 1867 and which opened in 1868. It had a congregation of about 450, while some 500 children attended its Sunday School. However the church was not just a place of worship but also a centre of social and sporting activity, sponsoring both young men and young women's fellowship associations, a girls gymnasium, and cricket and football (Rugby Union) clubs.[10] Its pews were filled with immigrants from around Edinburgh, the Lothians and Fife, Carthness and Dumfries, men and women who had a strong ethnic attachment both to Presbyterianism and to the Campbell Street Church in particular.[11]

Perhaps many Scottish immigrants were drawn to the fast growing suburb by the prospect of employment not only in the shipbuilding yards which included Drake's and Mort's Docks but also in the allied sail making and timber milling

trades.[12] Moreover, in the late nineteenth century Balmain became the home not just of small craft based workshops but a growing number of large-scale industries, including iron foundries, engineering workshops and soap factories.[13] In any case, even as early as 1871 Scottish Presbyterians comprised more than 18% of the Balmain population, twice the colonial average. Their numbers also included a high proportion of white rather than blue-collar workers, architects, managers, employers and teachers—constituting a Balmain elite of sorts.[14]

David Drake lived largely within an extended Scottish family and community, the latter centring on the Presbyterian Church, and so in marrying an English Anglican he was embracing a family outside his Scottish 'clan', although at some stage Mary converted to the Presbyterian faith. The fact that Taylor later became a customs officer perhaps suggests that in his earlier role as a broker he dealt either with ships or cargos or both, which might explain how the Drake and Taylor families came in contact. In any case, I suspect that David Drake's identification with Scottish Presbyterianism had more to do with ethnic identity than a specific commitment to Calvinist Christianity, because while the Drakes were married and buried from Campbell Street David Drake never served as an elder, nor did he hold any other office in the kirk.

David and Mary had seven children.[15] Although many years younger than David, Mary was the first to die, passing away on February 2 1898, when her youngest child was only three years old.

The Golden Era of Drake's Dock

After its establishment at Bald Rock (White Bay), Balmain in 1889, Drake's Dock enjoyed a golden age that lasted into the early years of the Great War. Employing some 60 workers the shipyard was responsible for the building of wooden barges, lighters, river droghers (small paddle steamers), tugs, pearlers, and both small passenger ferries and large vehicular carrying vessels designed to ply the route between Fort Macquarie, where the Opera House now stands, and Milson's Point. More ambitiously, it also produced larger ships, in the form of schooners and steamers, built to serve the Australian coastal as well as the inter-island Southwest Pacific trade covering areas ruled both by the British and German colonial authorities.[16] In 1913 Drake's Dock launched a ferry named *Kuramia*, designed to carry 1600 passengers, which it claimed as the largest steamer yet built in Australia.[17] When he died in 1922 David Drake was hailed as responsible for launching more ships than any other man in Sydney.[18]

To take advantage of these prosperous times in 1913 Drake registered his shipbuilding business as a company with a capital of £25,000 in £1 shares. Signatures to the registration included one of his daughters by Ann (Alexina) and three by Mary (Maggie, Jessie, and Rebecca). The two other signatures were H. Drake and I.D. Drake, which don't match the names of any of his children, so perhaps they represent misprints. Most importantly, the First Directors were listed as David Thomas Drake, his first son by Mary, and Isabella, his first-born daughter by Ann.[19] In naming David Thomas as First Director I suspect David Drake was anointing him as his successor. William, his first-born child by Ann, was not included in this list, despite the fact that he had qualifications as a naval architect, and almost certainly worked for his father's company. As it turned out, David Thomas didn't possess the management qualities

needed to deal with a series of serious challenges which the company faced, beginning in the second decade of the century.

World War 1 provided the first challenge to the company. The commissioning of ships to service the German Pacific colonies ended immediately and as the War dragged on there was a lessening demand for coastal steamers and Sydney ferries. By 1916 the Dock was producing few large vessels and concentrating instead on building barges and lighters as well as placing a new emphasis on repairs to both small and large ships. During this time too, David Drake became less active in the administration of the company, which is not surprising given that he turned 80 in 1918. Perhaps he focussed on his extensive family, and spent more time at the Balmain Bowling Club where at one time he was club champion. The family also were avid supporters of and participants in sailing skiff racing, which he may have continued to watch in his now more leisurely schedule. He died on August 17, 1922 at his home in Batty Street Balmain, only a short distance from the shipyard he founded at Bald Rock. Acknowledged as 'a shipbuilding pioneer of Sydney', he was buried near his second wife, Mary Florence Drake, in the Presbyterian section of Rookwood cemetery.[20]

The Failure of a (Brief) Dynasty

Born in 1882, David Thomas Drake lived in his parents' house in Batty Street Balmain until his marriage in 1914. He attended Balmain Technical School to study Mechanical and Model Drawing in 1907, and by 1911 was playing a prominent role in the company supervising the building of ships like the *Greycliffe*, and acting as the company's spokesman. In 1914 he married Florence Wheeler. Although born in Petersham in 1891, by the time of her wedding, her family had moved to Katoomba in the Blue Mountains. As a result of his marriage David Thomas was drawn out of the tight Scottish, Presbyterian, Balmain community which had marked his early life. He and his wife purchased a house at Springwood in the Blue Mountains, in which she probably lived most of the time. Their son later became a boarder at All Saints Anglican School, at Bathurst.[21]

David Drake the Boatbuilder
Sydney Morning Herald 18 August 1922

The post-War years were increasingly difficult times for Drake's Dock. The German colonies were now in British and Australian hands but that did not lead to an increase in the commissioning of ships to cater to a larger Anglo-Australian Pacific Empire. At the same time, with improvements to the roads that ran along the Australian east coast to cater to the burgeoning motor vehicle traffic, the demand for cargo and passenger carrying coastal steamers progressively diminished. In Sydney too, people and goods were more and more carried by motorised vehicles and less and less by ferries and calm water cargo vessels. One indication of the decline in demand for Sydney Harbour vessels was the withdrawal of the *Narrabeen* from the Sydney Harbour cargo trade in 1928. Instead, it was sailed to Victoria where it was converted to a passenger ferry and used on the Phillip Island run.[22] Drake's Dock had also built large vehicular ferries for the Sydney Harbour service between Fort Macquarie and Milson's Point but the completion of the Harbour Bridge in 1932 also spelled the end of that service.

The onset of the Depression, which reached its worst in 1931 was also of critical importance in weakening the viability of Drake's Dock and also destroying David Thomas Drake's personal finances. As a result of the Depression the value of his Drake company shares as well as the worth of his own properties at Strathfield and Springwood had steeply declined, which meant that the total sum earned from their sale didn't meet his bank debt requirements. Drake claimed that he had accumulated a large amount of debt in part because he had to pay for medical treatment for his son, who suffered from bronchitis and asthma, although he also owed debts to a number of non-medical providers, including the department store, Anthony Hordern. He was declared bankrupt in 1931. The company, which moved to Drummoyne in about 1930, limped on, now reduced to building tugs and fishing trawlers, and probably also relying on repairs to make ends meet. In 1936 it went into voluntary liquidation, selling its remaining assets, which included a floating dock, furniture, anchors and chains, a steam drogher, a steamer, two deck lighters and a steam launch.[23]

Effectively this was the end of Drake's Dock and the Balmain dynasty that its founder, David Drake, created. His son, David Thomas, left Sydney for Burrinjuck to work as a shipwright, for the Water Conservation and Irrigation Commission. He was discharged from bankruptcy in 1938. By 1943 he had returned to Sydney and was living in Croydon Park where he died in 1954 aged 74. Still listed as a shipbuilder, he left a modest estate of £920.[24] When I was a child my mother often referred to Drake's Dock and the prosperous enterprise her great grandfather created. Over the course of my life I sometimes wondered why, as a consequence, we weren't wealthy. Now I know why. There is a saying that the first generation creates wealth, the second builds on it, and the third fritters it away. But, as this story illustrates, sometimes the brutal fickleness of capitalism can't even guarantee two full generations of family prosperity.

William and Frances Maria

William, David's eldest child by his first wife Ann, is a far more elusive figure than his father David because, as a direct consequence of not succeeding him as the company's head, he left only a modest imprint on the historical record of Sydney shipbuilding. Born in 1864, like his younger half-brother, he also studied naval architecture at technical college and was awarded a Grade 1 certificate in 1885.[25] Three years later he married Frances Maria Francis in the Presbyterian Church in Ultimo.[26] Born in 1834 her father, John Francis, came to Australia from Portugal sometime before 1861, because in that year he married Caroline Mary A. Robinson whose family lived in Surry Hills, Sydney.[27] Francis is a name of Latin origin meaning Frenchman, which is nevertheless found in many languages and countries. So, we can't tell from his name whether his family was Portuguese or whether Portugal was a transient country which he passed through on a migratory route. It is possible that he was a sailor and that he continued to crew ships after his arrival in Australia.[28] The fact that he signed the marriage register with his mark further suggests he was of humble social origins. Surry Hills housed many of Sydney's poorest inhabitants, which indicates that Caroline Robinson's family belonged to the unskilled or semi-skilled working class. There is a story in my family, which my mother often repeated, that Frances came from a Catholic background. However, her parents were married in St Paul's Anglican Church on Cleveland Street in 1861 and she subsequently wed William in a Presbyterian Church, no doubt in deference to her husband's wishes. On the basis of this evidence this is clearly a false family narrative. Francis is however also a common Irish name so it is possible that John came from a Catholic Irish family and gave up his religion when he married the Anglican Caroline Robinson. Despite formal changes to their religion by John and his daughter Frances, perhaps the influence of Catholicism lingered in the family, which is why my grandfather, Frances's son David, called for a priest when he was dying in Caroline Chisholm Aged Care Home in 1976.[29]

William and Frances had five children.[30] The family lived at 23 Smith Street, close to Drake's Dock and to the house occupied by William's father. He was a shipwright for the whole course of his working life, and I suspect he spent most if not all of his career contributing to the construction and repair of vessels in Drake's Dock. However, there is evidence that he also owned at least one vessel, for when the small ship, *White Bay*, was wrecked on Stockton Beach near Newcastle in 1928, he was listed as the owner.[31]

Frances died in 1931 and was buried in the Presbyterian Section of the Field of Mars Cemetery in Ryde. In 1936, when the family business went into voluntary liquidation, William was 72 so I suspect he was already retired. He died in 1950 at a house in Nicholson Parade, Cronulla, probably in the care of his daughter, Alexina, who lived in the suburb throughout her married life.

His eldest son, David, chose not to follow his father and grandfather into the shipbuilding industry, but within an established career path of Balmain Scottish Presbyterians, he became a teacher. His brother, John Francis, on the other hand, remained in Drummoyne and worked as a shipwright for his whole working life. He died in 1968 and was buried in the Field of Mars Cemetery. A decade later his wife Carmen was laid beside him. William's oldest daughter, Ann Dalgleish ('Nancy') Drake, married James Coates in 1921. They lived in St Ives, and I can recall my mother taking me to visit one of her relatives who I think was 'Nancy' in the 1960s. I wish I had listened more closely as the two exchanged family stories from their respective youths. Her younger sister Alexina, who I remember visiting in her ramshackle Cronulla house with its unkempt garden when I was only about five or six years old, married John Fahy in 1923. They are both buried in Woronora cemetery.[32]

William and Frances had a strong sense of Drake family heritage. All five of their children, David, Isabella, John Francis, Ann Dalgleish, and Alexina were named after members of the Drake and Francis families. John Francis remained loyal to the Drake cultural faith, working as a shipwright and living in Drummoyne until the last years of his life. But the stories of the other children are those of a family diaspora into the suburbs and rural New South Wales, and an effective abandonment of ship building, Scottish Presbyterianism and Balmain.

Endnotes

1   Ancestry, bricksandbranches, *The Cornish Side*; *Elgin Courant and Morayshire Advertiser* 18 September 1846; *The Land* 26 October 1949. In this article, Walter Finegan, who was a correspondence school superintendent, argued that his grandfather, James Drake, was William and Ann's oldest, while David was their seventh child.

2   (Sydney) *Sunday Times*, 11 June 1922. William was the son of John Drake, a carpenter, and his wife Agnes (Williamson) who lived in Limekilns. See Ancestry, *Old Parish Registers, Births, 424/80 577, Dunfermline*

3   *Evening News* 3 March 1913; *Sydney Morning Herald*, 18 August 1922

4   *Sydney Morning Herald*, 5 September 1863; Ancestry, *Balmain Cemetery Records, 1868–1912*, Alexander McKay Drake, 24 April 1873

5   *Evening News*, 3 August 1870; *Sydney Morning Herald*, 3 August 1870, 18 August 1922 1806–1881)

6   State Records of NSW (hereafter SRNSW), NRS 13564-1-{2/9620}-12997; *Maitland Mercury*, 1 August 1876; *Sydney Morning Herald*, 18 February 1880, 20 June 1884, 18 August 1922; *Daily Telegraph*, 8 October 1885

7   SRNSW, NRS 13564-1-{2/9620}-12997

8   William (1864–1950), Isabella (1867–1914), Ann (1868–1959) Elizabeth (1869–1871), Daniel (1872–1880), and Alexina (1874–1956). In locating the children of David Drake and his two wives, Ann and Mary I have relied on the NSW Register of Births and on the *Auntie Peg Williams Family Bible* which in 1989 was in the possession of 'Margaret', whose grandmother was Mary Florence Drake, David's second wife. 'Margaret'copied the names of the 13 children of the two wives of David Drake and included them in a letter to my mother Nancy, great granddaughter of Ann, dated 20 April 1989. The letter is in the Waterhouse family collection.

9   Ancestry, Kent, England, *Church of England Baptisms, Marriages, and Burials, 1538–1914*; *Sydney Anglican Parish Registers 18114–2011*

10 Anon., *A Brief History of Presbyterianism in Balmain*, Balmain: Balmain Presbyterian Church Campbell Street, 1948, passim.

11 Max Solling and Peter Reynolds, *On the Margins of the City: a social history of Leichhardt and the former municipalities of Annandale, Balmain and Glebe*, St Leonards: Allen and Unwin, 1997, p.111

12 Benjamin Wharton, *Changing Tides: A Cultural Landscape Study of the Maritime Community in Balmain 1860–1910*, BA Thesis, University of New England, 2016, p.116

13 Solling and Reynolds, p. 123–6

14 *ibid.*, p. 109, 111

15 David Thomas (1882–1954), James (1884–1960), Jessie (1886–1959), Maggie (1889–1967), Rebecca (1891–1944), Christina (1894–1968) and Alexander Mackay (1895–1925).

16 *The (Sydney) Sun*, 7 August 1912. The building and launching of ships from Drake's Dock were widely reported in the Sydney press. For a list of ships launched up to mid-1909 see *The Star*, 26 August 1909

17 (Sydney) *Sunday Times*, 16 November 1913

18 *Sydney Morning Herald*, 18 August 1882

19 *Evening News*, 4 November 1913. Isabella died in 1914 so her prominent position in the company was not long lasting.

20 *Sydney Morning Herald*, 18 August 1922

21 *ibid.*, 18 January 1907, 13 January 1914; (Bathurst) *Advocate* 19 November 1927

22 *Sydney Morning Herald*, 30 October 1928

23 National Archives of Australia (hereafter NAA), *Drake, David Thomas, Bankruptcy Sequestration File*: Box 195 29/4/1931–20/7/1962, Series, SP414/1, Control Symbol, 1931/193, Item ID, 14446899, *Sydney Morning Herald*, 6 June 1936

24 NAA, *Drake, David Thomas, Bankruptcy Records*; Ancestry, *Index to NSW Deceased Estate Files, 1859–1958, (Drake, David Thomas)*

25 *Sydney Morning Herald*, 7 March 1885

26 ibid., 21 November 1888

27 Ancestry, *Sydney Anglican Registers, 1814–2011, St Paul's Cleveland Street Marriage Register*, 25 November 1861

28 Ancestry, *NSW Unassisted Immigrants 1878*, includes a list of passengers and crew for the ship *Bowen* which includes a John Francis, with a birthdate of about 1835, as a crew member. Given that John was born in 1834 this seaman could be the father of Frances

29 My mother, Nancy Waterhouse told me this story after her father's death in 1976

30 David (1889–1976), Isabella (1891–1927), John Francis (1892–1968), Ann Dalgleish, and Alexina Frances, known as 'Ena' (1897–1968). I have compiled this information from NSW, *Register of Births Deaths and Marriages*, Ancestry, *Sydney Anglican Registers*, Ancestry, *Australian Electoral Rolls*, and records of deaths in the *Sydney Morning Herald*. At the time of her mother's death Ann Dalgleish was referred to as 'Nancy', a common nickname for girls and women called Ann/Anne. See *Sydney Morning Herald*, 10 August 1931

31 *Newcastle Morning Herald and Miners' Advocate*, 11 August 1928

32 In tracing the lives of John Francis, Ann Dalgleish and Alexina I have used Ancestry, *Births, Deaths and marriages*, Ancestry, *Electoral Rolls*, and Ancestry, *Find a Grave*

Chapter 9

Breaking the Boatbuilding tradition: David Drake the Younger and his career in Education

MY GRANDFATHER, DAVID DRAKE, was born in Balmain in 1889 and grew up within a stone's throw of Drake's Dock and the White Bay waterfront. Bathing regularly in Sydney Harbour turned him into a strong swimmer and by the time he was eleven he had already saved two other children from drowning by diving into the water and dragging them ashore.[1] As a student at Fort Street Primary School in The Rocks, to which he travelled each school day by ferry, he was an outstanding scholar, awarded the General Proficiency Prize in grade 5A. His aunt Rebecca was the first member of his family to become a teacher, listed as an assistant teacher at Auburn Primary School in 1925, but David was the second.[2] Like Earle's father, Percy, David began his career as a student teacher, first at Unanderra and then at Leichhardt. The opening of the Sydney Teachers' College created new training opportunities for teachers and after successfully passing the admission examination, David was admitted to that institution in 1907. When he completed his Teaching Certificate he probably returned to teaching at Leichhardt. In 1912 he was appointed to Taree District School where he remained for nine years.[3]

Sometime before May 1914, either when he was a teacher at Leichhardt, or at home for the holidays from his school at Taree, David met Caroline Ruth Franklin. They married on May 21, 1914, in the Campbell Street Presbyterian Church,

with his sister Isabella acting as a bridesmaid and his brother John Francis serving as best man. At this time, the Drake clan Balmain connection was still strong, although the fact that David was now teaching in Taree was a sign of the beginning of a wider family exodus. After their marriage David and Ruth lived for another six years six years in this Manning Valley town.

David Drake the younger. *Waterhouse Family Collection*

The Franklins

On her father's side, Ruth's grandfather was Joseph Franklin (1815–1882) who was born in County Tipperary in Ireland. He immigrated to New South Wales in 1841 with his wife, who was born Johanna Ryan (1815–1892), and was also a native of Tipperary. They had at least two children, including Joseph (1849–1926) and James (1856-). Although Joseph was born in Parramatta, James was born in the inland town of Wellington, and the elder Joseph and wife Johanna died and were buried in Failford, a timber town located on the mid-North Coast of NSW. All of this suggests that perhaps the older Joseph was an itinerant worker connected to the timber trade.

However, his son Joseph spent his adult life in Sydney where in 1881 he married Annie Jane Richards. She was the daughter of a Pyrmont mariner, Thomas Moses Richards (1802–1870) and Caroline Victoria Richards (Watson). Joseph and Annie married in 1881 and had six children. The first, Robert (1880–1880), was born before they wed while the others included, Frederick (1881–1953), Ellora May (1883-), Sydney (1885–1885), Blanche (1886–1966) Ernest (1889–1902) and Caroline Ruth (1891 – 1960).[4] Two of them I knew personally, my great aunt Blanche and my grandmother Caroline Ruth, who was always called Ruth. The family lived in Pashley Street Balmain, where Joseph worked as a salesman. My mother told a story, which my sister Susan remembered and wrote down sometime in the 1990s, that Annie Jane was the daughter of a rich Jewish merchant in London who disowned her when she decided to marry Joseph Franklin, who, as the story goes, had previously trained in Ireland to be a Catholic priest.[5] As the above narrative indicates, this story has no basis in fact. Perhaps it was constructed purely on the premise that because Annie's father's second name was Moses, there is the possibility he was Jewish, and on such a flimsy foundation a Franklin/Drake family myth was created.

Perhaps Ruth constructed this story because her social origins were quite modest and she had pretensions to belong to the respectable middle class. Marrying David Drake, a white–collar

Ruth Franklin (Drake). *Waterhouse Family Collection*

schoolteacher and member of a modestly wealthy and well-known Balmain family was a start, but she still had to deal with her own family background and may have constructed a narrative of wealthy origins to obscure reality. Ruth was an uneducated woman who was also a social snob. She insisted that her daughter Nancy leave school when she reached fifteen or sixteen, believing that girls from respectable and well-off families didn't need to work and that their time was best spent mixing in the best local social circles in order to find a suitable husband. When Nancy met Earle, Ruth was keen for them to marry, because he was a young man with a degree and therefore had bright career prospects in the Department of Education. But she was far less keen on Earle's family, considering Percy and Maude to be far below her in social status, and that led to tension between the families, an issue that was resolved by Percy and Maude, Ruth and David, having few social interchanges, especially after Earle and Nancy married. This was, of course made easier, by the fact that the two families always lived at some distance from each other. It is also worth adding that Percy and Maude were not warm towards their daughter-in-law either, believing that Nancy was not Earle's intellectual equal and that she had inherited too much of her mother's snobbishness.

Ruth and David were far from an ideal match. She could be excessively effusive and sentimental in her attitude towards her pets, which included dogs and budgerigars, and the manner in which she treated her grandchildren. Even as a small child, I found her excessive expressions of affection towards me to be quite smothering. She was also a very outgoing personality, not afraid to express strong views and prejudices. Ruth was also capable of being quite abusive, especially in the language she used towards her husband. She had also inherited and retained from her father and grandparents some vestiges of Irish folk culture, including anachronistic expressions, and deeply held superstitions. David, in contrast, although possessed of an imposing physical stature, and very confident as a public figure, was shy in his conduct of personal relations. That reticent trait became stronger as he grew older and became increasingly deaf. I don't remember him ever hugging or expressing affection towards me, although I found his simple modesty to be very endearing.[6]

Ruth and David: Married Life and his Teaching Career

During the years David Drake spent teaching in Taree he was prominent in the local amateur musical community, performing cornet solos at concerts, organising at least one eisteddfod and conducting both the choral society choir and the Taree Brass Band.[7] Ruth was also active in the local musical scene indicated by the fact that a silver serving tray presented for outstanding contribution to the Choral Society was engraved with both their names. David was also an active sportsman. During his schooldays he had played Rugby but in Taree he and Ruth took up the less physical but highly exacting sport of golf, becoming founding members of the Taree Golf Club.[8] He was 24 when World War 1 began, and I wonder whether, at least in part, this strong commitment to the cultural life of Taree was prompted by a sense of guilt that he had not enlisted. Perhaps his reluctance to join the First AIF was driven, at least in

part, by the arrival of the couple's first daughter, Nancy, who was born in Taree in 1916.[9]

In any case his Department of Education career took a turn for the better in 1921 when he was appointed to Fort Street to teach Science. I am sure he was delighted to be posted to what was considered a highly prestigious School, which was also his alma mater. It also meant that he was able to enrol as an evening student at The University of Sydney, where he completed an Arts degree in 1925. As a science teacher, he mostly chose to study science rather than humanities subjects, especially Geology. On one occasion, when I was an undergraduate at the same university, he spoke to me of his own experiences there. Referring to a field trip he made to the Snowy with the Professor of Geology, Sir Tannatt William Edgeworth-David, he related how the Professor declined Drake's offer to carry his backpack down into the valley where the group planned to collect rock specimens but then handed him the rock filled bag when students and teacher began the long climb back up to the ridge.

The family didn't return to live in Balmain, perhaps because it was now marked as a relatively poor working-class suburb, but instead lived in Drummoyne, an area which was characterised as middle class. The move to Sydney involved another bonus too, because their second daughter, Margaret was born in 1923, during their residence in Drummoyne.[10]

David's completion of his degree led to a series of rapid promotions within the Department of Education. In 1926 he was appointed Headmaster at Bega, followed by appointments at the same level at Ballina (1928) and Cowra (1929). In 1931 David was promoted to the rank of Inspector of Schools and sent to Murwillumbah. In 1936 he was moved to Mudgee in the same position and four years later in 1940 he became Inspector at Maitland. He was subsequently promoted to the position of Senior Inspector a position, which in 1952 was reclassified as Area Director of the Newcastle Public Schools system. He retired at the end of 1954.

Three characteristics marked his life during his career as a teacher and Inspector. First, he

An elderly Sir Tannatt William Edgworth-Davies (at front of group) leading a University of Sydney undergraduate field trip to the Snowy Mountains in the early 1920s. David Drake is not in the picture perhaps because he took it. The picture is labelled in David Drake's handwriting as including the famous professor.

was a keen sportsman. As might be expected of a man who had learnt to become a strong swimmer growing up adjacent to the Balmain waterfront, he quickly adapted to swimming in the surf and was a member of the surf clubs in the beachside towns in which he was based, that is Bega and Ballina. On one occasion he swam from Ballina Beach in a dangerous surf in a vain effort to save a drowning surfer. The coroner praised him for his courage and persistence.[11] When he and Ruth moved to Mudgee he turned to lawn bowls with such success that he became a member of the fours team that won the club championship. When he returned to the coast he took up fishing with a vengeance. During the War, and despite the government regulations forbidding the construction of private dwellings in wartime, he and Ruth built a modest waterfront holiday home at Salamander Bay on Port Stephens. Subsequently, during the week they lived at their house at 106 Memorial Drive, Bar Beach, Newcastle (now an apartment block), but on weekends and during school holidays they resided at Salamander, referred to simply as 'the Bay'. Ruth also took up lawn bowls and they both became members of the Nelson Bay Bowling Club. David had a tendency to become a leader of any

organisation he joined and inevitably he served as President of the Club.[12]

Second, in a modest way David also committed himself to serving his local community. In this role he occasionally gave public lectures on matters of public interest, for example, the issue of unemployment. He was also involved in Rotary for many years serving as President of the Mudgee Club and also working as an active member of the Newcastle and the Nelson Bay Clubs.[13]

Finally, the style he adopted in his role as Inspector was rather different from the norm. My father, like most of his contemporaries, was a stern inspector, who was held in awe and sometimes fear, by both teachers and schoolchildren. But the mild-mannered David was more measured and approachable in his inspectorial role. When he and Ruth departed Mudgee he was praised 'for the justice of his judgements', as well as his 'tolerant attitude and friendly approach'.[14]

A Tale of Two Sisters: Nancy and Margaret

There is no record of Nancy's early childhood activities in Taree, Drummoyne and Bega. In Ballina she attended Ballina Intermediate School and also became an amateur performer, appearing as a singer, dancer and a recitation presenter. This last activity probably required her to memorise well known poems, speeches and essays and demonstrate her skills as an orator.[15] When each inspector in the state was authorised to choose four children from the schools in their area, to march in the procession to mark the opening of the Sydney Harbour Bridge in 1932 David Drake chose his own daughter as one of the fortunate students. With other children from the country, she stayed at Stuart House in Manly and earned a certain degree of fame when a photograph of her in her swimsuit and posing on Manly Beach was published in the *Daily Telegraph*.[16] I suppose this made her a pioneer of sorts, a prototype of what subsequently became the page 3 swimsuit girl.

At fifteen or sixteen she left school and entered conspicuously into Murwillumbah's social life, attending charity parties, balls and dances and participating in mannequin parades organised to raise funds for such causes as the local ambulance service.[17] She also continued her local stage career, and while performing as a minor cast member in a comedy, 'The Red Mill', staged by the local amateur opera company, met a young schoolteacher, Earle Waterhouse. They were both listed as amongst the 'artists, models, gossips, rustics'. I suspect Nancy played a model and Earle a rustic. The story of their subsequent life together is continued in chapter 9 below.

Born in Drummoyne in 1923, Nancy's sister Margaret also began her stage career in Murwillumbah at a young age. In her early teens Nancy was a member of the Young Crusaders, a performance group associated with the local Presbyterian Church. Margaret became the troupe's mascot, although she was also a performer, appearing as Bo-Peep when she was five, and later appearing in a school play about Robin Hood.[18] Nancy left school early for her mother believed respectable middle-class girls didn't need more than a basic education. She understood their object in life was not to work but to engage in an extensive social life as a means to find a suitable husband. In her teens Margaret's life and career paths took a different fork than the one chosen

for Nancy by her mother, perhaps simply because she insisted on finishing school and completing the Leaving Certificate. She was a high achiever and won prizes both at the schools she attended in Murwillumbah and Mudgee. She was also Girls' Captain at Mudgee High School.[19] Leaving school she chose a career over marrying young. At this time qualifying as a pharmacist didn't involve undertaking a university degree but working in a pharmacy while studying for a series of qualifying examinations. Margaret moved to Newcastle with her parents, qualified as a pharmacist and by 1946 was working in that capacity in Tamworth.[20]

In 1948 Margaret married Herbert Walter ('Bob') Hosking, a metallurgist from Warracknabeal in Victoria, who worked in Newcastle for BHP. For a brief period after her marriage Margaret continued to work but left employment when her first child Dianne was born in 1949.[21] A son, David, arrived during the time the family spent in the United States in the mid 1950s where Bob was studying for a PhD in Metallurgy at the University of Pittsburgh, all paid for by BHP. Eventually the company decided to move Bob to Melbourne where the family settled in the outer suburb of Glen Waverley. He had already undergone surgery for a defective heart valve at the Mayo Clinic in the US but the symptoms returned and he died a tragic early death in 1975 at the age of fifty-three. Margaret remained in the house at Glen Waverley for many years, before moving to an aged care facility where she passed away in 2005. I remember her both as a more practically minded and contented person than her sister Nancy. As the second daughter I suspect she was less subject to Ruth's misguided directions than her sister. Her completion both of the Leaving Certificate and her qualifying course to become a pharmacist reflected her strong determination to make her own decisions about her life.

Ruth and David's Latter Years

In his final year with the Department David reached what he probably considered to be his pinnacle as a public education figure when in 1954 he took on the roles as organiser and host of a visit to Newcastle Showgrounds by Queen Elizabeth II

David Drake hosts the Queen at Newcastle Showground. *Waterhouse Family Collection*

to meet thousands of local schoolchildren who had assembled in her honour. What then followed after his retirement was a popular public servant ritual of using his accumulated long service leave entitlements to fund a trip for Ruth and himself around the world. In 1955, leaving Sydney on the *Orsova*, the same vessel that later carried me to the United States in 1969, they first travelled to the American West Coast and then on to Pittsburgh to visit their daughter Margaret and her husband Bob. They then travelled on to continental Europe, where they accumulated a great many kitsch tourist souvenir items, including a cuckoo clock and slides of famous buildings and landscapes which fitted into a hand-held projector. In later years these became the preferred playthings of visiting grandchildren at Salamander Bay. However, the greater period of their time was taken visiting sites in the United Kingdom, especially those in Devon, Cornwall and Scotland which David considered to be his ancestral homes. As a small child in Gosford, I was excited to receive postcards from David, detailing what they had seen in precise schoolmaster's language and always asking me about my fishing successes.

On their return they moved to live full-time at Salamander Bay, David dividing his time between fishing, bowls and Rotary and Ruth focussing on bowls and the care of her latest budgerigar. Now that my family lived in Gosford, we had stopped our annual pilgrimage to Salamander, although we still made occasional short visits. Unexpectedly, Ruth died of a stroke in 1960. David continued to live alone in his beloved cottage for the next 15 years. Occasionally Susan and then Annabel visited him, bringing with them his great grandchildren. But as he grew older David became less and less physically capable. He was forced to give up bowls and fishing ceased to be an option when his boat *Susanna*, which was usually anchored in shallow water in front of the house, was swept away in a storm. Typical of his generation. David didn't make regular visits to a GP or dentist. Finally, he was forced to undergo dental treatment involving the extraction of several severely decayed teeth and an eye operation to remove cataracts. In 1975 he suffered a severe stroke and my parents moved him to an aged care facility in Lane Cove, near to their own home. In true David Drake fashion, he remained stoically cheerful and active too. He never missed the bus excursions to scenic places around Sydney and he kept abreast of what was happening in the world. I remember visiting him on one occasion when he expressed how glad he was that the War in Vietnam was coming to an end and expressed regrets that the US and its allies had ever intervened. He died, peacefully, on June 2 1976. He didn't carry on or revive the boat building dynasty but together with Ruth, Percy and Maude he co-founded a dynasty of teachers, that is now into its fourth generation.

Endnotes

1   *Sydney Morning Herald*, 14 September 1900

2   Ancestry, *NSW Public Service Lists,* 1925, Rebecca Drake

3   SRNSW, NRS 15320, *School Teachers Rolls, 1869–1908 and Teachers Career Cards* (Drake, David). In the following pages I have used this record to list all of Drake's Department of Education appointments

4   Ancestry, *Australian Marriage Index, 1788–1950.* The births are recorded in NSW Register of Births, Deaths and Marriages, with the exception of Ellora May. Her baptism is recorded in Ancestry, *Anglican Parish Registers, Balmain West 1875–1897* (17 October, 1883)

5   A copy of Susan's recollection of this story as told to her by her mother is in the Waterhouse family Collection

6   These assessments of David and Ruth are based on the recollections of Annabel Agafonoff and myself

7   *Manning River Times Advocate*, 28 May 1913; *Northern Star,* 17 November 1913; *Maitland Mercury*, 23 December 1916; *(Grafton) Daily Examiner,* 4 August 1919

8   The Drake family album contains photos of David as a member of the Rugby side during his schooldays at Fort Street. The same album contains an unsourced newspaper clipping featuring a photo of the foundation members of the Taree Golf Club, including Ruth and David

9   *Sydney Morning Herald*, 21 October 1916

10 Ancestry, *Australia Find a Grave Index*, Margaret Ruth Hosking

11 *Northern Star*, 29 February 1928

12 *Dungog Chronicle*, 9 August 1950

13 *Northern Star*, 9 July, 1928; *Mudgee Guardian*, 25 May 1939

14 *Mudgee Guardian*, 5 February, 1940

15 *Northern Star*, 13 September, 11 October, 1928, 19 March, 2 August, 7 November 1929,

16 *Tweed Daily*, 17 March 1932

17 *ibid*, 7 June 1933, 1 May, 26 October, 14 December 1934, 18 October 1935

18 *Northern Star*, 1 October 1928, 5 May 1932

19 *Tweed Daily*, 20 February 1935; *Mudgee Guardian,* 21 December 1936, 28 January 1938

20 *Manning River Times*, 13 July 1946

21 *Newcastle Sun*, 10 May 1948

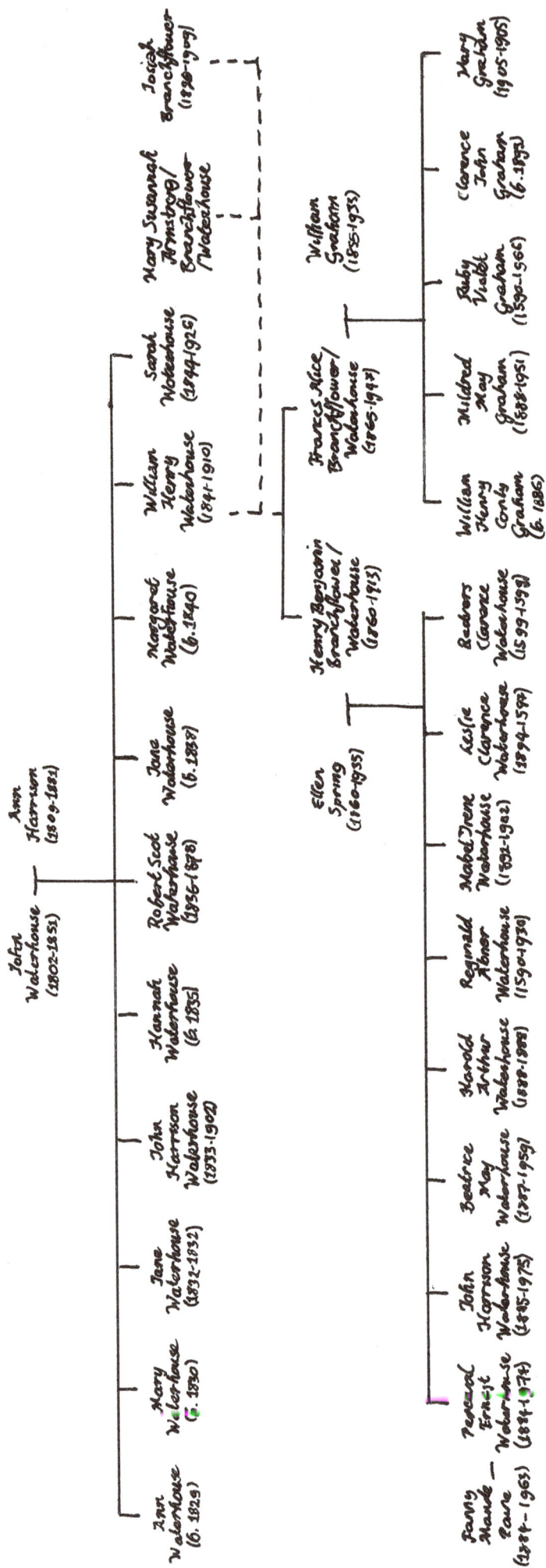

Family tree — Waterhouse

John Waterhouse (1802-1851) = Ann Harrison (1809-1881)

Josiah Brandtflower (1828-1909)

Mary Susannah Armstrong / Brandtflower / Waterhouse

William Graham (1855-1935)

Children of John Waterhouse & Ann Harrison:
- Ann Waterhouse (b. 1829)
- Mary Waterhouse (b. 1830)
- Jane Waterhouse (1832-1832)
- John Harrison Waterhouse (1833-1902)
- Hannah Waterhouse (b. 1835)
- Robert Scott Waterhouse (1836-1878)
- Jane Waterhouse (b. 1837)
- Margaret Waterhouse (b. 1840)
- William Henry Waterhouse (1841-1910)
- Sarah Waterhouse (1844-1926)

Henry Benjamin Brandtflower / Waterhouse (1860-1915)
Ellen Spring (1860-1935)
Frances Alice Brandtflower / Waterhouse (1865-1947)

Children:
- Percival Ernest Waterhouse (1884-1974) = Fanny Maude Rowe (1884-1965)
- John Harrison Waterhouse (1885-1975)
- Beatrice May Waterhouse (1887-1959)
- Harold Arthur Waterhouse (1889-1988)
- Reginald Elmer Waterhouse (1890-1970)
- Mabel Irene Waterhouse (1892-1982)
- Keife Clarence Waterhouse (1894-1994)
- Beatrice Clarence Waterhouse (1899-1998)

- William Henry Corns Graham (b. 1886)
- Mildred May Graham (1888-1951)
- Ruby Violet Graham (1890-1966)
- Clarence John Graham (b. 1895)
- Mary Gretton (1905-1905)

Chapter 10

Earle Waterhouse, the Schoolteacher who became a War Hero: and Nancy Drake, the Woman who wanted to be more than a Wife

From the Northern Rivers to the Big Smoke and Back Again: Earle's later educational adventures

Although he was dux of fourth year, Earle's high school career was not otherwise marked by academic distinction. On weekend visits home from Kempsey his attention was focussed on exploring the wetlands and emulating his father by learning to shoot ducks on the wing, that is, when they were in flight. At school he concentrated on sports, specifically cricket and rugby league, although he also appeared on stage with his sister Ella in a sketch called 'Smith's Unlucky Day', in a role in which he was required to smoke a cigar throughout the performance. A local press critic suggested that they both acquitted themselves 'remarkably well' but some morally minded students and teachers were outraged.[1] Earle achieved a pass in the Intermediate Certificate with commendable A results of in two subjects and Bs in another four. But in his final year his lack of effort and his poor performance concerned his parents to the extent that they feared he was likely to fail the Leaving Certificate outright and become a landless farm labourer. Stung by the comments of his Maths teacher who told him he was sure to fail Maths 1 and Maths 2, he put in a last minute effort and managed not only to pass the Leaving Certificate but to matriculate, by gaining Bs in five subjects.[2] This bare minimum level of matriculation was not sufficient to earn Earle

a University Bursary Scholarship, so rather than place a financial burden on his parents, involving payment of his University fees and his bed and board expenses, he chose to accept a scholarship to undertake a two year teachers' certificate qualification at Sydney Teachers' College. Not only were there no fees involved but he was paid an annual stipend of £50.[3]

Graduating from Teachers College at the end of 1927 Earle was appointed to teach Science at Granville Junior Technical High School. In 1928 he enrolled as an evening student in Economics at the University of Sydney. At first, because of the long distance he had to travel after school from Granville to Camperdown, he was often late for lectures. After persistent lobbying he eventually persuaded administrators in the Department of Education Head Office in Bridge Street, to transfer him to the more conveniently located Ashfield Junior Technical High School.

During the five years it took him to complete his degree he lived first in boarding houses in Glebe and subsequently in rooms he rented in private residences in Petersham and other inner west suburbs. His standard of living rose when he became a salaried teacher but fell again when public service pay was slashed during the Depression. Earle focussed hard on becoming a good teacher and apart from coaching school cricket and rugby league teams he also played on the wing for the Sydney University second grade league side. As

Earle Waterhouse in the early 1930s: teacher and University of Sydney evening student.
Waterhouse Family Collection

the product of the rural NSW public school system, he had grown up in a culture of rugby league. In contrast Rugby Union was played by private school educated boys who as young men became university college residents when they attended the University of Sydney. Unlike his sister, Earle never penetrated the University's more exclusive social circles. Instead, he attended the 'dress night' dances at the Palais Royal, a large ballroom at the Sydney Showgrounds. Of slight build with blue eyes and a strangely alluring half circle scar on his left cheek, he was a handsome man who had limited knowledge of city culture and people, and little experience of dealing with women, at least those outside his immediate family. He had grown up and lived in a world of outdoor recreational masculinity both in the Macleay and Sydney. To his embarrassment and chagrin, he was once thrown out of one of these dances for being drunk when in fact he was completely sober and simply carried away by high spirits and a lack of

knowledge of 1930s style 'cool' urban etiquette. He later claimed to be one of the 'neatest and smoothest dancers' at the Palais Royal although one also anxious to avoid being 'snared in matrimony'. He probably wanted to complete his degree and become more senior in his profession before getting married. But the number of young women who sought to ensnare him were probably fewer and the quality of his dancing less talented than he remembered more than fifty years later.[4]

At the beginning of 1933, with his degree completed, Earle received a telephone call from Head Office informing him of his appointment as a commerce teacher at Murwillumbah High School. From the time he was told of his appointment it took him nine hours to pack all of his belongings, with the exception of his books, and to board a Murwillumbah bound train at Sydney's Central Station. I think it's likely this was a sign that he was excited not only to be taking up a more senior teaching position but also to be returning 'home' to the familiar landscape of the northern rivers. Thirty years later, after a long residence in NSW country towns, Earle returned to Sydney where he spent the last 28 years of his life. But he loved the landscapes of rural Australia too much to ever become a fully city person and I always noticed that he seemed more comfortable with the people he associated with when he was on holidays in the Lower Macleay than he was in the Longueville community in Sydney. In 1987, chronically ill from emphysema he made a rare effort to attend an 80th birthday party of an old friend, and found enormous enjoyment in meeting a man who knew a large number of the boys and girls with whom Earle had attended high school.

At Murwillumbah High School Earle taught Economics, Book-Keeping, and Business Principles. He also led an active life outside school, joining the cricket, rugby league and tennis clubs. In addition, he completed his Bronze Medallion surf life-saving proficiency qualification, which could only be achieved through a surf-life-saving club. He probably belonged either to the Tweed Heads or Ballina surf life-saving club, travelling on weekends to Tweed Heads by bus, or to Ballina using the now closed railway branch line. In the

The glamour girl: Nancy Drake, the
Northern Rivers society belle.
Waterhouse Family Collection

year that he spent at Murwillumbah, which he later acknowledged as one of the happiest periods of his life, he also joined the dramatic society and appeared in a small role in a production of a romantic comedy set in The Netherlands, called *The Red Mill*. As I mentioned earlier, Nancy Drake, the shy sixteen-year-old daughter of the local Inspector of Schools, David Drake, and his wife Ruth was also an actor in this play.[5] In my family a story that was often repeated both by my father and my sisters was that Ruth strongly encouraged the development of a romantic relationship between her daughter and Earle. He was, after all, a handsome man with strong career prospects, for the number of teachers with university degrees was still quite small, and those who possessed this qualification were favoured for promotion. In any case, by the time he left Murwillumbah at the end of the year a romantic relationship had developed.

Earle was moved to Ballina Intermediate High School at the end of 1933 to teach Commerce and English. But that didn't mean the end of his courtship of Nancy because he made regular weekend trips to Murwillumbah to visit her. He concluded that the educational standards at Ballina were poor, which was something of an indictment of his future father-in-law, David Drake, formerly the school's headmaster. To improve results, he and other teachers conducted extra voluntary classes on Saturdays for Intermediate and Leaving Certificate students. The venture was an extraordinary success, with every eligible student choosing to attend and every one of them passing. His career prospects also received a boost when a long thesis he wrote to qualify for promotion to classification class 1 as a teacher was accepted. Just as in Murwillumbah Earle also led an active sporting and social life. He kept fit with daily swimming

The Newly Weds: Earle and Nancy c.1936
Waterhouse Family Collection

and running and on weekends played competitive golf, winning at least one competition. He also joined the local male voice choir and was an active member of the Anglican Church, serving as superintendent of the Sunday School.[6]

Earle's courtship proved successful, for his engagement to Nancy was announced in October 1935. But the following year the engaged couple had to deal with a long-distance relationship, when David Drake was moved from Murwillumbah to become Inspector of Schools at Mudgee. At first, David moved to his new posting alone, while Ruth and her daughters, Nancy and Margaret, lived in Sydney until suitable accommodation was found in Mudgee. In September Nancy returned to Sydney to buy her trousseau, and it was announced in the press that her marriage was to take place on December 19 at St Stephen's Church in Macquarie Street in Sydney. This church was one of the most exclusive wedding venues in the city and I suspect its announcement was an act of Drake family wishful thinking rather than reflecting a firm booking. Both Nancy and her mother Ruth had serious social ambitions and

pretensions that didn't match the reality of the family's social standing outside Murwillumbah and Mudgee. In any case, Nancy and Earle were married on December 19, 1936, but it was in the Mudgee Presbyterian Church, which was a more accurate reflection of the family's status and the Drake family's Scottish heritage.[7]

Earle often recalled that Ruth sought to dominate her daughter and influence her in ways he considered to be detrimental both to Nancy and himself. So, he was deeply disappointed when David Drake used his influence within the Department of Education to secure Earle's transfer from Ballina to Mudgee more or less at the same time that the marriage took place. It was reported that Nancy was 'elated by the transfer' but her feelings were not shared by her new husband who was perhaps also saddened to be leaving the familiar and much-loved northern rivers environment.[8] Mudgee is now a fast-growing rural town whose economy is driven by coal, wine and tourism. It has also emerged as a regional cultural hub. However, in 1937 it was a small town with an economy reliant on wool, merino studs and wheat. It was particularly known for the quality of its fine wool, with the local flocks known collectively as 'Mudgee blood'.[9] At the same time, the thirties was an era both of Depression and drought, which meant that the main rural staples, wool and wheat, declined in profitability, resulting in diminished economic contributions to towns like Mudgee. As the prices of these staples fell on foreign markets the burden of debt on Australian farmers rose by at least one fifth. Founded in the mid-nineteenth century, the wine industry also went through a lean period that extended well beyond the Depression era, with a number of the long-established winemakers shutting their doors. Indeed, for some years after the 1929 crash there were only two commercial wine producers in the district.[10]

In Mudgee they rented a new brick cottage furnished with items purchased from Sydney department stores, Bebarfalds in particular. These included lounge and dining room suites, grandfather hall clock and entrance table, and beds and wardrobes, all finished in the same dark varnish that was the dominant furniture colour of this era. Through the hard times of the Depression and War and the more prosperous times of the post War era this was the furniture that decorated their homes not only in Mudgee, but Dubbo, Grenfell, Orange, Gosford and Longueville. Occasionally,

there were modest additions of bookshelves and kitchen tables but they never replaced their entire furniture collection to match changing post War fashions. The hard times of the thirties and forties instilled a financial parsimoniousness in them that was to last both their lifetimes.

Endnotes

1   *Macleay Chronicle*, 6 May 1925; letter from Earle Waterhouse to his granddaughter, Ingrid Agafonoff, 19 May 1986. Ingrid asked Earle to write a letter about his life for a school project she was working on and while he wrote the letter he never sent it to her. I strongly suspect he kept it because he thought it would prove valuable to whoever delivered his obituary. In keeping with what I understood to be his wishes I relied on it in writing the address I delivered at his funeral. The letter is in the Waterhouse Family Collection.

2   Letter from Earle Waterhouse to Ingrid Agafonoff. A student needed to pass four subjects to achieve an overall pass in the Leaving Certificate. Matriculation, which was the qualification required for entry to university, required passes in a minimum of five subjects. All students who matriculated had the right to attend university. There were no student quotas at either university or individual faculty level.

3   *Macleay Chronicle*, 10 February 1926; letter to Ingrid; Earle Waterhouse, memoir letter, 4 June 1987

4   Letter to Ingrid; Katherine Brisbane, ed., *Entertaining Australia: an illustrated history*, Sydney: Currency Press, 1991, p. 181. He repeated the story of his ejection from the *Palais*

Royal to me on many occasions during both my childhood and adult years. He never lost his sense of moral outrage at being wrongly accused of drunken behaviour.

5   *Tweed Daily*, 31 August 1933; Letter to Ingrid

6   *Richmond River Herald*, 29 December 1933; *Tweed Daily*, 27 November 1934; *Northern Star*, 22 July 1935 *Daily Examiner*, 9 November 1935 Letter to Ingrid

7   *Tweed Daily*, 8 October 1935, 7 February 1936 18 September 1936; *Mudgee Guardian and North-Western Representative*, 3 December 1936

8   *Tweed Daily*, 2 February 1937. In later life Earle sometimes told me that Ruth had a controlling and negative influence on her daughter and that the move to Mudgee once again made Nancy subject to Ruth's attempts to promote her family members as socially exclusive, in short as small-town snobs

9   Godfrey Harris, *Mudgee*, Mudgee Guardian, 1960, no pagination

10   Julie McIntyre, *First Vintage: Wine in Colonial New South Wales*, Sydney: UNSW Press, 2012, p. 184; C. J. Connelly, *Mudgee a History of the Town*, Glebe: Fastbooks, 1993, p. 123

Chapter 11
The War Years

ARLE TAUGHT COMMERCIAL SUBJECTS as well as English at Mudgee High School. When they lived in the northern rivers the local press often reported on Nancy's social and Earle's sporting activities, but their public lives in Mudgee went virtually unrecorded, either because the local paper was less interested in everyday life in the town, or more likely because there were fewer social and cultural activities available here than in Murwillumbah and Ballina. However, in this period Earle coached one of the local boys' rugby league teams and indicated that he had aspirations to be a local public intellectual and political commentator when he delivered a lecture on 'The League of Nations and its Future' at the local Methodist Church.[1]

Earle Waterhouse, second from the left, as a member of the Mudgee Militia. *Waterhouse Family Collection*

But momentous events first in Europe and then in the Pacific were about to transform the world and even cause upheaval in the lives of a Mudgee schoolteacher and his young wife. During his time as a student at the Teachers' College, Earle had served in the Sydney University Regiment and in September 1939 with war threatening in Europe he joined the 20/19 Militia Battalion. Because of the colour of their uniform, these part time soldiers were referred to as 'chocolate soldiers' or by the abbreviated term 'chocos'. However, his career in the army was short and inglorious. Returning from military duty in early November 1939 Earle was sent home from school by the headmaster because he was obviously sick and exhausted. He was subsequently admitted to hospital with severe pneumonia and was unfit for work for a month.[2]

Earle was later discharged from the militia with the rank of private. Although this release was not formalised until June 1941, he had already enlisted in the RAAF Reserve in September 1940. He may not have met the army's physical stamina requirements but the RAAF placed more emphasis on intellectual skills and mental suitability. The number of those seeking to enlist in the RAAF was high but Earle drew on a mathematical knowledge that might have surprised his Kempsey High School Maths teacher to pass the entrance test for potential aircraft navigators. By September 1940

he had officially joined the RAAF, although he continued to teach at Mudgee High School while also studying mathematics and navigation from materials provided by the RAAF education office. In June 1941 he was called up for service, receiving his initial training at Bradfield Park, in the Sydney suburb of Lindfield, where he learnt mathematics, navigation and aerodynamics. This Initial Training School was intended to provide basic training for aircrew bound for Europe as part of the Empire Training Scheme, but the European War was not to be Earle's destiny. Instead, in September he was posted to the RAAF facility at Cootamundra to learn dead reckoning. In December he flew to Evans Head to study and practice bombing and air gunnery, and then completed his training at Parkes with a course in Astronomical Navigation. Throughout this period he made a series of entries in a small exercise book recording the meaning of signal pendants and very lights, navigation formulas, photographic, flare, compass, radio and astro procedures, and allied and enemy ship identification [3]

In April 1942 Earle qualified as a pilot officer and was assigned to 100 Squadron, which was flying Beaufort Bombers out of Richmond Air Force base near Sydney. This squadron was the first to receive Australian manufactured Beaufort Bomber aircraft. They were classed as medium

A Beaufort Bomber, probably the one in which Earle Waterhouse was a crew member.
Waterhouse Family Collection

bombers that could also be used for torpedo and dive bomb attacks and so fitted the requirements of anti-submarine patrol aircraft. While stationed at Richmond Earle flew on a number of training flights as well as anti-submarine patrols. In early May the squadron transferred to Queensland, where it was based at Mareeba, inland from Cairns. From there the squadron flew reconnaissance patrols in support of United States Navy convoys extending from Amberley RAAF base at Ipswich to as far north as New Guinea. In late June a detachment of 100 Squadron Beauforts, now based in Port Moresby, carried out a bombing raid against Japanese shipping. In September the whole squadron moved to Milne Bay and subsequently attacked Japanese targets both at sea and on land, bombing enemy facilities at Lae and Wewak and participating in the Battle of the Bismarck Sea.[4]

But Earle didn't move to New Guinea with the Squadron. Instead on July 13 he flew from Rockhampton to Richmond en route to the Base Torpedo Unit at Nowra, where until May, 1944, he was an instructor, with the role of teaching Beaufort crews how to engage in aerial attacks. This involved training aircrew in formation torpedo bombing attacks, radio procedures, radar reading, flare dropping and gunnery, which included firing at a drogue (target) dragged behind an aircraft. The training took place at Jervis Bay and surrounds, although the aircraft also occasionally flew anti-submarine patrols between Nowra and Evans Head. The course that Earle taught was not part of initial training but was designed to provide more specialised schooling for already experienced aircrew.[5]

There is no surviving written record explaining why he was chosen for this instruction role after one tour of duty. Perhaps his schoolteacher training provided him with communication skills that were effective in training aircrew. At the same time, he must have demonstrated high knowledge and skill levels as a Beaufort navigator to qualify him as an instructor not only in navigation but gunnery, bombing, flare dropping and formation flying. In his later role as the mine laying office for 76 Wing he was assessed as possessing a superior ability to

express himself, decisive, energetic and productive, and as a leader who was admired and trusted by the Catalina aircrew who flew the missions he planned. Surely it was these same attributes that led to his extended appointment at the Base Torpedo Unit at Nowra.[6]

But Nowra wasn't the safe sinecure that one might expect. Beauforts were difficult to fly, especially when loaded with torpedoes. Moreover, the training exercises required the crews to possess cool nerves and high skill levels, as they practiced flying in tight three plane formations to maximise the prospects of at least one torpedo hitting the target. Tragically there were training flights that resulted in accidents and deaths. For Earle such tragedies were made worse by the fact that they took place when 'the enemy was still far off'.[7] In the Waterhouse family collection there is a photograph of a clearly grief struck Earle leaving a grave in Nowra War Cemetery at the conclusion of the burial of a Beaufort crew. I remember us looking at that photo together sometime in the 1980s and him saying he wished it was never taken because it reminded him of a particularly tragic event, one that I could tell, still troubled him.

Earle Waterhouse leaving the funeral service for the Beaufort crew of A9–27, killed in a training/demonstration flight.
Waterhouse Family Collection

The accident occurred at Jervis Bay on April 14 1943 when three Beauforts were participating in an attack formation demonstration watched by war correspondents who were stationed on HMAS *Burra-Bra*. Led by Pilot Officer R.S Green in Beaufort A9–27 the three aircraft had completed their torpedo run and were pulling upwards into the sky when the pilot of A9–268, Flight Lieutenant David Dey, probably believing that the low flying planes were too close to the *Burra-Bra's* mast, moved to port (left) and as a result the wingtip of his aircraft struck the tailplane of A9–27. Both planes plunged into the sea and all crew members were killed. The wreckage of A9–268 was spread across several hundred yards of water, the bodies of the crew sank about 100 feet to the bottom of the Bay, and were not recovered. A burial at sea ceremony was held subsequently above the site where the accident took place. Aircraft A9–27 remained whole and sank in much shallower water, which allowed the bodies to be recovered and buried in the Nowra War Cemetery. A subsequent official investigation determined that Dey was primarily responsible for the accident, noting that he had a reputation for taking risks and that he lacked recent formation flying practice. It attributed a minor portion of the blame to Green for flying the formation too close to the *Burra-Bra*.

The accident was recorded by a newsreel camera and film of the tragic event can still be found on Youtube. During his previous tour of duty Earle had flown as the navigator on Beaufort A9–268 with pilot David Dey, and wireless operators and air gunners Jack Norman and Rex Solomon. It was this plane with the same crew, plus a new navigator, now stationed at Nowra for advanced torpedo training, that was one of the Beauforts involved in the accident. Earle later told his grandson, Stephen Oakley, that he was observing the flight demonstration from another aircraft at a much greater height, and his plane circled the area in a futile attempt to locate survivors. This account is confirmed by evidence given before the Investigating Officer. The cemetery burial photograph must relate not to Dey's but to Green's crew and now that I understand the full context of the accident it seems even more sadly poignant.[8]

Earle never forgot this event and related it on numerous occasions not only to me but to other family members as well. Although his version of the story varied as his memory faded, I doubt he ever came to terms with this tragic loss of life that took place in this period of his war service. As he acknowledged many years later, the fact that

Earle's 100 Squadron Beaufort Crew. He is on the left and the pilot, David Dey is next to him. Dey and the other two crew members all died in the training accident. *Waterhouse Family Collection*

the deaths occurred in a non-combat context made them seem much more futile and pointless. Nancy had moved from Mudgee to Bomaderry to be close to Earle when he was moved to Nowra and it seems that the Waterhouse and Dey families were on close terms. Sometime in late 1943 or early 1944, Dey's widow, Ruth, sent Nancy and Earle a photo of her infant child who was clearly born sometime after the accident. Perhaps Earle's sadness was deepened because not only did he feel his own sense of loss but he also witnessed the trauma experienced by Dey's widow.[9]

Promoted from pilot officer to flying officer in October 1942, Earle was promoted again, this time to Flight Lieutenant on April 2 1944. At the same time, he was also appointed as a Staff Officer with responsibility for mine-laying operations, attached to the RAAF Headquarters, North Western Area.[10]

RAAF Catalina Seaplanes had begun laying mines in 1943, while they also conducted anti-submarine patrols and flew supplies to coast watchers hidden on Japanese controlled islands. At first, Darwin was only used as a Catalina refuelling base because it was still vulnerable to Japanese attacks. So, Catalinas flew from Cairns to Darwin to refuel and from there moved on to their targets. However, beginning in May 1944, Earle was a member of an advance party that set up Catalina bases at Doctors Arm and East Arm

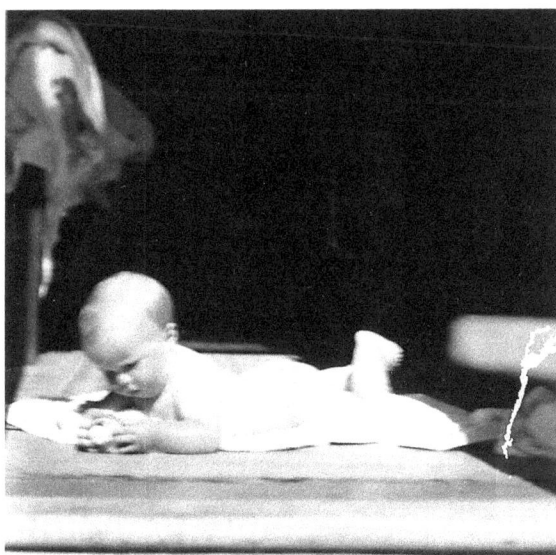

Susan Dey's 1944 'Christmas Card' to Earle and Nancy. *Waterhouse Family Collection*

in Darwin Harbour as well as Melville Bay on the Gove Peninsula. These three Catalina Squadrons were in fact seconded to the Commander of the 7th Fleet, United States Navy. In September this arrangement was made more formal with the movement of 76 Wing Headquarters to Darwin, while three Catalina squadrons-20, 42 and 43—were assigned exclusively to minelaying. Between May and August 1944 Catalinas operating from Shecat (Yampi Sound) and Melville Bay mined harbours and shipping lanes in the Dutch East Indies. In advance of those missions Earle flew in a Catalina from Darwin to Shecat and Melville Bay to brief the crews. The targets were identified by USN officers, but the missions were planned by the 76 Wing mine laying officer, Flight Lieutenant and subsequently (acting) Squadron Leader, Earle Waterhouse.[11] He also flew on at least some of these operations. More than 40 years later he recalled to his grandson Stephen Oakley that when the raids were carried out in daytime the Catalinas always approached the target with the rising or setting sun behind them to limit the vision and response capability of the Japanese anti-aircraft gunners.[12]

On June 26 1944 Earle navigated a Catalina skippered by S.L. Hurt, Squadron Leader of 43 Squadron, which led a torpedo strike mission on Japanese merchant shipping in Bima Harbour in the Dutch East Indies The torpedo was successfully dropped but Hurt was seriously injured when he was hit by flak. Earle pulled the pilot out of his seat '…and with great presence of mind and skill administered first aid.' He remained cool while staunching the flow of blood, and giving morphia, his actions in the words of the subsequent bravery citation '…undoubtedly saved the life of the captain…' In the meantime, the second pilot, B. A. Titsall managed to fly the damaged aircraft back to its Darwin base. For his bravery, coolness and resourcefulness Earle was subsequently awarded a Mention in Despatches bravery award. However, the post War official history of 43 Squadron, which included an account of the Bima torpedo strike mission, carried no acknowledgement of his role in saving the pilot's life.[13]

The missions flown by the Catalinas involving

Earle Waterhouse the Navigator.
Waterhouse Family Collection

mining harbours and sea lanes in the Philippines and Dutch West Indies were usually carried out at night and involved between two and six planes which flew below 1,000 feet en route to the target and up to 10,000 feet on the return flight. Soerabaya and Macassa were the harbours which were the object of the largest number of operations. Soerabaya was also the most heavily defended target for it was surrounded by more than 100 anti-aircraft guns and 15 searchlights.[14]

As the Japanese forces retreated, the distances that the Cats were required to fly were so long that they often needed to refuel at advance bases, which also served as briefing stations. So, in the later months of 1944 and through until August 1945 Earle not only briefed Catalina crews at Shecat and Melville Bay, but beginning in November 1944, he also flew to Moratai, Woendi and Jinamoc Islands, to instruct crews flying mine laying missions to Brunei Bay, the Balabac Straits and most significantly of all to Manila Harbour. Although most missions featured a small number of planes that sometimes needed to return to the target on subsequent nights, this last assignment was a complex operation involving Cats from 20

and 43 squadrons operating from Darwin, 42 squadron from Melville Bay, and a reserve squadron from Rathmines at Lake Macquarie in NSW.

The purpose of the Manila raid, part of the American campaign to capture the city, was to prevent Japanese ships entering or leaving the harbour by mining the entrance, in the process denying supplies of fuel to the Japanese aircraft stationed at Clark Field. With the American invasion of the Philippines imminent, there was a need for this task to be accomplished quickly and therefore in one mission.

According to Earle's later recollection intelligence calculations indicated that sixty percent of the Catalinas were likely to be lost on this raid but in fact only one plane failed to return. Earle later claimed that this aircraft attempted to return via the harbour entrance rather than following the briefing direction to fly over rising wooded land south of the harbour. Its wreckage was not located until 2019 when it was found near Cape Calavite at the north-western end of Mindoro Island. Earle flew on one of a group of Catalinas that left Darwin for Woendi Atoll on December 12. Here the crews were briefed, and then the planes moved on to Jinamoc Island in the Leyte Gulf the following day. On December 14 the aircraft were

ROYAL AUSTRALIAN AIR FORCE.

HONOURS AND AWARDS.

MENTION IN DESPATCHES.

FLIGHT LIEUTENANT EARLE WATERHOUSE. (412303)

CITATION:
                    Flight Lieutenant WATERHOUSE is the Area Mines and Torpedo
officer in North-Western Area.

                    On the 25th June,1944,he flew in a Catalina circraft of
No.43 G.R./F.B. Squadron on a torpedo mission against an enemy vessel
in Bima Harbour, Soembawa. During the attack, intense flak was
encountered and the captain of the aircraft received serious wounds.
Flight Lieutenant WATERHOUSE took charge of the seriously wounded
pilot and with great presence of mind and skill administered first
aid. He injected morphia,and succeeded in staunching the pilot's
wounds,from which he was losing a great amount of blood.

                    Flight lieutenant WATERHOUSE revealed outstanding coolness
and ingenuity in an emergency,and undoubtedly saved the life of the
captain of the aircraft.

                              (signed)

                                   Group Captain.
                           DIRECTOR OF PERSONAL SERVICES.

Mention in Despatches Awarded to Earle Waterhouse
for bravery over Bima Harbour.
Waterhouse Family Collection

serviced by RAAF technicians, mines were armed and the crews were briefed again. The aircraft were airborne by late afternoon and when they reached Manila Bay they made their minelaying runs on the required tracks and the mines were released at the prescribed intervals. It was a sign of the success of the mission that US intelligence later indicated that no shipping left or entered the port during or after the attack. Although Earle probably played a major role in the planning and briefing process, an American US Navy Mine Warfare Operations Officer based in Brisbane may also have participated in the preparations for the raid.[15] Following the capture of Manila, 43 Squadron participated in rescue flights from Manila to Jinamoc, carrying US civilians freed from Japanese internment camps. Many years later, when he saw television footage of American POWS just released from North Vietnamese prisoner of war camps, Earle was reminded of the emaciated and physically weak status of the former American prisoners whose transportation from prison camps to hospitals he had organised.

Between February and August 1945 Earle made flights from Darwin to Leyte, Labuan (DWI) and Jinamoc to plan assignments and brief RAAF Catalina crews conducting mine-laying missions in harbours at Amoy (Xiamen, China), Swatou (Shantou, China), Hong Kong, the Pescatores Islands (Penghu Islands, Taiwan Straits) and Taipei (Taiwan). Only one Catalina was lost in this time, although a total of 20 missions were flown. He also organised rescue flights for badly wounded American aircrew. On 29 July 1945 he received a mailgram (telegram) from the US Navy thanking him for organising a flight to take four seriously wounded American servicemen to hospital even though the rescuing RAAF aircraft was stationed twice as far away from the pick-up airfield as USAF planes. It was a sign of his key role in the 76 Wing mine laying and other operations that he was promoted to Acting Squadron Leader at the beginning of March 1945.[16]

Operating from the forward bases close to Japanese occupied territory was not without risk. The Catalinas were slow and cumbersome aircraft and there was always a likelihood of encountering Japanese fighters. Molokai, for example, was still in part occupied by Japanese forces at the time it was used for a forward re-fuelling and briefing base. The briefings were held in two stages. First, all crews participating in a mission gathered together to receive a general briefing relating to intelligence, navigation and meteorology. Second, each crew received an individual mining briefing from the mine-laying officer, Earle Waterhouse.

At some bases, when the Cats were ready to take off for the target, Earle rowed from plane to plane in a small dinghy, giving each crew last minute instructions. Some aircrew were superstitious enough to believe that it was critically important that he brief each crew in the same order before each mission. On one occasion, when he forgot to follow the accepted order, the crew of one Cat lamented to him that he had put them at great risk. But the crew survived the mission and 'House', as he was called by most of the Catalina crews, was forgiven.[17]

In planning the missions and briefing the crews that undertook them, Earle displayed high qualities of leadership, reflected in the fact that the crews not only 'relied upon and valued his instructions, but were also inspired by his abilities as a capable and versatile organiser. His senior officer also acknowledged that Earle had developed a method of minelaying that became standard practice in the Catalina Squadrons. Both the commanding officer of 76 Wing and the Senior Staff Officer of North West Area gave Earle much of the credit for the success of the Catalina minelaying operations and the second Mention in Despatches which he was belatedly awarded in 1946 gave an even greater acknowledgement of his contribution:

> He has shown organising ability of a high order, and the success of operations by units of No. 76 Wing against targets in China, Sumatra, Java and the Philipine (sic) Islands, and the fact that the casualties were so light have been largely due to his careful planning and attention to detail.[18]

And what specifically did these missions achieve? Well, an official RAAF account reported that they resulted in the sinking and damage of a significant number of ships, disrupted and delayed enemy vessels, forced the Japanese to divert valuable resources into minesweeping and salvage and led to the loss of valuable supplies of oil.[19] It is in this context that the praise of his commanding officers, and the second award of a Mention in Despatches, must be understood.

Unfortunately, those who have written about the Catalina minelaying missions, noting both their successful outcomes and the minimum loss of aircraft, have not sought to explore the role of planning and briefing in achieving such extraordinary success. Earle Waterhouse deserves better. However, I suppose it is also true that it wasn't until late in his life that Earle spoke or wrote about his major role in this whole enterprise. Although he died in 1988 even now his excessive modesty infuriates me.

It was the Vietnam War and all the moral issues that surrounded it that made me question why men and women volunteer to fight in wars. I remember that in about 1974 I asked Earle why he had joined the armed forces and then gratuitously added that I hoped he hadn't done it for the sake of 'King and Country'. At this stage of his life Earle was anxious to please, even including a self-righteous son, and so he answered that in a time when a Japanese invasion seemed a distinct possibility, he had decided to fight to protect his family. I don't think this answer fully explain Earle's motivation in 1939–41, for he was then living in a different world, one in which loyalty to Empire and King as well as country, was widely accepted. However, in a speech in Grenfell in 1949 proposing a toast in commemoration of Armistice Day, Earle spoke of the common purpose of Australian service personnel in World Wars 1 and 2 in defending freedom from want and fear, freedom of speech and worship. His implication, of course, was that Australia fought in both wars in defence of liberty and democracy. He acknowledged that the contemporary world was still mired in conflict but suggested that it was still a better place for the role that Australian armed forces personnel had played in 'shaping history'. And he emphasised his own belief in a simple version of the Digger Legend, one that focussed on the 'determination, courage and loyalty' embodied in the characters

Chart of Catalina Excursions in the Western Pacific. *Drawn by Ray Byfield. Reproduced courtesy of South Australian Aviation Museum.*

of his fellow comrades in arms. These qualities were not some genealogical inheritance from the Gallipoli generation but resulted from the shared experience of combat of service personnel in both wars.[20] These comments provide the best explanations I have found to explain why he enlisted and what he thought he had contributed in the context of Australia's overall war effort.

Unfortunately, the gratitude of the RAAF for Earle's major contribution to the minelaying success of the Catalinas was short-lived. When the atomic bombs were dropped on Hiroshima and Nagasaki, Earle was back in Darwin having recently returned from Labuan via Jinamoc. He was owed 120 days of leave on Squadron Leader's full pay. Presumably, because of his demonstrated leadership and organisational skills, he was offered permanency in the RAAF. As he later told me, he thought life in the RAAF in peacetime was likely to prove extremely repetitive and boring, so he declined the offer. Perhaps he was also influenced by the dysfunctional culture which emerged amongst the Catalina Squadrons with the coming of peace. At the time of his discharge and in the months that followed, poor leadership and a discharge process that was sometimes too fast, sometimes too slow and sometimes quite arbitrary, created an administrative 'shambles' and low morale amongst the members of Earle's former squadrons. The fatal crash of a Catalina en route to Manila further lowered spirits at a time when servicemen surely deserved to saviour their achievements and look forward to lives lived in peace.[21] I suspect that he also wanted to get back to school teaching, a profession to which he was devoted. When he decided to return to civilian life the RAAF discharged him from service in late September, not at his existing rank of Acting Squadron Leader, but as a Flight Lieutenant, and also cancelled his owed leave. After his release, Earle flew to Sydney, probably in a Black Cat that landed at the Rose Bay flying base, and was immediately manpowered to begin teaching at Homebush Boys High School. 'Lest We Forget' is a promise that those who served, both living and deceased, will never be forgotten, but Earle's treatment by the RAAF hierarchy in 1945 makes these words sound quite hollow.

In his 1949 Armistice Day address in Grenfell, Earle reminded his audience to remember not only those who served on the frontline but those who waited anxiously and with steadfastness for their loved ones to return. I suspect when he wrote and spoke those lines he had Nancy in the front of his mind. During the War she raised two small children on her own and moved regularly. Earle and Nancy's first child, Annabel, was born on December 10 1940 while they were living at Mudgee. When Earle left Mudgee to start

his more formal training in June 1941 Nancy remained there and a second daughter, Susan was born on March 17 of the following year at Broughton Private Hospital. Earle was given a short period of leave to visit Mudgee just before Susan's birth and he returned again briefly in June of the same year.[22] As I have indicated, Nancy and the two girls relocated to Bomaderry in 1943 to be closer to the Nowra based Earle. However, when he was posted to Darwin in May 1944 Nancy moved to a flat in Sydney's Cremorne. While living here Annabel remembers walking down to a park on the water on a path with bluebells growing on each side.[23] As the War drew to a close Nancy became eager for Earle's return and wrote to him, in Darwin, indicating that every time she looked across the Harbour and saw a Black Cat land at Rose Bay Seaplane Base, she hoped he was on board.[24]

By the end of the War Nancy and the two girls had left Sydney and as a result of pressure from her mother had moved to Newcastle to live with her parents at their Bar Beach home.[25] David and his wife Ruth had moved to the Hunter from Mudgee in 1940. Annabel remembers listening to her grandparents' radio and hearing news about the War. On the night the Japanese surrender was announced there was a fireworks' display celebration in Newcastle but Annabel must have missed the news that day because she became terrified, thinking that the Japanese were attacking the city.

Not long afterwards Annabel was playing in the front yard of her grandparents' house when a man in uniform carrying a kitbag over one shoulder, and a small round leather shoulder bag over the other, came through the gate. He emptied the contents of the shoulder bag, which consisted of a collection of shells from the islands that he had visited, on to the ground. Annabel wasn't sure who he was so she asked. He answered that he was her father. Shortly afterwards an intimate family photo was taken of Earle, Nancy and the two girls in that same front yard. On the one hand it portrays a happy and united family. On the other, Earle's drawn and lined face reflects years of trauma and intimates his personal post-War demons.[26]

Earle's Newcastle reunion with his family. *Waterhouse Family Collection*

Endnotes

1   *Mudgee Guardian*, 15 April, 16 July, 1937

2   SRNSW, NRS-3829-2-5/16984, Mudgee High School 1931–39; Letter to Ingrid; National Archives of Australia, (hereafter NAA) A9300, Waterhouse, Earle, War Service Record

3   NAA, Earle Waterhouse, War Service Record; untitled exercise book, used by Earle, to collect data during training, Waterhouse Family Collection

4   George Odgers, *Royal Australian Air Force, 1939–1942*, Official History of Australia in World War 2, Series 3, vol. 2, Canberra: Australian War Memorial, 1957, pp. 552–54

5   Waterhouse Family Collection, Earle Waterhouse, *Flying Log Book,* 16 August 1942–2 April 1944

6   Earle Waterhouse, *Service Record*

7   Earle Waterhouse, Letter to Ingrid

8   NAA, Series A705, 166/9/62, Dey, David George — Service Number 627-File Type-Casualty-Repatriation-Aircraft-Beaufort A9–268.' pp. 1–42 (The material includes evidence of eyewitnesses and a concluding assessment titled, *Statement by Investigating Officer*); Colin M. King, *Song of the Beauforts*, Keperra Queensland, no publisher, 2004, pp. 42, 281, lists Earle as crew of A9–268 in 1942, and records the other members of his crew as the three men who were later casualties of the 1943 crash. Earle not only flew with Dey during his tour of duty but also during his early months as an instructor at Nowra which suggests they knew each other extremely well; Richard Waterhouse, Interview with Stephen Oakley, 11 November 2022, Waterhouse Family Collection

9   The photograph of an infant child lying in the sunshine, with Ruth Dey's new year message directed to Earle and Nancy scrawled on the back, is in the Waterhouse Family Collection. Earle never showed it to me and I first located it hidden in a fold in the cardboard storage carton which held the family photographs in 2023.

10   Earle Waterhouse, letter to Ingrid

11   George Odgers, Australia in the War of 1939–1945, pp.359–64; Robert Cleworth and John Suter Linton, *RAAF Black cats; the secret history of the covert Catalina mine-laying operations to cripple Japan's war machine,* Crows Nest: Allen and Unwin, 2019, pp. 95–115; Earle Waterhouse, Flying Log Book; Earle Waterhouse, letter to Alex Agafonoff, 7 December 1976. I am grateful to my sister Annabel Agafonoff for providing me with a copy of this letter. At this time Earle's son-in-law, Alex was a member of the Executive Board of the Asian Development Bank and Earle and Nancy had recently visited their daughter Annabel and her family in Manila. Alex had subsequently written to Earle asking about his role in RAAF attacks on Japanese targets in the Philippines. The comments on his War Service Record by the Squadron Leader commanding 76 Wing, M. Robertson, and those by Air Commodore E. G. Knox-Knight indicate clearly that Earle planned the missions and briefed the air crews for 76 Wing mine laying expeditions.

12   Earle Waterhouse, Logbook, 16, 18, 22 June 1944; personal conversation with Stephen Oakley 11 November 2022

13   Earle Waterhouse, *Log Book*, 26 June 1944; Mention in Despatches Citation, Flight Lieutenant Earle Waterhouse (412303), original in Waterhouse Family Collection; RAAF Museum, *No. 43 Squadron, Royal Australian Air Force,* http//www.airforce.gov.au/raafmuseum/research/units/43sqn.htm, accessed 9 November 2022

14   NAA, Series A1196, Item ID 201657, *Mine Laying Operations of the RAAF Between 22 April 1943 and 31 July 1945*

15   Earle Waterhouse, *Letter to Alex Agafonoff.* His account of the Manila Raid is largely confirmed by Joseph Robert Cleworth, *The Night Shift*, Hill Top NSW: Macquarie University Lighthouse Press, 2015, pp, pp. 165–9. This book contains a very detailed account of the Catalina mine-laying operations. Unfortunately, it is a poorly organised book, which makes reading and accessing information difficult

16   Earle Waterhouse, *Letter to Ingrid*; Earle Waterhouse, *Log Book:* George Odgers, *Australia in the War of 1939–45,* Series 3 vol.2, p. 368; Captain W.C. Jennings, USNR, to Squadron Leader Earle Waterhouse, *Mailgram* , 29 June, 1945, Waterhouse Family Collection; Earle Waterhouse, War Service Record, comments by Squadron Leader Robertson and Air Commodore E. G. Knox-Knight

17   Cleworth and Linton, pp. 108–15; Earle told me the story of briefing aircrew by rowing from one Catalina to another just before take-off on a number of occasions in the later years of his life.

18   Earle Waterhouse, Mention in Despatches (1946), copy in Waterhouse family collection; Earle Waterhouse War Service Record, comments by Squadron Leader Robertson and Air Commodore E.G. Knox-Knight

19   NAA, Series A1196, Item ID 201657, *Report on Results of RAAF Minelaying Operations*

20   *Grenfell Record and Lachlan District Advertiser*, 31 October 1949

21   Flight Lieutenant J. Bellis to Earle Waterhouse, 9 November 1945, Waterhouse Family Papers

22   Mudgee Guardian, 5 March, 22 June 1942

23   Earle's first Mention in Despatches was mailed to Nancy at 75 Bennelong Street Cremorne. The nearest water side park is Primrose Park, Middle Harbour; for her Bomaderry address see Ancestry, *Electoral Roll, Eden-Monaro*; Annabel Agafonoff, personal communication with Richard Waterhouse, 11 February 2022

24   Two Letters, Nancy to Earle, undated but probably both written August/September 1945, Waterhouse Family Collection

25   ibid.

26   Annabel Agafonoff, personal communication with Richard Waterhouse, 29 May 2019

Chapter 12

Earle and Nancy's Return to Rural and (later) City Life

ARLE'S POSTING TO HOMEBUSH BOYS High was brief for in early 1946 he was promoted and at the same time sent to Dubbo High School as Commerce Master. I suspect that he was probably glad to leave Homebush High for he had found it difficult to adjust from instructing RAAF personnel to teaching teenage boys.[1] Dubbo was a modestly prosperous wheat town on the western plains, a town which also functioned as a service centre for large areas of rural north western NSW.[2] Nancy had enjoyed life in Sydney, despite the difficulties

Nancy with Annabel, Susan and Richard in Dubbo ca, 1947. *Waterhouse Family Collection*

associated with raising two small children on her own. She had expectations that she and Earle would live in Sydney after the War and she had already envisioned renting a flat with Sydney Harbour views.[3] She was reluctant to move back to a rural town and family lore records that at first she resisted the move. Her resentment towards Earle for this relocation, even though it was not a decision over which he had control, marked the beginnings of a strain in the marital relationship which widened in subsequent years. In any case Earle found that the School faced low morale amongst the teachers, poor standards and results and, like many public schools in this era, difficult financial circumstances. At this time, he felt he had lived another life for five years and that he now had the opportunity to make up for those years of lost civilian time. When he looked back on his life in Dubbo he thought that he had achieved success in returning to normal family and work life. He made good friends, worked hard as a teacher, abandoned golf for bowls, and received (with Nancy) a post war reparation in the form of a son, for I was born on November 20 1946.[4]

This was also a period of drought in rural NSW. Annabel remembers how hot it was and how she and Susan cooled down by running under the garden hose and bathing in the Macquarie River. Plagues of grasshoppers were common. As I explain below the returned Squadron Leader maintained a distant and severe manner, but he endeared himself to his two daughters by following

Percy's example and reading them bedtime stories from Greek and Roman mythology. He also sang Stephen Foster minstrel songs to them. These songs had soothing bedtime melodies although I'm sure they found the words, which caricatured the lives of African-American slaves, alien and bewildering.[5] The house was modest, although it possessed an air-raid shelter in the backyard, which the girls viewed as a forbidden cubby house.

Unfortunately, Nancy left little record of her activities and thoughts about life in Dubbo, Grenfell or Orange. She later told Annabel that when Earle returned to his family he sought to 'manage' it along the lines that he had organised RAAF aircrews. My own childhood memories, which begin with Grenfell, confirm that he continued to do this at least until the time that he was hospitalised in the mid 1950s. There was an emphasis on punctuality as well as tidiness both in the house and in dress and grooming. He woke early every morning and then made and brought a cup of tea to every family member, with strict

instructions not to spill. He polished the children's shoes as well as checking the family car oil level and tyre pressures on a daily basis. Dinner was a formal affair with Earle issuing regular instructions relating to the proper use of cutlery and the need for us all to eat everything on our plates. Throughout their marriage, Earle and Nancy's roles within the family were fixed and traditional. Nancy cooked, cleaned and looked after the children and Earle earned a salary, cultivated the garden, repaired broken household items, and engaged in recreational sporting activities on Saturday afternoons. His only 'inside' household duty was the washing up after every evening meal, with Annabel and Susan assuming 'drying up' duties once they were considered old enough.

In 1948 Earle was appointed Headmaster of Grenfell Intermediate High School which taught classes from kindergarten through to the Leaving Certificate. Apparently, he was chosen for this role, at least in part, because of his reputation as a stern leader. The headmaster he replaced,

Earle, centre front, and teaching staff of Grenfell Intermediate School. *Waterhouse Family Collection*

and some of the teachers, were alcoholics and it was Earle's task to have them removed from the Education Department. The school facilities were primitive, indicated by Annabel's fifth class room which was a portable structure with fly screens but no glass in the windows. It was bitterly cold when it snowed and when it rained the water came through the mesh.[6]

A modestly prosperous town that relied on wool and more especially wheat, Grenfell was also a town divided by class and religion. There were schoolyard brawls between Catholics and Protestants and I remember that when I was still a pre-schooler and often played in our front yard, the Catholic kids from across the road sometimes lobbed stones at me. Annabel was also teased both because she was the headmaster's daughter and because of her middle-class manners and accent.

The house we rented was small and, because it was built of fibro, cold in winter. However, Earle was very proud of the fact that it possessed sewerage. The girls shared a room and I slept on the veranda. It had walls that extended less than half way to the ceiling with the gap filled by flyscreens, so in winter I was given a hot water bottle, although my mother always claimed it back for herself when she went to bed.

In Grenfell Earle continued to play bowls and joined the local Rotary Club. He also revived a Belmore River tradition of hunting game to provide meat for the family table. Ducks were not prevalent in the Grenfell region so he took to shooting rabbits instead. On Saturday afternoons the family bundled into the car and Earle drove out to whichever rural property he had secured access. Usually, he shot several rabbits which he then skinned by hanging them on the backyard paling fence, stripping off their fur and cutting open their entrails. The rabbits were then baked in our wood fired oven, which had minimal temperature controls, so the rabbits were rarely evenly cooked. I can still remember the awful smell that exudes from rabbits when their guts are removed and the tough, dry taste of overcooked wild bunny. I dreaded those Saturday night meals.

But there were activities to enjoy in Grenfell, activities that later passed into pleasant family memories. Most Saturdays Annabel and Susan attended the Grenfell cinema and once, when I was about four, I was also allowed to go with them, only to be frightened by my first film and my first Western. I also became friendly with a one-armed Council gardener with a hook on the stump of his arm, who was probably a World War 1 veteran. I followed him around when he tended the Council gardens and once, with my parent's consent, he took me home to lunch. His wife cooked a two-course lunch in honour of the four-year old son of the school's headmaster.

The major family event of the year was our annual two-week holiday at Salamander Bay. With three children packed into the back seat of an eight horsepower Ford Anglia sedan, later marginally upgraded to a ten horsepower Ford Prefect, the family set out from Grenfell at about 5am on an early January morning each year. As I have recorded above, we always stopped at Glenbrook for the night to visit Percy and Maude, before departing for Port Stephens at about mid-morning on the following day. Even then there were ways to circumnavigate Sydney via Parramatta and Hornsby but my father insisted on driving into the City along Parramatta Road and then turning left at Central to follow the road over the Harbour Bridge and then join the Pacific Highway leading to Newcastle. I think he took the route in part because he wanted to catch glimpses of the University of Sydney, which is, of course, located on Parramatta Road. I really loved the last part of the journey, particularly the trip over the newly opened Hawkesbury River Bridge and also the ride across the Hunter River from Hunter Street to Stockton on a punt which held both cars and people. The Hunter and the Hawkesbury seemed such vast stretches of water to a boy from Grenfell and Orange.

In any case the prime activities at Salamander Bay were swimming and fishing. On mornings when the tide was high my sisters and I swam in the zone between the beach and oyster racks. We were forbidden to go further out because our parents feared sharks lurked in the deeper water, and the long weeds that grew on the bottom of the water outside the racks sheltered stingrays

Salamander Bay in the 1950s. *Waterhouse Family Collection*

My grandparent's house at Salamander. Ruth is at the window.

and other forms of dangerous 'flappers'. On those mornings when the tide was low, we made sand castles, while waiting for it to rush in and overwhelm them.

My grandfather owned a large 5 metre (approximately) long wooden clinker-built boat with a one-cylinder motor, which was started with a hand crank and stopped by preventing the cylinder from moving up and down by holding it down with a gaff. Called the *Susanna*, after my two sisters, it usually rode at anchor in the shallow water between the beach and oyster racks, although in

Tide's Out! David Drake and his boat

the winter it was hauled by winch along two rails which ran from the water into the garage.

The afternoons were often spent gathering worm and nipper (yabby) bait by extracting them from the short weed that was exposed at low tide. We trod in the weed to force the nippers out of their burrows and used pitchforks to extricate worms from their deeper hiding places. Both these practices are now outlawed as damaging to the environment and a threat to the survival of important fish food sources. Early most mornings my grandfather, father and sometimes our reluctant uncle, Bob Hosking, who were referred to collectively as 'The Men', set out in the *Susanna* to motor across to fish the sandbanks and oyster leases on the other side of Port Stephens. Usually, they returned with at least one sugarbag full of bream, flounder, flathead and especially whiting. The catch was then cleaned at a fishing table, which was simply a tree stump dug into the beach. By the time I was seven or so my father and grandfather decided I was old enough to scale and clean the catch, particularly on days when they returned home late and were in a hurry to change and head to Nelson Bay to play bowls. Frankly, I was daunted by the task, especially when there

were large numbers of fish to scale and gut, and my father usually had to redo the scaling and cleaning when he returned from bowls. Eventually I learned to be good at this task, although when I reflect, I can't imagine ever asking any of my children when they were seven or so to scale and gut fish with a sharp knife.,

On days when the men didn't fish together my father took my sisters and myself fishing, although these expeditions only extended to the sandbanks a few hundred metres off Salamander Bay. We didn't catch a lot of fish, usually only a few barely legal sized whiting. However, on one occasion my father took us several kilometres out into the middle of Port Stephens where the wreck of a small ship lay on the bottom of about 20 metres of water. It was a famous mulloway fishing spot. At first, we had no luck but then something very large took the bait on Susan's handline. It was too strong for her to handle and so Earle played the fish for about 10 minutes before getting to the surface what turned out to be a large grey nurse shark. This caused panic in the boat because we feared that if our father brought it on board, it would surely bite us. Instead, he calmly cut the line and the shark swam away. We know now that grey nurse sharks are harmless but in the 1950s, they were still seen as deadly predators.

This experience didn't diminish my growing love of fishing but rather made it seen even more entrancing and exciting. Joining my father fishing at Salamander Bay also deepened my sense of him as a charismatic and highly competent authority figure. But I am not sure that my sisters were quite so enamoured of this masculinist fishing culture because it seemed to be organised for the convenience of men and boys. Many years later my sister Susan complained to me that there was always an empty bottle on board for men and boys to go forward and pee into but the women and girls simply had to 'hold on.'

Our diet on these holidays consisted almost exclusively of fish fried in butter and oil with sides of mashed potato and slices of white bread with lashings of butter, the latter as a precaution in case anyone found a fishbone stuck in their throat. Eating bread and butter was considered effective in dislodging these bones.

There was no electricity at Salamander Bay so everything was cooked on small, gas stoves, lighting was courtesy of ('tilly') lanterns powered by methylated spirits or kerosene, and the refrigerator was kept cold by daily delivered ice. At night we read in bed and turned in early, although on those early evenings when it was half-tide, we waded amongst the oyster racks carrying lanterns and landing nets which we used to attract and net blue swimmer crabs.

Around Easter in 1969 I was preparing to spend the next four years of my life in the United States when I was struck by an unexpected wave of nostalgia for my boyhood holidays at Salamander Bay. As a twenty two year old student focussed on my studies I didn't spend much leisure time with Earle so when I suggested a trip to Salamander Bay to visit 'Da' Drake and go fishing with him he was both surprised and delighted. So, for the last time I found myself sleeping in the backroom and then seated at the front of the *Susanna* as we motored across Port Stephens to the whiting grounds on the Tea Gardens side of the estuary. In keeping with tradition, we caught a large number of fish, and once again I scaled and gutted them,

while David and Earle headed for bowls at Nelson Bay. Only now do I realise that on this day, aged 22, I was finally accepted by Earle and David as one of 'The Men'.

Beginning in the 1970s most of the modest fibro and wooden houses that lined the beachfront at Salamander were replaced with luxurious two storey holiday dwellings. At the same time much of the wetland on the western side of the road that ran from Salamander to Soldiers Point was filled in to allow the construction of shopping centres and housing estates. On a recent holiday trip with Grace in 2023 I discovered to my great surprise and even greater delight that my grandparents' house has somehow managed to survive the redevelopment of Salamander over the past fifty years. Renovated, and boasting a new front deck the rectangular structure now features as the front section of a large two-storey house which is built behind it. The fact that it is integrated into an attractive modern dwelling hopefully guarantees its future survival, a rare example of what the original Salamander 'shacks' looked like.

The annual trips to Salamander Bay continued through our three years living at Grenfell and three further years at Orange. As I discuss in more detail below, we moved to Orange when my father became an Inspector of Schools, which meant he also had to attend the annual Inspectors' Conference at Department of Education Headquarters in Sydney. Now, at the end of our Port Stephens holidays, we drove to Sydney and stayed either with Nancy's Aunt Blanche and Uncle Jack at Balmain or in a guest house on the lower north shore. Nancy enjoyed the trip to Sydney because she could return to her old wartime haunts, especially David Jones, with its women's clothing store and upmarket teashop and cafeteria. Annabel loved visiting Sydney because she had already fallen in love with art and always lobbied to visit the Art Gallery of NSW. I was excited too, because I was taken on excursions both to Taronga Park Zoo and the wonderfully old-fashioned and stuffy Australian Museum. While our parents had their own agendas on our Sydney trips it was our Great Uncle Jack who accompanied us on our gallery and museum excursions. I think he enjoyed it because Blanche and he had no children of their own and so we served as brief substitutes. A man of limited education and strong Protestant prejudices he was less a cultural guide than a benevolent child-minder.

After two years in Grenfell Earle was rewarded for his service in forcing the heavy drinking members of staff out of the Education Department with a promotion to the position of Inspector of Schools. Normally, Secondary School Staff who were elevated to this status became Secondary Inspectors of particular subjects. However, Earle was made a Primary Schools Inspector with responsibility for all primary school staff in his assigned district. For the first few months of 1951 he was a relieving Inspector for the Hurstville-Kogarah Inspectorate and then was transferred for the rest of the year to another acting position which encompassed the Bathurst-Orange area.

During this year Nancy remained in Grenfell, this time with three children to look after. For some of the time she had access to the car because Earle didn't always need it. She was an extremely nervous driver and when the car was in motion children in the back seat were ordered to keep their heads down so she had a complete view through the rear mirror. Nor could we talk because she believed that distracted her. Even at the age of four I found Nancy's driving a nerve-wracking experience. Occasionally, she drove us out into the country for picnics and once the engine overheated. Several passing cars stopped to help and one man ran over to a nearby dam and filled his hat with water to replenish the radiator. In later years when the marital relationship had worsened Nancy recalled this period with some bitterness and accused Earle of abandoning both her and the children. The kindness of neighbours and strangers, which I still recall, and which the example above illustrates, were insufficient compensation for her.

In 1952 Earle's role as relieving Inspector for the Bathurst-Orange area was confirmed as a continuing position and as a result the family moved to Orange. Because they expected regular transfers to new school districts my parents always rented rather than purchased houses in the rural towns in which we lived. The house we moved to, at 30 Kite Street, was the most substantial of all the dwellings in which we lived during our family's country town era. It was a solid brick federation house with three bedrooms, one for our parents, one for Annabel and Susan, and for the first time, one for me. However, it lacked modern gas and electrical appliances, which meant that Nancy washed clothes in a copper and cooked on a primitive gas stove. Apart from a coke burning fire in the dining room, it also lacked any form of heating. In winter we always felt cold and were perpetually plagued with chilblains. The house was located directly opposite Cook Park, featuring gardens planned and planted in European style, complete with deciduous trees, fern house, sunken rose garden and a duck pond. I came to view it as my own personal backyard, and played there nearly every day

Orange was a prosperous rural town, featuring substantial public buildings and solid brick houses. In the mid-nineteenth century, its economy was given an initial stimulus from servicing the miners who flocked to the goldfields at Ophir (Summer Hill Creek), the site of Hargreaves' discovery of the metal in 1850. But the town subsequently became more dependent on sheep raising for wool and meat, as well as fruit and vegetable growing on Canoblas Mountain — apples, cherries, pears. stone fruit, peas and potatoes. My sisters cycled out from the town to the surrounding orchards each summer to earn pocket money picking cherries. The Cherry Blossom Parade down Summer Street was an important event, held every Spring, and attended by large crowds.

Annabel attended the last year of primary and the first two years of high school at Orange. The high school, in particular, was a fine educational institution which ran outstanding programs in debates and music. Unlike Grenfell, she felt at home here. In Grenfell Annabel had discovered a love of painting and became so good at it that in 1951, aged 11, she won first prize in the junior section of the Commonwealth Jubilee Art Competition. In Orange, she maintained her passion for painting and we often made weekend excursions to the surrounding countryside so she could paint landscapes en plain air.[7]

Annabel, Susan and Richard in Orange. I am wearing the shorts with the flap for a fly made by my grandmother Maude

Although the three children developed different recreational tastes we shared a devotion to *The Argonauts,* an ABC children's radio program featuring serials, educational segments, music and competitions. Annabel performed so well in the competitions that she was awarded several books as prizes whereas I failed to accumulate any book prize points at all.

As in Grenfell, Annabel and Susan shared a bedroom. Susan's personality could sometimes be volatile and I remember she often became emotional about people, causes and animals she cared about. The three of us attended Sunday School at the local Presbyterian Church at the insistence of my mother who was not at all religious but seems to have felt obliged to genuflect to her Scottish heritage. Neither Annabel nor I liked it very much, in her case because she was not naturally inclined towards Presbyterian Christianity, and in mine because it just seemed too much like an extra day at school. For me Sunday was a day

to catch freshwater yabbies in the local creek and enjoy the playground equipment in Cook Park. But it inspired Susan to become very religious and she enthusiastically embraced Sunday School projects and homework. She took most pride in making a cross out of butterflies, which were pinned to felt in a display box with a glass top. Her engagement with Christianity proved, despite a brief late teen interruption, to be a life-long devotion.

I have very few memories of Nancy in Orange. And it troubles me that apart from remembering her carrying out household duties I cannot recall what recreations and social activities she pursued, apart from joining occasional Saturday night family outings to the cinema. She also enjoyed weekend drives to the countryside, although when a picnic lunch was not included, she remained in the car while Annabel painted or Earle hunted.

Earle had engaged with the Anglican Church both in his boyhood and during his early years as a teacher in the northern rivers. In Orange he often put on his suit on Sunday mornings and took himself off alone to the local Church of England. As I found out later, when I heard him recite sections of the Old Testament off by heart, he was extremely familiar with the Bible, but his Christian belief was a highly personal faith, which he didn't share or ever try to proselytise. The essence of it always remained a mystery to me. He also loved the Australian natural environment, although his care for the country around Orange was probably not as deep as his affection for the familiar river valleys of his earlier life. Still, he hunted rabbits on the sheep properties of friendly graziers and he also delighted in taking me to watch sheep shearing each spring. There was an atmosphere of excitement and industry in the woolsheds we visited that I found enthralling and indeed unforgettable. Some fifty years later those memories, at least in part, served to inspire me to write a book about the history of rural Australia.

Although it was not nearly so apparent as it later became, I think his wartime experiences also haunted him. I vividly recall walking along Summer Street with him in what must have been 1953 and he told me that the UN and opposing forces had signed an armistice to end the three-year old conflict in Korea. Even at the age of (almost) seven I thought it odd that he seemed so relieved that such a far-away war had ended but I guess his empathy with those who had suffered from the effects of combat was a continuing emotion.

The high-level organisational skills he had demonstrated in the RAAF were also in evidence in his role as a primary school Inspector. His most high profile undertaking during his Bathurst-Orange tenure was organising the large assembly of all school children in his district at the Bathurst Showground at a ceremony attended by Queen Elizabeth II on February 12 1954. I was one of those children and remember that we rehearsed a short dance that was performed in her honour. We had to stand for what seemed like hours waiting for Her Majesty to arrive and then listen to what seemed like endless speeches from local dignitaries. I can't recall a word that was spoken although I am sure those speeches were suitably obsequious. The students from Orange Infants School were located too far from the dais for us to catch any kind of decent view of the monarch. In any case we were too short to see over the hundreds of other students between us and the official party. However, at the end of the ceremony the Queen drove up and down the cleared spaces between the various school groups and I caught a glimpse of the Queen and the Duke of Edinburgh in the back of an open Land Rover as they passed my school group.

Earle received only a modest acknowledgement for his central role in organising the Queen's Bathurst visit. Although in its account of the occasion the *Mudgee Guardian* recalled that Earle was a former resident of the town and praised his mustering of the children as 'excellently done', contemporary photographs reveal that despite his central contribution he was not included with the official party on the dais.[8]

In 1955 Earle was moved to the inspectorate of Gosford, an area which extended from the Hawkesbury to the northernmost tip of Lake Munmorah. The Central Coast is now classified as Outer Metropolitan and about 35% of its workforce commute to Sydney by train or car. But at this time, it consisted of a set of mostly coastal villages

Gosford Show ca. 1955: Richard, Nancy and Earle are all smiles but friction was already building between my parents. *Waterhouse Family Collection*

together with two modestly sized towns, Wyong and Gosford. The economy depended heavily on citrus growing, reflected in the fact that the co-operative sorting and packing warehouse was located on Gosford's main street. When tourism first flourished here most visitors were accommodated in guesthouses at places like Woy Woy and The Entrance. But in the 1950s the majority of holiday visitors were caravaners and campers who parked their vans and set up their tents not only in the year-round camping grounds but also in Council reserves at places like Terrigal which were only opened for camping at Christmas and Easter. These holiday makers provided a stimulus to the local economy, but caravaners and campers were not big spenders and so the economic impact was limited. Tourism and citrus growing did not provide the level of prosperity that pastoralism and agriculture generated for the Orange community. So, Gosford was a town featuring modest public buildings and private dwellings, and the prospects of 'getting on' were limited. There was a popular local saying at this time that reflected the limited economic opportunities offered by the town and indeed the area as a whole: 'If you want a job go to Gosford. If you want a career, go to Sydney'.

In a sense the Central Coast must have seemed like familiar territory to my parents, although its beaches lack the length and wildness of those on the north coast and Brisbane Water does not match the majesty of the Richmond or the Macleay. However, Earle was probably determined to recreate, at least in part, the lifestyle he had known in the Macleay, Richmond and Tweed Valleys. After renting so often Nancy and he made their first purchase of a house, an extremely modest two-bedroom fibro cottage built on an enormous block that stretched from Albany Street in Point Frederick (Gosford) all the way down to Brisbane Water. The facilities, to say the least, were very basic, with Nancy once again forced to wash the family clothes in a copper. With no sewerage my parents installed a septic system with a pan that revolved when the lid was opened and closed. It came to be known as 'the chocolate wheel'. The two girls again shared a bedroom while my bed was located in a corner of the sunroom, which extended across two thirds of the back of the house. It had great water views but provided little privacy because the sun room was the most used recreational area in the house.

Earle's work life was extremely demanding, for it included managing a large number of schools over a wide geographical area. Those located in areas of disadvantage, including settlements both on the Hawkesbury and Tuggerah Lakes, posed challenges for Earle and the teachers who staffed them. Parents sometimes viewed young male teachers as suitable marriage partners for their daughters, even when their offspring were only fifteen or less. And sometimes the teachers were tempted. Earle's solution was to organise the transfer of vulnerable and weak-willed teachers to schools far from the Central Coast. He also was required to manage schools with particular educational needs, such as the one at Peat Island which catered to boys with physical and mental disabilities. Another important task he faced was

determining where new schools needed to be built or old schools expanded to meet the demands created by growing populations in some areas of the Central Coast. Here his greatest achievement was in securing the building of a separate complex ('The Annex') to house all first year (now called Year 7) students attending Gosford High School. Subsequently, this complex was expanded to house a second high school in Gosford, Henry Kendall High School

Nancy became more socially active in Gosford. She joined a tennis group that played on a private court, and which provided her with access to a fairly large social circle, consisting of professional and business families. Earle had served on the Board of Grenfell Rotary Club and he now joined Gosford Rotary, a conservative club dominated by Mann Street businessmen, most of whom were ex-servicemen. He also joined Legacy, for which he worked tirelessly, both from his understanding of the need to provide for the wives and children of deceased servicemen, and perhaps also from a sense of guilt that he had survived the War while some of his closest RAAF comrades had not. In any case, my parents often held card parties on Saturday nights, inviting the men and women they had met through tennis, Rotary and Legacy. The women sipped sherry and the men drank Toohey's Flag Ale, a really sweet beer that my father preferred. Occasionally they entertained themselves with piano accompanied sing-alongs, focussing on a repertoire of sentimental songs, many dating back to the Victorian era. In retrospect such a cultural ritual, both in its form and content, seems rather anachronistic in a post war world of records, radio, and rock and roll. But I suppose it also reflects the reality that this vibrant new musical popular culture appealed to and was claimed by the rising generation, teenagers unmarked by Depression or War.

Earle also became a more dedicated bowls player, competing not just in social games but also skippering a fours team in inter-club Pennant competition. But his main recreation became fishing. When my family bought their house it came with a boat house consisting of a casuarina timber frame and sheet iron walls and roof, which sheltered a small clinker built rowing boat. Earle repaired the rotten sections of the boathouse framework, replaced the missing pieces of sheet iron and caulked the gaps in the boat timbers so the vessel didn't leak. Once he secured permission from the neighbours to moor the boat at their jetty the shed was only used to house the vessel when it needed its bottom cleaned and painted.

Almost every week day afternoon after work, except in Winter, Earle rowed the boat 30 strokes out from the jetty, cast out the anchor and then fished for crabs, bream, flathead, whiting and flounder. He still scorned fishing rods and used a light handline which was wrapped around a small olive oil bottle He didn't catch fish in anything like the numbers we had at Salamander but he usually brought home enough for fish and crab dinners once or twice a week. But in a way, as I only realised some forty years later, catching fish was really not what mattered. For him sitting out on the water, was a time of peace and reflection, where he could try to forget about the stress of his work and vanquish those wartime memories. Sometimes, I was allowed to join him and even bring my homemade bamboo rod, to which I had attached reel and eyelets with electrical tape. Mostly, I caught small tailor, which he then used as live bait to attract flathead. But what entranced me about these trips was that after some pleading, and while we waited for the fish to bite, he told me tales of fishing and hunting in the Lower Macleay. His boyhood seemed so much more exciting than mine, and I suppose it was.

Annabel and Susan both completed the Intermediate and Leaving Certificates at Gosford High School. It is now an elite, selective school but in her time there Annabel found that it lacked the cultural activities that marked Orange High School in the form of debating and play nights, and musical concerts.[9] Instead, there was a strong focus on sports, especially the state wide University Shield Rugby League knockout competition. On those Saturday afternoons when Gosford High hosted visiting high school teams, Gosford's main sporting field, Graham Park, was packed with spectators.

In Murwillumbah Nancy had left school at

15 not to work, but to pursue a social life involving dances, charity events and performances with the local amateur dramatic society. Her mother required her always to be glamorously dressed and groomed. In Gosford she sought to make Annabel replicate the activities that her mother had wanted her to perform. She chose Annabel's clothes and insisted that she enter the Miss Gosford competition organised by the *Gosford Times*. Annabel found this extremely oppressive and painful both because she was shy and in any case, she was much more interested in securing the qualifications that would allow her to pursue a tertiary education.[10]

When they were in high school a sibling rivalry also developed between Annabel and Susan. Annabel played hockey but Susan, despite the fact that she was short and lightly framed, played with a fierce intensity that intimidated her opponents. Annabel endured the Miss Gosford competition but Susan acted as if she thought it was fun. Annabel was elected School Girl's Vice-Captain but Susan subsequently became Girl's Captain. Annabel believed that Susan tried to do better than her 'in everything'.[11]

If there was one thing that the family shared it was a love of the beach and, in particular, Avoca Beach. Complete with packed picnic lunch, we visited Avoca every Sunday during the warmer months. Earle disappeared around to the rocks at the base of the cliffs to catch bait and then fish for groper, drummer and morwong. In short, he was replicating his boyhood holidays at Hat Head. I retrieved used soft drink bottles from rubbish bins to collect the deposits, swam in the surf using my air-filled rubber surf mat to catch waves, and fished off the only rock shelf that my father considered safe. Annabel and Susan headed for the beach to swim, sunbake and organise their social lives with friends. In their final years at Gosford High School, they both began to go out with boys and young men. Annabel dated serious young men, at least one of whom had his eyes on matrimony. However, she had no intention of settling for a life in Gosford. She had ambitions to live in a wider world and university was her pathway. Susan dated boys for fun, choosing those with revved up cars who smoked and flashed well-greased flattop haircuts. She achieved excellent results in the Leaving Certificate but the kind of social life she tested in Gosford was a harbinger of her immediate life to come.

When, in response to a question from Billie Crawford about his post Macleay Valley life, Earle described his family's life in Gosford in somewhat idyllic terms:

> Tiny waterfront house, vast grounds, boat, lots of fish, hundreds of crabs, lovely beaches.[12]

But family life in those seven years was more complicated, and less happy than Earle intimated. Nancy became increasingly resentful towards him and developed a habit of sometimes taking to her bed late in the afternoon and staying there until morning. Alternatively, she packed her suitcase and announced she was leaving. When I once asked whether she was planning to stay with her parents, she just shook her head. With no plans, she inevitably unpacked her bag, and returned to her usual household routines. It all became worse after Annabel, followed by Susan, left for University in Newcastle. Now my parents often argued and slept in separate rooms more frequently. On one occasion Nancy physically attacked Earle while he was sleeping. Then she came into my room and sat on my bed stroking my cheek. I felt I wanted to brush her hand away but instead, lay there not moving. Over the more than 60 years since that incident I have often thought about it with the realisation that although I always tried to love both my parents equally, my feelings and respect for my father ran far deeper than any positive emotions I had for my mother. I had no understanding, and no desire to comprehend, the underlying causes of her dissatisfaction with her husband, family and life.

In the 1950s in the UK, the United States and Australia, there was a renewed emphasis on the domestic roles and responsibilities of women. In part this resulted from both men and women seeking refuge in the stability of the nuclear family after decades of uncertainty caused by Depression and War. The family as an institution was also now more carefully sponsored and nurtured by governments as a means of promoting an homogenous society, which was seen as an essential prerequisite for victory in the Cold War. Some observers of Australian society in this era concluded that Australian women were content to live in a world of domesticity but others suggested that suburbia had created a generation of frustrated and dissatisfied women, deprived of the opportunities to pursue careers.[13] With hindsight I can see that like many of her middle-class peers my mother found that domestic life was simply insufficient to provide her with a complete sense of fulfillment, while at the same time she could see no path to a work life outside the home. Confinement to a stifling role as homemaker was of course not unique to her but was an experience shared by millions of women in the United States, as well as Australia.[14] She was one of many middle-class women, who because they left school and lived at home until they married, lacked the qualifications to enter the workforce once their children had grown. In any case many public and private employers adopted policies forbidding the employment of married women. As her children became more independent, I'm sure Nancy became increasingly frustrated and dissatisfied with her prescribed role as wife and mother. She resisted her own children leaving home almost certainly because she couldn't imagine what her own life would be like without them. She didn't object to Annabel and Susan living away from home while they studied at university, but she was adamant that they should return to live at home once they had either graduated or discontinued their studies. I remember that in the 1960s, as she took up international travel as a means of finding a more interesting and rewarding life, she often spoke about becoming a travel agent, but that never eventuated, because she lacked the qualifications, experience and the confidence to pursue such a career.

Earle also contributed to the growing disharmony. Before he met Nancy, he had little experience of women outside his own family group. Without much practical experience to learn that women were not stereotypical characters but represented an infinite range of personalities he adopted understandings that were widespread amongst Australian men of all classes and professions, that is, that women tended to be less intelligent and more emotionally unstable then men. Nancy's frustration with life, I am sure, was in part caused by the fact that Earle did not treat her as his intellectual equal.

Both Earle and I marched in the Anzac Day marches in Gosford. I was a member of the Gosford Boys' Brass Band, which led the procession, while Earle joined the Second Word War contingent which followed the (still large) First World War group of veterans. Earle very rarely drank alcohol, confining himself to a few glasses of beer at Easter and Xmas, and occasional tastings of sherry with everyday evening meals. However, on Anzac Day he usually drank quite a lot, before and after the march, surreptitiously sipping from a small bottle of brandy tucked in his pants backpocket, and then joining other veterans in one of the Mann Street pubs for an hour or so after the ceremony at the cenotaph was complete. He always parked the car several hundred metres down the road from the main shopping strip, strategically pointing it in the direction of our house at Point Frederick. Driving home from there

was easier and hopefully less likely to be noticed. The prosecution of the Inspector of Schools for drunken driving was a frightening prospect.

But apart from Anzac Day Earle tried to keep his World War 2 memories at bay. In the 1950s there were a plethora of books and movies about the War, most of them focussed on retelling the stories of heroic participants and major battles and events. Amongst the most influential books about the War were Paul Brickhill's biography of the legless British fighter pilot Douglas Bader (*Reach for the Sky*), and his account of the Lancaster Bomber attack on the German dams in the Rhine Valley, in a book called *The Dambusters*. Both of these stories subsequently became highly popular British-made films featuring valorised heroes committing extraordinary acts of bravery. I was fascinated by these accounts of the War and read all the best-known books and saw all the most popular films. But I remember Earle forcefully declaring on more than one occasion that he didn't want to stir up memories of the War in his head and so he refused to read or watch anything to do with the War.

Anzac Day Gosford 1950s. I marched with the Gosford Boys Brass Band (foreground) and Earle with the World War 2 contingent (not in view). *Waterhouse Family Collection*

There was an exception, one that I think he made reluctantly. Each year students at Gosford Primary School were required to prepare picture posters of their favourite book as part of Book Week. Of course, I always chose a book about the War, including *Reach for the Sky*, *The Dambusters* and *The Sea Shall Not Have Them*. I was not a good painter and so the paintings of a Lancaster lurking above a breached Moehne Dam wall, and the crew of a shot-down bomber sitting in a rubber dinghy floating in the English Channel were in fact almost exclusively Earle's work. But the worst of it was that in only demonstrating interest in the European War I was not only forcing World War 2 memories on my father but displaying a high level of insensitivity by showing no interest in the equally important Pacific War and his role in it.

But in 1956 the War memories and workload of the Inspector caught up with him. One day he simply didn't get out of bed. For some days he slept intermittently and when he was half awake mumbled incoherently. He refused to get dressed, shower or shave. Eventually the local GP came to visit him and as a result of his examination Earle was transferred to Concord Repatriation Hospital for treatment. At that time Concord was exclusively a war veterans' hospital. He was probably undergoing a severe episode of psychotic depression, a very deep expression of Post-Traumatic Stress Disorder.[15] However, in an era when PTSD was not well understood or defined, his doctors referred to his illness as constituting a 'nervous breakdown'. In keeping with her own inability to cope with stressful situations Nancy inevitably took to her bed. At the age of 15, Annabel became the effective Head of the household, cooking the meals and ensuring that Susan and I got out of bed in time for breakfast before catching the school bus.[16] The members of Legacy helped out too, organising weekend working bees to mow the lawn and weed the garden. Two months or so later, and against the wishes of Nancy who for reasons of her own believed Earle should stay in Concord, he discharged himself and came home. After a few weeks rest he went back to work.

I don't know what treatment he was given in Concord, although this was an era when physicians increasingly turned from psychoanalysis to drugs in treating serious psychiatric conditions.[17] In any case, the treatment worked because he returned to his family as a less stern man, laughing more and caring more about being liked. He also ensured that he and I spent more time together, especially when Nancy was away. We camped at beaches further up the Central Coast and fished until late at night. We also went night fishing in the rowboat, which I found really exciting because we landed some big bream, not to mention those mostly nocturnal feeders, eels, catfish and porcupine fish. We also started to make trips to Sydney together to watch the Rugby League Game of the Week, which was always played at the SCG. In some ways it was like having a different father, I respected the old one, but this new father was also my friend.

I suspect that the psychological problems from which Earle suffered, and which came to a head in the 1956 episode were caused by two specific episodes and one underlying issue. The death of his RAAF comrades in the accident at Nowra in 1943 was an incident which preyed on his mind for the rest of his life. The photograph of him walking from the gravesite of his former aircrew disturbed him when he and I looked at it together some 40 years after the accident. In the late 1980s, when his grandson Stephen Oakley asked him to reminisce about the War this was the first incident he talked about and it upset him so much that he had to walk out of the house to calm himself.[18] He was always very reluctant to talk about the torpedo strike attack on Bima Harbour on 25 June 1944, except to indicate how glad he was that Squadron Leader Hurt recovered from his injuries. However, on one occasion, after I asked him if he had kept in touch with Hurt after the War, he indicated that he hadn't and added that when the anti-aircraft shells first ripped into the Catalina, he thought that the plane was doomed. These two events aside, between June 1944 and July 1945 Earle planned many missions to lay mines in harbours and sea lanes, missions that in some cases cost men their lives. The choices Earle made were necessary but he almost certainly also felt a sense of guilt for planning and sending men on flights that put all of them at risk and resulted in some deaths. Perhaps what deepened his sense of guilt was that some of his closest wartime friends had died but he had lived. The philosopher Nancy Sherman has called the form of psychological injury that Earle almost certainly carried with him for the rest of his life 'moral injury'.[19]

This aspect of his trauma was never diagnosed or treated. He later told me that he first consulted a physician about the stress and anxieties he was feeling while still serving in the RAAF. To relieve these emotions the prescribing doctor recommended that he take up smoking. Unfortunately, there were serious long-term consequences of Earle following this advice because in the early 1970s he developed emphysema, a disease that ultimately resulted in his death. To its credit, when the disease was first diagnosed the Department of Veterans Affairs acknowledged the culpability of the RAAF in prescribing smoking as a remedy and awarded Earle a War Service Disability Pension. I don't think he was interested in the money, but simply wanted an acknowledgement that the life-long severe psychological stress from which he suffered was caused by his wartime experiences. Perhaps he also sought official recognition that the originally prescribed cure had eventually resulted in him developing a severe and painful illness that limited his mobility and shortened his life. In any case, he deposited the pension in a bank account every fortnight, and judging from the amount that was in that account after he and Nancy had both died, I doubt he ever spent a penny of it. But I think he enjoyed the moral victory.

The Sisters Rebel

In 1958 Annabel moved to Newcastle to undertake a three-year Bachelor of Arts degree followed by a one-year Diploma of Education course at the local teacher's college. Her Teacher's College Scholarship only provided a meagre stipend and so she found cheap accommodation by renting a room at the YWCA. When Susan arrived a year later she was pursuing the same tertiary qualifications and held the same form of scholarship. She joined Annabel at the YWCA, where once again they found themselves sharing a room.

In rather different ways the two sisters rebelled against their parents' authority, values and expectations for them. Annabel was determined to complete her teacher qualifications, although the discipline in which she became most interested was psychology, not a subject taught in schools, but one which eventually opened the opportunity for her to become a student counsellor. Her rebellion focussed first on deciding that her own psychological well-being required her to refuse to contact or visit her parents for an extended period. During this time, at the age of thirteen or so, I became the conduit between daughter and parents, making weekend visits by train to be spoilt by Annabel and her then boyfriend who took me to sporting events and introduced me to the delights of 'continental' food. For the first time I discovered that not all spaghetti came in a tin. Second, living in Newcastle allowed Annabel to embrace a modestly non-mainstream counter-culture that was symbolised by jazz, cappuccino and cheap Italian restaurants.

Susan's rebellion was far more dramatic and consequential. Sometime during the course of the 1959 University year she lost all interest in studying at all. Instead, she spent the rest of the year sampling and enjoying University social life. At the end of the year, she came home to tell her parents that she was sure she had failed her first-year studies. At that time all university results were published in the newspapers and when the Newcastle University results came out Earle anxiously scanned the results page. Her name was missing which meant she had not passed a single subject. He was extremely nervous about telling her about her results, and I recall that he looked extremely disappointed when she laughed. At some stage, I suspect she had stopped submitting tutorial papers and essays and it was unlikely that she presented herself for any of her end of year exams. Earle probably found both her actions and reactions inexplicable. As a man who grew up in modest circumstances and who lived through Depression and War, he believed that opportunities for advancement needed to be seized and fully exploited because they were rare and not likely to be repeated. Fortunately, in Susan's case, she was later given a second opportunity to enrol for a university degree, and this time she grasped it with both hands.

In any case Susan then decided to study nursing and, in an era before nursing qualifications required university study, enrolled in a nursing training course at a major Sydney hospital. But she found that neither studying nursing nor living in hospital accommodation were to her liking. Not only did she drop out of the course, but she also changed her address without informing her family and for some time our parents simply had no idea where she was living. They were distraught by her actions and my mother set out on a determined campaign to find her, making regular trips to Sydney for that purpose. I have no idea whether she was following any clear leads, or if that was the case, where they came from. Nancy was probably not just concerned to ensure that Susan was safe but was also deeply concerned about what people might think about what kind of life her daughter was living. As a woman who still lived in a world of anachronistic Victorian values, my mother assumed that it was obligatory for women to live with their parents until they married. Otherwise, she believed, people would certainly question the moral standards both of the daughters and their parents.

Eventually Nancy located Susan in Sydney and I remember the day they came home together. Susan was poorly dressed and groomed. Some of her luggage was in a small battered suitcase and the rest of it in a string shopping bag with a packet of cigarettes at the bottom. I later learned that Susan had agreed to return home after negotiating certain conditions, including one that she be allowed to smoke. In retrospect this seems highly ironic because she subsequently became a fierce anti-smoking advocate.

Only recently did I learn that when Susan first left the hospital, she went to live with the family of Earle's sister Ella. This must have proved extremely inconvenient to them because they were crowded into a small two-bedroom semi-detached house in Rose Bay. As I described in the last section, both Ella and her husband Rod had joined the communist party in the 1930s, and Rod at least, remained

a fervent supporter even in the late 1950s. Through them she was introduced to Sydney's communist counter culture, including finding a boyfriend who was also a party member.

I suppose joining this world proved to her that she had successfully rebelled against her parents and their culture but it provided her with no lasting emotional support or spiritual comfort, which, as it turned out, is what she really craved. When Nancy found Susan it was not difficult to persuade her to return to her family in Gosford where she obtained employment with a prominent local law firm, Taperells, became a regular member of the Gosford Anglican Church and joined the local branch of the Young Liberals. What this remarkable turn-around suggests is that while Susan strongly felt the need to rebel from her parents, she also craved security, and had no strong commitment to radical politics or an alternative bohemian lifestyle.

During the brief period between Susan's return and our family's move to the Sydney suburb of Longueville she also met Bill Oakley, a state public servant who was the local Soil Conservation Officer. Bill was religious, politically conservative, and possessed of a gentle and calm personality. In him, the emotionally changeable and volatile Susan found her rock, a man who was loyal and supportive of her ambitions for the rest of his life.

Nancy's Camelot: Longueville

In 1962 Earle was appointed Inspector of Schools for the Mortdale area. He was moved to Burwood in 1966 and remained the Inspector there until he retired in early 1972. However, although I remember making one weekend trip to Sydney to look at real estate in the Hurstville area with both my parents, my mother had her heart set on the north shore, and I can't remember Earle opposing her wish. She had followed him to a succession of country towns and I suspect that in the interests of family harmony and her own happiness he decided to let her choose both the suburb and house where they were likely to spend the rest of their lives.[20] After many train excursions from Gosford to Sydney, Nancy finally decided to buy a mostly unrenovated Federation house which she had located in Longueville. It was a suburb of decaying old wealth, with Sydney's newly rich families preferring to live in more recently developed harbourside suburbs like Middle Cove, which featured modern houses. To cater to this demand there was a major expansion of home building in localities fronting both the north and south banks of Middle Harbour.

I found Longueville very different from Gosford. For the first time in my life, I encountered high levels of class consciousness. There were only two kinds of schools in the previous towns in which I had lived — Public and Catholic. But almost all the children in Longueville attended wealthy private schools, including Shore, Grammar, PLC (Pymble) and Ravenswood. On the first occasion that I caught the school bus I learnt that which school I attended determined my Longueville social status. There were no more than ten public school children on the bus, and the fact that almost all of us were enrolled in selective schools — North Sydney Boys, North Sydney Girls, and in my case, North Sydney Technical High — did nothing to elevate our status in the eyes of the private school passengers. What I also soon discovered was that social life in Longueville centred on the tennis and sailing clubs. I joined the latter but my inexpensive sailing craft and my extremely limited sailing abilities ensured that I was never accepted into the social circle of the other teenage members. I didn't try to join the tennis club because once when I was walking past

Nancy's Camelot: our Longueville home (now renovated beyond recognition)
Waterhouse Family Collection

the courts a girl, who was probably at least two years younger than me called out, 'Little boy, will you get my ball, it's on the road?'. This seemed a clear indication of what kind of patronising treatment a recently arrived public school boy who was not a good tennis player might expect from this club's younger members.

I lived in Longueville with my parents for six years, completing the final two years of high school at North Sydney Technical High School and then a four-year honours degree in Arts at the University of Sydney. But despite my dislike of Longueville and the loneliness I experienced in those years I also knew the move to Sydney was beneficial. In Gosford as I grew older and became a teenager, I became increasingly uncertain about the direction of my life and whether I had any control over it. I seemed to be mediocre at everything. I was one of the worst musicians in the Gosford Boys Brass Band, and my high school results were extremely uneven. I was of slight build and short stature and always thought I had to prove myself physically, which is why I played cricket, baseball and rugby league. At first, I was regarded as better than average at sports, because I played with enthusiasm and determination. But by the time I was fifteen I was playing against boys who had grown to be much taller and heavier than I was and my sporting limitations were increasingly exposed. In a town and at a school in which sporting ability was highly valued I began to develop a strong sense of inferiority, which only increased as I also began to realise that in any case I really didn't enjoy playing competitive level team games.

I didn't make many friends at North Sydney Technical High School. Surfing culture had taken a hold on Sydney teenagers by 1962 and the cooler kids at my school wore stove pipe pants, pointed black shoes and put peroxide in their hair to turn it blond. I was regarded as an immature country boy who was seriously uncool. But the fact that I had few friends and participated in minimal social activities meant that I could concentrate on studying. I was motivated to work hard at school because I was now determined to attend university. To achieve that goal, I needed not only to matriculate but earn sufficient marks to qualify for a fee-paying Commonwealth University Scholarship.

At Gosford High School I had usually performed well in English and History but not in my other subjects. There was an emphasis on science and technical subjects at North Sydney Technical High School, which certainly didn't suit me because my interests and strengths lay in the humanities, but with the help of additional tutoring in Science and Maths I managed to achieve four As and two Bs in the Leaving Certificate in 1963. This was not a brilliant result, but I was not an outstanding student, and I achieved what I needed—matriculation and a Commonwealth University Scholarship.

The other advantage in moving to Sydney was that to my great relief my behaviour and academic performance were no longer regularly monitored and judged according to the standards that the community expected of an Inspector's son, standards that I was often judged to have failed. Inspectors of Schools in Sydney did not have the same stature and high profile as they did in rural towns and in any case we didn't live in the areas included in Earle's inspectorates. Finally, our family was not well known in the Longueville community either, and given the nature of the suburb's class structure, I suspect that those neighbours who were aware of Earle's profession, probably classified him fairly low in the local social hierarchy.

Susan and Annabel: Work and Family

I suppose it was a sign of changing times that whereas Nancy's mother insisted that her daughter pursue husband and family, but not work, her two daughters were able to choose both to marry and have families and also to pursue careers.

When we moved to Sydney Susan came with us and soon obtained employment working in the branch of a bank at North Sydney. However, not long after we moved to Sydney, she and Bill became engaged. The following year on April 20 1963 they were married in St Aidan's Church in Longueville and Susan returned to live in Gosford with her new husband. On this occasion Nancy could hardly object to one of her daughters leaving home.

Their first son, Stephen (1965), was born in Gosford, and their second child, Patrick, arrived in 1967 after they moved to Yass, where Bill took up another position with the Department of Soil Conservation. From Yass the family moved to Scone, a town which Susan hated both because it was so small and because she disliked how cold it became in winter. At this time, she was undertaking a BA degree by distance education at the University of New England as well as working part-time as a typist at Scone High School. From the principal, who owned a holiday house at Hat Head, she learnt that this coastal village possessed a beautiful beach and a camping ground with at least adequate facilities. Her interest in spending summer holidays camping there was increased when Earle explained his boyhood connection to Hat Head. For a few years the family travelled from Scone to Hat Head for their annual camping holiday but in 1982 this wheel of the Waterhouse family story completed a full circle when Bill was posted to Kempsey, in the Macleay Valley. Here both Stephen and Patrick enrolled in and completed their HSC qualifications at the same High School, now renamed Kempsey High

Bill and Sue's wedding. *Waterhouse Family Collection*

School, which Earle and his siblings had attended. Susan worked as an assistant librarian at Kempsey High School while she studied for her Dip Ed. She then obtained employment at Kempsey's new High School, Melville High, which was attended not only by children from South Kempsey but also those from Hat Head, Crescent Head, Kinchela, Gladstone and Belmore River[21] It also possessed a large enrolment of First Nation students. One of the subjects in which she acquired a reputation as an outstanding teacher was HSC Ancient History, a reputation which would certainly have pleased her grandfather, Percy Waterhouse. A teacher who achieved outstanding HSC results, she was also highly respected both by her students and fellow teachers. At her funeral in 2022, which was delayed because of Covid restrictions, former staff from Melville High told me that when the students stood outside their rooms waiting to be admitted for their first classes of each school day, they could often be unruly, but those in line to enter Mrs Oakley's class were patient, quiet and respectful. Like Earle she was a charismatic teacher and also like her father she took a particular interest in Indigenous students. In his memoir letters Earle lamented that he had tried unsuccessfully to implement Indigenous advancement policies in a number of the rural schools in which he taught. Susan had more success, encouraging Indigenous students to finish school and pursue further education. Her daughter-in-law, Natalie Atherton, recalls that when walking through the Newcastle suburb of Hamilton with Susan some 15 years after her retirement from Melville High School, an Indigenous man greeted Susan with a huge smile and spent some time fondly reminiscing with her about his time in her classroom. She had clearly left a lasting impression on him.[22]

Ill health and a departmental reconstruction forced Bill to take early retirement. His death in 2002 was nevertheless sudden, unexpected and left Susan devastated, for they had enjoyed a long and extremely happy marriage. In retirement she studied to become a Deacon in the Anglican Church and after her ordination in Grafton Cathedral, the site of her great grandfather, Henry Benjamin Waterhouse's funeral ceremony, she

regularly conducted services at Macleay Valley churches, including Kempsey and Crescent Head. More completely than any other member of her Waterhouse generation Susan returned to her deep family roots as a teacher, as a committed Anglican and as a woman deeply engaged with the Macleay Valley and its culture. She always believed that she was following in Earle's footsteps, in particular, and her life stories suggest she was right.

After he died, she missed Bill and in mourning him she neglected her own physical and mental well-being. Six years or so after his death she was diagnosed with early onset dementia and although she continued to live alone in her beloved river front home for a year or so she finally agreed to move to an aged care facility in Newcastle close to her two sons and their families. Because of the love and care she received from family and health care professionals she lived far longer than anyone anticipated, finally passing away in 2021. She had lived a life that was both reckless and measured, tragic and joyful, although from the time she met Bill, her family, both immediate and extended, was always at the centre of what most mattered to her.

Following their graduations from Kempsey High School both Stephen and Pat studied medicine, Stephen at UNSW and Pat at Newcastle. Stephen also engaged in postgraduate study, completing a PhD at the University of Sydney and then undertaking postdoctoral research at Guy's Hospital in London. Stephen qualified and now practices as a rheumatologist. Pat studied to become a toxicologist and is now a staff specialist in General Medicine and Aboriginal Chronic Diseases at the John Hunter Hospital in Newcastle. In these capacities he supervises Advanced Training in General Medicine and makes frequent trips to inland towns to treat Indigenous patients.

Stephen married Natalie Atherton in 2002. They have three children Alexandra (2003) William (2005) and Flynn (2008). On November 30 1991 Pat married Kim Wheatland, the daughter of a '£10 Pom' Tony Wheatland and his wife Shirley, a native of Dubbo. They have three children, Gemma (1997), Ben (2000) and Sam (2006).[23]

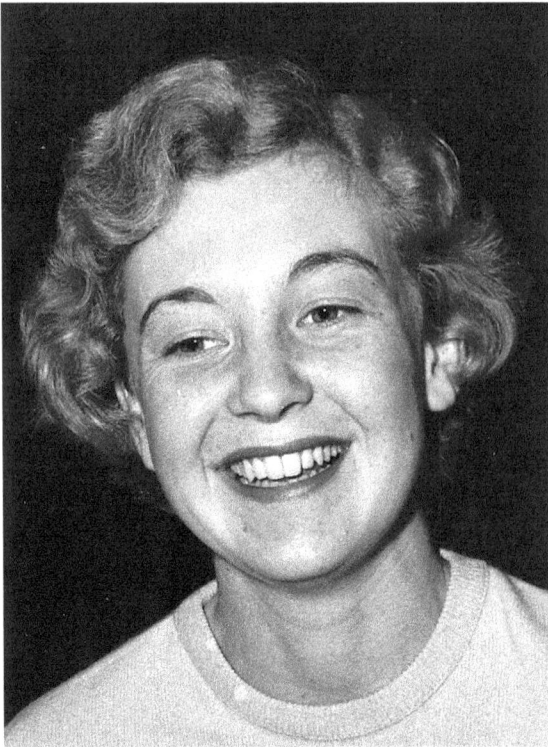

Annabel as a young woman. *Waterhouse Family Collection*

After completing her BA/Dip Ed at the University of Newcastle and Newcastle Teachers' College, Annabel joined the family in Longueville in 1962, at the same time taking up a teaching position at Northmead High School. In 1965 she moved to Ballina to take up a position at the local high school. She returned to Sydney in 1966 for training as a school counsellor with the NSW Department of Education, and was then posted to Wollongong for three years as a counsellor. Although she lived with the family in Longueville for some of these Sydney years she also lived for part of the time in Waverton, sharing a flat with an old schoolmate from Gosford. I was envious of her independence and flat living, which was not common at that time, seemed to me to be exotic and even bohemian. However once again Nancy strongly disapproved of Annabel's decision to move out of the family home, believing it put Annabel in moral danger and the family's social reputation at risk.

During the time she lived in Wollongong Annabel met Alexander (Alex) Agafonoff, a research economist for the Reserve Bank, who subsequently resigned to take up and further develop a grazing property near the village of Taralga about 230 kilometres southwest of Sydney. Annabel travelled to the property most weekends to be with Alex and his two small children, Roxanne (1962) and Katherine (1964), from his first marriage. They were married in 1970 in the Presbyterian (later Uniting) Church in Longueville. I didn't attend because by this stage of my life I was a 'graduate student' at Johns Hopkins University in Baltimore. However, I was sent some photographs of the occasion, including one of my grandfather, David Drake, then in his mid-eighties, delivering a speech, and relishing it.

Annabel and Alex had three children together, Ingrid, Alexander ('Sasha'), and Nicholas. In 2023 Roxanne married Leon Pollard and now lives in Victoria where she is an ordained Anglican minister. She has two sons from a previous marriage, Gabriel (1993) and Joshua (1995). Katherine married Rupert Hucker and has a daughter, Isabel (1999). Rupert works in the energy industry. The family lives in Miami, Florida. Ingrid married Chris Dick, an expert in IT and they subsequently moved to 'Silicon Valley' in California. They have two children, Veronica and Zac. Sasha married Maree Ringland and they have three children, Max (2001), Katy (2004) and Lily (2007). Maree works for the Department of Foreign Affairs and Trade and so the family has spent many years overseas, including China, Chile and Peru. She was recently appointed Ambassador to Peru and Bolivia. Nicholas married Belinda Heath and they have two children, Peter (2008) and Zena (2010). Nick runs his own advertising market research company, while Belinda is a high school teacher.

Nancy and Earle's Later Years

Earle and Nancy seemed to get on better in Longueville than they had in Gosford and I think there were two reasons for this. First, Sydney gave Nancy more freedom and opportunity to pursue her own leisure and social activities. She joined North Sydney Inner Wheel—an organisation dominated by the wives of Rotarians because at this time women could not join Rotary—and eventually served a term as President, which I suspect was a great confidence booster. There were also regular Thursday trips to 'town' on the Longueville to Wynyard bus to shop in arcades as well as in her favourite store, David Jones. Second, Nancy decided that she wanted to travel, and once again, Earle let her have her way. Her first trip was on a P and O passenger vessel that made a round trip to Japan and Hong Kong. In Japan she developed an appreciation for a culture different from her own and in Hong Kong she acquired a liking for buying precious stone jewellery both for herself and her (female) relatives. Although she asked Earle to join her on this trip, he refused to go, admitting both to me and other family members that he was unsure how he would respond when he arrived in Japan and encountered its citizens. He feared that his long-held hatred of Japan, its culture and people might overwhelm him and lead him to behave badly. However, a few years later when Nancy decided to join another cruise ship voyage to Japan, in part to re-unite with a young Japanese family who had befriended her on her first trip, Earle agreed to join her. As he later admitted, he found he no longer hated the Japanese and that he was attracted by their politeness and concern and found the countryside truly remarkable. It was, in the end, not just an enjoyable holiday but a voyage of reconciliation that carried inchoate psychological benefits.

Earle retired in early 1972 and he and Nancy enjoyed what was to be their last joint major trip that encompassed north America, Europe and Africa. After World War 2 a tradition emerged amongst Australian state and federal level public servants that when they retired, they collected their long service benefits in a lump sum which was then used to finance a return voyage to the United Kingdom and which usually included a guided trip to 'The Continent' as well. David and Ruth Drake, as I have already described, had already participated in this ritual. Apart from their trips to Japan my parents had also sailed on cruise ships to New Zealand and the South Pacific, reaching as far east as Tahiti. But their 1972 voyages involved the circumnavigation of the globe.

In 2012 Grace and I travelled on a river cruise from Budapest to Amsterdam along the Danube, Mein and Rhine Rivers. Because the cruise

company was an Australian organisation most of the other passengers were Australian retirees. One night we sat down to dinner at a table occupied by a couple we had not yet encountered. The table talk soon turned to which places in Europe we and they had visited on our various European excursions. I quickly realised that our dinner partners saw our conversation as a competition, when they asked 'Have you done Dubrovnik?' and so on as they listed all the places they had visited throughout Europe. They looked quite disgusted when I revealed that I had made only a couple of previous short trips to Europe and that most of my previous travel had involved University work related visits to the United States.

But I am sure that neither Nancy and especially not Earle, conceived of their great odyssey as an exercise in simply seeing as many of the most popular tourist places in Europe as possible. For him, and Nancy, apart from the fact that it provided the opportunity to spend time with me in Baltimore and London, it allowed Earle to pay homage to those cultural spaces and places which had inspired the great British literary figures he so much admired and those sites which were the source and inspiration of the Greek and Roman legends and myths which he had learnt in his father's classroom at Belmore River.

Conveniently, my ancient dog Bill died in early March and so they set sail on March 26 1972 without needing to persuade my sister Susan's family to look after him in their absence. The first leg of their journey involved passage on ss *Canberra* to Vancouver, then travel by train and bus across Canada to Niagara Falls, and then a brief detour to New York City before another bus journey to Baltimore.[24]

For them Baltimore was a shock and a revelation. Much of the inner city was burnt down in the 1968 riots, very little reconstruction had taken place, and so many of the old inner city row house neighbourhoods looked like war zones. The high-rise downtown shopping and business district was still standing but it was deserted and unsafe after dark, once all the white middle-class office-workers and shop assistants had fled back to the outer suburbs. In his diary Earle described the hotel they stayed in on their first night in the city as 'in decay'. As I explained the safety rules they needed to follow I remember that looks of horror appeared on their faces as they realised that their experiences in Baltimore were unlikely to be those of typical Australian retirees on the European grand tour.

But in the three weeks they stayed in Baltimore we had some good times together. One of the few recreations I could afford was to attend Baltimore Orioles baseball games and I took them to Memorial Stadium to watch some night matches. To my surprise, Nancy, who never attended sporting events in Australia, loved the atmosphere and the games. My PhD supervisor, Jack Greene, a man who I had learnt had a gruff and tough exterior, but a soft heart underneath, also invited them to his house for lunch, which I think pleased them immensely even if their son demonstrated an immature embarrassment to some of the answers they gave to Jack's questions. They also organised a small number of overnight excursions to rural areas in Ohio, Virginia and Maryland. I had spent the previous nine months before they arrived carrying out research on my PhD thesis in South Carolina, spending most of my time in the State Archives in Columbia but also a few weeks in the South Carolina Historical Society in historic Charleston. In my letters I had praised this eighteenth century city for its grand architecture and its stunning location. Deciding to see for themselves, and not realising it was at least a 10-hour trip south, they actually booked bus seats on a trip that took them west to Cincinnati, returning via Charleston West Virginia, a mining and industrial city, with few heritage or natural environment attractions. Their confusion in mixing the two Charlestons lived on in family memory and was often retold with suitable exaggeration over Sunday family lunch gatherings.

From Baltimore my parents returned to New York on a greyhound bus, in the process mixing with America's poorer inhabitants, and calling in at bus stations located in the most depressed neighbourhoods of declining east coast industrial cities. They gained a very different perspective of American society from the multitude of Australian travellers flying on package tours promising Disneyland, Las Vegas and San Francisco. However, they returned to the status of luxury tourists when they reached New York and boarded the ss *France* en route to Southampton and London.

After our first meeting in three years our second took place only a few weeks later. Needing to complete my PhD research before settling down to a year of writing my 100,000 word thesis I travelled to London to work in the British Library, the Public Record Office, the Bodleian Library and the Somerset Record Office in Taunton, where various MSS collections relating to the history of colonial South Carolina were located. I joined Earle and Nancy in their tiny apartment in Kensington, conveniently located close to the Gardens and the Central Line underground train service. Both the shower and the toilet were located in converted closets and the kitchen barely held a single adult. Each morning we went our separate ways, with me setting out on my research visits and my parents visiting galleries and museums in London that held the artefacts both of Empire and European civilisation, or taking excursions to nearby county points of interest. In particular, they made repeated visits to the British Museum and National Gallery to ensure that they took full advantage of the wealth of cultural artefacts on display. They travelled to Stratford-on-Avon to attend a performance of *The Merchant of Venice*, to Oxford and Cambridge to pay homage to these venerable educational institutions, and to Stonehenge because it seemed so connected to a mysterious British past. Ironically, their travels also took them to Taunton, the home of Josiah Branchflower, and through the Lakes District where William Henry Waterhouse's family had lived for several generations. Of course, Earle knew nothing about his family's English history and was certainly oblivious to the connection.

On what turned out to be a memorable occasion my father asked me to accompany him on what can only be described as a pilgrimage to Stoke Poges to visit St Giles Churchyard, the subject of Thomas Grey's poem, *Elegy Written in a Country Churchyard*. It was a poem that Earle had learnt from his father in the school at Belmore

River and when we arrived, he stood in the vicinity of Grey's grave and recited several verses from memory, verses which began as follows:

> The curfew tolls the knell of parting day,
> The lowing herd wind slowly o'er the lea,'
> The plowman homeward plods his weary way

At that time, I didn't fully appreciate his great love and knowledge of English literature, and how that connected to what his father had taught him, as well as serving as a means of remembering and honouring Percy. But I was at least aware of how much this performance mattered to him and felt a gratitude, which I was too embarrassed to express, that he had invited me to share in his carefully planned spiritual experience.

Better late than never, I suppose. Thank you, Dad.

During their stay in London which extended from mid-May through until early July they also made a quick trip across the Channel to the Netherlands and Belgium. In an extended visit to the Rijksmuseum, Earle carefully recorded the names of the painters of the Dutch and Italian Renaissance masterpieces that were on display, I suppose as a means to help his later reminiscences.

In early July they set out on a much more ambitious and demanding European journey that extended across Belgium, France, Germany, Italy, Greece, Yugoslavia (Croatia) and Austria, travelling by bus and sometimes by small ships or ferries between towns and cities in Italy, Greece and Croatia. I am sure Earle was particularly fascinated by the sites that related to the Greek myths and legends with which he was so long familiar and so it is not surprising that Athens, Corinth, Corfu, Mycenae and particularly Delphi were all on their destination list. Earle later recalled that it 'was one of my life's highpoints to assist an elderly New York librarian locate the very place at the Delphi temple ruins from which the oracle was delivered.' I rather suspect that this moment was as much a highlight and memorable trip event for Earle as it was for the librarian, an occasion that he still recalled in 1987.[25]

Returning to England for a few more London gallery and museum visits, excursions to Scotland and the West Country, and finally a visit to Dorothy and John at Petts Wood, the intrepid couple finally sailed from Southampton in mid-September on a long sea voyage that took them around the Cape, finally reaching Melbourne on October 16. Already suffering from emphysema when they set out on this massive excursion Earle nevertheless only recorded himself as too sick for tourist duties on one day during the entire trip.

Although Nancy continued to travel extensively, Earle only made one more overseas excursion and that was in to visit his daughter Annabel and her family in the Philippines where Alex was working for the Asian Development Bank. In those days customs officials walked through the aisles of just landed international flights spraying for insects that had managed to find their way on board at the departure city. When Earle and Nancy returned to Sydney the plane was sprayed on arrival, which had an immediate effect on his disease impacted lungs, leading to a doubled up coughing fit. This episode combined with the fact that the advancing emphysema increasingly made living, let alone travelling, difficult meant that Earle's future travel was limited to the annual Christmas holiday trip to Hat Head. In any case I suspect he felt that he had made the pilgrimage to the sites that most mattered, that is, those had inspired the literature that had shaped his education and his cultural understandings, and that was enough.

In the next few years, he joined the Ex-Inspector of Schools Association and became a highly active campaigner for the indexation of Public Service pensions, even joining demonstrations at the gates of State Parliament. He also took up lawn bowls again, a sport he had abandoned when we first moved to Sydney. He had begun to create his own eclectic style of garden when we first moved to Longueville a decade beforehand but now he spent several hours a day cultivating it, which also involved a determination not to allow any tree to grow above head height. He was certainly a vicious pruner. He also loved fires. At a time when the burning of rubbish in backyard 'incinerators' was still legal he built a crude brick 'barbecue' enclosure and delighted in setting alight bundles of small tree branches, shrub cuttings and flammable household waste, not always to the convenience of neighbours who had left their windows open. His conviviality and love of conversation were well known and neighbours often dropped in for a chat and a cup of tea or a beer. Self-described 'poet, painter and lapsed scientist', Edwin Wilson, who lived across the road was moved to write a poem *Voyage to Colchis* from listening to Earle's recounting of the story of the Golden Fleece. In another poem, Wilson succinctly and perceptively captured Earle's retirement life:

> My old Mate the Squadron Leader
> Has emphysema, water in his
>   fuel line leaves him spluttering.
> Tends his garden of chokos
> And runner beans, planted
> An *Arburus* for Horace and Ovid.
> Crossed the state in his career,
> But his heart is in Kinchela
> On the lower Macleay.
> Pours me a beer and talks
>   of schools, war, and literature
> And of course, The Department
> Laughs a lot and feeds the
>   parrots and kookaburras–
>   flew by the stars
> Grounded, he dreams of his river,
>   and sometimes has trouble
>   mounting the kerb and guttering[26]

He also became a favourite with a number of the small children in the neighbourhood, who often turned up to listen to him read stories to them, stories which inevitably involved the myths and legends of ancient Greece and Rome.

In the early 1980s, when Grace was trying to balance her share of raising two small children with work and the completion of her first postgraduate degree, a routine to give her more time to study was established by which I took our two children Margot and Eliza to Longueville for lunch most Sundays. I thoroughly enjoyed the time I spent with my parents, especially the conversations that involved reminiscences about Nancy's travel and Earle's boyhood and wartime experiences. In reality, however, most of my time was spent in supervising the girls and in ensuring that they ate as much of the lamb or chicken roast that my mother had cooked that I could persuade them to swallow. My parents hated wasting food and required that other family members, grandchildren in particular, demonstrate their gratitude for a home cooked meal by eating the lot, a notion that my children didn't fully understand. On some Sundays, when she was not faced with work overload, Grace also attended these lunches with my parents and on these occasions both of us waited with bated breath for Susan to make her usual Sunday lunchtime phone call. As soon as my parents heard the phone ring and headed into the hall to speak to their daughter, Grace and I each grabbed a child's plate and stuffed ourselves with the food that our kids had left uneaten. Only through such drastic measures were Margot and Eliza, Grace and Richard saved from parental and grandparental wrath.

I was convinced that my visits showed I was a good son, but looking back there are so many more personal conversations we didn't have, so many subjects my father in particular probably was eager to discuss, especially more detailed accounts of his wartime achievements, but they never happened. And that is one of the great regrets of my life.

Earle's health worsened through the 1980s to the extent that he no longer travelled to the city to meet old friends and colleagues, he gave up lawn bowls and he spent more time in the garden leaning on the hoe than using it to chop out weeds. As I have described earlier, his growing incapacity even to write letters was reflected in the ever-briefer messages he sent to Billie Crawford in 1987. In the last few years of his life, he seemed not only more anxious to record and speak about his own life experiences but also to reflect on what mattered most to him. Writing to his grand-daughter Ingrid in 1986 he listed his 'treasures' in what he determined to be their order of importance. First, he referred to his 'boundlessly loved' family; second he valued his memories and experiences as a student and teacher; third he acknowledged his love for 'my country', by which he meant both the natural Australian environment and the wildlife which inhabited it; fourth, he noted his war experiences, including the places he travelled and the people he met; and finally, with characteristic and infuriating modesty, he insisted that his overall contribution to society was a modest one, although he implied a level of pride that he had carried out his responsibilities and duties cheerfully.[27]

Earle stoic in the face of illness and pain. This photo was taken on his seventy-ninth and last birthday.
Waterhouse Family Collection

In reading Earle's acknowledgements of what values and experiences had shaped his understandings about the nature of his relationship to the environment and nation in which he lived I can't help but compare his path to the different fork which Dorothy chose. Both siblings valued their English cultural heritage but Dorothy chose to embrace it exclusively while Earle, whose love of the rural landscapes he lived in as a child on the northern rivers, combined with the awe he developed for the wild northwest of the Northern Territory that he encountered in World War 2, increasingly identified himself as simply Australian. His journey from identifying as British-Australian to thinking of himself as Australian, nothing more, nothing less, was one shared by many women and men of his generation,

including, ironically, Manning Clark. I wonder if Earle would have been surprised to learn that they had something in common after all.

In early July 1988, after a severe and prolonged coughing fit Earle was admitted to Concord Repatriation Hospital. After a day or so his condition seemed to improve but then he complained of chest pains and lapsed into a coma. He died a day or so later of pulmonary oedema, cardiac and liver failure, and the long-term impact of emphysema.[28] His life was commemorated in a simple ceremony attended by family and neighbours in the Longueville Uniting Church. The marker on his grave in the cemetery at North Ryde reads *Respected and Loved By His Family and Friends,* which are words I chose unwillingly as a compromise with my mother, who wanted another, even more restrained iteration: *Respected By All Who Knew Him.* But I concluded that he was a man who was deeply loved by many members of his family and as well as by his close friends. He deserved that acknowledgement on his grave and indeed so much more, for his extraordinary contribution to education, nation and family. He had looked forward to the arrival but died before the birth of another granddaughter, Isabel, who was born in September, two months after his death. Grandson Leo Earle was born 20 months later in March 1990.

In his last years, conscious of his physical weakness and vulnerability, Earle frequently expressed his gratitude to Nancy for the care she provided. She was understandably sometimes impatient with him, and expressed the view that his mental facilities were in decline, a view that his letters to Billie and Ingrid contradict. She also felt captured and confined by the need to be constantly available to assist his growing needs. When he died, I suspect she felt that that she would now be free to live a full life on her own. As it turned out she was wrong, because two factors combined to compromise her spirit of independence. In the first place, she had lived too long with him not to miss his conversation and his presence and found herself unexpectedly lonely. Her behaviour became erratic as she struggled to find a new direction in her life. Developing insomnia, she began to listen to late night talk back radio, and became an occasional caller, eager to discuss matters on which she claimed to be informed. Restless in Longueville she also began to discuss the prospect of moving to Salamander Bay and recreating for herself the retirement lifestyle of her parents. However, in late 1989, finding walking increasingly difficult, she consulted a specialist who in a cold clinical manner informed her that she was suffering from Motor Neurone Disease, which he simply described as a very serious illness. For some months after this diagnosis Nancy continued to live at home, aided by a live-in Dial an Angel and building modifications that enabled wheel chair access. Eventually, in mid-1990, she agreed to be admitted to an aged care facility at Terrey Hills, one of the few such institutions that was willing to admit patients with her condition. But she could not make peace with her illness or her life and was always dissatisfied with the level of care and the facilities. She constantly asked me to have her moved back to Lady Davidson Hospital, a repatriation facility in which she had stayed briefly as a respite patient, forgetting that during her previous stay there she had disliked it intensely. Fortunately, she didn't live long enough to experience the full force and symptoms of the disease, for she died suddenly of a heart attack on September 20 1990.[29] It was her tragedy that she lived what she clearly felt was an unfulfilled life, and resented the injustice of what fate had dealt her as much at the end as during the course of her life. Her ashes and gravestone sit next to Earle's in North Ryde Cemetery, inscribed with the words *Beloved Wife of Earle*, reflecting my hopes, I suppose, that they are reconciled in death as they never quite became in life.

Endnotes

1   Alan Waterhouse to Earle Waterhouse, 16 January 1946, Waterhouse Family Collection

2   Bill Hornadge, *Dubbo: The Story of Dubbo's Growth from Village to Town and City*, Dubbo; Council of the City of Dubbo, 1976

3   Nancy to Earle, undated letter, August/September 1945

4   Letter to Ingrid; *Dubbo Liberal and Macquarie Advocate*, 30 December 1948

5   Annabel Agafonoff, personal communication with Richard Waterhouse, 29 May 2019

6   *ibid.*

7   Richard Waterhouse, personal communication with Annabel Agafonoff, 29 May 2019; e-mail communication from Annabel to Richard 18 May 2023

8   *Mudgee Guardian*, 18 February 1954. In this context I note that Earle's father-in-law, David Drake, who played a similar role in organising the Queen's visit to Newcastle was also appointed the Queen's official host at the Newcastle Showground event.

9   Richard Waterhouse, personal communication with Annabel Agafonoff, 29 May 2019

10   ibid.

11   ibid.

12   Earle Waterhouse, letter to Billie Crawford, 20 October, 1987

13   Richard Waterhouse, *Private Pleasures, Public Leisure: A History of Australian Popular Culture Since 1788*, Melbourne, Longman, 1995, pp. 200–01

14   Betty Friedan, *The Feminine Mystique*, passim., New York: W.W. Norton, 1963

15   In coming to this conclusion, I have relied on the assessment of Leo Waterhouse, a highly experienced psychiatric nurse. His suggestive diagnosis is based on my recollections of my father's behaviour when he became ill.

16   Richard Waterhouse personal communication with Annabel Agafonoff, 29 May 2019

17   For the treatment of psychiatric disorders amongst War veterans see Stephen Garton, *The Cost of War Australians Return*, Oxford: Oxford University Press, 1996, pp. 143–175

18   Richard Waterhouse, personal communication with Stephen Oakley, 11 November 2022

19   Nancy Sherman, *Stoic Wisdom: Ancient Lessons for Modern Resilience*, Oxford: Oxford University Press, 2021, passim. I am grateful to Stephen Oakley for drawing my attention to this work

20   I am grateful to Grace Karskens for the suggestion that Longueville was most likely Nancy's choice. I should add that Earle didn't accompany her on her train excursions and she found the Longueville house on her own.

21   Jo and Jesse Gifkins, whose family purchased the residence and schoolhouse at Belmore River when the school closed in the early 1970s both attended Melville High School

22   Stephen Oakley e-mail to Richard Waterhouse, 4 July 2023; Stephen Oakley, personal communication to Richard Waterhouse, 3 July 2023

23   Patrick Oakley to Richard Waterhouse, 26 June 2023 (email); Stephen Oakley to Richard Waterhouse, 3 July 2023 (e-mail)

24   Earle Waterhouse, 1972 Diary, Waterhouse Family Collection

25   Letter to Billie Crawford, 20 October 1987

26   Edwin Wilson, *New Collected Poems 1952–2012*, Armidale: Kardoorair Press, 2012, pp. 146–47

27   Earle Waterhouse to Ingrid Agafonoff, 19 May 1986, Waterhouse Family Collection

28   NSW Register of Deaths, Waterhouse, Earle, 6 July 1988, copy in Waterhouse Collection

29   NSW Register of Deaths, Waterhouse, Nancy Franklin, 20 September 1990, copy in Waterhouse Collection

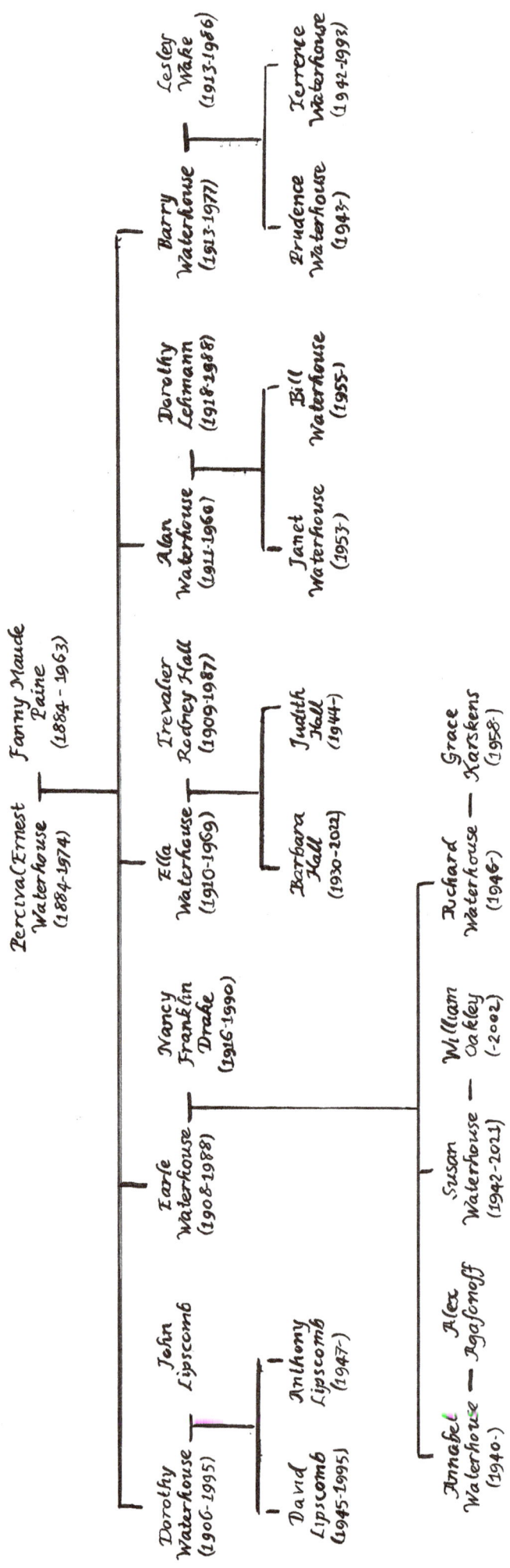

Percival Ernest Waterhouse (1884-1974) — Fanny Maude Paine (1884-1963)

Dorothy Waterhouse (1906-1995) — John Lipscomb

Earle Waterhouse (1908-1988) — Nancy Franklin Drake (1916-1990)

Ella Waterhouse (1910-1969) — Trevalier Rodney Hall (1909-1987)

Alan Waterhouse (1911-1960) — Dorothy Lehmann (1918-1988)

Barry Waterhouse (1913-1977) — Lesley Wake (1913-1986)

David Lipscomb (1945-1995)

Anthony Lipscomb (1947-)

Annabel Waterhouse (1940-) — Alex Agafonoff

Susan Waterhouse (1942-2011) — William Oakley (-2002)

Richard Waterhouse (1946-) — Grace Karskens (1958-)

Barbara Hall (1930-2022)

Judith Hall (1944-)

Janet Waterhouse (1953-)

Bill Waterhouse (1955-)

Prudence Waterhouse (1943-)

Terrence Waterhouse (1942-1993)

PART 5

The Longest Afterword:
my Public and Private Journeys

Chapter 13

Undergraduate Education: the University of Sydney

W HEN I COMPLETED THE Leaving Certificate in 1963, I had no clear idea about what university degree I wanted to pursue. My mother wanted me to enrol in Law, believing that working as a solicitor was likely to bring me both wealth and status. Because I had no strong personal degree preferences, I drifted into a lukewarm decision to follow her wishes. First year Law students were required to attend an interview with a member of the Law faculty's academic staff and the first question directed at me by the academic who I consulted was to ask my age. When I replied that I was seventeen, he told me that I looked about thirteen and that I was too immature to cope with Law, which had a high first year failure rate. But he suggested that if I enrolled in Arts-Law, spending the first two year of the degree studying humanities and social science subjects at the Camperdown Campus, I would have no difficulty coping with Law subjects when I moved to the Phillip Street Law Campus.

So, at the beginning of 1964, I enrolled in Arts at the University of Sydney. My mother disapproved but surprisingly didn't try to make me change my mind. My father was really pleased, telling me that he believed that studying for an Arts degree was an excellent preparation for life as well as work. The subjects I chose were Government, Psychology, English and History. I quickly decided that I couldn't understand exactly what discipline Government represented. Was I learning contemporary politics or political history? As a result, I couldn't figure out how to approach my first essay assignment and so I discontinued the course.

The Psychology lectures were heavily oriented towards Physiology and difficult for me to understand. However, I soon discovered that they were irrelevant to the course. For the purposes of sitting for exams and writing essays, all that was needed was a knowledge of the textbook. I hated everything about 'Psych 1' but managed to survive the course and scrape a pass.

At this time the Head of the English department was Sam Goldberg, a devoted disciple of the Cambridge-based English Literature scholar, F. R. Leavis. The latter was a man of strongly held views, who tended to be aggressively dismissive of those who opposed his arguments. Leavis strongly believed that the greatest novelists adopted complex but responsible attitudes towards the characters they created and the fictional societies in which they lived. It was an indication of his dogmatic approach that he claimed with great certainty that the great English novelists were Jane Austen, George Eliot, Henry James, Joseph Conrad and D. H. Lawrence. Needless to say, the Goldberg-designed syllabus at Sydney prominently featured these novelists. This curriculum was also very narrow because not only did it focus on the works of a limited range of English writers but it also concentrated on a very small number of their writings.[1] It is true that we were required to study novels by other writers but they were only included for purposes of demonstrating their inferiority to the works of Leavis's anointed five demi-gods. However, while it was easy for the disciples that Goldberg had appointed, namely Jock and Maggie Tomlinson, to teach the Leavisite creed to demonstrate the literary weaknesses in Alan Sillitoe's *Saturday Night and Sunday Morning*, compared to the greater dimension of Lawrence's *Sons and Lovers*, I thought they were less successful in denigrating Dickens' *Great Expectations* in comparison with Austen's *Emma* and Eliot's *Middlemarch*. I still think that the novels of all three bear some strong similarities as romantic melodramas. In a minor way I rebelled against the gospel of St Leavis and wrote essays and tutorial papers that praised Dickens and were highly critical of Lawrence, who impressed me as a bombastic bore. It didn't occur to me that my arguments were no less dogmatic than those of the Leavisites. But in the wake of the poor marks awarded to my written work I surrendered to pragmatism and wrote exam essays that were suitably obsequious towards the works of the 'fab five'. I managed to pass with a mark that an English Department staff member, acting in the role of academic advisor, acknowledged was probably higher than the one I earned in Psychology, a comment which was not intended as praise. This undistinguished pass nevertheless qualified me to enrol in English 2, although given my reluctance to adhere to the teachings of the Leavisite Gospel I knew I couldn't expect to achieve outstanding results. In second year, I developed a keener appreciation of the novels of Austen and Conrad but not of Lawrence. I found *The Rainbow* to be filled with exaggerated characters and language. I achieved the predicted mediocre pass but decided that enrolling in a third year of English was beyond my level of patience and masochism.

The course I chose in first year History covered the period of the European Renaissance and Reformation, from the fifteenth to the mid seventeenth centuries. The English history section was taught by Ken Cable and the rest of the European syllabus by Bruce Mansfield. Cable later taught and wrote Australian history, with an emphasis

on religious subjects while Mansfield published a series of major books relating to the influential Renaissance scholar, Erasmus of Rotterdam. Both these men were charismatic teachers, whose lectures were informed by a deep knowledge of Christian theology and European religious history. What I think contributed to their mutual passion for this course was their shared and deeply held Protestant beliefs. In their lectures Protestantism was portrayed as a movement marked by truth and progress, and Catholicism as an anachronistic medieval institution whose teachings were dominated by superstition. From the perspective of the twenty-first century a course on the Renaissance and Reformation taught from such a biased Protestant perspective is impossible to justify but in 1964 my seventeen-year-old self found it absolutely compelling. The course requirements included writing two essays based on primary sources. I found this difficult and challenging but also intellectually stimulating. My first essay was about the life of a sixteenth century English bishop, Stephen Gardiner, in which I was required to base my arguments about his religious life on my reading of his published letters. The second related to the causes of the Scandinavian Reformation, using the published and translated tracts and letters of the main Swedish Protestant reformers. By the time I had finished this course I believed that I had begun to understand some of the skills and judgements required of a professional historian.

It was this course that changed my career ambitions. About half way through the academic year I informed my parents that I had lost all interest in an eventual career in Law and instead wanted to become an academic historian. My mother was very unhappy about my decision, although she didn't try to make me change my mind. My father was very encouraging, although I suspect that, given my academic record to date, he probably thought my prospects of qualifying as a university lecturer were non-existent. Instead, he assumed I would become a high school history teacher, which in his view was an admirable outcome.

At the end of 1964 I was awarded passes in Psychology and English and a bare credit in History.[2] I probably needed to reflect that scraping a credit in History 1 didn't augur well for my academic ambitions but all I could think of was that it was a mark that qualified me to enrol in Honours in History 2 and was therefore a small step towards achieving my goals to become a university teacher.

For my second year at University, I enrolled in English 2, Archaeology 1 and History 2 honours. The second-year English course, as I indicated above, was essentially an extension of Leavis 101, although, apart from grudgingly developing a liking for Austen and Conrad I really enjoyed the poetry section of the syllabus, with its focus on the English romantic poets, Coleridge and Wordsworth. At North Sydney Technical High School our English teacher had avoided the optional poetry section of the Leaving Certificate English syllabus, arguing that boys lacked the sensibility to relate to this genre of literature.

In Archaeology lectures and tutorials students literally spent most of their time in the dark. Teaching consisted almost exclusively of slide presentations, focussing on artefacts and architecture, but almost no time was set aside for discussion. There was little emphasis on theoretical approaches to Archaeology or on locating material objects in their cultural and historical contexts. Assessment was partly based on slide tests, in which students were required simply to identify a series of archaeological artefacts from images projected onto a screen. I enjoyed writing the essays but was frustrated by the lack of feedback, which usually consisted of a brief written comment, such as, 'a well-argued essay', and the mark, which was invariably 6 ½ (out of 10), effectively a bare Credit grade.

The pass level History course in which I enrolled, covered European History from the French Revolution to the Treaty of Versailles. The English section of the syllabus was taught by a newly appointed lecturer, Ken Macnab. He was very nervous, and chain smoked throughout each lecture, which was delivered in a monotone. Nevertheless, the content was detailed and up to date in historiographical terms, reflecting the new interest in 'history from below' amongst an influential group of English historians. I found reading

my lecture notes on the bus home more interesting than listening to the lectures themselves. The lectures on continental Europe, with a focus on France, Russia and Germany, were delivered by Fred Stambrook, whose iconoclastic approach was to challenge standard understandings relating to such momentous historical problems as the causes of the French Revolution and World War 1. I found his lectures fascinating, although sometimes deliberately perverse, and I not only learnt a great deal about modern European history but also about the need for historians to be sceptical about both primary and secondary sources.

Because I had become fascinated by European religious history, I chose to enrol in an honours seminar focussing on the history of the Catholic Church in Europe from the French Revolution to the outbreak of World War 2. The lecturer who taught this course was also a recent appointee, Tony Cahill. Educated at Sydney and Oxford, along with Cable and Mansfield, he belonged to the last generation of academics who were appointed without PhDs. He was a shy man who was incredibly well read both in European and Australian history. Like Cable, he had what ultimately became unrealised ambitions to publish a series of major books.

But he was a fine teacher who encouraged the students in his seminar to perform to their highest ability and focussed on making constructive criticisms in his assessments of oral and written presentations. His encouragement gave me confidence and allowed me to begin to form my own ideas about history as a discipline and find my own voice in expressing my understandings and arguments about the meaning of the past. The subject of my first essay for the seminar related to assessing and explaining the changing political and religious ideas of the nineteenth century French radical priest Lamennais. I wasn't confident about the quality of what I had produced and at the appointment I had made with Tony Cahill to collect the marked essay I began by pleading to be given another chance. He gently cut me off, handed me the essay, and invited me to read the comments and mark which were written on the essay's last page. In fact, the mark was 18 out of 20,

Tony Cahill, my teacher, colleague and friend, attending our wedding in 1981. The bride, Grace Karskens, is in the foreground, and her parents Francine and Bill are on the rear left. *Waterhouse Family Collection*

which was High Distinction level. It was the highest mark I had ever received for any major piece of work in any subject, either at school or university level. I received the same mark for my second essay on the French Catholic fascist organisation, the Action Francaise. At the end of the year I was awarded a High Distinction in History, a Credit in Archaeology and the inevitable pass in English. My History results by no means confirmed my chances of a future academic career but they did make them seem a little more plausible.

When I returned to teach History at the University in 1973 Tony Cahill became my colleague instead of my teacher, a man I worked with and admired throughout his career in the Department. He had fallen ill with polio early in his life and always wore calipers and walked with two sticks. Although he was by then retired and experiencing a recurrence of polio, he attended my inaugural professorial lecture in 2002, which meant a great deal to me because I valued his approval far more than that of most of my other Sydney History Department colleagues.

The undergraduate history syllabus at the University of Sydney was still based on the principles established in the interwar period by the department's second Challis Professor, Stephen Roberts. In the first two years students enrolled in courses in European history extending from the Medieval through to the post World War 2 period. This emphasis was based on an understanding that Europe was the birthplace of modern civilization. Not until third year were students finally allowed to study the histories of South-East Asia, India, the United States and Australia. However, because this was an old-style imperial history driven syllabus, the countries and cultures studied were located within the context of the spread of European 'civilisation'.

I chose not to enrol in Australian history as my third-year history subject because the course syllabus was limited to say the least, and the lecturer, Duncan MacCallum, a staunch supporter of the British Empire and its achievements, delivered lectures that each covered a minuscule time period while also including massive amounts of detail. The First Fleet did not depart England until near the end of first term and spent most of second term slowly making its way across two Oceans to New South Wales. Third term was devoted to covering the early years of the European occupation of Sydney and its near environs. The course usually ended with the so-called 'Rum Rebellion' of 1808, although in some years it finished without even reaching the nineteenth century.

There were two courses in American history, one taught by Christina Campbell, the other by Neville Meaney. They were very similar in content although Meaney's course contained a greater emphasis on diplomatic history. There was no real educational justification for two such courses, but they existed because the two lecturers had difficulty co-operating and were incapable of partnering in teaching a joint subject.

I chose Neville Meaney's course for no other reason than the timetable fitted with my other subject which was Archaeology 2. The honours segment of the course focussed on the history of American foreign policy from the Revolution to the Cold War. I found Meaney a very different honours teacher from Cahill, because Tony encouraged students to find their own voices and develop their own arguments while Neville enforced his own strong ideas about American history and its interpretations. For my first essay on the origins of the War of 1812 I received only a mid-Distinction mark, while his written comments indicated that although my argument was strong and consistent it was 'the wrong argument'. My second essay dealt with the origins of the Monroe Doctrine and because my analysis was more in accord with his own understandings, I was awarded a (bare) High Distinction accompanied by the comment, 'Keep up the good work and you could do well'.[3] In my exam papers at the end of that year I was careful to focus on developing arguments that at the very least were not in disagreement with Neville Meaney's own interpretations. Perhaps this contributed to the fact that I not only earned a High Distinction mark in History 3 Honours but also moved up the table to be placed equal second in the Honours rankings. Achievement at this level also prompted Meaney to adopt me as one of his students, someone to be nurtured and directed through the Honours and (potentially) postgraduate years.

In 1966 I also avoided a possible hurdle in my hoped-for pathway towards an academic career. In 1964 the Federal Government introduced a national service scheme to boost army numbers to fight the war in Vietnam. In the year in which they turned 20, Australian men were required to register and the names of conscripts were selected by a birthday ballot, involving drawing numbered wooden marbles from a barrel. To the relief of my parents and myself, in September 1966, I learnt that I was not to be called up for army service.

In 1967 I enrolled in History 4 Honours for which students were required to enrol in two seminar courses and write a 20,000 word thesis. The History Method seminar, which was taught by Professor John Manning Ward was compulsory. For my second seminar I chose the Ken Cable and Gwynne Jones taught course on English history covering the period from 1559 to 1660. And Neville Meaney persuaded me to write my thesis on Australian Naval Defence Policy, 1901–1922, under his supervision. Although he taught American history he was in the process of researching and writing a book on the history of Australian foreign policy in the first twenty years of Australian federation and he was keen for me to work under his research interest umbrella. It was an offer very difficult to refuse.

I enjoyed and learnt a great deal from the Method Seminar. In the first few weeks the students sat bunched at one end of Ward's enormous office while he sat at his desk at the other. Using examples from his own research relating to the history of nineteenth-century British imperial policy he delivered a series of lectures about approaches to the writing of history that were very conservative and failed to take account of recent historiographical trends which focussed on class, race and the dark side of the British Empire. However, in succeeding weeks the students set off on a kind of historiographical Cook's tour as we attended classes led by staff members whose expertise extended across a range of periods and cultures. So, we studied Herodotus and Thucydides with Bob Sinclair, the Venerable Bede and William of Malmesbury with Ian Jack, Machiavelli with Ros Pesman, and Gibbon and Macaulay with Alastair MacLachlan. But the teacher who I found most fascinating and from whom I learned so much about history and the processes involved in writing it was Ernest Bramsted, a Jewish refugee from Nazi Germany, who subsequently not only taught European history at the University of Sydney but wrote one of the most important studies of the Nazi regime, *Goebbels and National Socialist Propaganda (1965)*. His talks on Friedrich Meinecke and Karl Mannhein were particularly fascinating and insightful because he had studied under them and knew them personally as well as professionally. Overall, this seminar provided me with a wonderful grounding in historiography and broadened my understanding of the forms that history has taken and the different ways historians have shaped our interpretations of the past. For the last few weeks of the seminar we returned to Ward's room to listen to his pragmatic and empirically based reflections on historical practice. It seemed something of a let-down.

I found the English history seminar to be less stimulating than I expected. Cable's first year lectures were challenging, and he came across as a charismatic figure, but as a seminar teacher he seemed detached from the subjects we discussed and not very interested in the students enrolled in the class. This was probably because he was dealing with a major health issue. I have no idea what marks I earned for the two seminar papers I wrote for him. On one he wrote 'an interesting paper' and on the other 'a very interesting paper'. Jones was much more enthusiastic about the seminar paper I produced for him but I also found him to be an historian who distrusted the study of political events within a wider cultural context in favour of a narrow, one event after another, narrative style of political history.

The History IV thesis I researched and wrote was based heavily on official Australian Government records held in the National Archives, together with the personal papers of Government Ministers and departmental officials deposited in the National Library of Australia. The thesis was deeply researched but not well organised, in part because it was not divided by chapters or headings, and it was written in a very formal and somewhat anachronistic style. When I read it now, I realise

that in that Honours year I was still an historian at the very beginning of my apprenticeship.

At the end of the year, I sat for three exams, one for each of the seminars, and another general History paper which in theory covered any subject taught in the History Department extending over the whole four-year syllabus. It was a formidable paper, almost impossible to study for, but fortunately it carried very few marks. In fact, the history staff rarely referred to its existence and never offered advice on how we could prepare for it. Nor did the Department provide a stated justification as to why such an exam even existed.

My handwriting had deteriorated badly during my university years and my fourth-year exam answers were indecipherable. So, I was summoned into the Department to read two of them out loud to my examiners, Cable and Jones in the case of the English history seminar and an avuncular Ernest Bramsted, substituting for Ward, as the marker of the Method seminar. I was later told by a disapproving Ken Cable that my persuasive enthusiasm in reading out my answers probably earned me some extra marks.

One afternoon just before Christmas I made my way to the University to check the Honours results, which were posted on boards in the Quadrangle just after 5pm. I learnt that I had obtained First Class Honours and come equal second in the History IV honours cohort. These days most students who complete an honours year at an Australian university earn First Class Honours but at that time only a small number of Firsts were awarded and the majority of students earned Second Class Division 1, Second Class Division 2, or even Third Class Honours. That year, in a class of 32 students, four earned Firsts in History and for me the results were both a relief and a delight. Most importantly, I had passed another milestone in my bid for an academic career because I had not only achieved a good honours result and qualified for a Commonwealth Postgraduate Scholarship but also increased my chances of earning a postgraduate fellowship at a prestigious overseas university.

During my undergraduate years I lived at home. A Commonwealth Scholarship paid for

My first step on my road to life as an academic historian: graduation day 1969 with my sister Annabel and parents, Nancy and Earle, Peter Herman my friend from high-school and his girlfriend Chery.l
Waterhouse Family Collection

my university fees but my father earned too high an income for me to qualify for the means tested scholarship living allowance. Instead, I relied for my travel, clothing, eating and entertainment expenses on a fifteen-shillings a week allowance I received from my father, supplemented by salaries I earned working in department stores, factories and the local post office over the Christmas holidays. My greatest expense was the £150 which I spent on an ancient Morris Minor which was mostly used to drive to and from Longueville and the University of Sydney. However, once I had completed my undergraduate studies, I decided it was time to leave home.

Endnotes

1   Christopher Hilliard, *English as a Vocation: The Scrutiny Movement*, Oxford: Oxford University Press, 2012, p. 237

2   At that time the marks awarded to students in each subject in Arts 1 included Credit, Pass with Merit, Pass, and Fail. Second and third year pass students were awarded marks at Pass With Merit, Pass and Fail level. Honours students were awarded marks of High Distinction, Distinction, Credit, Pass and Fail. An Honours student who received a Pass (or Fail) mark could not proceed with the Honours component in the succeeding year.

3   My History 1 and History 2, 3 and 4 honours essays are in the Waterhouse Collection

Chapter 14

Life at 'the Hop': my American Odyssey

AT THAT TIME AUSTRALIAN students who studied for PhDs at overseas universities, especially Oxford, Cambridge and London, were more likely to obtain lectureships in Australian universities than those who remained in Australia to complete their higher degree research degrees. In a pre-internet age, when it was still cheaper and therefore more common to travel from Australia to overseas destinations by ship rather than by air, this country was perceived both at home and abroad, as a remote destination, lagging behind in education and research. At the same time, an Australian 'cultural cringe' was still very much in play in this country in the late 1960s, involving a sense of intellectual inferiority that was reflected in the widely held belief that no matter how much Australian universities improved their educational standards they would never be capable of matching those of the best British institutions.

Supported by a Commonwealth Government Postgraduate Research Fellowship I enrolled as an MA (research) student in the History Department at the University of Sydney in 1968. My plan was to research a thesis at Sydney while applying for postgraduate fellowships at overseas universities, fellowships that would allow me to commence study for a PhD in the northern hemisphere Autumn of 1969. In the event that I failed to secure an overseas postgraduate fellowship I intended to convert my Sydney MA into a PhD, although I knew my future academic job prospects were likely to diminish as a result. My original intention was also to choose a research topic in American

history. However, Cable and Ward informed me that the Department had determined that early modern English history was the field in which I was most talented and I was duly, and unwillingly, assigned to Gwynne Jones. Under his supervision I embarked on a thankfully still uncompleted thesis on Puritan Legislation in the Elizabethan House of Commons. In that era Australian academics basically followed the English model of supervision, which involved supervisors providing very little advice to their postgraduate students until they handed in a full draft of their thesis. I can only remember holding one supervision meeting with Dr Jones in the eighteen months I was enrolled for the MA at Sydney. On that occasion I was invited to drive to his house at Epping for a discussion about my progress. But as soon as I arrived, he remembered that the Laurence Olivier/Greer Garson film version of *Pride and Prejudice* (1940) was scheduled for screening and so our meeting was abandoned for a night in front of the family television.

Neville Meaney was disappointed that I would not be researching a topic in American history under his supervision. In fact, I still had aspirations to undertake postgraduate study in American history, although not at Sydney. Unlike most Australian history postgraduate students, who had ambitions to complete their degrees at English universities, I was disillusioned with British culture because of what I considered to be its suffocating influence on Australia. As I have already indicated there was a widespread belief amongst antipodean academics that

Australian culture was and would remain inferior to its British counterpart. This belief hindered the nascent movement to assert an Australian history and culture. I had also heard a number of anecdotal stories that existed on the 'postgrad grapevine' about the patronising attitude of English academics towards Australian postgraduate students in England, including usually referring to them as 'colonials'. However, the United States of the late sixties seemed in the process of becoming a progressive, albeit also a divided country, in terms of technology, culture and higher education.

After carrying out my own research and assessment into which American universities might best suit my needs to study for a PhD in early (colonial) north American history I finally applied to Harvard and Johns Hopkins. I chose the former for the obvious reason that it enjoyed a reputation as an educational institution of the highest quality. More specifically, Bernard Bailyn, its colonial specialist, was regarded as a leader in the field. I chose Johns Hopkins, in part because I was impressed by Jack Greene, who was the History Department's young colonial American historian. His book, *The Quest for Power: The Lower Houses of Assembly in the Southern Royal Colonies, 1689–1776* (1963) impressed me as containing an ambitious and important set of arguments relating to the causes of the American Revolution. I thought it was the kind of book that I would like to write in the future and the high praise it received in the reviews in the most influential academic history journals suggested that Greene was already a major figure in the field. Frankly, I was also somewhat intimidated by Harvard and questioned whether I would measure up to its high standards. I concluded that Hopkins was a safer bet. There seemed to be something re-assuring about it, reflected in its handbook which featured photos of columned Georgian style buildings covered in snow. As it turned out my assumptions about Hopkins were completely wrong, for the History staff encouraged the highest levels of excellence and competitiveness amongst its graduate ('grad') students, levels which were too exacting to qualify as comforting. As I later learned, most Hopkins History graduate students lived in a permanent

state of concern that they couldn't perform at the expected level.

During the eighteen months I spent as a postgraduate student at the University of Sydney, while researching and partly writing my MA thesis, preparing my applications to Harvard and Hopkins, and waiting nervously to learn the results, I lived at International House, which was located just across City Road from the University. I benefitted enormously from moving out of my parents' home and enjoying a social life that included IH organised cultural events as well as informal and spontaneous room parties, usually involving the consumption of large amounts of alcohol. Now, a high proportion of Australian university students are from overseas, but in the late 1960s international student numbers were small. Most of the overseas students who lived in International House were Asian students who came from India, Singapore, Malaysia, Hong Kong, Taiwan, Thailand and the Philippines. There was also a sprinkling of students from Africa and north America. Some of the Asian students were financed by the Columbo Plan, while others came from families with the financial means to support their children's education at the University of Sydney.

I made some wonderful friends in International House both amongst the Australian and overseas students. I also learnt how to cook some basic Chinese dishes, namely Soy Sauce Chicken, and acquired a rudimentary knowledge of Asian cultures. I also found out something about what these very intelligent (mostly) young students thought about Australia and its racist attitudes and policies towards Asian countries. Living in International House with students from such a rich and diverse range of cultural backgrounds led me to challenge my own ethnocentric understandings about my country and its place in the world. My 'world view' remained Eurocentric but at least I began to understand the value of other cultural inheritances.

When I left Sydney for Baltimore I maintained an extensive correspondence with my International House friends, a correspondence that lasted throughout my four Hopkins years and extended through the first five years or so after my return to teach at the University of Sydney. I kept the letters I received but I only read through them again in 2024, some 50 years later. In response to this belated second reading I found myself wishing that I had maintained my connections to my International House friends, both in Sydney and abroad for much longer, because these men and women had enriched my life and contributed enormously to the education of young Richard.

In early 1969 I learnt that I had succeeded in my applications to both Harvard and Johns Hopkins. However, I was only awarded an 'alternate' or reserve scholarship to Harvard, which meant I was only offered funding for tuition and living expenses if other students turned their scholarships down. In contrast, I was awarded a junior teaching fellowship at Hopkins, which included payment of fees and a one-year stipend of $US2000. Given that I had some modest savings from the part-time tutoring I had undertaken at the University of Sydney and that I had succeeded in my application for an overseas travelling scholarship from P&O, which consisted of a first class return voyage to the United States, I had sufficient funds to provide for my first year of study at Johns Hopkins. I was sanguinely and naively optimistic that I would easily perform sufficiently well to earn successive fellowships for my latter years of graduate study. I wrote to Johns Hopkins accepting the teaching fellowship and I also contacted Harvard to decline the offer to enrol at that University. So, I never found out whether any students declined their offer of Harvard fellowships, in the process turning my 'alternate' into a 'real' scholarship. However, my mind was set on Hopkins and I was determined to accept its offer, no matter what the circumstances.

I was excited both about my first overseas trip and my acceptance at Hopkins but my buoyant mood was dampened somewhat by a conversation I had with John Ward when I spoke to him in his capacity as Head of the History Department to tell him I was leaving to take up a PhD scholarship at an overseas university. He smiled when I told him this and then asked which British University had accepted me. When I told him that

I planned to study colonial American history at Johns Hopkins a look of mild disapproval came over his face. He then congratulated me on the award of the fellowship and informed me that with the recent establishment of several Colleges of Advanced Education in (mostly regional) Australia my job prospects at one of these institutions when I returned home would be strong. However, I understood his underlying meaning to be that a PhD from an American University, with Harvard and Yale perhaps the exceptions, was unlikely in his view to land me a future lectureship at one of Australia's established universities.

At this time, I was also traumatized as the result of an encounter with a Sydney University academic. Congratulating me on the award of the Hopkins fellowship he shouted me a celebratory dinner at a Cleveland Street restaurant. After the meal, at which we had consumed quite a lot of red wine, he suggested we buy another bottle of wine and take it to my room in International House where we could continue to drink and talk. But as soon as we reached my room he made a sexual approach, which involved trying to unbutton my shirt. I resisted and told him several times that I wasn't interested, that I was heterosexual and had never felt sexually attracted to any man. Nevertheless, he persisted in his attempts to undress me and in the end I pushed him away with all my strength and he landed on my bed. Then came a series of accusations in which he claimed I had led him to believe that I wanted to engage in sexual relations with him and at the last moment I had lost my nerve. These insinuations had an immediate impact because I began to feel guilty and believed that the whole incident had taken place because I had unintentionally led him on. I found myself apologising to him then and again on a subsequent occasion when we met at his suggestion at a public eating space in the University Union. I carried this sense of guilt for many decades, even into the 1990s, until it finally dawned on me that this was a classic case of blaming the victim. But I think there was also a positive outcome from this incident, because when I finally became an academic administrator and found myself dealing with several complaints of sexual harassment from (mostly postgraduate) students against academic staff, my recollections of my own experience of sexual torment and its long-term consequences, sharpened my determination to understand the impact on the victims, as well as punish the predators and deter them from repeating such abusive behaviour.

Finally, on July 19 1969 I left Sydney on the ss *Orsova*, bound for San Francisco via Hong Kong, Kobe, Yokohama, Honolulu and Los Angeles. Most of the passengers travelling first class were wealthy Australian retirees, although there were a few English and American travellers. Within a day or two of leaving Sydney I concluded that the stuffiness and conservative nature of the decor, food and entertainments were reminiscent of a classy English hotel of the interwar era, at least as portrayed in English films.[1] However, there were also a small number of other P&O Scholarship winners bound for north American universities in first class, as well as a handful of young schoolteachers with contracts to teach in Canadian schools. We tended to congregate together both around the pool during the day and at the dances and concerts held in the evening. The only means for us to find a way into tourist class was through the medical centre waiting room, which served both classes, I suppose because P&O considered all ill people to be equal. Sometimes we used this room to find our way into the tourist class entertainment area where the music was more contemporary and the average age of the passengers about 40 years younger than in first class. The ship's officers also liked to enjoy the entertainments offered in tourist class, particularly because of the prospects of meeting attractive young women. When they recognised that we were interlopers we were escorted back to first class, with the officers claiming that our presence made tourist class too crowded.

In any case, I enjoyed the company of my fellow young first-class passengers and when on shore we often travelled together. Most memorably, seven of us left the ship in Kobe and travelled overland for three days by bullet train, stopping at Nara, Kyoto and Tokyo before re-joining the ship in Yokohama.[2] In Honolulu five of us hired a car

and drove around the island, while in Los Angeles we took the inevitable tour of Disneyland. I was excited to be introduced albeit briefly to what seemed such different and exotic cultures in Hong Kong and Japan. However, my exclusive exposure to tourist venues in Oahu and Los Angeles did little to prepare me for the vastness and diversity of American culture.

My mother had conceived of my trip to the US as a giant tourist pilgrimage, and aware of her experience in planning overseas excursions, I had allowed her to organise mine. In accord with her plan, a few hours after I left the ship in San Francisco I boarded a bus at the Greyhound Bus Station, en route to Baltimore, with only two scheduled overnight stops. I quickly noticed that the Bus Station was in a very poor and run down section of town and that the vast majority of the Greyhound patrons were African-Americans. As a suit-wearing European, I certainly stood out. Because I was so inappropriately over-dressed for an American bus traveller, I was panhandled in every bus station between San Francisco and Oklahoma whenever I stepped out of the bus to buy food or use the toilet.

My first scheduled stop was in Tulsa, Oklahoma, where Bob Kuzelka was living and working. I had met Bob at International House, when he held a Fulbright Fellowship in the Town Planning Department at the University of Sydney. In Tulsa he was employed in one of the Great Society programs established by Lyndon Johnson, in this case to encourage and provide support to African-American small businesses. Bob took me along to some of his meetings with African-Americans who were seeking support from this program and this experience made me aware of the difficulties these men faced in establishing and maintaining such enterprises, especially outside the unofficially prescribed African-American residential areas. In walking the streets of Tulsa, it was also apparent that de facto racial segregation was the norm because I didn't encounter any 'mixed' neighbourhoods. On Sunday Bob drove me some 64 kilometres (40 miles) to his parent's home in Okmulgee where I attended a rousing revival style service in a Methodist Church and enjoyed a Sunday lunch of roast chicken and blueberry pie. However, I was surprised and disappointed to also find myself listening to some disturbing anti-semitic comments from Bob's father.

In Oklahoma I began to realise how different the US was from Australia. Religion was more fervent and more pervasive, reflected in the fact that there were few bars and clubs in Tulsa and the only beer available contained a maximum of 3.2% alcohol. In Sydney people drank alcohol at parties, in Tulsa they played party games. African-Americans constituted a strong cultural presence, but perhaps because of the riots following Martin Luther King's death in the previous year, tension and a sense of mistrust, were certainly evident in Tulsa and I guessed in other cities too. To me America seemed far less comfortable than Australia.[3]

After the long bus trip from San Francisco to Tulsa I decided against resuming my road trip in favour of a much quicker and more comfortable journey by air. Arriving at Baltimore Airport I was met by Fred DeKuyper a Johns Hopkins administrative staff member, who together with his wife Mary and son Gordon constituted my Johns Hopkins appointed host family. Over the next four years they often invited me into their home for dinner, especially at Thanksgiving, in the process introducing me to American family life and allowing me to enjoy brief moments of domesticity.

I had arrived in Baltimore only a week or so before the beginning of the Fall semester and after a few days enjoying the hospitality of the Dekuypers in their house in an affluent area of north Baltimore, characterised by large Georgian style houses set in azalea-filled gardens, I moved into a studio apartment in a Hopkins-owned residential building adjacent to the Homewood campus. It was disappointing to discover that the apartment possessed neither cooking facilities nor a refrigerator.

I was also introduced to some of the History graduate students from whom I learnt a great deal about the Hopkins requirements for the PhD degree and about the University's 'grad school culture'. First, I discovered that although

the official name of the university was The Johns Hopkins University, graduate students referred to it as 'The Hop'. Second, and to my dismay, I learnt that I had not done enough homework on the PhD requirements at Hopkins. I knew students needed to fulfill certain coursework demands but I had assumed that these were cursory and that once I had met them, I could get on with the job of writing my dissertation, with all tasks completed within three years. Instead, I was told that initially students were required to engage in two years of coursework involving four areas of study. Only the final two years were set aside for researching and writing a dissertation, although my informants told me that very few students managed to complete their 100,000 word thesis in the allocated time. I began to realise that I was facing a minimum of four years of really hard work and study. In acknowledgement of this I wrote back to my parents to warn them that I was likely to be in the United States longer than they or I had anticipated:

...that to be lost here is the easiest thing in the world. The whole thing is assuming the proportions of a much greater challenge than I had anticipated.[4]

Discovering the extensive nature of the PhD requirements made me concerned not just because I had learned that the degree would take a minimum of four rather than three years but also because I knew that Hopkins would not fund me beyond four years and neither I nor my parents had the money to cover an extra year of tuition fees plus my living and accommodation expenses. Soon after my arrival I was also informed by the University's International Office that it was not the practice of Federal Immigration officials to extend student visas beyond the allocated four years. So, right at the beginning of my Hopkins enrolment I made the necessary decision to work as much as it took to complete the degree in four years.

From my discussions with senior students, I also learnt more about Hopkins culture. Students were very much identified with their supervisor. Jack Greene's veteran students told me I was now a 'Greene student' and that what characterised members of his tribe was high morale and a sense of being special. No doubt students of other professors in the History Department were told exactly the same thing by their seniors. All first-year students were required to research and write a seminar paper of publishable quality which they presented either to the American or European graduate seminars at the end of their first year of study. Usually, the supervisor and his other graduate students were supportive in these seminars, but if one of the other professors such as David Donald, Alfred Chandler or Kenneth Lynn were critical of the presentation, their students were likely to join in with similar expressions of disapproval. To my deep concern I learnt that as a result the discussions in these seminars were often heated and the presenters frequently left feeling humiliated. The other graduate students suggested and I quickly accepted that this 'rigorous' and even 'ruthless' seminar culture contributed to 'an all-pervading air of scholarship'. I also came to believe that I would receive a far better education and more complete training as an historian than I was likely to achieve either in Australia or the United Kingdom.[5]

When I re-consider this ruthless hard work and high-performance culture from the distance of 50 years it occurs to me that it was partly shaped by masculinist values, reflecting the fact that Johns Hopkins was a male-dominated institution. At that time the University only admitted male students as undergraduates and although women were accepted as graduate students, they were in a clear minority. The vast majority of academic staff members in the Faculty of Arts and Sciences were men, and in History there was not a single woman appointee. Not long after my arrival, two of the more senior graduate students, Glenn Porter and Hal Livesay, decided to become my unofficial mentors, and began by explaining that the Hopkins mantra could be simply explained as 'work, study, get ahead.'

During my enrolment period at Hopkins and for many years afterwards I believed that this ethos was the norm in the graduate programs of all the best American universities. I only learnt otherwise in the late 1980s when a fine American

historian from the University of Maryland, Jim Gilbert, visited the Sydney History Department as a Fulbright Fellow. Given the proximity of College Park, where the University of Maryland is located, to Baltimore I asked Jim whether he had visited Hopkins to give a paper to the History Seminar. He looked incredulous and then told me he would never do that because it had a unique reputation as a snake pit.

What contributed to my acceptance that Hopkins provided the opportunity for me to receive an outstanding postgraduate education was my own subsequent experiences in these early weeks of the 1969 Fall Semester, in particular, my encounters with Jack Greene. I was told in advance of my first meeting with him that he was a 'kindly eccentric man' who nevertheless expected his students to work hard and perform to a high level.[6] Within a week or so of my arrival he asked me to meet him for our first supervisory session. He seemed to me to be filled with energy, incapable of sitting for very long and instead constantly standing and bouncing from one foot to another. He was also filled with ideas, drawn not only from his wide reading in American and English history but also from political theory and sociology. After that meeting I wrote to my parents that he was a genius who was not only tuned to the latest scholarship, but writing it.[7] Over the many years of our relationship that followed, years that extended beyond my time at Hopkins to include my tenure as a member of the academic staff at the University of Sydney, I also learnt that he was a much kinder person than most of his Hopkins colleagues. When my parents visited Baltimore in 1972 he generously invited them to lunch and treated them with much more consideration than their embarrassed son, who was continually trying to get them to say as little as possible. Moreover, whereas, most of his colleagues ruthlessly refused to allow their weaker students to continue after either their first or second years of study, Jack persevered with his poorest performers. Two of his students who were enrolled during my time at Hopkins took more than a decade to complete their theses, but in the end Jack steered them through. He also had the gentlest method I have witnessed of shredding the arguments in papers presented to the Hopkins seminar by graduate students, academic colleagues and visiting scholars. When the chair asked for questions or comments at the end of the presentation Jack would begin his critique with the phrase, 'What you're really saying...' and then proceed to advance a completely different interpretation of the evidence presented. This allowed the presenter to reflect to him or herself that with a slight tweak the paper would be fine, whereas in fact Jack had just executed a complete demolition. And finally, once you were a Greene student you were always a Greene student. In 2008, some 35 years after I graduated from Hopkins Jack asked me to present a paper on the history of the relationship between liberty and representative government in Australia to a conference in Cincinnati. The papers given there, on the relationship between liberty and representative government in a range of First and Second British Empire colonies, later formed a book, edited by Jack and published by Cambridge University Press. As it turned out my debt to him was career long.[8]

In my first year as a graduate student at Hopkins I was required to enrol in one reading course, and to write two seminar papers relating to colonial American history, one historiographical and the other a publishable level research article. I chose a reading course in Tudor/Stuart history in part because I was already familiar with the historiography but also because I remained interested in this area of history. The requirements involved reading all the books, chapters and articles on a ten-page reading list provided by the teacher of the course and sitting for a take-home exam at the end of the academic year, that is, in May 1970. The course teacher, Wilfrid Prest, was an Oxford educated Australian who had taken leave from a position at the University of Adelaide to become an untenured assistant professor at Hopkins. We shared feelings of unfamiliarity with the general American university system and of intimidation from Hopkins academic culture. As well as a fine scholar he was a sympathetic figure who provided me with some much-needed re-assurance.

For the two pieces of work required by Greene, I chose to write my historiographical essay on histories of New England Puritanism and my research essay on the English background of the first generation of New England puritan clergy, men who arrived in Massachusetts in the decade beginning in 1630.

Most of the first and second year history graduate students followed the same routine. The University Library was open from 8am until midnight and from Monday to Friday, and apart from meal breaks, we spent those hours seated at our assigned carrels. We ate breakfast and lunch in the university cafeteria while at dinner time students who lived in apartments with kitchens went home to cook, while the rest of us either returned to the cafeteria or ate in one of the cheap restaurants in the areas adjacent to the campus. Chilli Con Carne, a dish not yet known in Australia, became my staple meal, both because it was cheap and I enjoyed the taste. When the library closed, we either went home to bed or adjourned to the Grad Club, which was located in the basement of one of the University owned apartments, to drink cheap beer and watch one of the late-night talk shows on television. On weekends most students spent shorter hours in the library, setting aside time to shop for food, wash clothes and on those weekends when the Baltimore Orioles were playing at home, walk the five blocks or so to Memorial Stadium to watch a game. I had played baseball as a teenager and understood the rules of the game, so it was one American cultural institution with which I was familiar. I felt privileged to watch one of the great teams in American baseball, one that included such talented players as Brooks Robinson, Frank Robinson and Jim Palmer. In 1970 I was fortunate enough to attend the fifth game of the World Series between the Orioles and the Cincinnati Reds, which was the one in which the O's clinched the title

Comforted by learning that I had miraculously passed the two required translation exams in French and German, I did have a break over Xmas and New Year, travelling up to Boston with Dick Ryerson, a Greene student who was a year ahead of me, to spend Christmas with his parents at their home in Marshfield Hills. It was my first, but not my last, white Christmas.

During this time, I also felt lonely and home-sick. Living alone in an apartment without cooking facilities didn't help but I also found that not only was there no reporting of Australia and what was happening here but most of the Americans I met knew almost nothing about my country and didn't really care to learn. Occasionally I fielded questions as to whether we had supermarkets or electricity, and someone inexplicably once asked whether Australia was a country near Wales, but the ignorant nature of these questions usually provoked me into providing answers containing a minimum of detail. Occasionally I would talk about my family, Sydney and the University of Sydney but my American friends always seemed so uninterested that I gave up speaking about my Australian background.

Ironically, in 1971, when my graduate student cohort had dispersed to all parts of America and Europe to research their PhD theses, one student who was now researching in a French provincial city, wrote to me indicating how strange he found it living in a foreign country and adding that now he knew how I felt. I wrote back suggesting that in fact our circumstances were different because it would only cost him $US300 and take 9 hours for him to get home. In contrast it would take me more than 40 hours to fly to Sydney, including compulsory stops in San Francisco, Hawaii and Fiji and cost a return airfare amounting almost to a full year's fellowship. In short, a visit home was not a viable option for me. Many years later, I caught up with another former Hopkins student, now a professor at a university near Washington, who was visiting Sydney to attend a conference. After he had talked for some time over lunch about how much he liked Australia he then asked about my reticence in referring to my country during the time I spent in America. When I replied that no-one ever showed much interest, he looked doubtful, which I found ironic because he was one of those fellow students who had shown no curiosity about Australia during the years we shared in Baltimore.

Apart from loneliness, life was also hard because I needed to live on a very small income. The $US2000 earned as a teaching fellow was paid over the nine months of the academic year so I needed to save a portion of it to pay for my living expenses over the summer. My parents occasionally and generously sent me small sums of money, enough that I could treat myself to some necessary extras. However, when I bought new clothes, they were from Target, while my diet mostly consisted of comfort food, including some take-out. When I explained my financial circumstances to my parents, my mother worried that I wouldn't be able to afford a hair-cut and therefore I wouldn't look respectable. I couldn't bear to remind her that this was the age of the counter-culture and most men had long hair. At the same time, she revealed that she and Earle had always wanted me to go to England rather than the US for postgraduate study, implying, I suppose, that this difficult situation was of my own making. Despite these comments I found my parent's letters comforting, reminders of my former life and perhaps of my future one as well. I really enjoyed my father's letters, which often contained shrewd assessments of the writings of Tennyson and Eliot, Aristophanes and Freud.[9]

When I returned to Baltimore after Christmas I moved into a shared apartment, one that thankfully contained a kitchen. My new roommate was a Japanese student, Tsuneo Ishikawa, who was studying for a PhD in the Department of Economics. The son of a distinguished Economics professor at the University of Tokyo, he had completed brilliant undergraduate qualifications in the discipline at Tokyo and had come to Hopkins to work under the supervision of the internationally renowned econometrician, Carl Christ. In the Fall semester of 1969 Tsuneo had two successive roommates, both of whom moved out because they found his long working hours disturbing and unsettling. He worked seven days a week, for hours that extended from about 8am until 2am, with only brief pauses for meals. I liked him immediately for his determination, for his gentleness and for his genuine interest in my own background. I also decided very quickly that I couldn't work any harder than I already was and that I wouldn't try to match his incredible study ethos.

Occasionally, usually late on a Saturday night,

we would sit at the dining table in our apartment, drink whisky and beer, and talk about our families, our countries and our hoped-for academic futures. Only once did we talk about World War 2 and that revealed that our perspectives were very different — I blamed the Pacific War entirely on Japan and suggested that the Japanese armed forces were exclusively guilty of war crimes, while Tsuneo very politely suggested that the allies were partly responsible for forcing Japan into War and that Nagasaki and Hiroshima were crimes against civilians — that we never talked about it again. I later realised that in 1970 I still shared much of the hatred that Australia as a nation carried towards Japan, a hatred passed down from my parent's generation.

In early 1970 I handed in my first piece of written work, an historiographical essay on New England Puritanism. It was based on extensive reading and was very closely argued, albeit in an anachronistic British style using a surfeit of passive voice, a style still commonly used in Australia. In contrast, modern American English was more direct, in particular, disdaining the use of passive voice. Greene, who as I was later to discover, was not interested in either the history of Puritanism or New England, indicated that the essay was professionally competent, although I didn't gain the impression that he found its arguments particularly original.

In late April I presented my research paper to the *American History Seminar*. Perry Miller a former Harvard History Professor who was regarded as the leading authority on the history of New England Puritanism had written an influential article in which he argued that the Puritans who emigrated to north America in 1630 and founded the colony of Massachusetts were motivated to establish their society as a model Christian community, 'a City on a Hill', to quote the words of the leader of the enterprise, John Winthrop. Miller argued that the leaders of the Massachusetts Bay emigration believed that once this exemplary church was established it would influence England's church leaders to abandon the theology and system of government of the Church of England in favour of the Massachusetts

example, which in turn would enable the New England Puritans to abandon the New World and return home in triumph.[10] In my paper, I argued that the emigrant Puritan clergy left England reluctantly and for less lofty ideological and more practical religious and economic reasons. Kenneth Lynn, one of the Hopkins History Professors who was present at the seminar, was previously a Miller graduate student and then colleague at Harvard. He was unhappy that I had presumed to be critical of Miller's argument and described my paper as consisting of (whale) 'spume'. Inevitably, Lynn's students then joined in the criticism. I defended my arguments, but I was overwhelmed by this onslaught, and when the seminar finished, I knew that I had come out second best.

Greene didn't seem to be phased by it at all and told me not to worry because it was all part of the cut and thrust of academic life. He also offered words of encouragement, suggesting that by carrying out some further research I could address the criticisms raised in the seminar, and then place the article in a large brown envelope and send it off to be considered for publication by the most prestigious journal in the field of Early American History, *The William and Mary Quarterly*. Eventually, as Greene probably suspected it would, the *Quarterly* rejected the article. When I dejectedly informed Jack about this, he told me that I should just keep mailing it off to academic publications until it was accepted. After several more rejections the paper was finally accepted for publication by *The Historical Magazine of the Protestant Episcopal Church*, an acceptance for which I was extremely grateful because I don't think there were any more eligible or more modest journals to which I could submit the piece. In any case, although not published until 1975, it became my (equal) first academic publication.[11] Through this process I also learnt the lesson that Greene no doubt intended, that academic life consists of many setbacks and rejections which can be met by determination and self-belief. Without me adopting this mantra self-consciously or deliberately it became an ethos which shaped my subsequent approach to my academic career.

In May I sat for a take-home exam in English

At Baltimore Airport en route to London, 1970. Fellow Hopkins History graduate student Jim Hoopes is on the left. An English graduate student enrolled in Economics and on his way home for the summer, is on the right. Clearly the counter culture had not influenced my dress mode. *Waterhouse Family Collection*

history. This was a new experience for me because this form of examination was not yet a part of teaching practice in Australian universities. The exam took the format of requiring students to answer three essay questions over an allocated time period of 24 hours. I collected it at 9am and worked on it in my apartment until about 2 am the next morning, setting the alarm for 8am that morning so that I could return it to the History Department by 9 am. Within a week Prest wrote me a note to let me know I had passed. Effectively, this meant I had successfully completed all the first-year requirements and could look forward to a summer break. I planned to spend some travelling in the UK as well as beginning the research for the thesis proposal I was required to present early in the succeeding 1970–71 academic year

There were several reasons for my decision to spend the summer in England. In the first place I had no desire to stay in Baltimore, especially given that most graduate students went home at this time, which meant that if I stayed I was likely to be even more lonely than I was during the previous

two semesters. Second, several of my friends from International House, Ros Wood, Gwen Burrows and John Eliot, were planning to spend time in England and invited me to join them. This was an opportunity both to catch up and to travel with them, for we planned to make a major road trip, extending from London to Edinburgh via the west and northwest of England. Third, I had grown up in an Australia which emphasised the nation's British heritage and continuing cultural connections. At school and university, for example, there was a much greater emphasis on British literature and history than on Australian subjects and authors. So, my education in British culture at a distance of 17,000 kilometres had aroused my interest in experiencing it in person. And finally, because I purchased a charter flight airfare, and booked cheap accommodation in Lillian Penson Hall, a University of London Hall of residence, I had sufficient savings to cover my travel and living costs in the UK without needing to ask my parents for funds to help tide me over the summer. In 1970 the UK was still a comparatively cheap country to live-in, especially compared to the US.

When I first arrived in England, I felt relieved. London seemed so much safer and poverty much less apparent than was the case in Baltimore. I really loved learning how to use 'the tube' (underground rail system), although I only travelled on it irregularly because my hall of residence was located in Paddington, and so in walking distance of all the historic and entertainment sites of central London. So many things, including the sizes of main roads, food serves, cars, houses, and flats, were much smaller than in the United States. These proportions seemed familiar and comforting.

My road trip with my International House friends commenced soon after my arrival. From London we made our way to Winchester and then on to Salisbury, in the process visiting and admiring two beautiful and massive medieval cathedrals. We subsequently visited Stonehenge, the picturesque seaside towns of Beer and Lyme Regis, the classic eighteenth century resort city, Bath, and finally made our way to Edinburgh where we stayed in the apartment of another International House alumni who was undertaking a PhD at the University of Edinburgh. Elsewhere, we stayed in youth hostels where we encountered some really hard travelled Australians, including two who had hitch hiked through Biafra during the course of the Nigerian Civil War. I found it fascinating to sit outside these hostels at dusk listening to the stories of these and other travellers about their odysseys through Africa, Central Asia, and Europe. In that era many young Australians undertook two years of rough travelling from their homeland to the UK as a ritual of youth.

When I returned to London, I followed a routine which involved spending half my time visiting museums, galleries and historic buildings, including the British Museum, the National Gallery, St Paul's Cathedral and Westminster Abbey, as well as daytrips to Oxford, Cambridge and Hampton Court. Otherwise, I spent week days in the University of London Library preparing my PhD thesis proposal on community life in Connecticut in the seventeenth and eighteenth centuries. New England town studies, which focussed in particular, on the nature and structure

of families as well as on the unique religious and political cultures which characterised these towns, had received a boost with the publication of three major studies of colonial Massachusetts communities by Ken Lockridge (Dedham), John Demos (Plymouth) and Phillip Greven (Andover), exemplary histories which came to be referred to as 'The Books'. They were in the vanguard of the new social history, an historiographical movement that came to dominate the writing of colonial American history. It was strongly shaped by the French Annales School and the Cambridge Group for the History of Population and Social Structure.[12]

Given its growing dominance it was prudent for me to choose a topic that reflected the subjects and methods favoured by the new social history because it was important to research a subject that was 'cutting edge'. But there was an ironic degree of difficulty involved here as well because the new social history relied heavily on the use of statistics and my mathematical training involved achieving a B in General Mathematics in the Leaving Certificate.

It was a reflection of the isolation and conservatism of the History Department at the University of Sydney that the staff was largely indifferent to the emergence of the new social history and its rising influence. Discovering its importance was a complete revelation to me, a revelation that I had experienced during my first year at Hopkins. Particularly influential for me was a lecture I attended by Peter Laslett, one of the founders of the Cambridge Group. In his presentation he detailed the approaches which characterised the new social history, which he had helped develop. His aim was to reconstitute seventeenth century English families, in the process revealing that the composition of these pre-industrial families was quite different from accepted understandings. His researches had revealed that the modern nuclear family (consisting only of parents and children) was not a product of the Industrial Revolution, but pre-existed it.

In this context I thought I had made a wise choice in determining on this topic but in fact it had drawbacks. My proposal was very similar in nature to the subject matter of another PhD thesis which Ted Cook, also a Greene student, was already researching. I proposed to work on Connecticut, his thesis focussed on Massachusetts, but I began to realise that the topics and approaches were so close, that my completed thesis was likely to find itself in the shadow of Cook's work. I continued to prepare my presentation but my doubts about the wisdom of continuing with this topic steadily grew.

As I have recounted in the previous chapter, I also visited Dorothy and John Lipscomb shortly before I returned to the United States. I was accompanied on my train trip to Petts Wood by Barry's daughter, my cousin Prue, a part time actor and music student, demonised by her relatives in Australia, who I nevertheless found '… completely charming, unaffected and very, very interesting.' I think what I meant when I wrote these words in a letter to my parents is that she seemed very cosmopolitan from the perspective of a library dwelling, impoverished graduate student. As I also indicated in the previous chapter, I'm not quite sure what John and Dorothy made of me, although my aunt wrote to Percy indicating that she was pleased that I had visited.[13] I envied my cousins, David and Anthony, both relatively recently graduated doctors who I described to my parents as 'dashing young upper-class Englishmen, with MGs and expensive clothes'.[14] They seemed to have inherited nothing Australian from their parents, but rather were unambiguously English. John, Dorothy, David and Anthony were remarkably hospitable towards me but indicated only marginally more interest in my Australian family background than my fellow Johns Hopkins graduate students. I suppose this indicated the extent to which they had cut themselves off from their Australian heritage and embraced an English past, present and future.

By the time I left England in late August my opinion of and feelings towards 'Home' had shifted from my first impressions. I acknowledged that the country was indeed more familiar than the United States but it also seemed to me to be more foreign than I had anticipated, and not a country in which I would choose to live. First, I was taken aback by the low standards of living endured by much of the population, which produced a collective and I

suppose necessary financial meanness, as well as a widely shared pessimism about the nation's future. During the time I spent travelling with my friends we often stopped for lunch in pubs in rural towns and villages. When we were asked where we came from and identified ourselves as Australians the common response was to the effect of 'What are you doing in this dump?' Second, I found myself disliking the climate, because even though the summer of 1970 was considered warm and sunny, by Australian standards it also possessed a large number of days marked by cloud and drizzle. And finally, I found the class system to be frustrating and annoying. I disliked the baby-talking upper class Londoners I met with their suggestions of 'Let's have drinksies on the Thamsies'. I was also annoyed that the English academics and postgraduate students that I encountered, uncertain about the status of an Australian postgraduate student studying at an American university, usually took the course of treating me in ways that were excessively patronising. It also seemed that a sense of entitlement permeated the English upper class, reflected in residual visions of imperial glory and an unwillingness to accept that the UK was now a small country on the edge of Europe.[15] I had arrived in England reluctantly accepting that Australia's British heritage meant that a small part of me was English. I returned to America certain of my identification with and commitment solely to Australia, its present and future.

At the beginning of my second year I didn't feel as intimidated by Hopkins as I had during the whole course of my first year. I sometimes even gullibly referred to its ethos as congenial. What made life more pleasant was that I was now sharing an apartment not only with Tsuneo but also with a newly arrived Greene student from the West Indian Island of St Lucia, Barry Gaspar. He had first enrolled at Hopkins two years earlier but had quickly decided to return home when he experienced racial abuse when walking on a Baltimore sidewalk. As part of his plan to ensure that Barry didn't abandon Hopkins a second time Greene asked me to share an apartment with him, suggesting that because we both came from British Commonwealth countries, we were likely to have a great deal in common. This reasoning seemed somewhat dubious to me and I suspected that the only British inheritance that Australians and St Lucians had in common was cricket. However, I agreed to organise a shared apartment with Barry so long as there was a three-bedroom place available because I was also determined to continue to share with Tsuneo. As it turned out the three of us got on well, taking turns to cook Japanese, West Indian and (more boring) Australian/American meals. Dinner was a break we all looked forward to not only for the food but for the enjoyable conversations we had about what we were each reading, how we were progressing with our studies, and sometimes about our families and home countries.

Of course, Tsuneo was a workaholic and while I studied hard, I had learnt the previous year not to try to compete with him in the hours I spent in the library or at my desk in the apartment. Barry also worked diligently but he also believed that weekends were for leisure. Tsuneo didn't go out with women, while I had a few dates with women Hopkins graduate students, none of which produced any serious, long-lasting relationships. However, Barry had three girlfriends, each living in a different East Coast city. He managed to ensure that they didn't know about each other by inviting them to visit him in Baltimore on different weekends. But on one occasion two of them turned up uninvited. Tsuneo and I each tried to entertain one, leaving the invited girlfriend to Barry's care. But it was hopeless and late on Saturday afternoon all six of us found ourselves in the same apartment. By the end of the evening Barry only had one girlfriend.

Finally, when these two men graduated from Hopkins they enjoyed outstanding subsequent academic careers. After a brief period at Harvard, Tsuneo became a Professor of Economics at the University of Tokyo and produced two books, *Income and Wealth* and *Income Distribution Theory* which quickly became acknowledged as highly influential works in Asia Europe and the United States. He died, tragically in 1998, at the relatively young age of 51. Barry joined the History Department at Duke University, published the

influential study *Bondmen and Masters: a study of Master Slave Relations in Antigua,* and became recognised as a leading scholar of slavery and slave resistance in comparative perspective.

The second-year requirements for History graduate students included the completion of three reading courses, similar in form to the course we had taken in our first year, this time culminating in three 24-hour take-home exams timetabled over one week in May 1971. In addition, each student was required to present a long thesis proposal to a seminar attended by their supervisor and all other first and second year students working in the same field, meaning in my case, colonial American history.

Towards the end of this academic year, I came to the opinion that studying these three subjects, which included Eighteenth Century French and Nineteenth Century United States as well as Colonial American History, had broadened my historical perspective, providing me with deeper contexts into which I could locate my research, and opening up new areas of the past which I was now qualified to teach. But my study routine was repetitive and involved long working hours. I complained to my parents that my life consisted of reading books and articles, eating and sleeping. I might have added that most nights I drank at least one beer in the Grad Club and that every two weeks or so I watched either a movie or an Orioles baseball game.[16]

My thesis presentation was neither given nor received with enthusiasm. The fact is that as the academic year progressed my interest and engagement with the proposed topic continued to wane. On presentation day I announced that I had decided, that If Greene consented, I planned to change my topic. Not only did he embrace my change of mind with enthusiasm but immediately suggested an alternative topic, namely the emergence of a planter and merchant class in colonial South Carolina. Much of early American historiography focussed on New England as constituting the most influential and representative section of colonial society. But Greene held to the view that the most powerful and 'typical' English colonies were those slaveholding plantation colonies that stretched from Maryland south through Virginia and the Carolinas to include the British West Indian settlements as well.[17] My new plan was still to write my thesis using the methods of the new social history because although such approaches usually focussed on 'history from below', that is, on the lives of the (mostly)illiterate plebians, they could still be profitably applied to histories of colonial America's wealthy classes. In any case, Greene advised me to take an approach that relied heavily on the statistical methods utilised by the new social history as a means of making the thesis more marketable and myself more employable.[18] There was an irony involved here, because the new social history, particularly in its statistical form, was not influential in Australia and the approach I used in writing my thesis was not in the end a factor in my hiring by the University of Sydney in 1973.

I sat for my three 24-hour take-home exams on the Monday, Wednesday and Friday of a week in late May, 1971. I worked on the first two exams from 9am until 2am but when I worked on the third, I had to stop writing at midnight because I simply couldn't stay awake. Overall, the experience was like participating in an exam writing marathon. The exams in French and Early National American history each involved answering three straightforward questions but Greene's Colonial American History Exam required the examinees to address just one topic, that is, to write an essay on the periodisation of Colonial American history. This was not a question I was expecting and at the time I was unsure whether the answer that I produced was original and thoughtful or banal and cliched. Now lost, for many years I kept a copy of my completed exam, although whenever I read it I still couldn't make up my mind whether I had written a masterful overview or an answer that was both mundane and overgeneralised. But it was a huge relief when I learnt the next week that I had passed all three reading courses and effectively completed the first half of my Hopkins PhD.

I rewarded myself with a holiday. First, I travelled to Philadelphia to spend a few nights in International House and visit Dick Ryerson who was undertaking research for his PhD thesis in the city archives. By coincidence, Graeme de

Celebrating the completion of the coursework component of my PhD on the JHU campus. Gilman Hall is in the background

Graaff, the Director of the University of Sydney International House, a man who had turned it into much more than a hall of residence by making it a cultural centre for an impressive array of intercultural events and exchanges, was also staying there as part of a tour of International Houses across the United States. Graeme, to my surprise, turned out to be a circus lover, and invited me to accompany him to a performance of Ringling Brothers and Barnum and Bailey's Three Ring Circus, which was then in town. I had previously attended performances by some travelling Australian circuses, Wirth's in particular, but the Barnum performance, held in the 20,000 seat local entertainment centre, was on a far more spectacular level. In some ways it seemed that what mattered was the scale of the simultaneous three ring performances rather than their quality. From Philadelphia I caught a bus up to Newark to stay with the family of another fellow student, Lenny Berlanstein. His mother greeted me at the door with the announcement that I was the family's first ever non-Jewish visitor. Over the next few days, she introduced me to Jewish cuisine, Newark style, while Lenny took me on a tour of New York, including its art galleries and museums. We even attended a Broadway performance of *Man of La Mancha.*

I left New York on an overnight Greyhound bus to travel to Toronto to visit Roger Hall and Sandra Martin, two friends I had made in London. Roger was a PhD student at Cambridge who had returned to Canada to work on his thesis on Canadian history. He later became a Professor of History at the University of Western Ontario and a well-known Canadian historian. Sandra had not yet decided on a career although she subsequently became a high-profile *Toronto Star* journalist.

Canada, in general, and Toronto, in particular, were a revelation to me, in part because they seemed unexpectedly far more familiar than America and its cities. Baltimore was a city with poor public transport, a small CBD which was abandoned after office hours, and a freeway system that literally ran a ring around the city. Like most American cities it was dominated by a car culture, with shopping malls, cinemas, and restaurants located adjacent to the freeway. In contrast,

Toronto possessed a comprehensive rail and bus public transport system and a vibrant downtown complete with ethnically based dining neighbourhoods. Baltimore was tense and dangerous, Toronto was relaxed and safe. Out in the suburbs there were even lawn bowling clubs, complete with bowlers in white uniforms. It felt a bit like home to me. I remember the two weeks I spent in Toronto as a whirl of trips to Niagara Falls and other scenic places, visits to non-mainstream art house movie theatres, eating in cheap Chinese and Japanese restaurants, and several parties in which everyone consumed large amounts of wine and beer.

In July I returned to Baltimore, not as prepared as I had anticipated, to face the reality of a move to Columbia, South Carolina, where I planned to spend almost a year in the State Archives researching my PhD thesis. It was a typical Baltimore summer, the weather relentlessly hot and humid day and night. The sense of familiarity and comfort in my surroundings, which I had felt in my second academic year now abandoned me both because the campus was deserted for the summer and because I developed a growing sense of uncertainty about what life would be like in Columbia. However, after a week or two of indecisive time wasting, I caught an overnight Greyhound bus to South Carolina.

My first priority was to find somewhere to live. Fortunately, I quickly found a very small room to rent in a large house in a street conveniently located close to the University and the state archives. The young owner and his wife, both university students, lived at ground level, while upstairs there were three rented bedrooms, complete with a bathroom shared by the tenants. There were no cooking facilities.

Over the next week I introduced myself to the archives staff and began to compile a list of material that I needed to examine, a list which I quickly realised was dauntingly long. My exploration of the city of Columbia revealed a state capital that was not much bigger than a large country town, while the people were insularly minded, and hostile to outsiders, especially an Australian accented postgraduate student enrolled at an elite private Yankee university. It was a telling sign of the parochial and backward-looking perspectives of the state's population that the Confederate flag flew over the Capitol Building.

Faced both with a larger workload than I had anticipated, and needing to cope with an even more unfamiliar environment than I had in Baltimore, I began to have serious thoughts of giving up my PhD studies, settling on the MA which I was awarded at the end of my second year of studies at Hopkins, and heading back to Australia with a plan to perhaps join the Federal Public Service in Canberra.[19]

In the meantime, and while I pondered the consequences of abandoning an ambition I had nurtured with determination for about eight years, I decided to at least begin research on my thesis. I adopted a schedule which involved working in the archives from 9am through to 9pm each weekday and from 9am until 4pm on Saturdays and Sunday. These were the hours the archives were open and I knew that I needed to make use of all the time available to ensure that if I continued with the degree, I completed the necessary research within 12 months. I knew less about the history of colonial South Carolina than I did about most of the other 12 colonies. So, in the waking hours not spent in the archives I took advantage of the resources available in the University and South Caroliniana libraries to learn as much as I could from secondary sources about Carolina's colonial past.

Two factors combined to renew my determination to complete my PhD. Although I didn't suddenly become passionate about my thesis topic, I found myself challenged by certain questions relating to the origins and characteristics of the colony's planters and merchants. I also became fascinated by the sources I found in the archives, sources which I knew contained at least partial answers to those questions. These were not the kind of primary materials that I had previously used but consisted of tax lists, wills, and personal estate inventories, records measuring the export of rice, indigo and deerskins, and proceedings of the parish vestries (which provided local government services) and the elected colonial assembly. As I read this material, I began to plan strategies that allowed me to use these records to track the emergence of a merchant and planter class, and trace the

changing patterns of wealth distribution and slave ownership, evolving economic trends, and the role of particular institutions in the colony's governance. I began to realise I could write a thesis that was solid and comprehensive if not brilliantly innovative. The depression that I experienced at this time was probably caused in part by a lingering exhaustion from the exams I had studied so hard for in the previous academic year but with the thesis now under way I developed a renewed faith that I could complete the PhD within the time available. After six weeks or so in Columbia I also made a trip to Baltimore to re-enrol and when I used the opportunity to complain to Porter and Livesay about my lack of desire and indeed inability to continue with the degree I received in response a pep talk that was part encouragement and part tongue lashing. In the end I was encouraged by their insistence that I was capable of completing the degree and it was time to get on with it. So, I did.

My fellow boarding house residents consisted of John, a schoolteacher who was completing a Master of Education degree, and a final year undergraduate student from New York whose name I don't recall. John took great pleasure spending Saturday nights watching old John Wayne movies on a local television station, while waving his hopefully unloaded 38 calibre revolver at the bad guys when they appeared on screen. The New Yorker was trying, not very successfully, to balance completing his degree with the demands of his South Carolina girlfriend and his New York fiancée. It occurred to me that perhaps he needed Barry Gaspar's contact details.

I usually ate breakfast and lunch in the University cafeteria but I normally joined one of these roommates, and one or more of their friends, for dinner in one of the cheap local restaurants. Their company, which usually took the form of conversations about the fortunes of the USC football or basketball teams, was rather different from what I had become accustomed to in Baltimore, and I found myself often missing my friends Barry and Tsuneo. On Saturdays I sometimes attended a University of South Carolina football game with other USC graduate student friends I had made during the course of my stay.

Taking a break from the Archives with a brief camping holiday in the Smoky Mountains. My companion is a fellow boarder from the house where I lived. *Waterhouse Family Collection*

I took a brief holiday to spend Christmas again with the Ryerson family in Massachusetts and then left Columbia for the last time in March to travel to Baltimore to meet my parents. Once they had left for Europe, I caught a train back to South Carolina to spend a month working with primary material held in the South Carolina Historical Society in Charleston. I found it to be a far more interesting and exciting city than Columbia and I loved walking the streets to photograph the eighteenth-century houses, churches and public buildings. In May I returned again to Baltimore to read the microfilm collections of eighteenth-century South Carolina newspapers held in the Johns Hopkins University Library collection.

My final two PhD research trips were first to England to stay with my parents in their Kensington flat, and to work with MS material in the Public Record Office, the British Museum, the Taunton Record Office and the Bodleian Library at Oxford. In these libraries and archives I focussed on researching material relating to the economic and political relationship between England and South Carolina.

Second, I travelled to Barbados where I examined records in the Barbados Archives and Barbados Historical Society relating to the West Indian backgrounds of the earliest white settlers in Carolina. Here I stayed in a hall of residence of the University of the West Indies. As soon as I moved into my room the student in the adjacent one moved to accommodation further down the corridor, because, as I was later told he didn't wish to live next to a white person. When I learnt a few days later why he had moved I felt distressed and wronged. However, during my stay in Barbados, my friend Eddie Cox, a Greene student from Grenada, passed through on his way home and stayed in the same hall of residence. He listened patiently to my arguments about me not being racially prejudiced and therefore not deserving of this treatment and then gently explained that I belonged to a culture that still had a lot of ground to make up, a lot of trust still to earn. Listening to him was sobering, humbling and educational.

By the end of summer 1972 I had completed

the primary research goals which I had set myself and at the beginning of the Fall semester in September of that year I sat down and mapped out a five-chapter thesis outline, covering the rise of Carolina's slave owning merchant and planter class. I then constructed a writing timetable, allowing a certain number of weeks for each chapter, making sure to allocate extra time for the longest sections. I also had to ensure that I completed the dissertation several weeks earlier than the May submission deadline, to allow for the professional typing and binding of the final version of the thesis.

In some ways the routine I followed for the following two semesters was similar to the one that had characterised my life in the first two years I spent at Hopkins. Once again, my working hours were from 8 am until midnight on weekdays, and slightly shorter on weekends. However, now I spent my time seated writing at my desk in my apartment, rather than reading books at my carrel in the library. Because I had successfully competed for one of 200 Woodrow Wilson Dissertation Fellowships offered nationally by the Princeton-based Woodrow Wilson Foundation, I was also financially better off, because inclusive of funds specified to be used for typing and binding expenses it amounted to almost $4000. To be awarded one of these fellowships in a highly crowded and competitive field was a great honour and I even received a letter of congratulations from the Hopkins President. I was also awarded an additional fellowship of $500 by the Maryland chapter of the Colonial Dames National Honor Society, which probably came about on the recommendation of Jack Greene. I felt like I had won a very small lottery that allowed me to eat and dress better as well as to regularly attend movies, baseball games and even dine out on occasional weekends in Baltimore's Chinatown.

In many ways this was this was a very uneventful year for I was almost completely focussed on writing the thesis. I did share my apartment with another History graduate student but we didn't eat or drink together and I can't remember anything much about him, not even his name. My socialising mostly took the form of attending occasional spontaneously organised Saturday night parties

that usually involved heavy drinking, lasted until 5am the next morning and shrank the number of hours for which I was fit to work during the remainder of the weekend.

Yet in late July, right at the beginning of my thesis writing marathon, I received news that provided a powerful incentive for me to complete the dissertation as soon as I was capable, and indicated that my long-held ambition to become an academic historian was perhaps within reach. From about the time when I completed my dissertation research I began to apply for advertised lectureships in American history at Australian universities. My submissions to The University of New England and Macquarie University were unsuccessful, probably in part because the two selection committees considered my PhD was too far from completion. In any case Macquarie was also looking for an historian of modern America while Russel Ward, the Professor of History at UNE, had advertised the position with a specific candidate in mind. However, my application to the University of Sydney was successful and I received a letter from Patrick Collinson, who had replaced Ward as Head of Department, offering me the position, conditional upon completion of my PhD. I was incredibly pleased to learn that my application had succeeded but I also knew I was very fortunate because I had not yet completed my doctorate and my modest cv only included one forthcoming publication. My belief that I had experienced a degree of good fortune in securing this appointment was confirmed when I received a letter from Neville Meaney, who was a member of the appointment committee, informing me that the appointable candidates included applicants from Australia, New Zealand, America, Great Britain, Ireland and Ghana and that I had won in a 'close tussle'.[20] Much later, I also learned that Greene's highly favourable reference was the key factor in my appointment.

My parents, who were still travelling in Europe were even more delighted and when they received my letter conveying the good news decided to savour the occasion by taking a walk and shedding a few tears in the process. They later told me they had thought it unlikely that I would find a job at a university in Sydney and were resigned to me living in another state and feared I might even stay in the United States.

Sometimes I fell behind in my writing schedule, especially in the case of chapter 3 which relied on inventories of deceased estates and tax lists to measure the changing patterns of wealth distribution in colonial South Carolina. In tabulating some 4,500 inventories I needed to rely on an adding machine and spent three weeks sitting at the reception desk in the History Department crunching the numbers to the amusement of some of the professors and the disdain of others. Miraculously, by early April 1973 I had completed a handwritten version of the thesis. I then distributed the five chapters amongst three separate typists to ensure it was completed and bound by the April 21 submission deadline. The only hitch in the process resulted from the fact that because the typists used different brands of typewriters the font was not uniform.

The final hurdle that I had to cross was an interrogation by a dissertation committee consisting of representatives of disciplines across the University which met in early May. Greene gave me an advance heads up of his approval in a meeting in his office in late April. On that occasion he asked me what I thought I had left out that I would need to include when I revised the thesis for publication. I responded by acknowledging that it clearly needed a chapter on elite cultural life in Charles Town (Charleston), one that focussed on theatre, musical concerts, reading and the lavish private dinners that characterised the everyday lives of the rich. We agreed that as I revised the thesis into a book, I would focus as soon as possible on researching and writing this missing chapter.

I met the dissertation committee at 9am on May 2. The questions and comments lasted an hour but there was hardly any sharp criticism and for the most part my examiners were polite, positive and offered modest praise. At 10 am I was invited to sit outside while the committee considered its findings and ten minutes later the chair emerged to congratulate me on the award of the degree and to shake my hand. Never before had I

felt such strong relief as I did at that moment. Nor could I quite make myself believe that my postgraduate years were finally over. Against my own recurring doubts, I had survived and completed the PhD, one of only two students who had entered the graduate program in the Fall of 1969 to finish within four years. And I had a lectureship waiting for me at the University of Sydney, an institution to which I had only dreamed of returning. So, well before noon I celebrated by drinking four grasshopper cocktails (consisting mostly of crème de menthe) in a Greenmount Street bar not far from campus. Then I phoned my parents, who chastised me for possessing an even stronger American accent than when I had last talked to them face to face in London, and acknowledged their own residual difficulties in believing that I really had completed my PhD. I also remember thinking that despite the theme of one of my favourite novels, Thomas Wolf's *You Can't Go Home Again*, I would soon be homeward bound. I didn't drink any more grasshoppers that day but I did consume a lot of beer, sharing my good news with several of my fellow History graduate students, and introducing them to the Australian ritual of the 'shout'. They told me they thought it was a great custom, which was hardly surprising, since I was providing all the 'shouting'.

American Postscript. My very own unromcom

Despite the completion of my Hopkins degree and the fact that there was a university lectureship waiting for me at the University of Sydney, I didn't return to Australia immediately. The reason behind what became a more than two-month delay was that I had an appointment to marry in the small town of Brownton, Minnesota, in early June.

I had met Karen, a second-year graduate student enrolled in the German Department, during one of my visits to Baltimore from Columbia in early 1972. At first, we thought we had a great deal in common but over time it became clear that we only shared two things: loneliness and the Hopkins experience. Otherwise, our personalities and cultural tastes were quite dissimilar. She preferred a hometown, folksy life-style, while my commitment was to a more urban and academic focussed life. Because of our differing personalities and life goals we found ourselves disagreeing and arguing on a range of issues, large and small, personal and professional. We had announced our intention to marry before these conflicts began to occur and her family began to plan the wedding for June 1973. Visiting her family at Christmas in 1972, I had noticed that she seemed much more at ease in the cultural environment of the Midwest than in the world of an elite east coast university.

In early May 1973, now free, for the first time since I had arrived in the United States, to focus more on my personal life and to spend some time on amusing myself, I became devoted to watching the Watergate hearings on television. Belatedly, I also I began to think that it would be best if the wedding was 'postponed' and I returned to Sydney alone. Karen could visit at Christmas and if that was a success we could then once again contemplate the prospect of marriage. However, in the back of my mind was a sense that this was improbable because with time for second thoughts from both of us I anticipated that there would be no visit and no wedding. And that would be for the best, because apart from the fact that personality differences had made the relationship conflict ridden, it was also highly unlikely that Karen would like living in Australia even if she did visit and then decide, against her own better judgement, to settle. But, in probably the greatest mistake of my life, I was too much of a coward to call a halt to what was planned. I decided to hope that our relationship improved and that Karen adapted to life in Australia, although I knew in my heart that neither of these things was likely to happen. Above all else, I could never become the kind of person she wanted me to be, that is, an honorary mid-Westerner, with both the physical stature and mindset

of an American of German Lutheran descent.

So, the marriage took place and what followed was more than five years of shared unhappiness. Although we became increasingly estranged, for reasons are still not clear to me, I decided to wait and let Karen take the initiative to end our relationship. From the perspective of 2024 I can only acknowledge that I displayed poor judgement and a high level of indecision.

After three years in Australia, we returned to Hopkins in 1976 where I spent six months as a visiting fellow in the History Department, while she resumed completing her coursework requirements in the German Department. But living in America didn't improve the connection but only made both of us more aware of how little we shared both intellectually and emotionally. My happiest times were spent hanging out with some of the senior German and History graduate students and travelling alone to Charleston and Columbia on a month-long research trip. Nor did I have regrets about returning to Sydney alone in early 1977, while Karen remained in Baltimore for several months to complete her examinations. Finally, in late 1978, after she had spent a further 18 months in Australia, she told me that she had decided to return to the United States. She had worked teaching German in a prestigious private school in North Sydney, but she was dissatisfied with that role and had plans to find what she considered more rewarding employment in the cultural sector, employment that she wanted to find in America. In her understanding both my country and I had failed her. The unqualified relief I felt at the prospect of making a different life for myself, confirmed my belief that I had made a major mistake in not intervening earlier to prevent the marriage, and another subsequent error in allowing the situation to persist for too long. I suppose my behaviour could best be described as passively coward.

Endnotes

1   Richard Waterhouse to Earle and Nancy Waterhouse, 25 July, 1969, Waterhouse Family Collection

2   ibid., 8 August 1969

3   ibid., 22 August 1969

4   *ibid.*, 28 August, 1969

5   ibid., 12 October 1969

6   ibid., 31 August 1969

7   Ibid., 3 October 1969

8   Jack P. Greene ed., *Exclusionary Empire: English Liberty Overseas, 1600–1900,* New York: Cambridge University Press, 2010

9   Earle to Richard 23 May 1971

10   Perry Miller, 'Errand into the Wilderness', *in Errand into the Wilderness*, Cambridge Mass., Harvard University Press, 1956

11   Richard Waterhouse, 'Reluctant Emigrants: The English Background of the First Generation of the New England Puritan Clergy,' *The Historical Magazine of the Protestant Episcopal Church*, vol LIV, December, 1975, PP. 473–88

12   For a readable account of the findings of the Cambridge Group see Peter Laslett, *The World We Have Lost* London: Methuen Paperbacks, 1965: for my own interpretation of the new social history, its origins and nature, see Richard Waterhouse, 'Locating the New Social History: Transnational Historiography and Australian Local History', *The Journal of the Royal Australian Historical Society*, vol. 95, June, 2009, pp. 1–17

13   Earle to Richard, 7 September 1970

14   Richard to parents, 16 August 1970

15   Richard to parents, 11 July 1770, 31 August 1970

16   Richard to parents, 18 and 26 January, 13 March 1971

17   Jack P. Greene, *Pursuits of Happiness: the Social Development of Early Modern British Colonies and the Formation of American Culture*, Chapel Hill: University of North Carolina Press, 1988 sets out an argument that Greene had contemplated for 20 years. Other colonial historians ignored the West Indian colonies because they did not become part of the US in 1776 and they interpreted colonial American as a prequel to national American history. But before the Revolution, the British West Indies islands were simply conceived as an integral part of British America

18   Richard to parents, 12 December 1971

19   Richard to parents, July 20, 27 1971

20   Neville Meaney to Richard Waterhouse, 3 July 1972, Waterhouse Family Collection

Chapter 15

Return to Oz and my Unproductive 1970s

MORE THAN TWENTY YEARS AGO Australian universities introduced a new category for recently hired academics, categorising them as Early Career Researchers (ECRs). The new appointees included in this category are not only eligible for special research grants but also allowed to teach fewer hours per week than their more experienced colleagues. But when I returned to Sydney in mid-July 1973 no such regulations existed. Indeed, it was then the custom for newly appointed staff to assume heavier teaching responsibilities than their more senior colleagues and in my case, this was applied to an even greater extent than usual. There were two reasons why I was assigned an above normal load. In the first place, there was a degree of resentment from my History Department colleagues about the delay between my appointment and my return to Sydney. I gained the impression that some academic staff members believed that I had remained in the US for so long after my appointment because I had come to prefer American life. In their view I needed to catch up on the teaching I had missed. They seemed unaware that the terms of my hiring required me to complete my PhD before starting employment at Sydney. Second, I was caught up in the rivalry between the two senior American historians, Christina Campbell and Neville Meaney. Each one of them wanted me to teach primarily in their American history course, with the result that I carried a heavy load spread across both. In addition, in 1973, when I first commenced my appointment, Campbell's course was taught in the

evening and Meaney's during the day, so I often began my teaching at 10am and finished just after 9pm. I found difficulty coping with the workload, especially because I was required to give a relatively large numbers of lectures, all of them written from scratch. The work environment wasn't very helpful either because the power workers were conducting rolling strikes, which always led to blackouts. On several occasions the lights went out in the lecture theatre in the middle of my 8:15–9:15pm lecture, which I then continued by candlelight.

I had promised Greene that I would start revising my thesis for publication as soon as I returned to Australia but that project lost priority as I dealt with a heavy teaching load in courses which included aspects of American history with which I was unfamiliar. I also tried to pretend to my family and friends that my marriage was on firm ground when in reality it had already failed.

The History Department became a very large one in the 1970s with additional appointments in Ancient, Medieval, Early and Late Modern European, Asian, American and Australian history. At the same time the number of professors increased from one to three with the elevation of a long-term member of the Department, Marjorie Jacobs, and the appointment of an outstanding Reformation historian, the English scholar, Patrick Collinson. The non-professorial staff included academics recruited from Australia, the UK and the United States. There was a long tradition of Australian universities appointing academic staff from Great Britain but the arrival of so many academics from north America reflected a new trend. At this time the US was in a serious recession, which caused many universities to pause the hiring of new staff. The most highly qualified academic job seekers still found employment in the United States but many with solid but not outstanding cvs, were forced either to seek employment outside the university sector or apply for academic positions in other countries. In contrast, Australian universities had difficulties filling positions in some areas, namely European and Asian history. The Sydney History Department made a few outstanding appointments from north America, particularly Craig Reynolds, an historian of Thailand. However, driven by what they apparently considered an urgent need to fill positions, the professorial leadership also hired scholars whose applications indicated both limited qualifications and prospects for future professional growth. Unsurprisingly, their subsequent contributions to the Department's teaching and research profiles failed to raise the status of the Department either at the national or international level.[1] University departments, schools and faculties rarely go through periods of large-scale staff expansion and when this happens, they are opportunities not to be missed. But instead of developing a plan which involved identifying worthy subject areas in which to concentrate teaching and research resources, the professors simply followed an ad hoc process of filling staffing gaps as they appeared. This approach was in keeping with the dominant ethos of the Department, an ethos that was maintained by John Ward during his more than 25-year term as Head of Department, extending from the late 1940s through until 1970. He was an old-style English conservative who rarely initiated policy based on a carefully devised strategy but rather reacted to circumstances and crises as they developed. His legacy was an expanded Department that grew haphazardly, failed to create new or strengthen existing areas of research excellence or revise an outdated curriculum into a coherent and integrated History program.

Until the late sixties the History Department was largely staffed by British-educated Australians and appointees from the UK. They shared an Anglophile culture, reflected in a curriculum with a heavy influence on English and Empire history, and an acceptance that the professors alone were entitled to determine appointments, the structure and content of the curriculum, and the allocation of resources. But by the mid 1970s, with an expanded Department consisting of staff from a variety of educational and national backgrounds this management model came under challenge. At the same time, two of the leaders of the move for reform that emerged at this time, namely Richard Bosworth and Tony Cahill, although educated at Sydney, and Oxbridge, became advocates for the democratisation of decision-making. In their case, their experience of the 'god professor' system in Australia and the UK sharpened their awareness of the shortcomings of a structure without consultative processes rather than accepting that it was the norm.

Under the existing system the professors remained quite remote from the everyday life of the department. This is illustrated by the fact that while each working day teaching and administrative staff gathered for morning and afternoon tea, two of the professors never attended these social occasions, despite the fact that they offered important opportunities for the leadership to learn about the aspirations and grievances of the academic staff. Collinson was a regular attendee and as a result he was more aware than his two colleagues of the level of staff dissatisfaction with the existing system of governance and the strong support for a more consultative system.

The object of the reformers was to establish a system of departmental governance in which the staff were consulted about academic appointments, the allocation of teaching responsibilities and were given the right to elect the Head of Department. At this stage of my life, as someone modestly influenced directly by American university left wing student politics, and indirectly by the counter culture via music, movies and novels, I had a natural tendency towards opposition. So, I found myself on the side of the reformers. Ward ran a masterful defence of professorial authority, arguing that it was too late to introduce a management structure providing for elected Heads of Department because the previous year the University had adopted new by-laws which maintained the existing policy of the University appointing Heads of Department on the advice of the professors. No doubt, with tongue firmly planted in cheek, he suggested, without giving reasons, that next year might be good year for reform.

The Harvard economist, John Kenneth Galbraith, once indicated that whenever he didn't want anything acted on, he always appointed a committee, and that is what happened in the History Department. A committee, chaired by a professor was established, to write a formal constitution for the governance of the Department. Instead of requiring an elected Head of Department this document instead provided for the creation of a whole series of committees to advise on the curriculum, research policy, postgraduate matters and the administration of finance. But the Head of Department was under no obligation to adhere to this advice. It was an amazingly complex committee system which, if implemented, was likely to consume many hours of everyone's time, without guaranteeing a single positive outcome. Fortunately, only a few of the committees ever operated and over the years, with a little help from successive Heads of Department, they died of irrelevancy.

I have written at length about this movement for change because it had a strong influence on me, shaping my understanding of how governance at the departmental (and later School) level should work. I noticed that colleagues who were often discussed as suitable (potential) Heads of Department were usually mild-mannered men (never women) who believed in the need for consensus on all major issues. Even as a young and inexperienced member of the Department I found myself wondering whether such leadership was likely to lead to an improvement in teaching and research performance. Consultation was needed but effective governance also needed leaders who were willing to develop plans and strategies for the present and future even if these were not widely approved by their colleagues. They also needed to make hard decisions especially in relation to revisions to a curriculum that was still based on a model of the expansion of British 'civilisation', and in relation to creating a research and publication culture

across the Department. As matters stood there was a widespread view in the Department that research was an optional extra, while the professors monopolised the designated research funds which the University allocated to the Department

I also began to question whether the motives of some participants in the democracy movement were as pure as they seemed. I had complete faith that Bosworth and Cahill believed in the principle of an elected Head but from the careless comments of others I concluded that they had personal grievances to settle. Their disagreements with the three professors about what they could or couldn't teach and the resentment they developed towards the current leadership as a result strongly influenced their commitment to an alternative means of choosing the Head of Department. It was a valid question whether some of my more determined colleagues, who had already made up their minds about what the future curriculum would look like simply wanted to replace one authoritarian system with one that was no less rigid.

At this stage of my career, I had no future plans or desire to become an academic administrator and so I didn't think about whether my participation in these events carried lessons from which I could learn and profit. But the whole experience stayed in my mind, and while I remained committed to a model of governance that included widespread consultation, I began to think that the most popular didn't necessarily make the most competent leadership candidate. In addition, I concluded that an effective Head needed to be willing to make decisions that were in the best interests of the Department even if they were not widely supported. I didn't form these views overnight. Indeed, it wasn't until more than a decade later that I realised that they had become firm understandings in my mind, and that I was informally, and without intending to do so, assessing the performance of administrators at the Departmental, Faculty and even University level in terms of how far they operated in terms of these principles.

Endnote

1   This argument is based on my later assessment of the applications of those appointed to History Department positions in the 1970s. to which I had access in 1999.

Chapter 16

1979: The Year my Life Changed

ONE MAJOR CHANGE MADE IN THE Department in 1979 was the introduction of a new curriculum. This development involved an acknowledgement that the syllabus that had characterised the Department for decades was becoming increasingly irrelevant in the face of new historiographical developments as well as shifts in Australian culture more generally. The core of the new course structure consisted of 'General' and 'Specialist' units. The first were similar to the survey style courses which were the basis of the earlier curriculum. However, the 'Specialist' units covered more particular topics, and dealt with shorter time frames. This allowed staff to teach subjects that were more specifically aligned with their existing or developing areas of research. Previously most courses taught in the department had focussed on political, religious, diplomatic and intellectual history but this more flexible curriculum also allowed the introduction of units that emphasised social and cultural history. This was of critical importance because in Europe and north America, cultural history, which first emerged as a reaction to the labour intense, and statistically underpinned new social history, was now the dominant historiographical influence. Social science research methods were the basis of the new social history but the new cultural history, with its emphasis on relativism and the multiple meanings of texts, shifted the discipline to the humanities end of the History spectrum.

Significantly, this new framework allowed the Department to introduce a curriculum that incorporated the latest historiographical developments and which no longer placed an undue reliance on the British Empire and the systems of governance it established across its colonies. Instead, in the Asian component of the syllabus there was now an emphasis on the long independent histories of countries like India. Marjorie Jacobs deserved much of the credit for this because her support for this change was critical to its success. To my surprise, she revealed herself as a post-colonialist, not as I had wrongly believed, an advocate of British Imperial history as taught and written about by John Ward and his departmental disciples. Similarly, the syllabuses covering the histories of the United States and Australia no longer prioritised their colonial British heritages but rather the stories of how they became independent nations with their own unique cultures and institutions. One of Ward's more famous undergraduate lectures had focussed on the reasons why the American Revolution breached English law. It was a lecture that left undergraduates wondering whether that really mattered. Some, but not all the new Australian history units also placed a previously missing emphasis on women and First Nations people, historiographical updates that were long overdue. Although her influence in modernising the Australian history curriculum was subsequently forgotten, Heather Radi was the inspiration behind these changes, a role that received less acknowledgement than it deserved, probably because Heather, who possessed a blunt and direct personality, was not a popular figure in the Department.

In the later 1970s I had continued to revise

my PhD thesis with the intention of turning it into a book. I published two of the revised chapters, one as an article and one as a book chapter. I also researched and wrote a chapter on the cultural life of South Carolina's planter and merchant class which also became an article. But I was becoming increasingly weary not only of the new social history but also with the history of colonial South Carolina and indeed with colonial American history more generally. I found myself increasingly interested in reading books and articles about cultural history, especially those relating to nineteenth century Europe and America. I also realised that the new syllabus gave me the opportunity to teach a unit of study of my own choice and creation and that one way to learn more about the cultural history of America was to teach a unit of study in that field. I can't say I made a conscious decision to abandon colonial American history and I had no clear idea about where this decision to move into the nineteenth century might lead. However, if felt liberating to be taking on a new challenge and to finally be teaching a unit that I had created and now controlled.

The unimaginative title of the Specialist Unit as it was called that I began to teach in 1979 was Society and Culture in America, 1750–1914. It commenced in the colonial period because I wanted to emphasise how different America became culturally as well as politically as a result of the Revolution. The main theme focussed on how American writers, painters, architects and jurists, amongst others, sought self-consciously to create a distinct American culture that was mostly inspired by a unique American landscape and reflected a vibrant democratic political culture. This theme was inspired by my reading of several classic works in nineteenth century American history by Perry Miller, Leo Marx, R.W.B Lewis and Henry Nash Smith. Of course, in the last forty years or so this orthodoxy of the creation and existence of an American culture in the first half of the nineteenth century has crumbled as a result of a series of specific studies demonstrating that far from consisting of a consensus culture nineteenth century America included the existence of a whole range of contrasting and conflicting

cultures, including those created by African slaves, Native Americans and European immigrants. If I were to teach this unit again in the third decade of the twenty first century it would take a vastly different form and emphasize diversity rather than homogeneity. But at that moment I found discovering and teaching American cultural history to be an exhilarating experience.

The history of popular culture was not generally considered to be a legitimate topic for teaching or researching at the University of Sydney. However, simply because I wanted to know more about the history of this subject—a corollary of my loss of interest in the history of colonial elites—I decided to include a lecture and a tutorial on the topic. I thought about sport as a case study, but although some fine academic studies in this field appeared in later years, most of the books I came across at this time were valorising accounts written by sports journalists. Instead, after reading a fascinating and well researched book by Robert Toll, *Blacking Up: The Minstrel Show in Nineteenth century America*, I chose to base a lecture and tutorial on the minstrel show and its influence. I was fascinated by Toll's account of this popular stage genre, particularly his explanations about how it became so pervasive and influential. I was also intrigued by his account of the emergence of troupes of African-American minstrels after the Civil War, troupes that claimed to more faithfully present slave culture than white companies. I was also surprised and tantalised to read Toll's account of how in 1876 one of the most successful of the African-American companies, The Georgia Minstrels, sailed from San Francisco with the intention of touring Australia.

Toll did not research the Australian tour of the Georgias—American historians at that time were not interested in pursuing American history outside the boundaries of their own country—but I was intrigued to know how the company was received in Australia. I thought an article on the history of the tour would be fun to research and write, although I didn't see the project as central to my future as yet undefined research plans. I referred to is as my 'Friday project', the day I set aside to pursue this subject. I had some preconceived notions of what I was likely to find because given the reputation of the Australian colonies for racist legislation and behaviour I (wrongly) suspected that I would discover a story of failure, misfortune and even tragedy. So, without making a conscious decision to completely change my field of study from American to Australian history, and from writing about elite to focussing on popular culture, I set out on a research odyssey that in the end reshaped my academic career, turned me into a much more productive historian and contributed to rekindling my love affair with history.

My personal life also underwent dramatic change in this same year, in ways that brought unanticipated happiness and fulfillment that has never diminished. From the beginning of the year, I had begun to ask women that I considered as potential partners to join me to go out to dinner, see movies and attend social events. Mostly they were similar in age to me and tended to be schoolteachers, librarians or academics. I was determined to be very careful about entering into a long-term relationship or marriage. However, I thought that when I finally made the decision to

enter a more enduring relationship it was likely to be with someone of approximately my age who was employed in the education sector. My plan was to be rational and controlled, which was easy because no strong feelings of mutual attraction emerged from these outings. Instead, my carefully organised plan simply fell apart when over a frighteningly short period I found myself falling hopelessly in love.

That year, I was teaching Survey and Specialist units in American history which together made one subject. One of the students enrolled in both was a young woman, Grace Karskens, who had chosen the History subject I taught as the last one she needed to complete her degree. With her rainbow toe socks and dyed blonde hair, her effervescent and outgoing personality, she was noticeable and I found her much more attractive than I consciously realised. Filled with energy she sometimes organised social events and get togethers for the students and staff connected to these two units, a picnic at Balmoral Beach, the occasion I remember as most memorable.

Our Wedding Day, May 9 1981. In the back row are Earle, Annabel, Bill Oakley, Susan, Stephen Oakley, Richard and Alex Agafonoff. In the front row are Pat Oakley, Sasha Agafonoff, Nicholas Agafonoff, Nancy, Grace Karskens and Ingrid Agafonoff

Initially, I thought of her as a really fun person as well as an outstanding student who made thoughtful contributions to tutorials and wrote terrific essays. But one Friday afternoon, on the last day of second term, we ran into each other on campus and I invited her to join me for a cup of coffee. But I so much enjoyed our subsequent conversation that it seemed natural then to invite her out to see a movie that evening. We got on so well on our first outing together that I realised that I was already developing hopes of a serious, romantic relationship. The next day she left to spend her university break on holiday at a friend's house in Byron Bay. For the next few weeks, I looked forward to her return, and was excited when I received postcards she sent me from Byron and her home town of Coonabarabran. An hour or so after she attended the first tutorial of third term, I called in at the student house where she lived, giving the pathetic excuse that I wanted to know whether she thought the class had succeeded. Her two housemates, who witnessed this conversation, struggled to control their amusement. In any case, the next week was a succession of shared take-out and restaurant meals in which I experienced lightheaded exhilaration and a sense of rushing uncontrollably towards a confession. A week later, the man who had professed a determination to proceed carefully and slowly in any future relationship, acknowledged what he felt and told Grace that he loved her. I already knew that I wanted this to be a long-term relationship although it was almost another year before we became engaged. My connection with her changed my life far more than anything else that has ever happened to me. She became and has remained the love of my life, my best friend and my intellectual companion. She has enriched my world in extraordinary ways and from the time we became a couple I could never again imagine my life without her at its centre.

Chapter 17

The (Mostly) Best of Times: the Eighties and Nineties

Departmental Worst

In this twenty-year period the History Department experienced a decline in staff numbers that resulted from one major and one minor cause. In the first place, the number of students enrolled in History subjects declined, which meant that as members of the academic staff retired, they were not replaced. Second, the half dozen or so Ancient historians left History and became a separate department as part of the newly established School of Ancient History, Archaeology and Classics. Another development was the appointment of two new professors to replace Collinson (who had returned to an academic position in the UK), Jacobs (who retired) and Ward (who had become Chair of the Academic Board and was later appointed Vice-Chancellor). Deryck Schreuder, originally from Africa, but educated at Oxford, sought to improve research productivity by providing encouragement to those members of the Department with modest publication records. He also tried to increase student numbers, particularly in Asian history, by developing team-taught comparative history courses. The American and English educated Roy MacLeod worked in the field of the History of Science, which brought a new subject area to the curriculum, although his main focus was less on teaching and far more on his own research. Because they didn't belong to a University of Sydney tradition that stressed professorial authority, including the right and obligation of professors to serve as Heads of Department, MacLeod and Schreuder were more open to a culture of consultation, including the

right of all academic staff to have a voice in the choice of departmental Head.

Unfortunately, what also continued in some quarters of the Department in these years was a culture of complacency and indifference. Some staff were not interested in applying for research grants and only slightly more motivated to write, or attempt to write, articles and books. These same colleagues were also content to teach the same subjects featuring the same lectures as they had done for many years. In 1989–90, when there was an attempt by some staff to modernise the curriculum to meet changed Faculty and University requirements, introduce more innovative teaching practices, and encourage new fields of history, there was fierce opposition from a minority of staff members. They not only opposed changes to the curriculum but in a telling example of short-sightedness, objected to the holding of syllabus reform meetings on Fridays. They argued that Friday was acknowledged as a sacrosanct 'working from home day' and criticised the convenor of the curriculum reform meetings, who was me, for breaching a time-honoured tradition. In this culture advocates of reform faced a mixture of apathy and hostility.

In this era, Associate Professors as well as Professors were now eligible to hold the position of Head of Department. Trained within the Ward tradition the first few Associate Professor incumbents tended to be reactive in their decision making and unwilling to develop innovative policies and strategies designed to improve research production, grant application figures and student numbers. In the 1990s, however, Ros Pesman,

who later served as an influential University level
administrator, became Head of Department.
Supported by a small team of carefully chosen
reformers, she encouraged colleagues to revise
their courses and to improve their research performances. Under her leadership, the morale of the
Department improved and staff became more
willing to embrace reform. Her successor, Stephen
Garton, who later served as Dean of Arts, Provost
and Vice Chancellor, was also keenly aware of the
need for change. While continuing to promote
a culture of teaching and research improvement,
he also sought to stimulate the Department's
revitalization by encouraging a number of long
serving colleagues to retire. He planned to replace
them with a new generation of young scholars.
Although he had success in persuading some older
staff members either to retire or move to fractional
positions, the University and Faculty remained
reluctant to replace them, and the staff numbers
in History shrank to less than 15, an alarm-
ing decline from the figures of 20 years earlier.
Finally, the Department was given permission to
make a three-year appointment in Early Modern
European history, an appointment designed to
provide a temporary replacement for Ros Pesman,
now seconded to a senior University position. In
fact, the person offered the lectureship declined
the appointment. Although Stephen was no longer
Head of Department when this happened, he
advised his successor to omit the clause indicating
it was a temporary position from the re-advertise-
ment notice, in the hope that no-one in the Staff
Office would notice the change. The tactic worked
and Andrew Fitzmaurice, who quickly became an
internationally recognised scholar, was appointed
to a continuing position. It was a brilliant move
which would never have occurred to Stephen's
successor, who was me. No wonder he was later
called 'the silver fox'.

Ros Pesman and Stephen Garton laid the
foundations for turning the History Department
around, but they were not given the resources
to allow them to introduce more major changes.
Those only came about when in 2000 the University
decided to invest in a Faculty of Arts renaissance
by dramatically revising its management structure,
investing its new leaders with more authority and
providing the financial resources to implement
renewal.

Amazing Grace

After she graduated at the end of 1979 Grace
found employment as a clerk working for Telecom
Australia (now Telstra). It was employment that
lacked both present challenges and future prospects. She also enrolled as a Masters student in
Historical Archaeology choosing to write a thesis
on the history of the convict built Great North
Road. Over the next couple of years, we made regular excursions to Wiseman's Ferry which served
as a base for our walking and driving trips along
the road. On these trips Grace discovered, measured and photographed the still surviving material
remains of the Road, which consisted of culverts
and bridges, as well as work camps once occupied
by the convict labourers. Through her enrolment
in this course, she began to develop a network in
the heritage industry, a network that included the
leader of the Historical Archaeology program
at the University of Sydney, Judy Birmingham.
Through Judy, Grace found employment as the
Historic Buildings Officer at the National Trust,
where she gained valuable experience in Heritage
conservation and planning, while continuing
to research and write her MA thesis. Although
the thesis was officially supervised by Judy
Birmingham, succeeded by two members of the
History Department, Ian Jack and Brian Fletcher,
the form it took was very much determined by
Grace herself. She was determined to ensure that
the study was a genuine contribution to Historical
Archaeology, balancing and integrating the techniques and questions relating to both Archaeology
and History. This caused disagreements with Judy,
who understood Historical Archaeology simply to
be a form of Archaeology which studied relatively
recent rather than pre-historic sites. In contrast,
Grace understood the discipline to consist of a
partnership of Archaeology and History which
drew on the methods and approaches of both.
When this effectively self-supervised thesis was
submitted in 1985 it received highly positive
examiners' reports and was awarded the highest

grade possible, a Pass with Merit.

I enjoyed those excursions even though I often felt cold staying in a small, basically furnished caravan in the Wiseman's Ferry caravan park in the middle of Winter. What added to my fondness for the 'GNR', as Grace came to call it, was the fact that it was while we were walking up the Road on one of those excursions, we agreed to get married, even though our romantic relationship was not yet a year old. But I had no doubts about that decision, it just felt completely right, as it still does.

We married in May 1981 in the Longueville Uniting Church, in part because, although we could not wed in a Catholic church, we wrongly thought a Protestant church wedding might meet the expectations of Grace's Catholic parents. Because we didn't want a formal reception it was held at my parent's house, just a short walk from that same church.

When I first returned from the United States in 1973 my father told me that I was the most determined person he had ever met. If I had known then what I have since discovered in the writing of this family history, I'm sure I'd have disputed that suggestion, given his own record of resolve both in peace and war. But the longer I knew Grace the more I found myself in awe of her academic achievements, which resulted from her intellectual commitment, capacity for hard work and an exceptional talent for researching and writing history. Our four children, Margot (1982), Eliza (1984), Isabel (1988) and Leo (1990) were born over a short eight-year period and yet in the years from 1982 to 1996, while she balanced minding four young children with work and study commitments, what she achieved was quite extraordinary. During this time I was heavily focussed on my own teaching and research and although I shared in childminding and household duties, she carried by far the greater share of the load. In the period after Eliza was born, when she was a stay at home mother, our disposable income was quite small and our financial circumstances were made more difficult as home mortgage interest rates rose into double figures. I was so obsessed with ensuring we didn't find ourselves in debt that I ignored the financial needs both of Grace and

our children. Stuck in our house with two small children and a stingy allowance from me she had a far harder time of it than her not always understanding husband.

Her career prospects brightened because of her own determination. She left the National Trust to become a heritage consultant, developing a reputation for producing high quality reports. However, the nature of this work required the production of these documents in a relatively short period of time, which allowed a minimum period in which to research the specified subject. Because she wanted to produce complex studies in history based on extensive research, she applied for a Commonwealth Government postgraduate scholarship to undertake a PhD in Australian history at the University of Sydney. Her topic was the early history of European occupation of The Rocks, and the thesis was completed in 1996. Two years later when it was published in revised form as a book by Melbourne University Press, it received highly favourable reviews and was awarded the New South Wales Premier's Award for Local/Community History. Despite a multiplicity of other commitments her academic career was off to a brilliant start. Inevitably, ARC Postdoctoral and Queen Elizabeth 2 Fellowships followed, while her subsequent appointment to a continuing lectureship in Australian history at UNSW guaranteed her a long-term University career and the time and resources to pursue major research projects.

Research

Through the early 1980s I continued to teach in units of study in American history and to maintain a modest publication record in the field of colonial American history. This output included a chapter in a book of essays on officeholding in the American colonies and an article in the official journal of the South Carolina Historical Society. The book manuscript was despatched to three or four American university presses and rejected by them all. In each case too, the referees' reports, while acknowledging that the book was based on extensive research and made an important contribution to the history of the emergence and establishment of southern plantation slavery, argued against publication on the basis that because it used the methods and approaches of the new social history, it was out of step with recent historiographical trends, which now emphasised cultural perspectives. It was worthy, they agreed, but it wouldn't sell. By the end of the decade, I decided to cut my losses and not despatch the MS to any further presses. I convinced myself that I could take consolation in the fact that most of the material in the unpublished book had already appeared in one form or another as chapters in books or articles in journals.

But then out of the blue I was contacted by Garland, a small commercial press in New York, which proposed to include my book in their Early American History Series. The books were very much in the Franklins No Frills tradition, they had plain hardback covers and there were no illustrations to accompany the text. Despite that, they were high priced, reflecting a marketing strategy designed to sell expensively priced books with short print runs to university libraries, of which there are, of course, thousands in the United States. When I wrote to the publisher a year after publication, seeking to buy extra copies to give to family and academic colleagues, I was told all copies were sold. In any case, the book received some moderately favourable reviews, including in the flagship journal of early American history *The William and Mary Quarterly*.[1] I didn't exactly feel elated when the book was published but rather relieved, although perhaps also somewhat embarrassed that it had taken so long to happen and that the book itself was so modest in appearance.

In fact, there was still a twist in the tale of this book's story. Fifteen years after publication I was approached by *The History Press* in Charleston with a proposal for a second edition. This version, when it appeared in 2005, was a paperback with an illustrated cover, as well as maps, diagrams and pictures spread through the text. It also included a foreword by Charles Joyner, a noted historian of southern history, and a second edition introduction, in which I placed the book in its historiographical context, and apologised for simply treating slavery as a system and ignoring the contribution of

African-Americans to the colony's culture and economy. It didn't sell a huge number of copies, as my subsequent royalty cheques testified, and I'm not sure what the various reading groups in South Carolina, who wrote to let me know they were about to discuss it, made of a book that included several dozen tables and was written in an opaque, academic style. But I was pleased that a work that I had laboured over for almost two decades now existed in an attractive format.[2]

However, in the 1980s, my research was increasingly focussed on Australia. To my surprise I discovered that the Georgia Minstrels were a huge success in Australia between 1876 and 1879. Not only did the troupe attract large and enthusiastic audiences but in their private lives these men experienced less discrimination than they had in the United States. A few of them married European women and spent the remainder of their careers performing on the Australian popular stage with minstrel and vaudeville companies as well as featuring in melodramas, most notably *Uncle Tom's Cabin*. These findings led me to ponder questions that extended far beyond the scope of one minstrel troupe tour. Why were American minstrel shows so popular in the Australian colonies? And where did the minstrel show fit in the broader context of Australian stage entertainment? Because there was no secondary Australian theatre history literature that addressed these questions, I began to widen my own ambitions to explore the history of the Australian minstrel show as a fundamental element not only of the popular stage but of Australian popular culture more generally. My extended research revealed the genre as a major conduit for American popular music and humour, confirming that American influence on Australian culture long predated the arrival of the movies.

And so, with the help of my first grant from the Australian Research Council, which I applied for with the support of Deryck Schreuder, a professor who encouraged his colleagues to research and publish, the article on the Georgia Minstrels was expanded into a book about the Australian history of minstrelsy and its successor vaudeville. When I first began to approach publishers, I received some very negative responses and was told on repeated occasions that books on theatre didn't sell. Beginning to have a sense of déjà vu, I asked the most senior Australian history academic in the Department, Brian Fletcher, to read the MS and give me his honest assessment. His evaluation was a relief and an encouragement. 'I am at least glad that I played some part in directing your considerable talents to Australian history,' he wrote. 'We are clearly all going to benefit.'[3] That was a more generous assessment than I deserved but it was great for my morale and it helped persuade me to persevere in finding a publisher. In fact, a short time later, UNSW Press, as it was then called, agreed to publish the book in its Australian history series and it duly appeared in 1990.[4] In fact, it sold reasonably well, boosted by an extensive review in *The (Saturday) Australian* by Phillip Adams and an hour-long interview I had with him on the commercial radio station that he worked for in his pre-*Late Night Live* days.

During the course of researching this subject my reading of the sources persuaded me that if the popular stage was one main pillar of Australian popular culture in the nineteenth and early twentieth centuries, horse racing was the other. But given the size of the topic and the immense range of available sources I found the prospect of embarking on a history of Australian horse racing to be a daunting prospect. But one afternoon in 1988 when I was sharing a few after work drinks with some colleagues from the Department of Government and International Relations and expanding upon my views about horse racing as a critical Australian popular culture institution, one of them facetiously bet me one beer, that I could never persuade the Australian Jockey Club to sponsor me to write the Club's history. I found that an interesting challenge, one which I accepted and within days made an appointment to meet the secretary of the Club, Ray Alexander. Fortuitously, the Sesquicentenary of the AJC was due in 1992 and the Club, the oldest turf club in Australia, was anxious for the occasion to be marked with the publication of an authoritative history. So, Ray Alexander and I agreed that in partnership with my University of Sydney colleague, Martin Painter, who subsequently contributed the administrative

history chapters, I would research and write a history of the AJC, extending from its founding in 1842 through to its sesquicentenary year. The book was launched at a lavish occasion in the Queen Elizabeth Stand at the 1992 Easter Carnival.[5]

While I was researching and writing these two books, I found myself wondering how these two influential Australian popular culture institutions fitted into that culture more broadly. I also became increasingly curious about what other activities underpinned and shaped Australian popular culture at different stages of its emergence and transformation. So, I began to think about the prospect of writing a general history of Australian popular culture, one which I conceived of as argumentative and selective rather than descriptive and comprehensive. However, it was a challenging topic, both in terms of its enormous scope and also because of the obvious difficulty of prescribing its boundaries at different stages of its evolution. I also began to have second thoughts after I consulted David Walker, an Australian historian for whose work I had considerable admiration. He had co-edited a volume of essays on aspects of the history of Australian popular culture and I wanted to know why he hadn't attempted a comprehensive history. He answered that he thought that the subject was just too large and complicated for a general study and that in any case his Australian history interests had developed in new directions.

In the end I decided to attempt a broad study because I found it an intriguing challenge, one that interested me more than any of the other topics that I considered as alternatives. But I was also aware that given the increasing amounts of time that I was now devoting to teaching and, to my surprise, administration, it might be difficult to find time to complete this project within a reasonable period. The massive scope of the study and the wide range of primary sources, both printed and manuscript, that needed to be consulted required a considerable investment of time. Realising I needed help to complete the project I applied for an ARC grant, specifying that I proposed to use almost all the funds awarded to employ research assistants to help search out the primary sources, a task too extensive to undertake on my own. I knew that if I failed to secure the grant I would need to revert to a more modest and less labour-intensive subject. But not only was I awarded the grant but at the same time, John Rickard, who was commissioned by Longman Cheshire/Pearson International to edit a series of books in Australian history, approached me to write the popular culture volume. In writing this book I constantly questioned my ability to finish it because the subjects and the sources both seemed overwhelming. 'I doubt my ability to comprehend the subject', I wrote to a fellow historian of popular culture, Jim Gilbert, even as I had completed two-thirds of the volume.[6] But with the help of several experienced and hard-working research assistants, led by Hilary Weatherburn, I managed to complete the book in three years and it was published in 1995.[7] Some reviewers referred to it as a text book, perhaps because most of Longmans educational books were texts, and my book was edited in the same style. But text books are usually descriptive, based on secondary material and summarise the arguments of other scholars. In contrast, my book was based on primary sources, discussed a selective range of subjects, and articulated original arguments. For example, it established a periodisation of popular culture as well as enunciating the changing characteristics of that culture over a period that extended from 1788 into the 1970s. It also focussed on how popular culture interacted with other types of culture, especially middle-class and 'high culture'. It is still set for undergraduate courses in Australian history and almost 30 years later I continue to receive annual copyright payments. Of all my books, it is the one which captured the most international attention, reflected in an invitation to participate and deliver a paper at a conference held in Washington in 1997 to celebrate the opening of the Smithsonian's Ronald Reagan Building.

With this book completed I began to turn my attention to my next project which I decided was to be a social and cultural history of rural Australia, an endeavour that was no less ambitious than the previous assignment. There were three reasons why I chose this subject. First, my previous book, as some reviewers had pointed out, had focussed

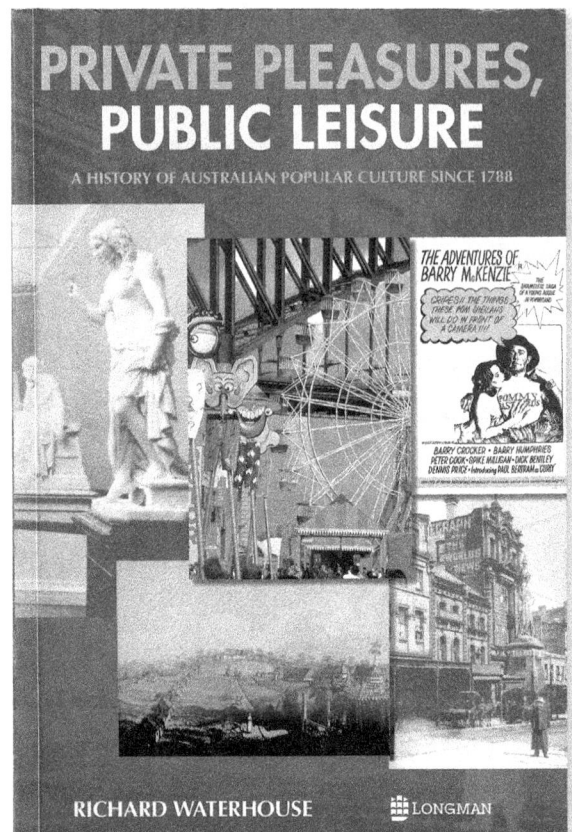

The cover of my book on the general history of Australian popular culture. It was designed to be as eclectic as its subject

heavily on urban Australia and I now became fascinated with the issues of how rural differed from urban culture and of how city and bush cultures interacted and impacted on each other. Second, although historians had once focussed heavily on rural history, from the late 1960s onwards their concentration moved towards urban history. Moreover, the trend of this new urban historiography was to emphasise the importance of the role of cities in Australian history to the detriment of the contribution of the Bush, socially, culturally and even economically. In my judgment the pendulum had swung too far the other way, a judgment that I considered was confirmed when I heard papers given by a number of academic historians at major History conferences in which they argued that historically Australia was *always* an *urban* country, an argument I knew to be untrue. So, my decision to write a book about rural Australia went against the current historiographical trend. But I was confident that my research would allow me to develop arguments that both re-emphasised the important role that rural Australia played in Australian history and enabled me to analyse the complex and evolving historical relationship between the City and the Bush. Third, I was born in rural Australia and lived there until the age of fifteen. As I indicated in the book's Acknowledgments my country origins were an important factor in motivating me to choose this topic because I wanted to know more about the complex cultural contexts that had contributed to shaping my life and character.

I was fortunate to receive ARC funding to support the research for this book because at this time, while my teaching load had diminished in the early 1990s, that was only because I was taking on an increasing share of administrative duties at the departmental, Faculty and University level. Even so its publication was delayed because I found I only had time to work on it during periods of SSP ('Sabbatical') leave. The book, entitled *The Vision Splendid: A Social and Cultural History of Rural Australia* was finally published in 2005.[8] I undertook a modest promotion tour, giving lectures in Orange, Kempsey and Wagga Wagga, and it was widely reviewed not only in academic journals but in rural Australian newspapers. One of my Sydney colleagues once sat next to an ANU Professor of History at a conference dinner who told him that no academic historian could claim to be in the first rank of Australian historians unless their books were reviewed in the (London) *Times Literary Supplement*. When this comment was repeated to me it struck me as constituting a classic example of cultural cringe, although I have to admit that when *The Vision Splendid* was reviewed in that publication, I took some satisfaction in knowing that my work had received a modest level of recognition internationally as well as in Australia.

In the years subsequent to the publication of that book I continued to produce a range of chapters and articles that included Australian social and political as well as cultural history. These included pieces that dealt with some central subjects in Australian history, including the changing relationship between liberty and representative government between 1788 and 1901 and the nature of popular political ideology in the early years of World War 2. But the publication of *The*

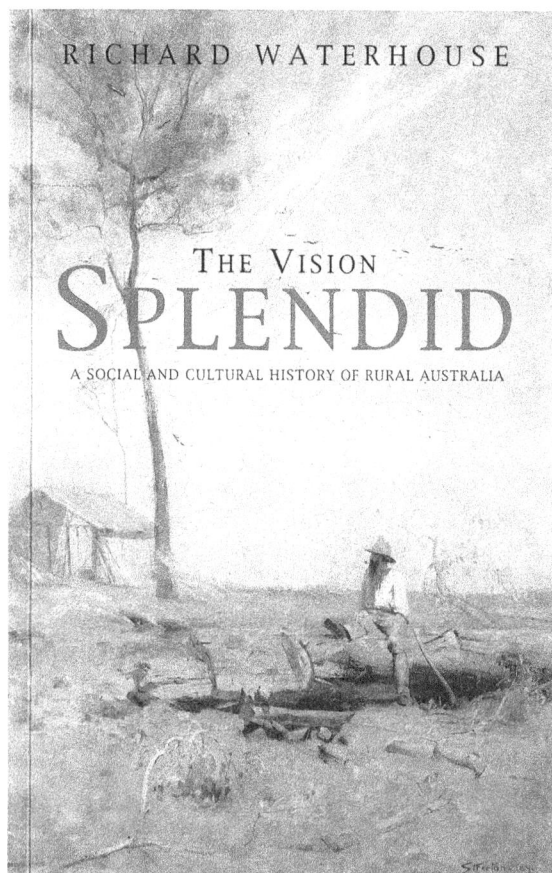

RICHARD WATERHOUSE

THE VISION SPLENDID

A SOCIAL AND CULTURAL HISTORY OF RURAL AUSTRALIA

Cover of The Vision Splendid a book my colleagues sometimes referred to as my autobiography in deference to my rural upbringing

Vision Splendid, which I like to think should be read as a companion piece to *Private Pleasures*, marked my last major contribution to the history of Australian popular culture.

A year or so before I retired one of my recently appointed colleagues who was teaching an advanced seminar course relating to the methods and practices of history, invited me to speak to her class about which individual historians and schools of history had influenced my own writings. I explained how the works of Raymond Williams, E.P. Thompson, and Lawrence Levine, with honourable mentions to Robert C. Allen (the importance of text in context), Roy Rosenzweig (how twentieth century cultural resolution replaced nineteenth century cultural conflict) and James Deetz (how people who have not left behind written records have nevertheless left material objects), had shaped my awareness not only of the importance of the histories of ordinary people but about the possibilities of recovering them through a wide variety of sources and set out paths that I could follow in recreating the lives of ordinary Australians. At the end of the seminar, when I had delivered my presentation and the students had asked a series of deferentially polite questions, my colleague summed up the discussion, which culminated in her asking me whether I agreed with her understanding that the approaches of these historians were now outdated and superseded. I thought about that suggestion for a few seconds before responding with the answer that although I accepted that the arguments and approaches of these scholars needed modifications in the light of subsequent research by succeeding generations of historians utilising new sources and approaches, their contributions were still relevant and important. When I later reflected on this response, I realised I might have cited Thompson's books and articles as an example. His work, as Anna Clark subsequently pointed out, focussed on working men, rather than working women, and subsequent research has revealed that women too were not only advocates of left-wing reform but in the process contributed more to the creation of a more comprehensive working-class consciousness than Thompson allowed.[9] However, her input and the contributions from other revisionist labour historians has enlarged upon rather than negated Thompson's pioneering work.

Jack Greene was the first historian to influence my understanding of history in ways that shaped my subsequent written work. This influence came about in two ways. First, when I attended meetings with him to discuss my progress he often spoke more generally about the purpose of history. He argued that history was about context and generalisation, which meant for him, in particular, locating British north American history within the broader context of the First British Empire. The north American colonies were not to be considered discretely, but together with other British colonies in the Americas, particularly the West Indian settlements. Second, he put these arguments into practice through a series of books specifying the relationships between Britain's north American colonies and the wider British Empire in the Americas.[10]

I chose my PhD topic, which subsequently became my first book, because I accepted Greene's argument that the plantation colonies which stretched from Maryland on the mainland down to Barbados in the West Indies were more typical and economically important than the (Puritan) New England Colonies. My later decision to write general studies of the history of Australian popular and rural cultures was also influenced by the Greene dictum of the value of generalisation in creating broader understandings of the past. And finally, in keeping with Greene's argument of the need to locate American colonial history within a wider Imperial context my books on the popular stage, Australian popular culture, and Australian rural culture, all sought to place their subjects within a setting of wider cultural influence and transmission, a setting that included the United States as well as the First and (more importantly) Second British Empires.

In reaction to the Frankfurt School, which had stressed the hopelessness of individual action and freedom in the face of capitalist hegemony, E. P. Thompson, Raymond Williams and Lawrence Levine rescued the term 'culture' from a narrowly literary meaning and applied it to the work and leisure practices of ordinary people, which in Levine's case included slaves. These historians also sought to give agency to the common people. In this context, while acknowledging that the creation of the English working class was pre-determined by the Industrial Revolution, Thompson suggested that the values that constituted working class consciousness were created by working men themselves. These historians also accepted that culture is a process, and that the changing forms that high, middle-class and popular cultures take are the result of interchange across time, race, class and gender. Strongly influenced by these understandings of agency and culture my book on Australian popular culture also included chapters on high and middle-class cultures, because popular culture did not exist in isolation, but was constantly changing in part due to the influences of other forms of culture, local and imported. And finally, agency is at the heart of my arguments throughout my studies in Australian cultural history, which stress that popular culture served not only to entertain and reflect the values of working people but on occasions became an oppositional culture challenging the proclaimed establishment orthodoxies.

However, over that last 20 years or so, I have become more flexible in my perspectives. The work of one outstanding Australian historian, in particular, reminded me that deeply researched studies of particular localities over a relatively short time frame can provide original and deep insights that are at least as important and influential as those developed in more general studies. And here the historian I am referring to is Grace Karskens. Her study of community life in The Rocks area during the early years of European occupation provided new understandings about the nature of Sydney's pre-industrial society and the role of the early convict system. The arguments in this study of a small community in fact have enormous implications for wider interpretations of the pre-industrial culture of early colonial Sydney. Her two major subsequent books, *The Colony: a History of Early Sydney* and *People of the River: Lost Worlds of Early Australia*, used multi-disciplinary approaches to explore the deep time history of Sydney and adjacent areas, the history and form of Indigenous occupation, the roles of convicts and ex-convicts in an emerging European society, and the causes and consequences of conflict between First Nations people and the European invaders, from the perspectives of both sides of the frontier. The local studies written by proponents of the new social history were statistical and schematic, providing only limited understanding of the cultural worlds of pre-Revolutionary New Englanders, but Grace Karskens' studies, relying on multiple approaches, especially the ethnographic 'action' method, are far more complex and intuitive in their arguments, and much more successful in bringing her historical characters back to life. Her books are demonstrations that studies covering a limited location and time period, nevertheless, can have major implications for understanding the history of cultures and peoples more generally. Although she published most of her major works after mine had already appeared, my conversations with her as she developed the arguments that later

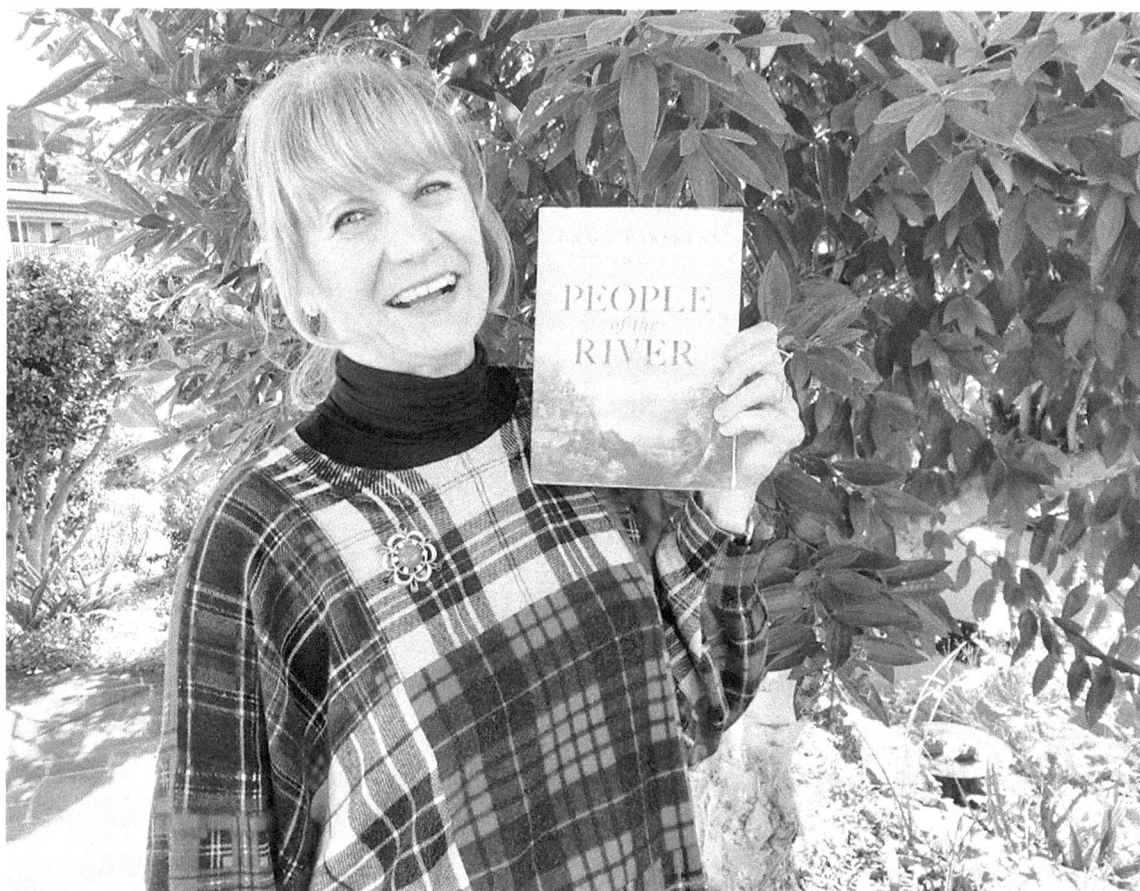

Grace Karskens holding a copy of her prize-winning book, People of the River

underpinned *The Rocks*, *The Colony* and *People of the River* proved invaluable to me as I formulated the chapters of both *Private Pleasures* and *The Vision Splendid*.

Teaching

In the 1980s, with my research interests moving more in the direction of Australian history I also decided that I also wanted to teach in that field both because it would provide the opportunity for me to learn more about my own country's history and result in the introduction of more cultural history into the Australian component of the History Department syllabus. In 1984 I approached my Australian History colleagues with a proposal to introduce a course in comparative Australian-American cultural history, covering the period from the late eighteenth century through to World War 1. It subsequently was titled Contact and Comparison: Society and Culture in America and Australia 1750–1914. I hadn't anticipated any opposition to this proposal and so I was quite surprised to discover that although Brian Fletcher, who four years later became the inaugural Bicentennial Professor supported the proposal, most of the 'Australianists' opposed it, suggesting I wasn't qualified to teach Australian history. In the end, they agreed to allow the course to proceed on condition that my former teacher, Ken Cable, delivered all the Australian history lectures while I focused on the American component. Ken was a brilliant teacher of the English Reformation, and he was also well versed in Australian religious history, but he was not well read in Australian cultural history. He taught the course during its introductory year but then decided that I was capable of carrying in with it on my own.

From 2002 it also became a joint course, taught simultaneously both at Sydney and the University of North Carolina at Chapel Hill. My colleague (and friend) Robert C. 'Bobby' Allen, a member of the American Studies Department at Chapel Hill, and a brilliant and influential American cultural historian, was the course co-teacher. The students at Sydney and Chapel Hill met once a week via (the then) advanced educational communication medium of teleconferencing. Sometimes, Bobby

also visited Australia to lecture to the Australian students, while I also made trips to Chapel Hill to teach at the American end. For its time it represented an innovative way of teaching and connecting students from different countries and cultures. It also influenced a number of the American students to come to Australia both for short and long-term study. Perhaps it deserved more recognition, which it might have achieved if Bobby and I had chosen to promote the course using the educational jargon that was becoming increasingly common in universities world-wide. But I was suspicious of the general approaches to teaching and learning embraced by the educational theorists which often seemed to me to be shallow and cliched, and I valued stressing subject learning over generic educational outcomes. In the end I preferred to let the course speak to the students and for itself.

Nor was this my only teaching partnership with UNC, Chapel Hill. Although the University of Sydney had established a Study Abroad pathway for students from Chapel Hill wishing to study at Sydney for a semester some years earlier, in 2001 I established a program for Honors Abroad UNC students, a program that involved a series of excursions to important historical and cultural sites both in Sydney and Canberra.

In the early 1990s, as a result of a recommendation from its Undergraduate Committee, the Department finally decided to allow the introduction of courses in Australian and American history into first year. Initially there was very little enthusiasm from staff in either of these fields to introduce such courses but I found myself thinking that I had never taught in first year and that it could prove to be an interesting challenge. So, I proposed a 'settler society' style course that involved the comparative social, political, and economic histories of the United States and Australia. Brian Fletcher was an enthusiastic supporter of this suggestion but was too heavily committed to other teaching responsibilities to partner in teaching this new course. However, to my surprise, Stephen Garton a relatively new staff member, who I had not previously worked with, not only agreed to become the joint teacher of the course but seemed to be enthusiastic about the project. In fact, team teaching this course with Stephen became one of the most enjoyable experiences of my career. First taught in 1991, the following year it was expanded to include a South African component led by Deryck Schreuder, an academic who was an enthusiastic supporter of team teaching.

In the late 1980s and first years of the 1990s I was concerned about the Department's future, but it was also the period in which I found teaching an incredibly rewarding experience because, apart from the first-year course, I also introduced two new honours seminars to the curriculum, seminars which addressed subjects and issues which were also the subject of my research. First, I offered an honours seminar called Contact and Comparison Part 2: The Twentieth Century, which extended the material covering Australian and American cultural history I dealt with in Part 1, and proved so popular that it had to be held twice a week to accommodate the numbers. Second, I introduced a fourth-year honours seminar, Writing the History of Popular Culture, because I was concerned that contemporary honours students were not receiving the same level of training in History Method as previous generations. I didn't have the knowledge to take my students on a tour that began with the Classical Greek and Roman historians and ended with contemporary approaches. Rather my aim was to introduce them to twentieth century Frankfurt School, Labour, Feminist, Social, Cultural, Ethnographic, Structuralist and Post-structuralist approaches. I liked teaching these courses because I found them intellectually stimulating, the students were generally of very high quality, and because when I taught subjects that were broadly connected to my research, my teaching stimulated my research and vice versa. I didn't realise it at the time, but I was fortunate to be teaching in an era when academic staff still had a high level of control over individual course content, as well as the overall syllabus offered by their departments. Now the curriculums of Departments, Schools and Faculties are much more determined by the central university administration and the influence of the educational theorists ensures that generic outcomes are too often emphasised at the expense of subject content.

Apart from teaching a wide range of courses over an extensive range of subjects I also carried a relatively heavy load as a research thesis supervisor. Altogether, over the course of my career I supervised more than one hundred History honours dissertations, at first covering American and then, from the mid 1980s, Australian topics. For the most part these focussed on eighteenth and nineteenth century topics although I also supervised a few theses that covered the twentieth century. During the course of his career Jack Greene supervised more than 100 PhD candidates. My record was rather more humble, altogether I supervised five MA (Honours) and 19 PhD thesis students to completion. During the time I taught and researched American history I supervised a total of four MA and three PhD students researching fields in English and American history, whose topics included the English image in the American mind in the nineteenth century and the impact of the end of slavery on New York City. However, once I switched my research interests to Australia and developed a profile as a cultural history scholar the number of postgraduate students who chose to work with me increased considerably. Between 1990 and 2013 one MA and 16 PhD candidates completed their research theses under my supervision. Their subjects included modernist dance, masculinity in Australian cinema, post-World War 2 actor training, conflict between Asian fishers and the Australian border force in the Timor Sea, the early wine industry in NSW, and the nineteenth century temperance movement. A number of these former students, including Shane White, Jennifer Clark, Amanda Card, Katherine Biber, Rachel Landers, Ruth Balint, Julie McIntyre, and Matthew Allen have enjoyed highly successful academic careers as teachers, researchers and, in the case of Landers, also as culture producers. White is probably the best known internationally, achieving a world-wide reputation as a leading scholar of the history of African-American slavery and culture. Others, including Mark St Leon, and Rosemary Kerr, have pursued careers outside academia, but nevertheless published significant books, based on their PhD theses, that have enlarged our knowledge of Australian cultural history. And Anna Wong, as a public servant, has made an important contribution towards the recognition and preservation of the built environment of rural NSW.

Some of these students wanted close supervision, others needed it, and a few quickly learned so much about their subject that they needed very little guidance from me at all. But in the light of my own postgraduate experiences of suffering from a lack of supervision at Sydney and benefitting from close oversight at Johns Hopkins I scheduled regular meetings with my students because, in my judgement, I could advise them on research processes, approaches and professionalism, even when I knew less about the subject than they did. I only abandoned regular meetings, when students, for one reason or another, needed to extend their candidatures into long term stays. In those cases, I figured that after four years of regular supervisory sessions my supply of wisdom had expired.

Promoting History

During the early years of my academic career, I was too preoccupied with a heavy teaching load, and lacked the experience, seniority and profile to promote my discipline in the wider community. But in the 1980s I was nominated by the University to serve on a number of History related NSW Board of Studies committees, namely the Modern History Syllabus (1986–93) and the Modern History Examination (1986–98) Committees. I also sought to promote the role of History in the community as a consultant to the National Maritime Museum, which involved writing a series of briefs documenting the Australian-American maritime relationship from the age of sealing and whaling through to the era of surfing. In the late 1990s I also attended a series of workshops organised by the staff of the not yet opened National Museum of Australia in which I set out my arguments about which Australian cultural values and institutions I considered mattered the most. I hoped that the extensive and important artefacts which the Museum had purchased would be exhibited in the context of a narrative about Australian cultural history to which I had

contributed in a very modest way. Unfortunately, the curators more often chose to exhibit the artefacts and objects for their own sake rather than in a wider historical context and an opportunity to use the material objects in the Museum to tell original and informative stories about the nation's past was only partially adopted.

But I found that I really enjoyed promoting history to a wider public and as my reputation as an Australian historian grew, I found myself giving occasional interviews to television news and public affairs programs and dozens of radio interviews, including a few on commercial, although mostly on ABC city and regional stations. I was fortunate to talk to some really professional and well-prepared radio journalists including Andrew Olle, Phillip Adams, Angela Webber, Richard Glover, James Valentine and Geraldine Doogue. The two interviews which I recall most fondly are first, *Mornings with Margaret Throsby*, in which I talked to Joe Gelonesi about my life in academia and my tastes in music, which focussed on those works like Dvorak's *New World Symphony* which crossed over between high and popular culture; and second, an interview with Scott Levi, breakfast presenter on ABC Central Coast, in which I reflected on my childhood in Gosford and my academic career at the University of Sydney. Later in my career, I contributed as a 'talking head' to two documentaries, *The Maitland Wonder: The Les Darcy Story* (1998) and *Bombora: The History of Australian Surfing* (2008). More significantly, I was the consultant historian as well as a talking head on the Chris Masters' narrated, three-part documentary, *The Years That Made Us: Australia Between the Wars* (1913). All of these documentaries were shown on ABC television, while *The Years That Made Us* also appeared on The History Channel, helping to ensure that films about Hitler were not completely dominant in that channel's viewing program.

I also had two excruciating experiences with television documentaries. In the early 2000s I was interviewed for a BBC documentary about the history of the Australian wine industry, a documentary that was eventually shown in Australia on SBS. To illustrate the view of the film's makers that

Australia's early European settlers were the flotsam and jetsam of the British Isles, I spoke about the character of the transported convicts while standing on top of a pile of garbage at a rubbish dump at Botany Bay. Many years later, another BBC television crew came to Australia to film a documentary about the *Cutty Sark*, as part of a series named *Ships That Made the Commonwealth*. As evidence of Australia's continuing ties to the UK I was interviewed standing beside the Bankstown Oval fence, while the Sydney First Grade Cricket Grand Final was played in the background. Fortunately, I don't think this series was shown in Australia.

For three decades, extending from the early 1980s through until my retirement in 1911, I was also regularly quoted on issues relating to Australian history mostly in the Australian, but sometimes in the American press. I was vain enough to fill several scrapbooks with cuttings from articles in which I was quoted although I found some of my more cliched comments so embarrassing that those clippings were filed in my office wastepaper bin. But I enjoyed my communication with the wider community extending from high school children to those who belonged to local and state level historical associations as well as to members of the wider reading public interested in a deeper understanding of their own country's history than they were given during their childhood education. One example of my interchange with a reader came in 2005 shortly after the publication of the *The Vision Splendid*, when I received a letter from a man who told me he had purchased three copies of the book. His adult children all lived overseas and he had sent each one of them a copy of the book to remind them of their distinct Australian heritage which he was concerned they had forgotten. Over the next few years, I sometimes wondered what impact the book had on his children, or if they even read it.

Endnotes

1   Richard Waterhouse, *A New World Gentry: The Making of a Merchant and Planter Class in South Carolina, 1670–1770,* New York: Garland, 1989

2   Richard Waterhouse, *A New World Gentry: The Making of a Merchant and Planter Class in South Carolina, 1670–1770,* Charleston: The History Press, 2005

3   Brian Fletcher to Richard Waterhouse, undated letter, but certainly written in 1989, Waterhouse Family Collection

4   Richard Waterhouse, *From Minstrel Show to Vaudeville; the Australian Popular Stage, 1788–1914.* Sydney: University of New South Wales Press, 1990

5   Martin Painter and Richard Waterhouse, *The Principal Club: A History of the Australian Jockey Club*, Sydney: Allen and Unwin, 1992

6   Richard Waterhouse to Jim Gilbert, 18 August, 1994, Waterhouse Family Collection

7   Richard Waterhouse, *Private Pleasures, Public Leisure: A History of Australian Popular Culture Since 1788,* South Melbourne: Longman, 1995

8   Fremantle: Curtin University Books/Fremantle Arts Centre Press, 2005

9   Anna Clark, *The Struggle for the Breeches: Gender and the Making of the English Working Class*, Berkeley: University of California Press, 1995

10 For a summary study of his arguments see Jack P. Greene, *Pursuits of Happiness: The Social Development of Early Modern British Colonies and the Formation of American Culture,* Chapel Hill: The university of North Carolina Press, 1988

Chapter 18
Becoming a Suit

One day in 1989 I was standing in the sandwich order line in the University Staff Club when I found myself in conversation with my colleague, Iain Cameron, who was then nearing the end of his term as chair of the History Department's Curriculum Committee. He asked if I was willing to stand for election as his replacement. I indicated that I would think about it and provide him with an answer within a day or two. As I thought about whether I wanted to take on this relatively demanding, and I suspected unrewarding, administrative position I was strongly aware that over the past few years I had acted as an outspoken critic not only of the Department's curriculum but of its overall lack of direction. Here I had an opportunity to make at least a modest contribution to improving the Department's curriculum by restoring the coherence it had lost since the major revisions of the 1970s. It seemed to me that given my propensity to argue for change I also had an obligation to participate in bringing it about. In the end I decided not only to nominate as chair of the Curriculum Committee but I persuaded several colleagues who were supportive of syllabus reform to join me in running for office on an announced and specified platform of reform. Usually, staff needed to be coerced into committee responsibilities so this marked a rare moment in the Department's history. The policies we proposed including (finally) introducing Australian and American history courses to first year, and requiring second and third year students to enrol in both Specialist (which involved the study of one country over a limited period) and Thematic (which addressed a prescribed theme over several countries and covering a long time period) units. In addition, it was proposed to require second year honours students to enrol in a compulsory method class which exposed them to a wide variety of philosophies and approaches to history. After these policies were discussed at a meeting of the Curriculum Committee, they were referred to a series of specially convened Departmental Meetings which were held on several consecutive Fridays. To my relief, all of the proposed changes were adopted, which produced a more coherent and rational curriculum, one that lasted for more than a decade.

However, this result was not marked by total consensus. Some staff indicated resentment towards the sequence of Friday meetings, arguing that it impinged on their rights to keep this day free of teaching and administration responsibilities. I suspect what really concerned them was what they considered my overzealousness in promoting the development of new courses. They were content with the way things were and preferred to be allowed to teach the same courses which they had offered for many years. Others were dissatisfied with the new second year honours curriculum, specifically the inclusion of topics that dealt with Structuralism and Post-Structuralism, which they viewed as potentially subversive of the very discipline of History.

I had also often spoken about the need for the Department to review its research production with the aim of developing plans to increase the

number of ARC grants and its research production
in the form of books, chapters and articles. One
or two colleagues expressed concern to me that I
might next mount a research 'reform' campaign,
although given that I was only a Senior Lecturer
and my own grant achievement and publication
records were still modest my capacity to influence
the department's research culture was far more
limited than my ability to contribute to curriculum changes.

Despite my interest in reforming the curriculum and changing the research culture I had no
ambitions as an academic administrator beyond
contributing to further improving the teaching
and (I hoped one day) the research environments
within my own Department. I had no idea that
my role as Chair of the History Department's
Curriculum Committee was the beginning of
a career in Department, School, Faculty and
University administration that was to last for most
of the remainder of my academic career.

A decade earlier, in 1980, I was promoted to
Senior Lecturer based on a solid record in teaching
and a much more modest research record. In 1991
with two books and a reasonably sizeable body
of chapter and journal articles now on my curriculum vita I applied for promotion to Associate
Professor. My application was unsuccessful, which
I half expected because in my judgement, while
my qualifications were solid, they were not exceptional. However, I was later told that a member of
the committee who had opposed my promotion
had made inaccurate comments about the quality of my research and teaching, which prompted
other committee members to believe that I had
received an unfair assessment. Normally when
a candidate was not promoted, she or he was
required to wait two years before applying again.
However, I was allowed and indeed encouraged
to apply the following year, and with my third
book now published, and a far more sympathetic
committee, I learnt in late September 1992 that I
had achieved the rank of Associate Professor. As
Head of Department Ros Pesman had supported
my role in curriculum revision and both my
applications for promotion to 'Aspro' and she
was instrumental in my second time success. The

first thing I thought when I read the congratula-
tory letter from the Dean was that I wished my
parents were still alive to witness my promotion
since I owed them so much for the way they had
supported my studies over some 25 years.

At this time universities in Australia also
began to pay more attention to raising and measuring the standards of teaching quality. In part this
was in response to the Federal Government determining not only to measure university research
output and quality but teaching standards as well.
In this context, in 1992 the University's central
administration directed the faculties to establish
teaching committees, whose roles were to create
Faculty teaching plans setting out teaching and
learning policies and goals. These committees
were also required to develop specific policies
designed to achieve these goals. The Dean, Paul
Crittenden, asked Stephen Garton to become
Associate Dean, Teaching and Learning, as well
as establish and chair a teaching committee. But
Stephen declined the role and as I understand it,
nominated me as his replacement. He probably
cited the role I had played in History Department
curriculum reform as evidence of my qualifications for the position. I suspect that in deciding to
offer me the role Crittenden believed my recent
promotion also ensured that I was senior enough
to have influence in promoting any future teaching
and learning agenda.

As an administrator I had now moved from
department to faculty level. But I did not consider
myself as belonging to the new wave of university
level educational theorists. As a member of the
NSW Board of Studies Modern History Syllabus
Committee for some years I had listened to other
members of the Committee, more influenced by
educational theory than commitment to History
as a discipline, as they spoke with depressing
regularity about 'the skills approach' and 'student
centred learning'. Metaphorically chanting these
terms as mantras, the advocates of these notions
neither explained what they meant in detail, nor
the process by which these educational approaches
were to be integrated into the school history curriculum without impinging upon the discipline's
integrity. Their most significant contribution was

the creation of a compulsory Australian History syllabus that was subsequently taught in all NSW High Schools. Lacking chronology, periodisation and context, and with no connection drawn between its various thematic strands it qualified as an Australian Studies but not as an Australian History curriculum.

My intent was to produce both a pragmatic and jargon-free teaching plan as well as specific policies designed to measure and improve the quality of teaching in the faculty. I drafted an initial version of the Teaching Plan, which was then modified at a meeting of the Teaching and Learning Committee. The Dean then called a special meeting of all Faculty staff to discuss and hopefully approve it. The meeting was characterised by extensive discussion with most of it negative, colleagues arguing in effect that they didn't wish their teaching to be inspected or subject to direction by Faculty. In the end the Plan was adopted when it was explained that the university insisted that Faculties adopt such plans and that in any case it was written primarily to satisfy the inspectors at University and Government level. It was in part intended as window dressing and not all of its requirements, especially those that required funding, were likely to be implemented. In keeping with the policies set out in the Plan the Committee also later adopted a specific scheme to allow for the orderly administration of student evaluation questionnaires in courses across the faculty, and for the establishment of a faculty level Teaching Awards program designed to recognise outstanding teachers. It also developed a Teaching Relief Program which provided selected academic staff with reduced teaching for a semester to allow them to develop innovative teaching methods.

At this time the Federal Government was implementing what was called a Quality Review Process designed to measure the quality of teaching and learning in Australian universities. Because of my role as Associate Dean Teaching and Learning I participated in the organisation of the University's presentation and attended a meeting with the Quality Review Assessment group. Sydney had slipped in the rankings in the previous round but was restored to Group 1 this time,

and as a result all the contributors to the Sydney University cause received a letter of commendation. Most of us were more relieved than pleased.

At the University level the Academic Board had established the Teaching and Learning Committee and the Committee for Undergraduate Studies. In early 1994 I was approached by Michael Jackson, a Political Scientist, to replace him as chair of these two committees. I don't know why I was picked but I suspect that both he and John Mack, the Chair of the Academic Board, were impressed that the Faculty of Arts had adopted a Teaching and Learning Plan, given the strength of opposition to it, and I was given the credit for that adoption. I probably deserved some kudos but the reality was that most Arts colleagues were resigned to what they saw was an inevitability and decided the faculty might as well adopt the Plan to satisfy what the Vice-Chancellor wanted.

During the two years I chaired the Teaching and Learning Committee it adopted a code of practice for teaching, learning and assessment, another code covering plagiarism, a revised policy relating to the award of merit grades that was designed to ensure uniform marking standards across all faculties, and the establishment of procedures and policies designed to require faculties to submit annual teaching reports to the Academic Board. On the one hand this was a reasonable achievement, on the other, most Deans had only limited respect for Board policies and only enforced those which they found convenient or which also were supported at other high levels of administration. So, not all these plans were universally adopted across the University. But, one great advantage for me in serving as Deputy Chair of the Academic Board was that it allowed me to develop contacts in a wide range of faculties as well as at the central administration level. I was also developed a deeper understanding of how the institution operated. Later, when I became Head of Department and then Head of School, I often drew on these experiences and contacts to make decisions, develop policies and hire staff.

At the end of 1996 John Mack completed his term as Chair of the Academic Board and his Deputy Chairs also stepped down so that the new chair, Ros Pesman, could put together her own team. After an extended and tense period in the administrative trenches I was looking forward to a long period of study leave which I planned to spend completing my book on the history of Australian rural culture. But, in the end, Grace's year and mine were totally disrupted by family matters. We had lived in Denistone, a suburb in Sydney's northwest since 1983, and had added an upstairs extension to accommodate our four children. But thinking that a more rural environment might be beneficial for our children and ourselves we decided to move to the Central Coast, close to where we had purchased a small house for her parents two years earlier. We hoped to find a five-bedroom house, with water views, close to a railway station, and not too far from her parents, Francine and Bill. After a short search we located a five-bedroom Pettit and Sevitt modernist house in Tascott, with water views and a short walk from the nearest station. We could even see Grace's parents' house located across the Bay and one train station further north. In subsequent years we have made this beloved house an extension of ourselves with its book lined rooms and Grace's beautiful European styled front and native Australian backyard gardens.

As we discussed our proposed sea change of sorts to the Central Coast, I began to lose my nerve and suggested that given the time we were likely to spend commuting, it probably made more sense to remain in Sydney. But Grace had more determination and courage than me and it was largely her will that in the end drove our relocation. I quickly found that I loved living at Tascott and on some days as I stood on the station waiting for the 7:12am train to Sydney, I found myself looking out over Brisbane Water and wishing I could go fishing rather than to work. Sometimes we found the commute exhausting because most days we had to rise early and return home late. But we also learnt to use the two and a half hours we each spent on the train most weekdays to good purpose, for it was a time that could be spent reading for work, research or simple relaxation. It was the only time in my working day that I had to myself for when I returned to work in 1998 most of my time

was spent attending meetings or holding conversations with university colleagues. But 1997 was certainly a year when my family life took precedence and the completion of *The Vision Splendid* was delayed until my next study leave in 2002.

Sociology Professor, Bettina Cass, and I had worked together when we were both Deputy Chairs of the Academic Board and when she became Dean of Arts in 1998, she asked me to serve as chair of the Faculty Undergraduate Matters Committee and as a second Pro-Dean. Most of the work of this committee was mundane, involving approving new units of study proposed by Departments within the Faculty. But I was also tasked with a more creative and substantive contribution, chairing committees that developed three new undergraduate Arts degrees in Languages, Social Science and Media Studies.

Despite the roles I had played at the Departmental, Faculty and University level I was uncertain about what the future held for me at the University of Sydney. I had ambitions to be Head of Department but I was also aware that I was not a popular figure in History. I began to explore the possibility of moving to another university and in fact applied for the position of Professor of History at a provincial university. As it turned out that university decided not to continue with a chair appointment, judging, quite rightly, that it was better using the available funds to fill several positions at lecturer level. However, more than 20 years later I met a former member of the History department from that university at a conference and he told me about running into one of my Sydney History colleagues at the time when the applications for the chair were under consideration and the decision not to proceed with an appointment was not yet made. It is university practice that the names of applicants for academic positions are kept confidential but my Sydney colleague was apparently aware that I was a candidate, and, determined to provide advice, said with pointed directness, 'Don't appoint him'. I was shaken to hear this story, even all these years later, because although I knew that I was not favoured by some of my History colleagues I had no idea that the resentment ran so deep that a colleague would seek to interfere in my plans to leave Sydney because of their determination to prevent the advancement of my career at Sydney or elsewhere.

Stephen Garton's three-year term as Head of the History Department was due to expire at the end of 1998 and towards the end of the year a small committee was established with the brief of sounding out the views of staff on which Professor or Associate Professor, they preferred to succeed him. Since the 1970s, the method of choosing a Head of Department had become more of a consultative process than was the case in earlier eras. Although not legally required to appoint the person favoured by a department Deans usually accepted the majority decision. The chair of the History Department search committee circulated a memo which, rather than simply indicating that most staff favoured a particular candidate, declared that the committee had found the next Head under a mushroom and his name was Richard Waterhouse. I guess this was either a sarcastic reference to my alleged undisguised ambitions to be Head of History, or an indication that I was full of excrement. Stephen Garton voiced his opinion that I was the most qualified candidate, given my experience as an administrator at both Faculty and University level, and I suspect he had lobbied amongst my colleagues in my favour. Perhaps, the memo was also expressive of a level of resentment towards Stephen's support for my 'candidature'. In any case, when I read the memo, it reinforced my suspicion that while it seemed most colleagues accepted that in terms of seniority, I was the logical person to succeed Stephen, there was also concern amongst the few that I might aggressively use the position both to promote change and my own career.

Actually, when I assumed the role of Head in 1999, I knew that the possibilities for making major changes to the Department were limited. During the course of the 1990s some twenty staff members had left the Department and because of falling student numbers only a few of them were replaced.[1] Student numbers began to increase in the late 1990s but given the precarious state of Faculty and History department finances there was a lingering reluctance from the University

administration to authorise new appointments. Perhaps it was possible to tinker with the curriculum but there was little scope for imaginatively re-creating it. However, two factors which I had not anticipated heralded the beginning of change and renewal. First, for the first time in many years History undergraduate enrolments accelerated to an unexpected level, which meant that the Faculty not only allowed the Department to re-advertise the lectureship in Early Modern History, which I referred to earlier, but also to fill two further positions, one in Late Modern European History, the other in American History. The Department was also the beneficiary of funding from the Cassamarca Foundation, which provided funding for a lectureship in Italian Renaissance history for four years, with the likely prospect of renewed financial support for the position at the end of that period.

Faculty appointment committees consisted of the Dean, Head of Department, a representative of the Academic Board, and one other member of the appointing Department. As Head I had the most influence on appointments and I used it to support candidates who not only possessed fine track records but who had also indicated outstanding potential to become major international scholars. In one case I successfully advocated for a candidate who lacked the publication record of his main competitor and had not yet completed his PhD. Nevertheless, his referees' reports indicated that he was headed for a brilliant career as a scholar of international renown. Andrew Fitzmaurice (now a Professor at Queen Mary College, London), Dirk Moses (now a Professor of Political Science at the City College of New York), Stephen Robertson (now Professor in Digital Humanities, George Mason University) and Nick Eckstein (Associate Professor Emeritus, Department of History, University of Sydney) all proved to be important appointments and contributors to the Department, although the eventual loss of three of them to prestigious overseas universities, while clear demonstrations of their international standings, was disappointing because they were neither replaced nor replaceable.

Second, within three months of me becoming

Head of History, the Faculty was informed that the University planned to restructure the Faculty of Arts by merging the twenty-three departments into four schools. This scheme was designed to streamline Faculty administrative resources, centralise authority through a structure of Dean and the Heads of four Schools, rather than through a Dean and Heads of 23 Departments, and increase the prospect of more co-operative and interdisciplinary teaching and research projects by reducing the barriers that the existence of discrete departments created.[2]

Although the Vice-Chancellor announced that the faculty was to reform itself into a school structure, surprisingly the central administration made no attempt to dictate the form of this new order. The number of schools and how the 23 departments were to be ordered within them was left to the faculty. Nor did the Dean, Bettina Cass set out a plan of arrangement. Heads of Department were told there were to be four schools and then left to negotiate which departments joined which schools. In fact, I had received advance knowledge of the Vice Chancellor's forthcoming announcement and I had held a series of discussions with the Heads of those departments that seemed to me to logical partners with my own, that is, Classics, Ancient History, Archaeology and Museum Studies. So, the School was in part informally organised even before there was a formal instruction for it to be created. However, once the policy was announced I was approached by the Head of the Department of Gender Studies (now Gender and Cultural Studies) who I think feared that her department would be swallowed or at least dominated by the English department if they both joined the same school. This request was quickly followed by one from the Philosophy department, whose head argued that History and Philosophy were a natural fit. When some of the Philosophers subsequently discovered that Gender Studies, which they didn't regard as a legitimate academic discipline, was also joining the School, they proposed that Philosophy withdraw from the arrangement. However, most Philosophy staff subsequently decided that the alternative School possibilities were far less satisfactory so

they reaffirmed their support for the partnership with History and its allies.

At this stage it seemed to me that the proposed School was big enough and when I was approached by a few other departments I announced that 'the inn was already full'. I probably didn't have the authority to make this decision and it was a mystery to me why the aggrieved Heads of the spurned departments didn't appeal for support to the Dean. As it turned out, the decision of the University and Faculty not to devise a plan for how departments were to be allocated was to be at a cost. When the negotiations were complete and three potential schools formed there were still a number of departments, most without much discipline connection to each other, which remained unattached. So, they were gathered together into a school of convenience, one which lacked clear intellectual connections. It was no surprise that within a few years it collapsed. Ironically, two of the departments that I had spurned were now allocated to the School of Philosophical and Historical Inquiry, of which I was now Head.

As progress was made towards setting up the new schools, which were scheduled to come into being at the beginning of 2000, it was decided that under the new arrangements the former Heads of department were to become chairs of department, with prime responsibilities for curriculum supervision and teaching allocation duties. In the School to which History belonged, which was given the awkward (and fortunately temporary) name of School of Philosophy, Gender, History and Ancient World Studies (SPGAWS) the most senior scholar, teacher and administrator was Kevin Lee, the Professor of Classics and also Faculty Pro-Dean. I fully expected to become the chair of History while Kevin became the Head of School. Neither I nor anyone else in the faculty, as far as I know, was aware that Kevin was suffering from a serious illness and no doubt wanted to avoid taking on a heavy administrative role at this stage of his career. It seems that he and Bettina Cass discussed who was the most suitable, qualified and available alternative Arts academic who could be appointed to the position and I was chosen. So, a few weeks before Christmas in 1999

I received a phone call from Bettina asking me to accept the role. There was still a process of calling for academic staff to nominate to be Head of School and for candidates to provide copies of their curriculum vitas for staff scrutiny, but as everyone was made to understand, this was all a formality. Inevitably only one CV was submitted, only one candidate nominated.

When the new School came into operation on January 1, 2000 each department, for the moment, kept its own professional staff in place while the new Heads were permitted to make just one appointment at School level. I chose Diane Ferrari, an extremely capable administrator, who had previously worked in both the History and Linguistics departments. Although not possessing any formal qualifications in accounting she was extremely knowledgeable about budgets, which proved invaluable, as together we explored the state of the school's finances, discovering that every single department was in deficit. In these early days I also commenced discussions with the Dean and the other three heads about the future forms that the professional staff arrangements in each School would take. Once this was decided, all administrative positions were declared open and existing staff had to compete for the advertised positions both with staff from other faculties as well as external applicants. Eventually all the newly appointed staff in SPHGAWS were located in a school administration hub, although accommodation shortages prevented this from happening immediately.

The early lack of administrative support at the School level placed a heavy work burden on both Diane and myself and we often found ourselves carrying out tasks more suitable to an entry level administrative assistant. While the appointment of the new staff solved this problem, we still faced a more difficult and enduring obstacle. Most of the academic staff had wanted to keep the old departmental system of government. They resented the school and had no sense of loyalty towards it. While I was pondering the consequences of this culture of disappointment and even anger, I was visited by a delegation from the History Department, whose members

insisted that I vacate the office I occupied as Head of School because it was the room previously occupied by the Head of History and so now, in their view, belonged to the chair of that department. Soon the story of this visit had spread widely through the institution and I even received a phone call from the Pro-Vice Chancellor of the College who told me not to accede to this demand. In fact, I knew that this was a calculated challenge to the authority of the Head of School, an attempt to assert that departmental was more consequential than School power. As a courtesy I had told the delegation that I would consider their request but I always intended to reject it, which I did. Subsequently, the chair of History publicly announced that despite the new University regulations, in practice the chairs were more important than the Head. In response, one Friday when he was presumably working from home, I had his books, papers and other belongings moved to an office close to mine, a clear indication that I had heard about what he had said and had decided he needed close supervision. When he complained about this peremptory move, I explained that I had become concerned about whether we could work together, and had moved him to an office where I could keep an eye on him.

Not long after this I had a meeting with Stephen Garton, who at that time was enjoying study leave. He asked me about who I considered were my supportive School allies. I responded by telling him that the newly appointed administrative staff were loyal to the School because they saw more opportunities for promotion in the new structure, but there were only a few academics who understood the potential of the new system. However, this was an issue that really troubled me because I knew that policies designed to improve teaching and research could only be adopted and meaningfully implemented if they had widespread support. So, I decided to think of myself as on a kind of pilgrimage in search of academic excellence and to share my plans and expectations as well as my frustrations with my colleagues. To fit in with this vision the School began to publish a regular on-line newsletter called *Sophistry*, which contained information about events and available resources in the School, Faculty and University. It also included a column which I wrote called *Headlines* where I shared my thoughts about University and Faculty policies, and my plans for the direction of the School. I regularly divulged information which I had learned both from my personal contacts and as a member of particular University and Faculty committees to which I belonged, information which was sometimes classified as confidential. But I did this because I wanted my colleagues to feel that they too were sharing in the creation of something important. I also knew that the proof was in the pudding and that developing policies that actually improved teaching, as well as the quantity and quality of research, and produced a higher level of grant achievement was vital in persuading academic colleagues that the school was capable of providing greater benefits than the previous departmental system.

One other factor that boosted my authority and confidence was my promotion to full Professor at the end of 2001, followed by the University's subsequent decision to appoint me as the Bicentennial Professor of Australian History in 2002. Ironically, the most important promotion of my career was also the least opposed, for my application was encouraged and later supported not only by the Dean of Arts but also by senior University level academic administrators.

As well as History, Classics, Ancient History, Gender Studies, and Philosophy, all benefitted from rising undergraduate student numbers, a development that allowed the appointment of more academic staff and improved the school's financial bottom line. Also of enormous importance in changing the culture was a generous voluntary retirement scheme that was introduced to the Faculty of Arts by the University Administration whereby those academic staff who chose to leave, were paid a lump sum based on years of service. There were a number of colleagues of retirement age with modest publication records who had taught exactly the same courses, albeit under different guises, for 20 years or more and I made a special effort to encourage staff who fitted that profile to take advantage of the scheme.

Because of the rising student numbers combined with the large number of retirements the School was able to appoint 54 academic staff in the period between 2000 and 2006, twelve of them in History, although there were also a significant number of hirings in Classics, Ancient History, Gender Studies and Philosophy. There were only a modest number of appointments in Archaeology because it was one department in which there was neither a significant rise in student numbers nor many retirements.[3]

In mid-2000 the Vice-Chancellor visited the faculty to meet the Dean and Heads of School to check on the press of the implementation of the new school structure. When my turn came to speak, I couldn't withhold my enthusiasm. I began by acknowledging that initially I was a sceptic, believing that the schools were likely to prove to be just another administrative layer, and an ineffective one at that. But I acknowledged that even my brief experience as Head had persuaded me that I was able to exert far more authority than Heads of Department had managed to do previously, with the result that school, faculty and university policies were now implemented rather than ignored. Apparently, I said what he wanted to hear and so I was invited to be one of the main speakers at the next Vice-Chancellor's Retreat. On this occasion, aware that the deans of other faculties regarded the Faculty of Arts as a financial drain on the rest of the University I focussed on demonstrating how in a period of nine months the school had turned an initial financial deficit into a surplus of $750,000. Arguing that the University could now have faith in the School to act with fiscal responsibility, I set out plans to improve the School's teaching and research performances, insisting that any funds allocated by the University to assist the School in implementing those plans would be spent in a manner that was targeted and responsible. That was the beginning of a reputation for excellence that the school enjoyed across the University for many years.

Over the succeeding months and years, a series of policies were implemented that were designed to improve the levels of research production and grant applications, measure and improve teaching standards, and introduce new subject areas to the curriculums of School departments. To stimulate the research environment each department was provided with a research seminar budget which allowed them to fund presentations from local and even overseas scholars. The underlying aim was to stimulate research environments in every School department. Staff wishing to apply for ARC grants were encouraged to apply for financial assistance from the school which funded teaching relief and research assistance in support of grant preparation. When staff members published books the school celebrated by sponsoring launches, which were usually held in Gleebooks, the State Library or the Nicholson Museum. It seemed important to always mark and publicise such important occasions, through acknowledgement of the authors' achievements.

In the early days there was also some tidying up to do. The school's name and acronym (SPGHAWS) were the butt of humour across the University and on one occasion referred to by the Vice-Chancellor as 'unpronounceable'. So, the School invited staff, academic and professional, to submit potential replacement names and then a ballot was held to decide the winner. A prize was promised of several bottles of wine, bottles which I had purchased from Orange Agricultural College, then affiliated with the University. The winning entry was School of Historical and Philosophical Inquiry, although the order was subsequently reversed to School of Philosophical and Historical Inquiry (SOPHI), at the request of the Philosophers, who argued that their department was older than History. It was an inclusive title because all the disciplines in the school were grounded in one or both of the disciplines of Philosophy and History.

From the beginning of my term as Head of History and extending into the years I spent as Head of what became SOPHI I was determined to develop and act in terms of a set of principles. First, I made a conscious decision to keep a distance between myself and staff, mostly because I didn't want there to be any appearance of favouritism. I accepted that the role didn't involve

winning any popularity contests and accustomed myself to learning that I was referred to as 'the hard bastard', 'the bastard upstairs', 'the 'tough nut' and more generously, the 'straight arrow'. Second, it seemed to me to be essential to develop a set of plans and policies relating to improving the quality of teaching and research and to have the determination to implement them. A series of these policies were successfully implemented although my endeavours to bring about extensive curriculum reform in some departments, especially Archaeology, were notable failures. Third, I knew I would experience opposition and conflict from those who opposed the changes that the School was implementing, and that there was a need to focus on ensuring that the major policies were put in place while sometimes giving way on less important issues. Fourth, mindful of Benjamin Franklin's dictum to the effect that the simpler something is the easier it is to implement and the less difficult it is to fix when it breaks down, I tried to focus on developing uncomplicated proposals and policies. For example, in consultation with the chairs, I devised a fairly simple workloads formula that measured the teaching activities, research output and administrative responsibilities of all academics in the School as a means of ensuring that there was a relatively even distribution of work. Workloads formulas were always controversial and some schools adopted formulas that tried to measure every aspect of staff workloads, focussing on indicators which were measured using complex statistical techniques. This led to constant debates about what to add and what to abandon with the end result that some Heads of School decided against even bothering with workloads policies at all.

As I indicated above, the School made a large number of appointments in the period from 2000 to 2006. As the Dean's delegate, I chaired most of the appointment committees in this era, making the decision that I would continue to have a major say in History appointments and follow my earlier policy of assessing applicants on their potential as well as their track record. However, when making appointments in other disciplines I determined to rely on the advice of representatives from those areas of study. There were two people who served on some of those selection committees in whose judgements I developed considerable faith, Shane White from History and Peter Wilson from Classics. When I saw the applications for two different positions in Classics and Ancient History, from Alastair Blanshard and Julia Kindt, I thought they were stunning candidates both in terms of their future potential and existing track records. I was greatly gratified to discover that Peter had come to the same conclusion. Overall, a whole series of outstanding appointments were made across the School, appointments that allowed it to flourish for the next fifteen years or so.

I took particular pride in the research culture that flourished in the School, which was reflected in an increase in publications, including books, book chapters and articles, and in a rise in the number of successful applications for ARC Research Grants. This culminated in 2004 when academics in the School were awarded 17 such grants, the largest number of any school or department across the University. These combined results led to university-wide acknowledgement of the School as a research powerhouse. When the University decided to hire a number of research fellows to boost the institution's output and reputation approximately ten of them were appointed to SOPHI departments. I should add that the University decided on these appointments, and in the process, there was no consultation with the School or its departments. The hiring of such important scholars increased the research status of the University, Faculty and School and they also made significant contributions to the School's research output. However, they were a costly extension to the School's long-term budget, and their presence inevitably prompted other staff to aspire to research only positions. I suppose this troubled me because I believed that the role of academics was both to teach and research and my observations over the years had led me to the conclusion that outstanding teachers usually were also highly productive researchers. However, when I reflect back on these appointments, I feel obliged to acknowledge that the School benefitted from the presence of most of these research-only

appointees and Iain McCalman and Mark McKenna made particularly important contributions to raising the History department's research profile both at a national and international level and as model research mentors.

In teaching, the School introduced a policy of requiring all teachers to administer student evaluation questionnaires in all their courses. To some extent I was sceptical of the results of these questionnaires revealed, but while I had doubts about their capacity to show excellent teaching, I was confident that they accurately indicated which course were taught badly. At the end of each semester, I examined the results of these questionnaires and where they revealed problems I referred the results to the chairs of the relevant departments, with a request that they counsel the teachers concerned and, if necessary, ask them to take advice from the Centre for Teaching and Learning.

To celebrate its Sesquicentenary the University asked schools to apply for 13 Sesquicentenary lectureships which were required to be in new subject areas of teaching. The School was successful in obtaining two of those lectureships, one in Philosophy and the second in Heritage Studies. Philosophy was not included in the NSW school curriculum but the first of these new lecturers was required to teach in a pilot program in this discipline in selected High Schools. This was a terrific scheme that originated in the Philosophy Department and proceeded with full School support. The second position was designed to revive the program in Historical Archaeology, which had once featured strongly in the Archaeology curriculum. Because Historical Archaeology was not a new teaching area, I needed to disguise it in the application under the nomenclature of Heritage Studies. As it turned out, Annie Clark, who was appointed to the position, devised a syllabus that was both innovative and more broadly conceived than a standard syllabus in Historical Archaeology, one that could indeed be classified as Heritage Studies.

Much of my time as Head of School involved attending Faculty and University level committees and writing reports relating to appointment and promotion applications. I also spent a great deal of time meeting with individual staff members to listen to grievances and provide advice. As more students turned to the internet for resources they could use to produce plagiarised essays and tutorial papers, the University responded by appointing Heads of School as the staff responsible for dealing with identified cases both of deliberate and unintentional copying. It was a difficult task, especially since some of the students whose work I penalised were aggressive rather than penitent in their responses. Apart from these normal Head of School duties I was occasionally asked by the Dean to undertake one off tasks on behalf of the faculty. In particular, when the University established a committee to determine whether the Department of Government and International Relations should be transferred to the Faculty of Arts (which involved an implicit understanding that if this was recommended several other Faculty of Economics departments were also likely to join Government in Arts) I became the Faculty of Arts representative on that body, with a brief to advocate for the move. In the end, the Committee recommended in favour of the shifting of Government into Arts. In response I received a nod of approval from the Dean and earned enduring resentment from Government department academic staff.

However, the most difficult issues I dealt with involved cases of sexual harassment which turned out to be more prevalent than I had previously imagined. On the one hand I found it to be deeply concerning that some of my male colleagues held such exploitative attitudes towards (mostly postgraduate) female students. On the other, I found it extremely frustrating, although also understandable, that after making initial complaints, the young women concerned often decided not to proceed with their claim. Although assured of confidentiality I suspect they feared the prospect of retribution. And despite promises to believe their stories I'm sure that they were worried that their accounts were likely to be treated with scepticism. In the end some of those accused decided to leave the university, but that was because they were found to have repeatedly transgressed other university

requirements and directions. Usually, I asked the accused academic why they engaged in this form of behaviour, and apart from the fact that usually I was given a denial that anything had happened at all, occasionally I received such gems as, 'It's a long tradition in my department', or 'Where else am I going to meet girls?'.

In this context, I should add that the University did not prohibit consensual sexual relations between staff and students. However, an academic staff member who entered into such a relationship was required to inform his/her supervisor and to ensure that there were no conflicts of interest by removing themselves from the marking of the student's work. Given how few staff members reported such relationships to me I suspect this was a policy that was mostly ignored.

In the last years of my tenure as Head of School the role became less concerned with trying to create a School of world class departments and more about dealing with mundane administrative issues. One of the Schools in the Faculty had become increasingly dysfunctional to the extent that it was finally disbanded and the departments dispersed into the other three schools. Two of them, Anthropology and Sociology, were assigned to SOPHI. When he informed me of this assignment the Dean indicated that he expected them to be inculcated with SOPHI culture, that is one which emphasised professionalism in teaching and research, and where departments were willing to obey and implement directives and policies emanating from the School, Faculty and University. Such characteristics were not central to the culture of the now abolished School. However, no matter how much I pointed out that SOPHI's success resulted from its adherence to a set of policies designed to produce both professionalism and improved teaching and research performances, the two departments resisted integration into this culture and stuck to values and policies that long pre-dated the creation of the school structure. It was probably my greatest failure as Head of School.

My third contract as HOS expired at the end of 2006. I felt completely burnt out, believed that I had lost my zeal and energy for change and reform, and had become simply a paper pusher.

The Dean offered me another contract, this time for five years, but I was certain that if I accepted, I would be doing a disservice to the School and myself. I was then offered a one-year contract as Head of the proposed School of Social Sciences, with the designated role of setting up the required administrative structures, hiring professional staff, and creating policies designed to improve teaching and research. The new School was scheduled to include Anthropology, Sociology and the incoming departments from the Faculty of Economics. But I knew I no longer possessed the determination and enthusiasm to take on this position. I needed a break, and anyway it was hard to develop a sense of commitment to another School when my heart belonged to SOPHI. I suppose too, that I was aware of certain levels of resentment towards me, not only from staff in Sociology and Anthropology but also from some senior academics in the departments in Economics who blamed me for their transfer into Arts and were certain that it would mean a decline in their access to services and resources. When rumours began to circulate that I had received an offer to be Head I was told by more than one Government department staff member that I was not a suitable person for the position because my discipline, that is History, was not represented in the new school. I was absolutely certain that this was not the main reason why some staff objected to my assuming the role of Head, but these conversations confirmed my view that I had made the right decision to take study leave in 2007 rather than engage again in the task of school building.

As I mentioned earlier, I spent most of my final five years of my tenure at the University teaching and researching. However, I didn't manage to entirely divest myself of administrative duties. When the Federal Government introduced its Excellence in Research Australia (ERA) which involved financially rewarding universities on the basis of their research performances, it announced that it would first trial the policy through an assessment of the number and quality of research publications in Humanities and Social Sciences in a select number of Australian universities. As one of the selected universities the University of Sydney was required to submit its staff research publications in Humanities and Social Sciences for a designated period. The Dean appointed me Associate Dean Research, with the particular brief to collect this data. As far as the Faculty of Arts was concerned this was a straightforward task but I found, that for reasons that still baffle me, at least one of the other 'Social Science' faculties refused to co-operate in providing lists of relevant publications. In the end I had to rely on unofficial contacts that I had established over the past 20 years or so, to provide me with the information I needed. It was a drawn-out and cumbersome process. There were some other modest achievements during my tenure as Associate Dean Research. Discovering that the faculty provided no administrative support to the Associate Dean Research or the Faculty Research Committee, I successfully argued for the establishment of that support. I also succeeded, in partnership with other members of the Research Committee, in creating a Faculty Research Ethics Committee, one whose establishment was long overdue.

In 2011, the last year of my service at the University of Sydney, I undertook one last major administrative task. Early in the year I was invited by Trevor Burnard, Head of the School of Historical and Philosophical Studies to visit the University of Melbourne to discuss the reforms I had introduced to SOPHI and how they might be applicable to the Departments of History and History and Philosophy of Science as well as the Centre for Australian Studies at Melbourne. After a long discussion, and just before he took me down to the Dean's Office to meet Mark Considine, he asked me to chair a committee to review the Centre and the two departments. I thought that taking on this task would prove an interesting and challenging and provide me with the opportunity to share what I had learned at Sydney with colleagues from another university. And so, without any premonition of what was to follow, I agreed to undertake the task.

I was very fortunate to be joined on the review panel by three outstanding scholars, including the Directors of the Institute of Historical Research at the University of London, and the Stout Centre at

Victoria University (Wellington) and a Professor of the History and Philosophy of Science at Vanderbilt. The panel convened at the University of Melbourne later in the year, and we conducted a series of interviews, including with the Acting Vice-Chancellor, the staff both of the two departments and the Centre as well as with postgraduate and undergraduate students. Drawing on these interviews, as well as documentation provided by the Faculty and University relating to teaching, research and finances, I drafted a report which after amendment by my fellow panel members, was submitted to the Dean. The Dean's response was highly positive. After an initial reading of the report, he expressed his relief that the Faculty and University now had '…an authoritative and imaginative document to help steer this group towards a new future'. After rereading the document, he was no less enthusiastic. 'The report itself is a landmark achievement', he wrote, 'and I have no doubt it will be talked about in the future as the turning of the tide for this group.'[4] Altogether the review committee made approximately 30 recommendations designed to rationalise and improve the curricula, raise the quality of postgraduate supervision, and restructure the Centre for Australian Studies. Some years later, when I sat next to Trevor Burnard at an Academy of Humanities Fellows' Dinner in 2016, he told that it was his judgement that the post review Hansen Trust endowment of a chair, a senior lectureship and three lectureships would not have happened without the Review and the implementation of its findings.

However, the response to the Review's recommendations from members of the History discipline area were more mixed and two of its most senior representatives used the pages of the *The Australian's Higher Education Supplement* to question the intentions of both the members of the review committee and of senior members of the University's administration. Their criticisms were extensive, exclusively negative and viewed by a number of senior academic staff from other universities as unfair. I was informed that as a result of the extreme nature of their strictures that the Vice-Chancellor would write an admonishing letter to the most senior of the transgressors,

although I don't know whether in the end that happened. Here I will give just two examples to illustrate the misplaced nature of the criticisms, one relating to a specific and the other to a more general criticism of the report. Noting that some staff in History were supervising up to a dozen PhD theses each, the Committee recommended that the School limit the number of candidates any one member of staff could supervise to five, a number which was in accord with the limits required in most universities across Australia. It was a policy that ensured academic staff were not overworked and that students received the necessary amount of time from their mentors. However, one senior and influential staff member argued that the intent of this proposed policy was to reduce the number of Ph D candidates in History at Melbourne and allow the University of Sydney to catch up to its southern rival which at that time ranked first in the number of enrolled History postgraduate research students. Behind this claim was the view, that History staff at Sydney, myself especially, considered the Melbourne History department to be its major rival and that the policies recommended by the Review panel were designed to boost Sydney's prospects of overtaking Melbourne in major areas of excellence, including the numbers of postgraduate students. However, apart from the fact that it was extremely unlikely that the three overseas members of the panel would agree to be part of such a conspiracy, many of the committee's recommendations were similar or identical to the policies that I had found *worked* in the rebuilding of SOPHI. And, in fact it was preciously because SOPHI was a success story that I was asked to chair the Melbourne Review in the first place.

The second more general criticism was that the whole exercise was, in the words, of a very senior Melbourne professor, 'a fix', which carried the implication that the Review committee had conspired with the Faculty and University administration to produce a set of pre-arranged findings. I did talk to the Acting Vice-Chancellor and the Dean in advance of the conduct of the Review but that was essentially a matter of courtesy and our findings were the result of our meetings with staff and students in the school, our reading of the documentation provided at the School, Faculty and University level, and our own experiences as university teachers, researchers and administrators. The Melbourne-Sydney rivalry, which involves comparisons of sporting, cultural and educational achievements, has a long history, more strongly acknowledged and encouraged in the southern capital than in Emerald City. I suppose I had anticipated that I might experience some degree of suspicion and resentment from Melbourne colleagues, although nothing prepared me for the fierceness of their response, or the degree to which notions of conspiracy were in the air. However, my fellow reviewers had not expected any serious objections to the establishment of the review or its findings. All three of them expressed deep concern about the reaction from some of the academics in the school, and one told me they would not have participated had they known they would face such 'unprofessional' conduct. After the Review was submitted and made public, I had no further communication with the two most outspoken opponents. However, there was reconciliation of sorts with other senior members of Melbourne's History discipline when we enjoyed a meal together at an Academy of Humanities Fellows Dinner in Sydney some years later.

But my last year as a staff member at Sydney didn't end on a sour note. At the end of the year my former PhD student and long-term colleague, Shane White, very generously organised a day long symposium in my honour. I didn't want the speakers to consist solely of the most distinguished scholars in my field of Australian history but also to include a number of my former PhD students who now held positions not only in academic but also in heritage and public service institutions, or who worked as public historians. I really enjoyed the papers given at the seminar, including those presented by my former students who were now distinguished historians, including Anna Wong, Rosemary Kerr, Katherine Biber and Shane White, as well as other outstanding scholars, namely Penny Russell and Grace Karskens.

Endnotes

1   Richard Waterhouse to Professor Jill Roe, President, Australian Historical Association, 23 May, 2000, Waterhouse Family Papers

2   One view that central administration staff consistently expressed was that the Faculty of Arts simply didn't possess 23 capable administrators, which meant that in the current system there would always be departments that were poorly governed.

3   These figures include appointments made in Sociology and Anthropology, two departments which only joined the school in 2006 when the school to which they formerly belonged was disbanded. They do not include the Research only appointments which were made by the University in the period from 2003 to 2005.

4   Mark Considine to Richard Waterhouse, 7 and 8 July 2011, Waterhouse Family Papers

Chapter 19

Other Lives to Live: Retirement

WHEN HE LEFT WALDEN POND after two years in the 'wilderness' and returned to live in the nearby town of Concord, Henry David Thoreau suggested he did so because he had other lives to live. When I retired, I had plans to engage in a couple of major research projects, to give some guest lectures in History at the University of Sydney, to travel, to involve myself more with state and national level professional organisations, to engage more with local community institutions, to spend more time fishing and most importantly, to provide more support to my family, including Grace and our now grown up children.

As I indicated earlier, although I have written a number of articles, chapters and encyclopaedia entries I have not produced any lengthy academic publications since I retired. In part this is because one of the subjects I was researching, the response of the Australian people to the Japanese bombing of Pearl Harbor and invasion of Malaya, turned out to be more suited to a modest article, rather than a scholarly book. At the same time, not long after my retirement I developed a serious illness, Polymyalgia Rheumatica, which in 2016 metamorphosed into Rheumatoid Arthritis. Both these illnesses made it difficult for me to sit for long periods or to travel, without experiencing considerable pain. Research and writing became activities that I could only practice for limited periods on a restricted set of days. But it is also the case that I increasingly found that I lacked the motivation to engage in large scale research activities. I much more enjoyed writing short pieces

on narrowly defined topics in Australian history, because this involved researching a limited body of primary and secondary material. Grace was aware that on the one hand I felt a sense of obligation, even as a retired academic, to research and write at least one more book, but that on the other I didn't have the motivation or energy to begin one. One day in 1919 she spoke to me about it, pointing out that because I was retired, I could research and write about anything I wanted to, including 'non-academic' subjects, which is how this book came about. However, I envisaged writing the family history as a short project that would be completed in six months. Instead, it has taken six years.

I did give some guest lectures to the Second Year Honours History class at the University of Sydney, lectures which focussed on my own odyssey from Social to Cultural history as a case study in a broader historiographical shift, but that contribution ended when the History department decided to change the Honours syllabus. I also served as a liaison officer between the Faculty and Taylor College, giving lectures and providing syllabus advice on the program in Australian Studies.[1] I also found myself giving lectures on a whole array of topics in Australian history to Rotary and Probus clubs, as well as local history societies. Most years too I gave these same lectures to interested residents of rural towns and Sydney suburbs as part of annual History Week celebrations. However, I suppose that the most prestigious public lecture I have given in retirement is the Premier's annual history lecture. It

Delivering the 2015 Annual NSW Premiers History Award Lecture

is a lecture delivered as part of the annual NSW premier's History Awards ceremony, and I used the occasion to set out a new set of arguments relating to the Bush, Pioneer and Anzac legends. It was an ambitious lecture to give in the allocated 12 minutes.

For the first time in my life, I also travelled overseas for leisure rather than work. During my university days I had made many working trips to the United States but now both Grace and I turned to Europe for both work and leisure. In 2012 we took a river cruise from Budapest to Amsterdam and then travelled to Munich where Grace took up a fellowship in the Rachel Carson Centre for Environment and Society and I became a fellow of the rather less well-endowed Centre for Nineteenth Century Global Theatre History. Both Centres were part of Ludwig Maximilian University. The latter was located in an attic and was furnished with a small number of chairs, desks and computers. I discovered that the postgraduate students didn't appear until well after lunch, and to avoid competition for a desk and a computer, I made sure to get there early in the morning and leave soon after lunch. While the weather was still

warm, I spent my late afternoons walking the city but when the weather turned bitterly cold, I was reduced to reading or watching television in our apartment. Because of my inability to understand German it was difficult to extract much enjoyment from my television watching. However, one channel was devoted to a man selling tickets in raffles which viewers phoned in to buy; another used stationary cameras in ski resorts in The Alps to broadcast the snow falling; and a third focussed exclusively on televising from within one of the Octoberfest tents, showing people eating pork knuckles and chickens, and drinking beer. Munich television was not exactly compelling entertainment.

We travelled back to Munich in 2014 to visit the museums and galleries we didn't have time to view in 2012. Strangely none of them carried exhibits that ventured beyond the end of World War 1. This was a city which still had a Hitler complex, with no insights on how it should represent and explain its most notorious former resident and his locally nurtured Nazi party. We caught the train to Salzburg where we didn't take *The Sound of Music* tour, and then travelled to Berlin, a gritty city compared to the baroque doll's house qualities of Munich. It is also a city that, unlike Munich, is prepared to confront its Nazi past, in the form of memorials to the victims of Hitler. Then we travelled to the Netherlands, beginning a tradition of visiting Grace's aunts, uncles and cousins that has lasted for our two succeeding trips.

Apart from Amsterdam, our 2016 travels included Venice, Budapest and a wonderful trip over the Swiss Alps on the Bernina Express. As an undergraduate student in Archaeology I had listened enthralled as a visiting Professor from the University of Athens, Spyridon Marinatos, gave a series of lectures on the Minoan Bronze Age site of Akrotiri on the Greek Island of Santorini. It was one place I had always wanted to visit and we met up in Santorini there with our daughters Isabel and Eliza and Eliza's partner Yiorgos Crespis. Amongst other places we visited Akrotiri, as well as a number of vineyards, which produce outstanding white wine, relying on very traditional methods, took a boat ride on the water filled caldera (volcano crater), and watched the sunset from Oia. Grace and I had stunning views from our hotel room perched right on the edge of the caldera, although we became a bit nervous about our safety when Yiorgos told us that the Greeks didn't follow the practice of underpinning their buildings. I began to think it would only take a slight volcanic tremor for our room, and indeed the whole hotel, to slide hundreds of metres down the cliff into the water. But my fears were unrealised and we travelled to Athens to meet and stay with Yiorgos's parents. His mother Barbara became our generous and knowledgeable tour guide, leading us to the Acropolis and the National Archaeological Museum in Athens, two sites which had been on my 'must see' list since the mid 1960s.

Our final overseas trip before Covid put an end to our overseas travel plans for some years was in 2018. It began with the obligatory visit to Grace's Dutch relatives, the highlight of which was our stay with one of her cousins who lived on a modern two storey houseboat moored on the Spaarne River. Even better, he also owned a small wooden boat with an inboard motor which was

tied up against the houseboat and on which he took us on a trip up the River to Haarlem and along some of the joining canals. Visiting him I also learnt to appreciate how people in Europe are unaccustomed to 'rough' or dirt roads. His houseboat is reached by dirt track which runs about 50 metres from a bitumen street. To navigate this strip, he sold his city suitable convertible and purchased a four-wheel drive. Maybe that dirt road becomes very muddy in winter.

Since 2015 I have held a number of interviews with the ABC Central Coast breakfast show host, Scott Levi to discuss a series of First World War battles fought by the First AIF, as each of the 100th anniversaries of these encounters came about. Preparing to discuss Gallipoli, Fromelles, Pozieres, Polygon Wood, Villers-Bretonneux, Hamel, Mont St Quentin, as well as the lingering impact of the conflict on Australian society after 1918, instilled in me a desire to see at least some of the battlefields. So, after a detour to Ghent, our next stop was the city of Amiens, where thousands of Anzacs were stationed and which is in easy reach of the battlefields where the First AIF secured some of its most important victories. It was a moving experience to stand on the site of the Windmill at Pozieres and look towards Mouquet Farm, across an area in which so many First and Second Division soldiers lost their lives. The Franco-Australian Museum at Villers-Bretonneux tells a false and overworn narrative about naïve and innocent rural Australian men drawn into a bloodbath created by cynical and soulless European politicians, and features digital displays, many of which don't work. But if the Museum disappointed me the walk through the cemetery at VB was a truly moving experience. That day on the Somme is one I will never forget.

Our subsequent stops included Paris, where we particularly enjoyed the Northern European Art section of the Louvre, which features great paintings and much smaller crowds than in the Salle des Etats, where the Mona Lisa is located. I also liked just mooching through the Marais. From Paris we caught a train to Besancon to meet with my cousin Janet and her husband, an experience I have referred to in an earlier chapter.

From Besancon we travelled to Le Puy, a beautiful town in the Haute Loire, which is also one of the starting places for the Comino de Santiago. Not only does it possess a beautiful cathedral but also several unique chapels built on the top of volcanic plugs that rise into the sky. Le Puy is also noted for its lentils, which we were served in our hotel. I know they are a very healthy food, but it doesn't seem to me that there is much to be done with them in terms of providing culinary variety.

Travelling on to Lyon we were fortunate to have as our guide Andrew Fitzmaurice, my colleague from Sydney, who owned an apartment in this city. Lyon has wonderful Roman ruins, including an amphitheatre. It also possesses a museum containing the artefacts excavated from the old Roman city, which include what were once the belongings of the poor as well as the rich. The curators have used these objects to create a narrative which explains the lives not only of the rich and powerful residents but also those of the plebeian inhabitants. I found the exhibits quite inspiring, but of course I am an historian of popular culture. The section of the city that housed the silk weavers and their workshops is still there but when we visited the city I had not yet researched and written the story of the Branchflowers so I had no idea that my family had a possible connection to Lyon.

Finally, we travelled by train and bus first to Tours, with its magnificent cathedral, and then to Clermont Creans in the Loire Valley to stay at in the Chateau d'Oyre, which Grace's brother Jeff and sister-in-law Angela had booked for an extended stay. I enjoyed visiting the small towns and their markets in this area as well as standing on the banks of the Loire and looking across its broad reaches. But we could only stay briefly with Grace's family because Grace was due back at work and so we had a plane to catch.

I suppose it was essentially because I had fairly extensive experience as an academic administrator across a range of areas that I was invited to join a number of professional organisations either as a board or council member or in an executive capacity. I took on these roles for the most part because I wanted to contribute to promoting history and other academic disciplines both within the university and the wider community. However, I think that ego was also involved because I had previously enjoyed speaking to the media on a whole range of subjects relating to Australia, its culture and history and I thought that holding office in professional cultural organisations would allow me to retain a profile as a public intellectual. I was invited to serve as a member of the Council of the Australian Academy of Humanities in 2012 which I thought would prove an interesting experience, and was an ideal gig because it involved a modest workload and a time limit of three years. However, not long after I joined Council the Academy found itself in a difficult financial position as a result of a Federal Government cutback of its annual grant. When Council debated what strategies to introduce to meet the problems created by the financial shortfall I spoke about the need to cut Academy spending to avoid 'structural deficits'. The consequence of this speech was that I was asked to become the Academy's Treasurer, which I agreed to because I saw it as an interesting challenge, although not realising that this position had no time limit. In the end I was the Academy Treasurer until the end of 2023, assisting in repositioning its investments into an ethical portfolio, and working with successive Presidents and Executive Officers to ensure that the annual budgets were responsible and (mostly) balanced. However, although my contribution to Council largely consisted of providing financial advice, I also loved the intellectual life of the Academy, which was manifested most strongly in the annual symposiums.

From 2012, until the end of 2014, I was also President of the History Council of NSW. I took on this role because I wanted to expand interest in history to a wider community audience, one that included more young people, in particular. The most ambitious project that the Council embarked on with this aim was a re-creation of the Artists' Ball that was once a hallmark of the Sydney social calendar. Held in the old tearooms of the David Jones Elizabeth Street Department store it succeeded in attracting a group of young people who were fans of big band music and the dances that went with it. But these 'twenties something' dance followers were not interested in actually joining the History Council or engaging in Australian history in a broader context. The Artists' Ball was a great deal of fun, cost more than the History Council could afford, and failed in one of its major objects. I did, however, have a measure of success with some other History Council events. To attract a wider audience to the Annual History Week lectures I occasionally secured speakers with major public profiles who were not professional historians. Chris Master's lecture, for example, attracted a very large and diverse audience. The History Council also successfully lobbied to maintain a separate Mitchell Library Reading Room for the convenience of serious researchers, rather than giving all the space previously utilised for that purpose over to general readers, who mostly consisted of students anxious to take advantage of the free wi-fi facilities that the library provided. All in all, my tenure at the helm of the History Council yielded some very modest outcomes.

I had served as chair of the judging panel for the NSW Premier's History Awards in 2008, at a time when this competition was administered by Arts NSW. When that management was transferred to the State Library in 2012, I became the initial Senior Judge serving in the role for three years. I was lucky to head a team of judges for the most part possessed of good judgement and high levels of common sense. Occasionally, I encountered judges who were determined to have their own way, and when the majority decision went against their own assessments, responded petulantly and sometimes even tried to challenge the majority verdict. Academic egos, as I discovered, not for the first time, can be distracting, and I spent more time than I wanted consoling those egos in the interests of committee harmony. Perhaps because of my experience on the NSW book awards panel, in 2017 I was asked to join the Australian History and Non-Fiction judging panel, one of the five such panels that judged the six categories of the Prime Minister's Literary Awards. Lynette Russell, served as the highly professional chair of the panel for three years and then I was asked to succeed her in 2020. Because there were so many entries, serving as a judge for these awards was really hard work. Because the panel I belonged to judged two categories, its members consisted of those who were historians and those who were more familiar with non-fiction writings, which meant that judges with different areas of expertise tended to value different qualities in the books under judgement. Although this inevitably led to disagreements, for the most part they were resolved relatively amicably. In any case, in 2020 I took particular satisfaction in the fact that that the winner of the Australian history award was a book about Indigenous history and the winner of the non-fiction prize was a book by Yolngu women about Yolngu Songlines and their meaning.

Commuting to Sydney most working days between 1997 and 2011 meant that I had only limited professional and personal connections to the Central Coast community. Because I wanted to contribute in a modest way to that community, I joined Gosford Rotary Club in 1999. In the end, along with some of my fellow members, I became dissatisfied with the fact that in defiance of the Rotary International Constitution that this Club, dominated by the conservative local business establishment, refused to admit women members. To overcome this problem the rebels resigned from the Club to form a new one which actively encouraged women to join. Over the years we have done some good in the local, national and international communities. We have raised funds for the Central Coast homeless, the victims of floods and fires across several states, and for those devastated by epidemics and natural disasters in Africa, Asia and South America. Rotary is in decline across Australia but this club, which encourages not only women but locals from a variety of ethnic backgrounds to join, is both growing in numbers and possessed with a vitality to serve. Rotary has given me fellowship, and a sense of connection to the community in which I live.

Endnote

1   Taylor College is an institution established by the University to teach programs which qualify (mostly overseas) students who have not sat for the HSC for entry to the University.

Chapter 20

The Final Word

WE LIVE HALF WAY UP A HILL surrounded by bush, and the top marks the beginning of a national park which, although intersected by the M1 Motorway, extends west for many kilometres. As a result, we have to live with bushfires and the summer of 2019–20 was a particularly fierce bushfire season. One day in in early January 2020, I caught an early train home from Sydney, and when it emerged out of a tunnel onto the Hawkesbury River Bridge the smoke was so thick that vision extended less than ten metres. But not much later our attention became focussed on Covid 19 and a preoccupation with trying to stay healthy while still having contact with our kids in Sydney as well as the broader community. Quite a lot of the early parts of this book were written at this time, which was marked by strict regulations about when people could leave their homes and how far they could travel. Fortunately for me, fishing was categorised as exercise and so my friend Jeff and I were still able to make our regular Tuesday morning excursions on Brisbane Water. At one stage all travel between the Central Coast and Sydney was banned, although for inexplicable reasons the authorities still allowed the running of the ferry that ran from Ettalong on the Central Coast to Palm Beach on Sydney's northern beaches. This seemed very odd because at that time the northern beaches were reporting large numbers of covid cases. One day as the ferry passed us on Brisbane Water, we decided to call it the SS Covid.

During the isolation years most of my administrative and committee duties were carried out via Zoom and Team meetings. But as times returned to normal, I also decided to cut back on my commitments to community and professional organisations. In part this was motivated by my belief that I was becoming stale and no longer had the enthusiasm for the tasks I was undertaking. Experience had taught me that when you feel like that it's a good time to leave because I was just going through the motion. I also felt that it was a good idea to step aside to give younger women and men the opportunities to experience the roles I had held. I really didn't want to be a boomer who wouldn't let anything go. And finally, I experienced a serious illness in 2021, an illness that eventually required major surgery. It seemed wise to spend more time just enjoying life.

So, in the last two years or so I have continued to reduce my community and professional commitments, and focussed my life much more on learning to cook a wider range of meals across European and Asian cuisine; becoming fitter through regular gym exercise; fishing every Tuesday morning with ambitions to get out on the water at least one more day a week; finishing this book and continuing to write modest scholarly articles; and most importantly of all, spending more time focussing attention on my grandchildren, children and their partners, and on Grace, to provide the support she needs to meet her bewildering number of commitments. Above all I want to be a better grandfather, father and husband because the family I love more than anything in the world deserves nothing less.

Our children have grown up in a world in

which they face a steep level of competition in finding employment and achieving professional advancement as well as a much higher level of difficulty in purchasing and paying the mortgages on houses and apartments. But I have taken great pride both in their educational, professional and family achievements.

Margot experienced successive careers as a model, actor and singer, highly competitive occupations in which she enjoyed brief successes, winning swimsuit model contests, appearing in brief roles in television comedies and recording a pop song. She then worked for some time promoting beverages in entertainment venues before experiencing considerable economic hardship in the Covid lockdowns. She is now seeking to establish new paths in her life. After a false start at the University of Sydney and sometime spent working in the catering industry Eliza undertook an honours degree in Media and Communications at UTS. Graduating with First Class Honours she was awarded a postgraduate research scholarship to undertake a PhD in Film Studies at the University of Sydney. Unfortunately, she completed the degree at a time when the impact of Covid was forcing Australian universities to release rather than hire staff. However, she had decided in any case that she didn't want an academic career and after working for a short period as a part-time teacher in the public high school system in 2023 she was employed as a casual and then in 2024 as a permanent staff member at Blue Mountains Grammar School.

In 2017 Eliza married Yiorgos Crespis, a project manager, and they now have two children Iannis (2017) and Ophelia (2019).

Isabel studied for an Arts degree at the University and then became an IT manager, working for such companies as Dell, Amazon Web Services and Delinea. In 2023 she married Luke Howlin, who has worked as a media administrator and media consultant. Their daughter Guinevere (Gwen) was born in 2025.

After completing his HSC equivalent qualifications Leo spent a year in Armidale where he enrolled in partying 101 at UNE. Returning to Sydney he completed Enrolled Nurse qualifications at Meadowbank TAFE. Subsequently, with the guidance and support of a fellow nurse whom he met working at Cumberland Hospital, Mai Nguyen, he successfully completed a Bachelor's degree (Nursing) at Charles Sturt, and a Masters degree (Nursing) at the University of Newcastle. He has now worked at Cumberland Hospital for many years, first in the wards and now as a Nursing Educator. He and Mai married in 2020 and they now have three children, Francine or 'Frankie' (2020), Celine or 'CeCe' (2022) and Lily (2024). We are a twenty-first century multicultural family but we are as tightly bound to each other as the generations of Karskens, Waterhouse, and Drake families who preceded us.

When I reflect upon my life, I find that three of the qualities that my father listed as most important to him are also on my most valued list. Grace, my children and their families, are at the very centre of my existence, the source of my greatest happiness. Second, I value the life I have lived in education as a teacher, researcher and administrator, which I have found stimulating and rewarding, and to which I have made a modest contribution. Third, the older I have grown the more I have come to love the natural environment of my country, including the beaches and estuaries, the native bushland and the birds that inhabit it, although I exclude the garden destroying bush turkeys from my list of beloved native fauna. Bert Facey entitled his autobiography *A Fortunate Life*, although his experiences in war and his life as a farmer living on marginal land, suggest that this naming was unintentionally ironic. If I had appropriated this title for my own life story that would also be ironic, because plagiarism constitutes serious academic malpractice. But it would also be a fitting and accurate title because it succinctly describes the privileged and fulfilled life I have lived.

Index

www.ingramcontent.com/pod-product-compliance
Lightning Source LLC
Chambersburg PA
CBHW051308270326
41929CB00028B/3452